TOURING
PACIFIC CULTURES

TOURING
PACIFIC CULTURES

EDITED BY KALISSA ALEXEYEFF
AND JOHN TAYLOR

Australian
National
University

PRESS

ANU PRESS

Published by ANU Press
The Australian National University
Acton ACT 2601, Australia
Email: anupress@anu.edu.au
This title is also available online at press.anu.edu.au

National Library of Australia Cataloguing-in-Publication entry

Creator: Alexeyeff, Kalissa, author.

Title: Touring Pacific cultures / Kalissa Alexeyeff and John Taylor.

ISBN: 9781921862441 (paperback) 9781922144263 (ebook)

Subjects: Culture and tourism--Oceania.
                 Tourism--Oceania.
                 Cultural industries--Oceania.
                 Arts--Oceania--History.
                 Oceania--Cultural policy.

Other Creators/Contributors:
                 Taylor, John, 1969- author.

Dewey Number: 338.47910995

Cover design and layout by ANU Press. Cover image adapted from *Culture for Sale, 2014.* Still from video installation by Yuki Kihara. Photography by Rebecca Stewart.

Contents

List of Illustrations

Acknowledgements

This book began as a conference session bearing the same name, held in 2011 in Wollongong as a part of the Australian Association for the Advancement of Pacific Studies biennial conference. We would like to express our immense gratitude to that association, now the Australian Association for Pacific Studies, and to all of the participants of that event. We also received generous funding and support from the ARC Laureate Project, 'Engendering Persons, Transforming Things: Christianity, Commodities and Individualism in Oceania' (The Australian National University, College of Asia and the Pacific), and we are especially grateful of the generous support received from Laureate Professor Margaret Jolly throughout the journey of this project. This work also received assistance from Kalissa Alexeyeff's ARC Future Fellowship project 'New Regional Labour Circuits in the South Pacific: Gender, Culture and Transnationalism'.

Editing and other aspects of production for this book were carried out with the assistance of several people. For their excellent and patient work during the early stages of manuscript collection, preparation and author liaison we warmly thank the assistance of Rebecca Clark and Karen Turner. We would also like to thank Natalie Araujo for her help with liaison and securing images, and are especially grateful to Carolyn Brewer for her meticulous and patient copyediting. Finally, we acknowledge ANU Press Pacific editorial board chair Stewart Firth and his initial enthusiasm and continued support for this project, and thank Emily Tinker for her expertise and patience in bringing the completed book through copyediting to press. We also thank the two anonymous reviewers for their generous and insightful thoughts.

We would like to thank Yuki Kihara for generously allowing us to reproduce an image from her artistically superb and critically challenging 2011 exhibition 'Culture for Sale'. We are extremely grateful also to Jane Desmond for so kindly and enthusiastically taking up our invitation to write the Afterword. We could not have hoped for a more engaged, original and insightful contribution. Finally, as volume editors, we would like to extend our heartfelt thanks to the individual authors, poets and artists who contributed to this book, including especially the late phone-ins and those who got in early and stayed the distance.

Kalissa Alexeyeff and John Taylor
Melbourne
November 2016

Notes on Images and Orthography

In preparing this volume, the editors have followed the individual contributors' own decisions with regard to certain issues of orthography, for example in the capitalisation of Indigenous and the italicisation of non-English words. This has been in keeping with an overall aesthetic preference towards giving priority to each individual author's stylistic voice over editorial conventions. The same aesthetic preference has been applied to images with regards to 'image quality', including especially original photographs taken by the individual authors. In taking this approach we have aimed to retain something of the 'touring' quality of many of the photographs, such as snapshots or mobile phone images, alongside more professionally styled images.

INSERT 20c TO WATCH ME DANCE

Source. *Culture for Sale, 2014*. Still from video installation by Yuki Kihara. Photography by Rebecca Stewart.

1

Departures and Arrivals in Touring Pacific Cultures

John Taylor and Kalissa Alexeyeff

Reframing perspectives in tourism studies

A Hawaiian Airlines flight from Honolulu has just landed at Kona International Airport on the Big Island, Hawai'i. Arriving passengers make their way across the tarmac and into the airport building, while those about to board the aircraft check in. In the buzzing terminal building itself, under the shade of a large, open-air roof inspired by local indigenous architectural forms,[1] people and luggage are everywhere. Negotiating the bustle, bumping into benches, rubbish bins, racks of postcards and each other, they make their way from plane to bus, taxi or car, vice versa, or from one flight to another. Others anticipate arrivals, to be greeted with hugs and tears, or silently await departure calls as they sit reading, stand alone, or cluster in chatty groups. Some appear easily recognisable as touring types: a young ukulele-strumming backpacker is a case in point, as is a group dressed in business suits and greeted with handshakes and flower leis by a similarly attired delegation. A travelling dance group, evidently departing, is also recognisable by their matching t-shirts and lava-lavas. Otherwise, it is difficult to distinguish businessperson

---

1   Winner of the US Federal Aviation Authorities' 'Beautification Award' for 1971, the Keahole Airport was described as a 'unique cluster of terminal structures resembling a Hawaiian village' and praised for its 'delightful melding of ancient with modern'. See 'Hawaii aviation: An archive of photos and historic facts', n.d., *hawaii.gov*.

from leisure-seeker. Those idly browsing the postcard racks or the gift shop souvenirs—tiki figurines and bottle openers, fridge magnets with images of volcanic lava flows and palm-fringed beaches, hibiscus-print bags—are as likely to be locals as tourists, or may be both, departing or returning home.

At the centre of all this activity, surrounded by a concrete bench edging a small square of raised lawn, stands a beautiful life-size sculpture in bronze—three hula dancers held in an eye-catching twirl. 'Just as the hula was built on a symbolic language of gesture and movement', as the plaque describes it, one group of travellers takes turns posing for photographs with the sculpture, mimicking the dancers' pose to produce a neatly choreographed snapshot moment. Evidently providing inspiration, they are followed by another group, one of whom asks a stranger to take the shot so the entire party can be included. This casual exchange is disrupted by an elderly couple who sit on a bench in front of the dancers, an unwittingly stifling act that has the effect of creating more space for arrivals and departures to flow and bump through the terminal. At last the couple rises at the sound of a final boarding call, and as both arrivals and departures depart, a quiet descends on the terminal and finally a roar of engines signals that the passenger jet has taken to the sky once more.

This scene is mundane in many respects to airports across the island Pacific, be it Rarotonga, Luganville or Pape'ete, and introduces the central metaphor that connects the contributions of this collection. *Touring Pacific Cultures* explores the incessant traffic in everyday items, people and performances of cultural production, consumption and exchange that have come to define the Pacific region, and the movement of the Pacific in the world. Here we are concerned with the myriad intersections inherent to the mobilities of people and creative culture across the Pacific and beyond; arrivals are threaded with departures, locals become tourists, and culture tours at the same time as it is toured.

This book takes us on a bumpy journey, exploring how culture is defined, produced, experienced and sustained through tourism-related practices. In doing so, it captures the importance of tourism to the visual, material and performed cultures of the Pacific region. 'Touring' is here approached in the plural sense of diverse cultures toured across multiple locales by equally diverse and cultured tourists, and also includes the travel of people and things on tour. This volume highlights the connections between tourism and other motilities and modalities, including the global movement of people, ideas, images and objects, the experience of class, status mobility and corporeal movement, and the ongoing importance of historical legacies to contemporary production, exchange and encounter.

The stylistic approach adopted here illustrates the complex and overlapping contours that comprise touring Pacific cultures. As such it includes a diverse range of written and visual strategies. The intention is not simply to subvert the conservative textual and analytic techniques of mainstream tourism studies, found especially in the majority of international academic journals where there is a continued reification of tourism as a simply identifiable set of practices. Despite the acknowledgement in tourism studies of an ever-widening set of touristic sub-genres—such as 'eco-tourism', more recently 'dark tourism',[2] medical tourism,[3] film tourism,[4] culinary tourism,[5] sports tourism[6] and voluntourism[7]—such diversions into niches,[8] we argue, fail to capture the diffuse, multi-faceted, fractured and elusive nature of the ideas, practices, values and processes tied up in that core concept, however tightly or loosely.

Here we have invited authors to examine the production, performance, movement and exchange of culture across and beyond the Pacific region in such a way that keeps in mind the idea of and material reality of a tourism industry, however historically inchoate, analytically slippery, or politically, socially and economically fragmented such an entity might be. In doing so, it has been possible to refocus our optics in such a way that recognises that culture often tours or is toured through contexts and for reasons that have very little to do with reified notions of 'tourists', 'tourism' or a 'tourism industry'. While recognising such intersections and departures, we have not

2   John Lennon and Malcolm Foley, 2000, *Dark Tourism: The Attraction of Death and Disaster*, London and New York: Continuum.

3   John Connell, 2006, 'Medical tourism: Sea, sun, sand and … surgery', *Tourism Management* 27(6): 1093–100.

4   Sue Beeton, 2005, *Film-Induced Tourism*, Series: Aspects of Tourism 25, Clevedon: Channel View Publications.

5   Lucy M. Long (ed.), 2010, *Culinary Tourism*, Lexington: The University Press of Kentucky.

6   Mike Weed and Chris Bull, 2012, *Sports Tourism: Participants, Policy and Providers*, London and New York: Routledge.

7   Stephen Wearing and Nancy Gard McGehee, 2013, 'Volunteer tourism: A review', *Tourism Management* 38: 120–30.

8   Marina Novelli (ed.), 2005, *Niche Tourism: Contemporary Issues, Trends and Cases*, Amsterdam and Sydney: Elsevier.

and do not advocate for a rash discarding of the notion of tourism. In fact, at very least, the very notion of tourism can be seen to act as a powerful ideological category or trope—or rather set of tropes—such that are as fundamental (and therefore unavoidable) to scholarship as they are to public discourse. There is something of a double irony in that as many leisure travellers and sightseers seek to move beyond or reject 'tourist' as a category of identification, they often tend to both reinforce and epitomise it. Through their repetition such tropes become endlessly sedimented as a 'self evident essence',[9] echoing through tourism statistics, national branding campaigns, and indeed in academic research centres and projects in the still burgeoning field of tourism studies. In the same way, depending on the particular example at hand, a focus on touring Pacific cultures may lead to both reifications *and* disruptions of the standard tropes of tourism and tourism studies for the Pacific. This is the same in academic analyses as it is in everyday life. In one context, for example, the idea of the Pacific as paradise may be eagerly repeated by Pacific Islanders. In others it may be vehemently rejected as a neo-colonial lie, one that says nothing of the many contexts of inequality and alienation that often travel hand-in-hand with tourism-related developments.

In short, the schisms and debates of tourism studies are also evident across local productions, performances and analyses. For this reason, we have invited a range of contributions to this volume—this includes identifiably academic offerings as well as those that are less so; personal reflections, poems, artwork, images and other creative engagements. In doing so, we hope to reflect the mobile and fragmented qualities of tourism's relations to touring Pacific cultures, as well as the creative and dynamic nature of production, exchange, performance and experience that such intersecting contexts, departures and arrivals entail.

---

9   Chris Rojek and John Urry, 1997, *Touring Cultures: Transformations of Travel and Theory*, London and New York: Routledge.

Touring Pacific imaginaries

Mobility, by definition, is a central aspect of both tourism and touring. It has, however, been curiously absent from many analyses that have instead tended to focus on static 'destinations'. One way we may critically reframe and refocus tourism-related research is by paying attention to such mobilities. This includes by observing the ways in which the material content and imagery of tourism moves and shifts, even as it is reproduced and consumed by people. As is widely noted, for many western tourists the Pacific is an imaginary awash with iridescent waters, white sandy beaches and curvaceous women reclining under swaying palms. Such highly gendered and romantic images of the Pacific as 'paradise' stretch as far back as those early 'voyages of discovery' that also arguably represent the first touristic excursions into the region.[10] So, too, do titillating images of savage cannibalism, sorcery and heathen gods. While pre-colonial Pacific Islanders undoubtedly also travelled near and far for reasons primarily or partially relating to pleasure, if not leisure, the particular historic and ongoing association of tourism with various forms and products of colonialism is a defining feature of that industry.[11]

---

10   Bernard Smith, 1960, *European Vision and the South Pacific* (2nd ed.), New Haven: Yale University Press; Bernard Smith, 1992, *Imagining the Pacific: In the Wake of the Cook Voyages*, Carlton: Melbourne University Press at the Miegunyah Press; C. Michael Hall, 1998, 'Making the Pacific: Globalisation, modernity and myth', in *Destinations: Cultural Landscapes of Tourism*, ed. G. Ringer, pp. 140–53, London and New York: Routledge; John Connell, 2003, 'Island dreaming: The contemplation of Polynesian paradise', *Journal of Historical Geography* 29: 554–81.

11   See Miriam Kahn, 2011, *Tahiti Beyond the Postcard: Power, Place, and Everyday Life*, Seattle: University of Washington Press; Jane C. Desmond, 1999, *Staging Tourism: Bodies on Display from Waikiki to Sea World*, Chicago: University of Chicago Press; Hall, 'Making the Pacific'; Margaret Jolly, 1997, 'From Point Venus to Bali Ha'i: Eroticism and exoticism in representations of the Pacific', in *Sites of Desire, Economies of Pleasure: Sexualities in Asia and the Pacific*, ed. Lenore Manderson and Margaret Jolly, pp. 99–112, Chicago and London: University of Chicago Press; Haunani-Kay Trask, 1993, 'Lovely hula hands: Corporate Tourism and the prostitution of Hawaiian culture', in *From a Native Daughter: Colonialism and Sovereignty in Hawai'i*, pp. 179–97, Maine: Common Courage Press; Tracey Banivanua Mar, 'Performing Cannibalism in the South Seas', this volume; John Connell, 'Fiji: Reflections in the Infinity Pool', this volume; Marata Tamaira, 'Native Realities in an Imaginary World: Contemporary Kānaka Maoli Art at Aulani, A Disney Resort & Spa', this volume; John Taylor, 'Pikinini in Paradise: Photography, Souvenirs and the "Child Native" in Tourism', this volume.

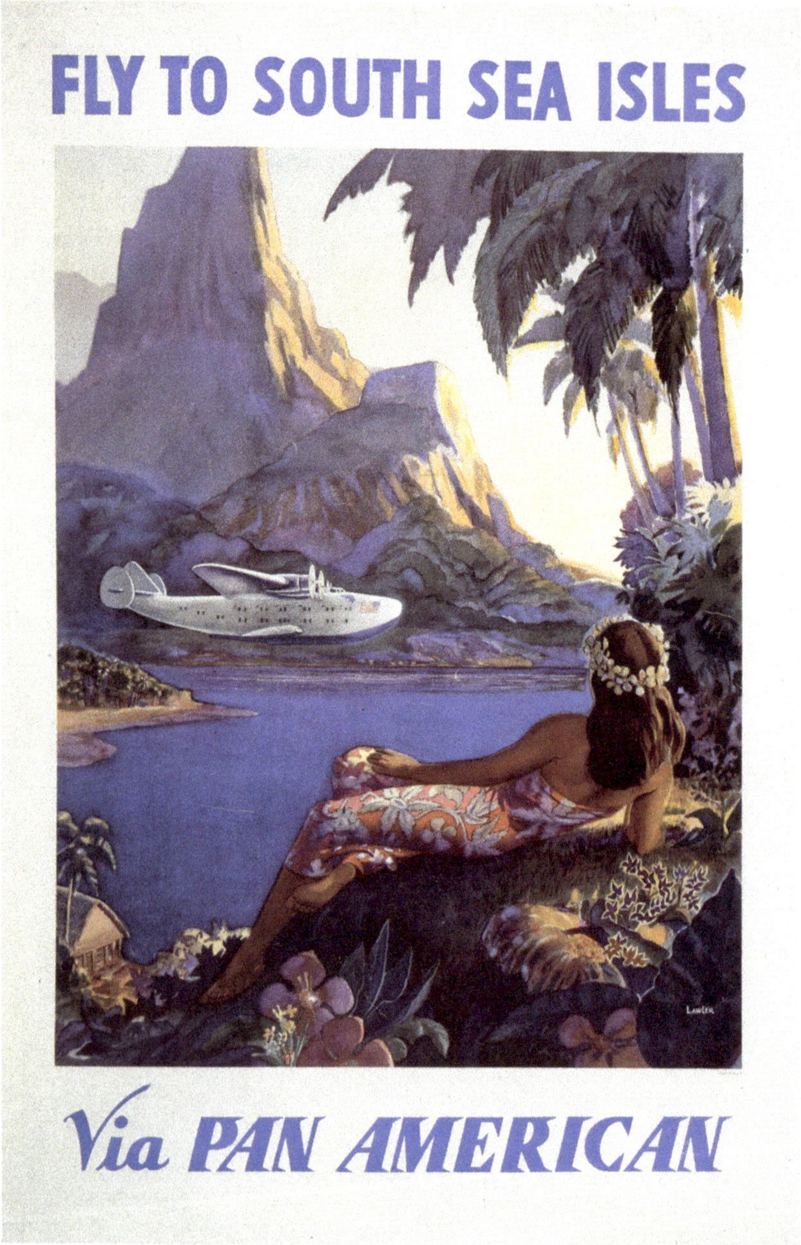
FLY TO SOUTH SEA ISLES
LAWLER
Via PAN AMERICAN

Figures 1 and 2. Reclining dusky maidens provide a tranquil frame for the romance of travel for leisure, and through the important inclusion of tourism technology and infrastructure, fantasy meets reality through the prospect of touring.

Source. Figure 1. 'Fly to South Sea isles via Pan American'. Lithograph by Paul George Lawler circa 1938, Library of Congress Prints and Photographs Division Washington, DC 20540 USA; Figure 2. Louis Macouillard artwork circa 1955, reproduced courtesy of Matson.

Many of the chapters in this volume reveal the work that has gone into creating these tropes, particularly in the nineteenth century. Mission imagery of the Pacific in the form of pictures, popular literature and lantern slides, toured metropolitan markets and, as Lamont Lindstrom shows,[12] created portraits that shaped and framed perceptions of the Pacific Islands and the nascent colonial tourist industry. On the early cruise vessels of the nineteenth century, Frances Steel argues,[13] cross-cultural encounters aboard ship were often unpredictable engagements that sometimes served to dismantle dominant tropes and their inherent opposition between savage and civilised, native and modern, toured and touring. This, it may also be noted, is a constantly recurring effect of the disjuncture between touristic imaginaries and real-world encounters everywhere.[14] The work of artist Yuki Kihara is a contemporary intervention that serves to unveil and disrupt the racialised and gendered genealogy of colonial tropes of travel.[15]

Despite such disjunctures, there is a remarkable historical 'durability' of colonially produced images of the Pacific.[16] Branding styles may disappear and mediums of communication change, but the images of 'soft primitivism' associated with leisure-related travel in the Pacific have for the most part remained remarkably consistent over time. While recent marketing strategies have dictated the generation of new themes within, due to an incessant replicability and 'pseudo-individuation'[17] of the core touristic tropes, there remains a remarkable consistency of content across these. So in the post-war period the image of a native maiden reclining above a sandy beach and native village served equally well for Tahiti as it did for Hawai'i, and was also used more generally to represent the entire South Sea Islands. In key stylistic terms, with the replacement of mode of transport to that of accommodation, it was even extended to the snow-capped peaks of New Zealand.

---

12 Lamont Lindstrom, 'Darkness and Light in Black and White: Travelling Mission Imagery from the New Hebrides', this volume.
13 Frances Steel, 'The Cruise Ship', this volume.
14 Kalissa Alexeyeff, 'Re-purposing Paradise: Tourism, Image and Affect', this volume.
15 Mandy Treagus, 'Yuki Kihara's *Culture for Sale* and the History of Pacific Cultural Performance', this volume.
16 Desmond, *Staging Tourism*, p. 11.
17 Max Horkheimer and Theodor W. Adorno, 1944, *Dialectic of Enlightenment*, New York: Herder.

Figure 3. Images of childlike fun speak to touristic fantasies of escape from mundane life while also echoing primitivist tropes of native innocence and spontaneity.

Source. Reproduced with permission of the Vanuatu Tourism Office, 2015.

The most recent 'rebranding' of Pacific neighbours Vanuatu and Fiji, under the respective campaign themes of 'Discover What Matters' and 'Where Happiness Finds You', demonstrate an equally remarkable interchangeability. Focusing heavily on images of frolicking indigenous children, often pictured in joyous play with tourists, both emphasise a quirky sense of childlike fun as the basis for what are simultaneously physical and existential journeys of discovery. While diverging in some respects from earlier images in terms of visual content, including by abandoning the image of the 'dusky maiden', the emphasis on carefree spontaneity represents a continuation of long-standing tropes of native primitivism measured in relation to western modernity. Such approaches also illustrate the historical durability of Polynesian–Melanesian divide in touring tropes. The romantic and bountiful 'Polynesian' princess versus the childlike or, as a flipside, the menacing cannibal that characterise 'Melanesia', have a long historical trajectory as a number of papers in this volume demonstrate.[18]

In considering the mobility of such images we also note the way in which visual tropes frequently slip out of the tourism sphere, featuring on products as diverse as cigarettes, beer and perfume. As the caption of one such product reads:

> Sun, sea, sand, palm trees … Sounds idyllic, right? Well, now you can escape to your own tropical paradise with the lush, exotic scent of the NEW Fijian Water Lotus range from The Body Shop.[19]

Touristic tropes and images relating to Pacific Island romanticisms not only migrate between 'products', they also seep into social contexts not typically associated with the tourism industry. This includes being appropriated as markers of identity or foci of critical engagement by Pacific Islanders themselves, as several inclusions in this volume examine. The dangerous warrior and the demure maiden are continuously 'played up' and both adopted and adapted in engagements with tourists.[20] At dance shows across the region, emcees describe local women as 'the most beautiful in the Pacific' and jokingly warn tourists

---

18 Banivanua Mar, 'Performing Cannibalism in the South Seas'; and Lindstrom, 'Darkness and Light in Black and White'.
19 International, T.B.S., 2013, 'Paradise beckons with Fijian Water Lotus!' *The Body Shop*.
20 For example, Michelle MacCarthy, 'Touring "Real Life"? Authenticity and Village-based Tourism in the Trobriand Islands of Papua New Guinea', this volume; and Taylor, 'Pikinini in paradise'.

to avoid late night walks lest they are captured, cooked and eaten.[21] Such 'appropriations' might in the former case seem ironic given their colonial legacy. Doubly so in the case of the nostalgic and nationalistic revaluing of vintage tourism advertising as 'kiwiana', and its transformation into coffee table art. Either way, such associations often suggest strong continuities across colonial and neo-colonial practices of objectification, production and capitalist enterprise.

Given the explicit centrality of mobility to tourism and touring, it is unsurprising that the depiction of modes of transport is so prominent in much tourism advertising. As such, it is not just romantic visions of 'destinations' and their inhabitants that have characterised tourism-related imagery. Equally from the outset, ships and later aeroplanes have also frequently featured as central visual components. Such inclusions reflect that the experience of travel by luxurious technologies of leisured motility is as saleable as the destinations themselves. This is particularly the case in the advertising of cruise ship tourism. They also, however, are often made to do the double-work of reflecting the trope of spatio-temporal juxtaposition.

Figure 4. A long-standing favourite—images of ultra-modern cruise ships looming over 'stone age', 'primitive' or 'traditional' outriggers remain a key signifier of tourism's magical powers of transportation, such that suggest journeys through time as well as space.
Source. Photographed by Colin Taimbari and used with permission.

---

21   See Maria Amoamo, 'Pitcairn and the *Bounty* Story', this volume; and Banivanua Mar, 'Performing Cannibalism in the South Seas'.

As several commentators have noted, in such instances the trope of paradise becomes coupled with that of nostalgia within the context of modernity.[22] The implication of such narratives, of course, is that tourists may somehow uncoil the ravages of modern time and the degradations of progress. By visiting a palm-swept beach on an island in the deepest, remotest Pacific, they may also rediscover their long-lost 'real' selves, reconnecting with nature and humanity alike.

Figure 5. Typifying the nexus of tourism and contemporary colonialism, Queen Elizabeth II is given an elevated royal welcome as she arrives on Rarotonga by British Airways to officiate at the grand opening of the Rarotonga International Airport, 1974.

Source. Photographed by Bill Johnson and used with permission.

---

22   Barry Curtis and Claire Pajaczkowska, 1994, 'Getting there: Travel, time and narrative', in *Travellers' Tales: Narratives of Home and Displacement*, ed. George Robertson, pp. 199–215, London and New York: Routledge; Desmond, *Staging Tourism*; Catherine A. Lutz and Jane Lou Collins, 1993, *Reading National Geographic*, Chicago: University of Chicago Press; John Taylor, 1998, *Consuming Identity: Modernity and Tourism in New Zealand*, Department of Anthropology, University of Auckland.

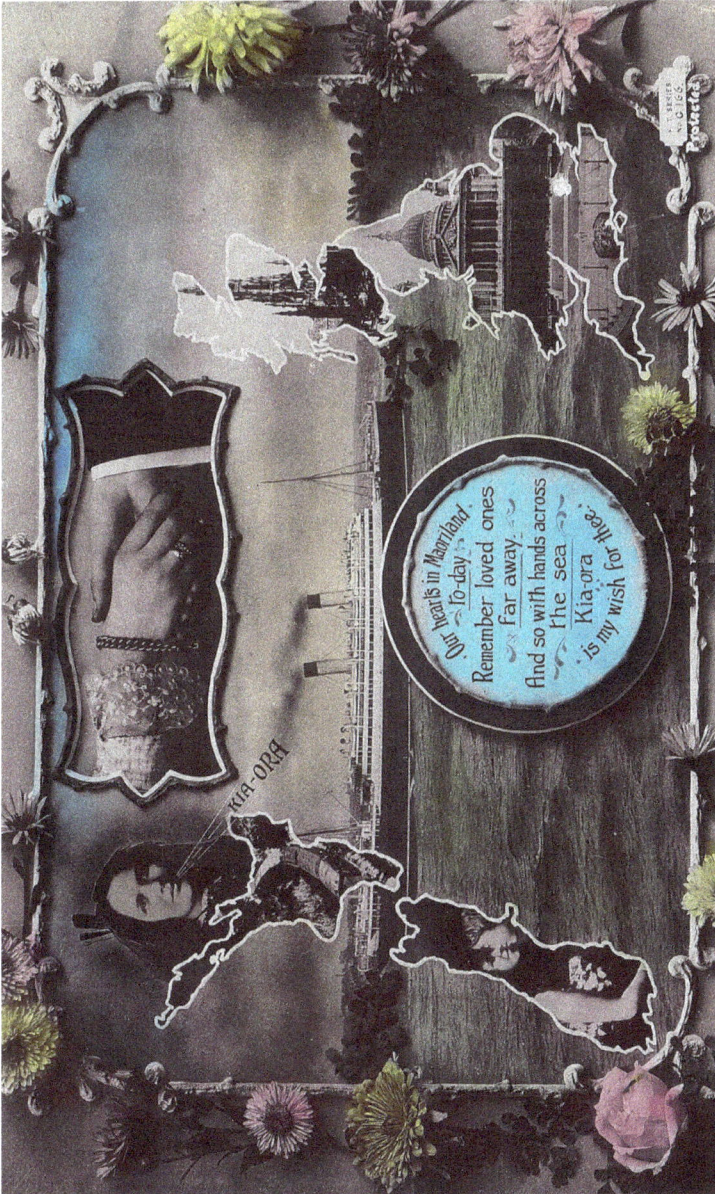

Figure 6. This example of touristic material culture and imagery can be read as being equally if not more reflective of class-related labour mobility within the context of colonialism than tourism *per se*.

Source. Postcard. Kia Ora. Our hearts in Maoriland today … F.T. series No. G 166. Protected. New Zealand postcard (carte postale). Made in England [ca 1911]. Ref: Eph-POSTCARD-Hearts-and-Minds-04. Alexander Turnbull Library, Wellington, New Zealand. Online: natlib.govt.nz/records/22801988 (accessed 9 March 2016).

From the earliest days, the inclusion of ships and later planes in tourism imagery has not only played into primitivist desires and fantasies, it has also reinforced in a much more tangible sense the link between tourism and neo-colonial enterprise. This was most explicitly witnessed during the nineteenth and early twentieth centuries, during which time the first inter-island tours were offered.[23] Here, as in the present, adventure-seeking travellers very often had multiple reasons for travelling, and were transported with cargo and other passengers largely dissociated from that still nascent tourism industry.

The voyages of missionary vessels such as the Melanesian Mission's *Southern Cross* similarly overlapped with and fed into the industrialisation of leisured travel. Indeed, both colonial and missionary writers contributed to much of the earliest travel literature.[24] By contrast, in New Zealand as the postcard came to represent an instantly recognisable material signifier of tourism and circulated Orientalist fantasies of a romantic 'Maori Wonderland', intersecting nostalgias were often apparent as longings for home referenced the lived experience of long-distance labour mobility alongside those associated with touristic nativeness. In sum, it would appear the images and affective sentiments associated with tourism are as mobile and multi-directional as tourists themselves.

This volume does not attempt to provide a complete picture of the intersecting and enmeshing of tourism and other forms of mobility in the Pacific region. It does, however, demonstrate the extraordinary historical and geographical mobility of Pacific culture in the form of objects, images and imaginaries. Most particularly, Jo Diamond's chapter takes us on a mystery tour to discover the origins of the *pari*, the bodice worn by Maori women in cultural performances.[25] This tour moves through archives, histories and images from across the globe and encapsulates the cross-currents that have created both the *pari* and academic disciplines that similarly tour the region: Pacific studies, anthropology and tourism research. In other chapters, many Pacific Islanders are depicted engaging in movement at very different

---

23   Ngaire Douglas, 1996, *They Came for Savages: 100 years of Tourism in Melanesia*, Lismore: Centre for Tourism, Southern Cross University.
24   Frances Steel, 2011, *Oceania Under Steam: Sea Transport and the Cultures of Colonialism, c. 1870–1914*, Manchester: Manchester University Press; Lindstrom, 'Darkness and Light in Black and White'; and Steel, 'The Cruise Ship'.
25   Jo Diamond, 'Writing Home on the Pari and Touring in Pacific Studies', this volume.

registers from displacement[26] and labour migration[27] to travel to cultural exhibitions and workshops,[28] regional festivals,[29] or for leisure and education. This diversity invites strategies of understanding that are equally enmeshed, mobile and multi-perspectival.[30]

Destination inequality?

Colonial migration, capitalist enterprise and the missionary legacy are imbricated within the dynamics and practices of tourism today. The latter for instance is witnessed in the growing trend of voluntourism that simultaneously satisfies the desire to undertake 'good works' and provides a quest for 'remote' adventure.[31] Likewise, for Pacific Islanders, church and business enterprise, as with political engagement and education, represent significant contexts of pleasurable travel. In Vanuatu, the link between tourism and neo-colonial enterprise is explicitly witnessed in the close association of tourism imagery and advertising with rapacious land sales, especially to expatriate Australian and New Zealander 'sea changers'.[32] Many of these touristic migrants go on to contribute more directly still to the presently booming tourism economy by setting up tourism-related businesses themselves.

In the most extreme cases, colonialism and tourism have intersected to both undermine and appropriate indigenous forms of cultural identity. As Marata Tamaira in her analysis of the Aulani, A Disney

---

26   Tamaira, 'Native Realities in an Imaginary World'; Greg Dvorak, 'Detouring Kwajalein: At Home Between Coral and Concrete in the Marshall Islands', this volume.

27   Alexeyeff, 'Re-purposing Paradise'.

28   Margaret Jolly, 'Moving Towers: Worlding the Spectacle of Masculinities between South Pentecost and Munich', this volume; Bomai D. Witne, 'A Trip from Port Moresby to Suva', this volume.

29   Katerina Teaiwa and Joseph Vile, 'New Pacific Portraits: Voices from the 11th Festival of Pacific Arts', this volume; Peter Phipps, 'Performing Indigenous Sovereignties across the Pacific', this volume.

30   Miriam Kahn, Teana Gooding and Moenau Holman, 'Cross-currents: Teana and Moenau, Tahitian Tourists in Seattle', this volume; Courtney Sina Meredith, 'Ibu & Tufuga' and 'Great Works', this volume; and Flora Aurima-Devatine, 'Carnet de Voyage en Irlande', this volume.

31   Mary Mostafanezhad, 2014, 'Locating the tourist in volunteer tourism', *Current Issues in Tourism* 17(4): 381–84.

32   Claire Slatter, 2006, 'The con/dominium of Vanuatu? Paying the price of investment and land liberalisation', unpublished paper.

Resort & Spa on O'ahu, Hawai'i,[33] demonstrates, such appropriations
entail a repackaging of place and history even as the original owners,
many of whom are excluded from such contexts, live in relative poverty
nearby. The inclusion of indigenous agency in the production of many
of these repackagings, however, ensures that they do not always
appear as simple sanitisations, but may be subversively shot through
with critical voices, images and perspectives. Similarly, here the
analysis of such violent appropriations and erasures comprises a key
feature of this volume, such that they often lead to further creative,
critical and reflexive interventions. In telling the story of his family's
residence on the military base of Kwajalein Atoll, Marshall Islands,
Greg Dvorak uncovers layers of American and Japanese history from
the half-buried bunkers, and then to the bottom of the lagoon where
the remains of Japanese war dead are presumed to be located. In doing
so, following in the path of both the analyst and of war pilgrims, we
are taken on a tour and detour through acts of familial and ancestral
memorialisation.[34]

Such connections not only suggest the complexly articulated nature
of the tourism 'industry', they also point to ongoing processes of
resource extraction and increasing inequality that have come to
define tourism 'investment' and 'development' across much of the
region and beyond.[35] It may be the case that in the current neo-liberal
climate, inequality is not only an unfortunate outcome of tourism
development, but a key driving force in touristic reproduction and
enterprise. At the most fundamental level, relative poverty not only
provides photogenic 'added value' to tourism destinations in the form

---

33   Tamaira, 'Native realities in an Imaginary World'; see also Anita Jowitt, 'Suva,
November '97', this volume.
34   Dvorak, 'Detouring Kwajalein'; on 'militourism', the strategic links between tourism and
military, see also Teresia Teaiwa, 1999, 'Reading Paul Gauguin's *Noa Noa* with Epeli Hau'ofa's
Kisses in the Nederends: Militourism, feminism, and the "Polynesian" body', in *Inside Out:
Literature, Cultural Politics, and Identity in the New Pacific*, ed. Vilsoni Hereniko and Rob Wilson,
pp. 249–63, Boston: Rowman and Littlefield; and Setsu Shigematsu and Keith L. Camacho (eds),
2010, *Militarized Currents: Towards a Decolonized Future in Asia and the Pacific*, London and
Minneapolis: University of Minnesota Press.
35   Donald V.L. Macleod and James G. Carrier (eds), 2010, *Tourism, Power and Culture:
Anthropological Insights*, Bristol: Channel View Publications; John Connell, 2013, *Islands at
Risk?: Environments, Economies and Contemporary Change*, Cheltenham and Northhamton,
MA: Edward Elgar Publishing; John Connell and Barbara Rugendyke, 2008, *Tourism at the
Grassroots: Villagers and Visitors in the Asia-Pacific*, Abingdon: Routledge; Regina Scheyvens,
2012, *Tourism and Poverty*, Hoboken: Routledge.

of exotically attired locals. It also ensures an abundance of cheap beachfront land and labour, thereby enabling the materialisation of those Pacific imaginaries of sand, sea and service.

The ever elusive promise of a significant financial 'trickle-down' ensures the continuing support of national governments for tourism-related development, including in creating infrastructure that often benefits expatriates more than locals. As described by C. Michael Hall, 'As a destination for the tourist, the Pacific is a creation of capitalism', and as such, 'has always been a component of the global system', however that may be defined.[36] We are mindful of the critical importance of this perspective and agree that much tourism industry enterprise represents the 'hedonistic face of neo-colonialism', and thereby amounts to 'leisure imperialism'.[37]

Leisure imperialism is not simply the purview of western tourists, it is also increasingly and ambivalently adopted by Pacific Islanders themselves. So, the island dream is not only consumed by visiting tourists but also by an expanding middle class in the region as well as in large transnational diasporic communities.[38] Such multidirectionality reminds us that class location is a further component that shapes touristic engagements. The economic and cultural capital available to local elites enables them to replicate leisure practices that are out of reach to the majority of local poor. This includes visiting resorts for a massage or to socialise by the pool, and it is embodied in leisure activities such as sun-baking and swimming, both foreign concepts to many Pacific peoples for whom the beach, ocean, reef and lagoon are places of work (for example, fishing or pearling, gathering seaweed or shells for necklaces).

---

36 Hall, 'Making the Pacific', p. 141; see Alexeyef, 'Re-purposing Paradise'. Also C. Michael Hall and Stephen J. Page (eds), 1996, *Tourism in the Pacific: Issues and Cases* (1st ed., series in tourism and hospitality management), London and Boston, MA: International Thomson Business Press.
37 Malcolm Crick, 1989, 'Representations of international tourism in the social sciences: Sun, sex, sights, savings, and servility', *Annual Review of Anthropology* 18: 307–44; and see Connell, 'Fiji: Reflections in the Infinity Pool'.
38 See Audrey Brown-Pereira, 'Local Tourist on a Bus Ride Home', this volume; and Audrey Brown-Pereira, 'Mixed Bag of Tropical Sweets Sitting Outside the Hotel R & R', this volume; Regina Scheyvens, 2007, 'Poor cousins no more valuing the development potential of domestic and diaspora tourism', *Progress in Development Studies* 7(4): 307–25.

Tourism is known to enact and effect wealth differentials within and across communities and nations.[39] Increasingly, such inequalities are explicitly defined through tourism-related engagement and conflicts within the region, including in ways that move beyond the tourist/ local divide. In the Cook Islands for example, Fijian contract workers are key to service industry provision associated with tourism as Cook Islanders choose to work abroad rather than at home. At another register, the New Zealand Government recently and controversially changed labour laws in order to bolster the international film industry, and by extension in the interests of benefiting the generation of film tourism. Even so, as in this case, it seems that the fetishistic desires and imaginaries of international tourism—whether they be of Pacific paradise or other fantasy landscapes, such as Hobbiton—often evidently overshadow such realities.[40]

By contrast, at a more localised level, tourism shapes cross-cultural understandings of work and leisure, notions of economic development and culture difference more generally. In this context, 'the tourist' operates as a highly ambivalent trope indexing both the promises of capitalism and the pitfalls of neo-colonial inequality. Throughout the Pacific, tourism is the focus of entrepreneurial ambitions, be it in opening a guesthouse, sewing handicrafts to sell at the airport, or purchasing a boat or taxi. Working in some sectors of the industry (such as tourist bureaus and as dancers and musicians) affords prestige if not wealth to some locals. Conversely, the term 'tourist' is used by Cook Islanders as a pejorative term to describe locals who dress immodestly or who conspicuously 'flash' around money or other signs of wealth. The numerous diasporic locals who return from Australia and New Zealand for holidays similarly embody this ambivalence. With cameras flashing, expensive clothing, and self-conscious expressions of local language and protocols, they are described, and as well describe themselves, as tourists in comparison to their local family members. By contrast, and differing once again to widely held if somewhat ambivalent beliefs about the economic benefits of tourism in the Cook Islands or Fiji, Tongans are often reticent about engaging explicitly in conventional tourism. As long as Tongans residing overseas support

---

39   See John Cox, 'Bandit Singsing: The Tourism Unexperience', this volume.
40   Carolyn Michelle, Ann L. Hardy, Charles H. Davis and Craig Hight, 2014, 'An unexpected controversy in Middle-earth: Audience encounters with the "dark side" of transnational film production', *Transnational Cinemas*, pp. 1–18.

their national economy by making regular visits home (itself a form of tourism), tourism in the more conventional sense of hosting foreigners is considered a largely unattractive enterprise.[41] As cases like these demonstrate, the trope of the tourist as well as the value of tourism is diversely and complexly constituted across the region.

Relations of gender further cross-cut engagements between 'locals' and 'tourists'. Classic analyses of tourism have rightly emphasised the role of stereotypes of 'hula girls' and 'dusky maidens' in generating a sexualised vision of the Pacific.[42] Such types often relate to geographic divides, with Melanesia by contrast often being marked in more masculine terms, including through tropes of the muscular savage and smiling 'pikinini in paradise'.[43] At the same time, however, we note that an awareness of gender does not only entail paying attention to the dynamics of relations between men and women, but also between different kinds of masculinities and femininities. In this way, Margaret Jolly eloquently details how the commodification of *kastom* and contestations surrounding the land dive in South Pentecost are enacted in a jostling performance of 'relational masculinities' between indigenous men of different status and between indigenous men and foreign men. Such insights demonstrate the ways in which gender relations are harnessed as a part of enactments and reenactments of power and authority, intersecting with class, race and other sites of social as well as economic capital.

Such analyses are vital to understanding the political-economic realities that underpin the tourism industry. However, recognising the link of tourism and other forms of Pacific touring to inequality should not eclipse an appreciation of tourism's many positive outcomes, for tourists and locals alike. Many local communities and individuals *do* enjoy significant financial and other forms of reward from engaging in tourism-related enterprise. Tourism-related engagements and activities also may play a key role in promoting aspects of indigenous culture. We should also be attentive to the many revaluations and relocations of tourism products that occur as a part of everyday life, both across the Pacific and beyond. Here, for example, we recognise

---

41   See Helen Lee, 'The Friendly Islands? Tonga's Ambivalent Relationship with Tourism', this volume.

42   Selina Tusitala Marsh, 'Hawai'i: Prelude to a Journey', this volume; Meredith, 'Ibu & Tufuga' and 'Great Works', this volume.

43   John Taylor, 'Pikinini in Paradise', this volume.

that locals who produce many such products—including especially forms of 'cultural tourism'—very often repurpose these to fulfil local purposes of performance and consumption. Thus the same choreographed cultural show that is produced for performance in a resort setting might also on later occasions be repurposed to welcome home returning political dignitaries, toured to a regional arts festival, or included in the program of a school fundraising event. In cases such as these, tourism is a crucial site for the meaningful engagement of ongoing strategies concerning personal livelihood, community development and the sustainability of cultural heritage.

Looked at through the lens of dynamically mobile touring culture, such that reframes tourism as an analytic category, the easy dismissal of tourism-related performances as shallowly inauthentic is rendered problematic at best, if not entirely inappropriate. As the many diverse papers of this volume demonstrate, the ascription of relative positive or negative cultural value as to the degree to which such traditions might be seen as more or less 'invented' is largely a matter of perspective. In the same way, just as tourism appears in diverse and ever changing inflections across the region, by refocusing our attention in such a way that recognises the mobile, fragmented and diffuse nature of tourism, perhaps we may find a space in which to celebrate even as we critically evaluate the performances, encounters and productions that the notion of tourism encompasses.

Reframing and remobilising tourism studies

Tourism today is vital to the economies of most if not all Pacific nations. Over many decades it has also represented an important albeit often contested site for the dynamic production and circulation of cultural practices, meanings and values.[44] In tourism industry and development literature especially, extraordinary statistics linking 'visitor arrivals' to 'capacity generation' are routinely marshalled to justify the bolstering of tourism-related infrastructure across the

---

44   Stephen Pratt and David Harrison (eds), 2015, *Tourism in Pacific Islands: Current Issues and Future Challenges*, Contemporary Geographies of Leisure, Tourism and Mobility, London and New York: Routledge; David Harrison, 2003, *Pacific Island Tourism*, New York: Cognizant Communication Corporation; Douglas, *They Came for Savages*; Connell and Rugendyke, *Tourism at the Grassroots*.

region.[45] Impressive though they may be, however, these say little about the complex social, cultural and environmental costs and benefits associated with these indices. More so, they rest on a largely discursive category of 'tourism' as a monolithic whole that ignores the many intersections that cross-cut the countless practices, processes and products encompassed by that term. In reality, tourism is difficult to pin down, being complexly articulated across multiple sites of production, consumption and lived experience.[46] Its diffuse yet ubiquitous reach means that tourism intersects in one way or another with the lives of all Pacific Islanders. Yet it does so unevenly. As such, the benefits and costs of tourism, however defined, are not distributed or experienced equally. In the same way, Pacific Islanders are involved in tourism to varying degrees and in different contexts. Some have daily face-to-face involvement as tour operators, hotel staff, business investors or in their roles as public servants, while others engage less directly with tourists through related industries such as farming, fishing and craft manufacture, or still more casually or sporadically as a part of day-to-day living. At the same time, clearly tourism revenues more directly benefit a minority elite, both local and expatriate.

Observations concerning the enmeshing of tourism in everyday life, and of the diffuse and fragmented nature of tourism as an industry are not entirely new. Neither are attempts to respond to such observations through deconstructing, expanding or otherwise rethinking our understandings of tourism and the tourism industry,[47] or broadening

---

45   As one example, the Pacific Islands Forum Secretariat report on *Tourism as a Pillar of Economic Growth* states that 'Tourism is vital to the sustainable growth of Forum Island Countries (FICs), contributing an estimated 10.7 per cent of the region's Gross Domestic Product (GDP) in 2012. In 2010 tourism accounted for 56 per cent of Palau's GDP, 44.4 per cent of Cook Islands GDP, 34.1 per cent of Vanuatu's GDP, and 23.4 per cent of Fiji's GDP. In most FICs, it continues to be the major driver of economic growth and foreign exchange earnings. The 2012 Economic Impact report by the World Travel and Tourism Council showed that total (direct, indirect and induced) contribution of tourism to the Pacific Island economies in 2012 was 2.7 per cent of total GDP (US$46.7bn). This is forecast to rise by 1.8 per cent in 2013.' See Pacific Islands Forum Secretariat, 2013, *Tourism as a Pillar of Economic Growth*, Nuku'alofa, Tonga, 3–5 July, Pacific Islands Forum Secretariat.
46   See, for example, Anne Campbell, 2009, 'Almost in paradise: The intrusion of tourism in the living/leisure space of local women In Waikiki', *World Leisure Journal* 51(3): 160–66.
47   Sohail Inayatullah, 1995, 'Rethinking tourism: Unfamiliar histories and alternative futures', *Tourism Management* 16(6): 411–15; Freya Higgins-Desbiolles, 2006, 'More than an "industry": The forgotten power of tourism as a social force', *Tourism Management* 27(6): 1192–208; Arthur Asa Berger, 2004, *Deconstructing Travel: Cultural Perspectives on Tourism*, Walnut Creek: Rowman Altamira.

the scope of tourism-related scholarship.[48] Chris Rojek and John Urry's serendipitously titled *Touring Cultures: Transformations of Travel and Theory* was premised on just such a project, proposing to move beyond previous visions by seeing tourism as a cultural practice that is both highly social and sensorial. Through his notion of 'traveling cultures', James Clifford has also insisted that we direct our analyses away from entrenched understandings of cultures as fixed wholes and instead pay better attention to the mobility and intermingling of people and things.[49] Just as we should look beyond the boundedness of anthropological 'pure cultures', so too we should look beyond the boundedness of 'pure tourism'. Instead, we might conceptualise the culture of tourism as infinitely diverse and mobile, and as characterised by long histories of travelling and meeting, gazing and exchanging, borrowing and producing, accommodating and resisting.

Remobilising our understanding of tourism includes at a most basic level refocusing questions regarding the stereotypical image of tourists as foreigners from 'big' countries (economically if not physically) who visit remote and exotic Pacific Islands and people in order to satiate their primitivist desires and for a short time live out romantic, barefoot, sun-drenched fantasies. Equally it includes refocusing stereotypical images of locals performing culture in staged settings, trapped in a devilish and divisive pursuit of capital, such that would quench touristic fantasies even as it degrades the traditions from which those performances are derived. Approaches such as these that continue to too easily see tourism production as consisting entirely as gratuitous spectacle, as consisting of sharply defined front and back 'stages',[50] or as endlessly producing a 'hermeneutic circle' of commodified culture,[51] merely reify the trope of tourism. Worse, they rehearse a negative meta-narrative that casts tourists and locals alike as slaves to a Kafkaesque machine of Destination Marketing.

---

48 Noel B. Salazar, 2010, *Envisioning Eden: Mobilizing Imaginaries in Tourism and Beyond*, New York: Berghahn Books; Claudio Minca and Tim Oakes (eds), 2006, *Travels in Paradox: Remapping Tourism*, Lanham: Rowman & Littlefield; Rojek and Urry, *Touring Cultures*.
49 James Clifford, 1997, *Routes: Travel and Translation in the Late Twentieth Century*, Cambridge, MA: Harvard University Press.
50 Dean MacCannell, 1976, *The Tourist: A New Theory of the Leisure Class*, Berkeley, CA: University of California Press.
51 Patricia C. Albers and William R. James, 1988, 'Travel photography: A methodological approach', *Annals of Tourism Research* 15(1): 134–58, p. 136; Erik Cohen, 1988, 'Authenticity and commoditization in tourism', *Annals of Tourism Research* 15(3): 371–86.

Just as some commentators are quick to vilify tourism as an industry for its deleterious effects on local populations and indigenous cultures, for politicians and tourism industry advocates the trope of tourism is often taken as a harbinger of development and prosperity, especially for populations typically figured as 'isolated' from significant flows of capital. This is reflected, for example, in the South Pacific Tourism Organisation's ministerial vision, that 'Tourism will inspire sustainable economic growth and empower the Pacific people'.[52] Coming from the other extreme, such visions are equally problematic for conviction and dependence on the monolithic trope of tourism. Clearly, just as tourism may be more or less present in daily life, as numerous case studies demonstrate, explicit engagement with tourism may be both positive and negative in its social and economic effects.[53] Just as the validity of Fiji or Vanuatu being identified 'the happiest country in the world'[54] is up for debate, even as it presents an effective tourism marketing slogan, measuring and scaling such impacts is a fraught exercise.

All such tourisms exist—happy, sad, corrosive and creative—as tropes and as material realities. But these descriptive fields are far from the be all and end all of touring Pacific cultures. Here we take seriously the simple observation that cultural products readily associated with tourism are rarely produced or consumed within the context of a discretely defined tourism industry. Neither are they toured exclusively by tourists. Tourism is not an isolated sphere of activity. Rather it denotes a loose conglomeration of political, economic and social phenomena that in reality intersect—in one way or another, be it directly or indirectly—with a great many other aspects of daily life and outcomes of material production.

---

52   South Pacific Tourism Organisation, 2012, *Pacific Regional Tourism Capacity Building Programme (Inception Report and First Work Plan)*, South Pacific Tourism Organisation.

53   On this tension, see Cluny Macpherson, 2008, 'Golden goose or Trojan horse? Cruise ship tourism in Pacific development', *Asia Pacific Viewpoint* 49(2): 185–97.

54   Worldwide Independent Network of Market Research (WIN), 2014. 'End of Year Survey 2014', *Gallup International*, Zurich, 30 December.

References

Albers, Patricia C. and William R. James. 1988. 'Travel photography: A methodological approach.' *Annals of Tourism Research* 15(1): 134–58.

Beeton, Sue. 2005. *Film-Induced Tourism.* Series: Aspects of Tourism 25. Clevedon: Channel View Publications.

Berger, Arthur Asa. 2004. *Deconstructing Travel: Cultural Perspectives on Tourism.* Walnut Creek: Rowman Altamira.

Campbell, Anne. 2009. 'Almost in paradise: The intrusion of tourism in the living/leisure space of local women in Waikiki.' *World Leisure Journal* 51(3): 160–66.

Clifford, James. 1997. *Routes: Travel and Translation in the Late Twentieth Century.* Cambridge, MA: Harvard University Press.

Cohen, Erik. 1988. 'Authenticity and commoditization in tourism.' *Annals of Tourism Research* 15(3): 371–86.

Connell, John. 2003. 'Island dreaming: The contemplation of Polynesian paradise.' *Journal of Historical Geography* 29: 554–81.

——. 2006. 'Medical tourism: Sea, sun, sand and … surgery.' *Tourism Management* 27(6): 1093–1100.

——. 2013. *Islands at Risk?: Environments, Economies and Contemporary Change.* Cheltenham and Northhamton, MA: Edward Elgar.

Connell, John and Barbara Rugendyke. 2008. *Tourism at the Grassroots: Villagers and Visitors in the Asia-Pacific.* Abingdon: Routledge.

Crick, Malcolm. 1989. 'Representations of international tourism in the social sciences: Sun, sex, sights, savings, and servility.' *Annual Review of Anthropology* 18: 307–44.

Curtis, Barry and Claire Pajaczkowska. 1994. 'Getting there: Travel, time and narrative.' In *Travellers' Tales: Narratives of Home and Displacement*, ed. George Robertson, pp. 199–215. London and New York: Routledge.

Desmond, Jane C. 1999. *Staging Tourism: Bodies on Display from Waikiki to Sea World*. Chicago: University of Chicago Press.

Douglas, Ngaire. 1996. *They Came for Savages: 100 years of Tourism in Melanesia*. Lismore: Centre for Tourism, Southern Cross University.

Hall, C. Michael. 1998. 'Making the Pacific: Globalisation, modernity and myth.' In *Destinations: Cultural Landscapes of Tourism*, ed. G. Ringer, pp. 140–53. London and New York: Routledge.

Hall, C. Michael and Stephen J. Page. 1996. *Tourism in the Pacific: Issues and Cases* (1st ed., series in tourism and hospitality management). London and Boston, MA: International Thomson Business Press.

Harrison, David. 2003. *Pacific Island Tourism*. New York: Cognizant Communication Corporation.

'Hawaii aviation: An archive of photos and historic facts.' n.d. *hawaii.gov*. Online: hawaii.gov/hawaiiaviation/hawaii-airfields-airports/hawaii/kona-international-airport-at-keahole (accessed 9 March 2012).

Hereniko, Vilsoni and Rob Wilson (eds). 1999. *Inside Out: Literature, Cultural Politics, and Identity in the New Pacific*. Boston: Rowman and Littlefield.

Higgins-Desbiolles, Freya. 2006. 'More than an "industry": The forgotten power of tourism as a social force.' *Tourism Management* 27(6): 1192–208.

——. 2012. 'Resisting the hegemony of the market: Reclaiming the social capacities of tourism.' In *Social Tourism in Europe*, ed. Scott McCabe, Lynn Minnaert and Anya Diekmann, pp. 53–66. Bristol: Channel View Publications.

Horkheimer, Max and Theodor W. Adorno. 1944. *Dialectic of Enlightenment*. New York: Herder.

Inayatullah, Sohail. 1995. 'Rethinking tourism: Unfamiliar histories and alternative futures.' *Tourism Management* 16(6): 411–15.

International, T.B.S. 2013. 'Paradise beckons with Fijian Water Lotus!' *The Body Shop*. Online: www.thebodyshop.com.my/fijian-water-lotus (accessed 9 March 2016).

Jolly, Margaret. 1997. 'From Point Venus to Bali Ha'i: Eroticism and exoticism in representations of the Pacific.' In *Sites of Desire, Economies of Pleasure: Sexualities in Asia and the Pacific*, ed. Lenore Manderson and Margaret Jolly, pp. 99–112. Chicago and London: University of Chicago Press.

Kahn, Miriam. 2011. *Tahiti Beyond the Postcard: Power, Place, and Everyday Life*. Seattle: University of Washington Press.

Lennon, John and Malcolm Foley. 2000. *Dark Tourism: The Attraction of Death and Disaster*. London: New York: Continuum.

Long, Lucy M. (ed.). 2010. *Culinary Tourism*. Lexington: The University Press of Kentucky.

Lutz, Catherine A. and Jane Lou Collins. 1993. *Reading National Geographic*. Chicago: University of Chicago Press.

MacCannell, Dean. 1976. *The Tourist: A New Theory of the Leisure Class*. Berkeley, CA: University of California Press.

Macleod, Donald V.L. and James G. Carrier (eds). 2010. *Tourism, Power and Culture: Anthropological Insights*. Bristol: Channel View Publications.

Macpherson, Cluny. 2008. 'Golden goose or Trojan horse? Cruise ship tourism in Pacific development.' *Asia Pacific Viewpoint* 49(2): 185–97.

Manderson, Lenore and Margaret Jolly (eds). 1997. *Sites of Desire, Economies of Pleasure: Sexualities in Asia and the Pacific*. Chicago: University of Chicago Press.

McCabe, Scott, Lynn Minnaert and Anya Diekmann (eds). 2012. *Social Tourism in Europe*. Bristol: Channel View Publications.

Michelle, Carolyn, Ann L. Hardy, Charles H. Davis and Craig Hight. 2014. 'An unexpected controversy in Middle-earth: Audience encounters with the "dark side" of transnational film production.' *Transnational Cinemas*, pp. 1–18.

Minca, Claudio and Tim Oakes (eds). 2006. *Travels in Paradox: Remapping Tourism*. Lanham: Rowman & Littlefield.

Mostafanezhad, Mary. 2014. 'Locating the tourist in volunteer tourism.' *Current Issues in Tourism* 17(4): 381–84.

Novelli, Marina (ed.). 2005. *Niche Tourism: Contemporary Issues, Trends and Cases*. Amsterdam and Sydney: Elsevier.

Pacific Islands Forum Secretariat. 2013. *Tourism as a Pillar of Economic Growth*. Nuku'alofa, Tonga, 3–5 July, Pacific Islands Forum Secretariat. Online: www.forumsec.org/resources/uploads/attachments/documents/2013FEMM_FEMT.06.pdf (accessed 9 March 2016).

Pratt, Stephen and David Harrison (eds). 2015. *Tourism in Pacific Islands: Current Issues and Future Challenges*. Contemporary Geographies of Leisure, Tourism and Mobility, London and New York: Routledge.

Ringer, Greg (ed.). 1998. *Destinations: Cultural Landscapes of Tourism*. London and New York: Routledge.

Robertson, George (ed.). 1994. *Travellers' Tales: Narratives of Home and Displacement*. London and New York: Routledge.

Rojek, Chris and John Urry. 1997. *Touring Cultures: Transformations of Travel and Theory*. London and New York: Routledge.

Salazar, Noel B. 2010. *Envisioning Eden: Mobilizing Imaginaries in Tourism and Beyond*. New York: Berghahn Books.

Scheyvens, Regina. 2007. 'Poor cousins no more valuing the development potential of domestic and diaspora tourism.' *Progress in Development Studies* 7(4): 307–25.

———. 2012. *Tourism and Poverty*. Hoboken: Routledge.

Shigematsu, Setsu and Keith L. Camacho (eds). 2010. *Militarized Currents: Towards a Decolonized Future in Asia and the Pacific*. London and Minneapolis: University of Minnesota Press.

Slatter, Claire. 2006. 'The con/dominium of Vanuatu? Paying the price of investment and land liberalisation.' Unpublished paper.

Smith, Bernard. 1960. *European Vision and the South Pacific* (2nd ed.). New Haven: Yale University Press.

———. 1992. *Imagining the Pacific: In the Wake of the Cook Voyages*. Carlton: Melbourne University Press at the Miegunyah Press.

South Pacific Tourism Organisation. 2012. *Pacific Regional Tourism Capacity Building Programme (Inception Report and First Work Plan*. South Pacific Tourism Organisation. Online: www.forumsec. org/resources/uploads/attachments/documents/EDF10_2012_ PRTCBP_Inception_Report_1st_WP.pdf (accessed 9 March 2016).

Steel, Frances. 2011. *Oceania Under Steam: Sea Transport and the Cultures of Colonialism, c. 1870–1914*. Manchester: Manchester University Press.

Taylor, John. 1998. *Consuming Identity: Modernity and Tourism in New Zealand*. Department of Anthropology, University of Auckland.

Teaiwa, Teresia. 1999. 'Reading Paul Gauguin's *Noa Noa* with Epeli Hau'ofa's *Kisses in the Nederends*: Militourism, feminism, and the "Polynesian" body.' *Inside Out: Literature, Cultural Politics, and Identity in the New Pacific*. ed. Vilsoni Hereniko and Rob Wilson, pp. 249–63. Boston: Rowman and Littlefield.

Trask, Haunani-Kay. 1991. 'Natives and anthropologists: The colonial struggle.' *The Contemporary Pacific* 3(1): 159–67.

Trask, Haunani-Kay. 1993. 'Lovely hula hands: Corporate Tourism and the prostitution of Hawaiian culture.' In *From a Native Daughter: Colonialism and Sovereignty in Hawai'i*, pp. 179–97. Maine: Common Courage Press.

Trask, Haunani-Kay. 1993. *From a Native Daughter: Colonialism and Sovereignty in Hawai'i*. Maine: Common Courage Press.

Wearing, Stephen and Nancy Gard McGehee. 2013. 'Volunteer tourism: A review.' *Tourism Management* 38: 120–30.

Weed, Mike and Chris Bull. 2012. *Sports Tourism: Participants, Policy and Providers*. London and New York: Routledge.

Worldwide Independent Network of Market Research (WIN). 2014. 'End of Year Survey 2014.' *Gallup International*. Zurich. 30 December. Online: www.wingia.com/en/services/end_of_year_ survey_2014/8/ (accessed 17 March 2016).

2

Hawai'i: Prelude to a Journey

Selina Tusitala Marsh
for Haunani-Kay

you go then
poppin' in bubble-gum jeans
you, wrapped bubble-gum teen
knowin' nothin'
'bout no Hawaiians
not living
in Waikiki
no more

you go then
floating on two-buck sunshine
courtesy of Longs
one of a dozen stores stacked
against a postcard beach
within reach of King Kamehameha's
you surface from under the slick of tourist

you go then
buy five key rings for ten
two hibiscus singlets for one
free Hershey bars softening in the sun of
Aloha Stadium fermenting
red-tipped toes in jandals

pale chests in floral shirts
necks noosed in fluorescent lei
wrists handcuffed in gold, etched with black enamel
detained by Reebok and Nike

you go then
to finish in Hale Mānoa
where student voices
rise above smoking black bean stir-fry
fa'alifu fa'i, tofu and udon noodles
breezing open pavilions
you go then
to class to find friends
kama'aina who surf and protest
he is writing on Hawaiian land rights and kalo
sings at the Royal Hawaiian
for his fees
she is writing on post-'80s sovereignty
like waves lapping a broken shore
we are one we
are more she writes
he is writing on wipe-outs of Kamehameha Schools
surfs Sunset
always goes for the barrel
no matter how he gets worked

you go then
and meet
Pele's pen
her black ink lava
ever pricking the night

you go then
to hula halau to
the picket sign to the
angry line outside parliament to
Greevy's photo exhibition to the
kalo plantation to
the valley of stolen waters to the
valley of ground bones and mortar to
the majesty of Kilauea

2. HAWAI'I: PRELUDE TO A JOURNEY

you go then
and smell embered Lincolns
wrapped in kalo leaves
wedged in creases
of Pele-'ai-honua
eater of the land

31

3

Darkness and Light in Black and White: Travelling Mission Imagery from the New Hebrides

Lamont Lindstrom

'Missi! come quick!' the caption reads, 'Miaki's men are stealing your sheets and blankets!' (Figure 7).[1] The 'missi' was John Gibson Paton. The thieves were men and boys from Port Resolution, Tanna, in what was then the southern New Hebrides (Vanuatu today). The caption comes from one of many hagiographic accounts of Paton's missionary exploits on that island between 1858 and 1862.[2] Paton's pilfered bed linen became a popular part of his storied travails, told and retold in several dozen books for children and adults that sprang from his own multi-volume autobiography.[3] Although this account offered no illustrations except for a dignified frontispiece portrait of the man himself, most subsequent versions of the story featured numerous photographs and line drawings. Illustrations of that crime

---

1   Bessie L. Bryum, 1924, *John G. Paton: Hero of the South Seas*, Anderson, IN: Warner Press, p. 34. Images discussed in this chapter are all now in the public domain.

2   Ron Adams provides a more tempered history of Paton's endeavours. See Ron Adams, 1984, *In the Land of Strangers: A Century of European Contact with Tanna, 1774–1874*, Pacific Research Monograph. Canberra: Australian National University Press.

3   John G. Paton, 1890, *An Autobiography*, London: Hodder and Stoughton; A.K. Langridge and F.H.L. Paton, 1910, *John G. Paton: Later Years and Farewell*, London: Hodder and Stoughton.

scene appear in other editions of Bessie Byrum's Paton bio, although they vary somewhat, and depictions of the stolen sheets and blankets likewise embellish several other Paton biographies (Figure 8).[4]

"Missi! come quick! Miaki's men are stealing your sheets and blankets!"

Figure 7. Stealing sheets and blankets!

Source. Bessie L. Byrum, 1924, *John G. Paton: Hero of the South Seads*, Anderson, IN: Warner Press, p. 24.

4   See, for example, John Paton, 1898, *The Story of John G. Paton Told for Young Folks, or Thirty Years among South Sea Cannibals*, London: Hodder and Stoughton, p. 89; John Paton, 1923, *The Story of John G. Paton's Thirty Years with South Sea Cannibals*, ed. Dr. James Paton, revised by A.K. Langridge, London: Hodder and Stoughton, p. 44; see also Charles D. Michael, 1912, *John Gibson Paton, DD: The Missionary Hero of the New Hebrides*, London: S.W. Partridge & Co., p. 43.

STEALING THE BEDCLOTHES.

Figure 8. Stealing the bedclothes.
Source. John Paton, 1923, *The Story of Dr. John G. Paton's Thirty Years with South Sea Cannibals*, London: Hodder and Stoughton, p. 45.

In the years before mass tourism, mission imagery helped shape metropolitan understanding of island life.[5] Mission imagery, whose heyday lasted from the 1880s through the 1930s, swamped the world market for views of the southwest Pacific, and particularly of the New Hebrides.[6] It dominated global circuits, shaping ways in which island life was 'pictured' and understood, until the outbreak of the Pacific War during which Vanuatu's principal airport was constructed and the subsequent development of mass tourism carried by plane and cruise ship,[7] most of these tourists arriving with their own cameras in hand. Before the Pacific War, however, Presbyterian missionaries in the New Hebrides and their supporters, during the late nineteenth and early twentieth centuries, generated a notable archive of island images illustrating their autobiographies and other accounts. They also produced illustrated mission periodicals, picture postcards, magic lantern slides, and even lapel pins (Figure 9). To help circulate their published and more ephemeral imagery, island-based missionaries regularly toured Australia, New Zealand, Scotland and North America to lecture, raise funds, and sell miscellaneous depictions of their labours to homeland congregations who thereby vicariously came to know South Pacific people and places.[8] The mission graphic archive is substantial and one can only sample it here to explore both the types of pictures it circulated and the views these portrayed.

---

5   Nicholas Thomas, 1992, 'Colonial conversations: Difference, hierarchy, and history in early twentieth-century evangelical propaganda', *Comparative Studies in Society and History* 34: 366–89, p. 371; Christine Weir, 2013, '"Deeply interested in these children whom you have not seen": The Protestant Sunday School view of the Pacific', *Journal of Pacific History* 48: 43–62. The illustrators and photographers who produced these images were often anonymous, typically unacknowledged or only quickly identified by signature or initials, for example J.F. and W. Hatterell in Michael, *John Gibson Paton, DD*; and James Finnemore in John Paton, 1898, *The Story of John G. Paton Told for Young Folks, or Thirty Years among South Sea Cannibals*, London: Hodder and Stoughton.

6   Weir, '"Deeply interested in these children whom you have not seen"', pp. 61–62.

7   Ngaire Douglas, 1996, *They Came for Savages: 100 Years of Tourism in Melanesia*, Alstonville, NSW: Southern Cross University Press.

8   For an analysis of two Presbyterian photo albums now in church archives in Dunedin, see Antje Lübcke, 2012, 'Two New Hebrides Mission photograph albums: An object-story of story-objects', *Journal of Pacific History* 47: 187–209.

Figure 9. John G. Paton lapel pin.
Source. A.W. Patrick (manufacturer), Fitzroy, Vic, 1924; author's collection.

Pictures

Until the 1860s, relatively few images of New Hebridean life and landscape had circulated abroad; these mostly prints by William Hodges who sailed as an artist on James Cook's second voyage, other illustrated voyage accounts, and scattered encyclopedic illustrations. Beginning in the 1860s, a flush of illustrated mission texts began to depict new stories of the archipelago—two of the first being George Patterson's *Memoirs of the Rev. S. F. Johnston, the Rev. J. W. Matheson, and Mrs. Mary Johnston Matheson, Missionaries on Tanna* (1864) and his *Missionary Life among the Cannibals: Being the Life of the Rev. John Geddie, D.D., First Missionary to the New Hebrides* (1882).[9]

Missionary writing then dominated popular literature about the southern and central New Hebrides, and associated pictures, postcards and lantern slides also travelled widely. Collector John Ferguson compiled a three-part bibliography of Presbyterian literature printed for diverse audiences that ran to 135 pages.[10] While missionary

---

9   George Patterson, 1864, *Memoirs of the Rev. S. F. Johnston, the Rev. J. W. Matheson, and Mrs. Mary Johnston Matheson, Missionaries on Tanna*, Philadelphia: W.S. & A. Martien; and George Patterson, 1882, *Missionary Life among the Cannibals: Being the Life of the Rev. John Geddie, D.D., First Missionary to the New Hebrides*, Toronto: James Cample & Son, James Bain & Son, and Hart & Co. This literature had a longer history in Polynesia; missionaries landed in Tahiti in the 1790s, Tonga and Hawaii in the 1820s, and Samoa in the 1830s.

10   John Alexander Ferguson, 1917–1943, *A Bibliography of the New Hebrides and a History of the Mission Press*, parts 1–3, Sydney: privately printed.

representations of the New Hebrides competed with other imagery offered by Royal Naval officers, administrative memoirists, occasional freelance journalists and writers like Beatrice Grimshaw,[11] Jack and Charmian London, passing professional photographers like J.W. Beattie and Martin and Osa Johnson,[12] and various early anthropologists including W.H.R. Rivers, R.H. Codrington, Felix Speiser, Bernard Deacon, John Layard, T.T. Barnard, and Clarence Humphreys, the journalists, photographers, and anthropologists who visited the islands themselves typically travelled along mission circuits.[13] Beattie, for example, sailed on the Melanesian Mission's *Southern Cross* and the Johnsons depended on the hospitality of Catholic priest Jean-Baptiste Prin on Vao.[14]

The Presbyterians circulated their island imagery in a variety of media and formats including books (missionary memoirs, accounts, and biography) and illustrated periodicals. These latter included *Quarterly Jottings from the New Hebrides* (which, published by the John G. Paton fund, ran from 1863 through 1966), *New Hebrides Mission Reports, New Hebrides Magazine, The Record: The Sabbath School and Missionary Magazine of the Presbyterian Church of Australia,* and *Our Missionaries at Work.* Presbyterian exploits were also selectively featured in *The New Zealand Missionary Record, The Outlook, Break of Day,* Canada's *The Presbyterian Record,* and also in several Scottish Presbyterian church journals. These publications featured both photographs and line drawings, some of the latter made from original photographs were more expensive to reproduce. As reproductive technology developed and rotogravure supplanted lithography, missionary texts were more abundantly illustrated.[15] Alongside these

---

11   Eugénie Laracy and Hugh Laracy, 1977, 'Beatrice Grimshaw: Pride and prejudice in Papua', *Journal of Pacific History* 12: 154–75; Douglas, *They Came for Savages,* p. 65.

12   Prue Ahrens, Lamont Lindstrom and Fiona Paisley, 2013, *Across the World with the Johnsons: Film, Photography, and American Empire,* Farnham: Ashgate.

13   For a summary of available pre–World War II travel literature that touched on Vanuatu, see Douglas, *They Came for Savages,* pp. 40–48. Burns Philp in 1903 did begin bringing intrepid tourists into the islands who shipped on that company's cargo steamers. To attract custom, in 1911 it began publishing a handbook, *Picturesque Travel,* later replaced by *The BP Magazine.* See Douglas, *They Came for Savages,* pp. 54–56.

14   The Johnson's 1918 silent features *Among the Cannibal Isles of the South Pacific and Cannibals of the South Seas,* with associated shorts, introduced New Hebrides people and places to early movie fans.

15   Illustrations in earlier volumes, reproduced more expensively, were often of higher quality. See, for example, the engravings in Patterson, *Missionary Life Among the Cannibals,* 1882.

publications, mission images also circulated as magic lantern slides and picture postcards—the same image often deployed in several different media as book illustration, magic lantern slide and postcard.

Missionaries on home leave typically lectured to church congregations, beating the bushes for cash donations and other forms of support. They captivated audiences with magic lantern slides depicting heroic lives and gripping examples of danger and salvation. Back in the field, beginning in the 1880s, they also deployed different limelighted slide sets illustrating the life of Jesus and other Biblical figures.[16] Tanna mission wife Agnes Watt, for example, reported that on 26 March 1885, 'In the evening, we had a Magic Lantern display to a crowded house, people have come miles to see it. The pictures were explained, and in that way we hope some heard the gospel who would not attend a service either in church or the open air.'[17] And, John Paton's missionary son Frank on east Tanna similarly reported that:

> A never-ending delight to the natives was our magic lantern. We were so thankful to get a box of beautiful Scripture slides from London. The picture that always made the deepest impression upon the natives was that of the Crucifixion. Even determined Heathen came to see the wonderful pictures which could only be seen in the dark![18]

If pictures of baby and crucified Jesus delighted on Tanna, missionaries when on leave instead lit up their lectures with pictures of savage heathen and cannibal killers. Few of these slides survive today, but examples that do (many once marketed by Australian photographers Henry King and John W. Lindt) depict various groupings of villagers and suggest the flavour of these presentations. A King lantern slide innocuously labelled 'Erromanga New Hebrides' (Figure 10) had appeared earlier in at least two mission books. Maggie Paton in 1894

---

16   For missionary uses of the magic lantern elsewhere, see Daile Kaplan, 1984, 'Enlightened women in darkened lands', *Studies in Visual Communication* 10: 61–77; Elizabeth Shepard, 1987, 'The magic lantern slide in entertainment and education, 1860–1920', *History of Photography* 11: 91–108; and Paul Landau, 1994, 'The illumination of Christ in the Kalahari Desert', *Representations* 45: 26–40. The Anglicans, in *The Southern Cross Log*, published a guide for successful meetings including how to stage a magic lantern show. Pointers included 'The best Lantern obtainable and an experienced operator having been secured', and 'Let a Collection be taken during a hymn in the middle of the address'. See Melanesian Mission, 1913, 'What helps to make successful meetings: Hints to Local secretaries', *The Southern Cross Log* (December): 197–99.

17   Agnes Craig Patterson Watt, 1896, *Twenty-five Years' Mission life on Tanna, New Hebrides*, Paisley: J. and R. Parlane, p. 242.

18   Frank H.L. Paton, 1903, *Lomai of Lenakel: A Hero of the New Hebrides. A Fresh Chapter in the Triumph of the Gospel*, London: Hodder and Stoughton, p. 152; at another lantern show Paton reported that 'Jesus as a Baby' also 'impressed them most'. Paton, *Lomai of Lenakel*, p. 165.

captioned this 'The Murderer of [missionary George] Gordon, and His Child' (attributing the photograph to fellow missionary William Gunn).[19] H.A. Robertson also used the same photograph in his own New Hebrides book, but his caption named the murderer: 'Uhuvili and His Child.'[20]

Figure 10. Magic lantern slide, Erromanga New Hebrides (Uhuvili and his child).

Source. Henry King (photography studio), Sydney; author's collection.

King, Lindt, Beattie and other photographers who converted mission negatives into lantern slides also sold postcards. Beattie churned out 800 New Hebrides postcards reproduced from photographs he shot

---

19   Maggie Whitecross Paton, 1894, *Letters and Sketches from the New Hebrides*, London: Hodder and Stoughton, p. 126.
20   H.A. Robertson, 1903, *Erromanga: The Martyr Isle*, London: Hodder and Stroughton, facing p. 74.

during his 1906 visit to the archipelago,[21] and missionaries themselves went into the postcard business.[22] A contemporary Melanesian Mission guide for staging successful magic lantern shows highlighted associated possibilities for card sales: 'Stands for post cards, as used on railway platforms can be easily borrowed.'[23] Like lantern slides, images first featured in missionary books also sold as postcards. 'The Miracle of Water from the Well', a drawing included in Michael,[24] celebrated the divine assistance that guided Paton in digging for water on Aniwa, a small atoll that neighbours Tanna: 'It was the Missi's God, the mighty Jehovah, who had wrought this great and wonderful thing.'[25] This image also appeared as a coloured postcard (Figure 11) to be purchased and posted by Presbyterian supporters.[26] Missionary texts featured these illustrations, missionaries displayed and sold them, while their supporters appreciated and circulated them further in church lending libraries and by post.

Figure 11. John Paton, as postcard.
Source. Anonymous, printed in Germany; author's collection.

---

21 Frédéric Angleviel and Max Shekleton, 1997, '"Olfala pija blong Niuhebridis blong bifo": Old pictures of the early New Hebrides (Vanuatu)', *Pacific Studies* 20: 161–85, p. 164.

22 Ibid., p. 169.

23 Melanesian Mission, 'What helps to make successful meetings', p. 197.

24 Michael, *John Gibson Paton, DD*, p. 131.

25 Ibid., p. 132.

26 Lübcke quotes missionary William Milne who wrote to a colleague that 'our photo is pretty good' when the celebratory postcard featuring his portrait had sold out. See Lübcke, 'Two New Hebrides Mission photograph albums', p. 193n22.

Portrayals

Designed to cultivate support and to justify Presbyterian endeavour, missionary imagery illustrated the master story of savagery and its salvation. The chief trope was one of darkness and light, of Christian enlightenment. This was a hugely popular and long-standing Christian metaphor borrowed immediately from Biblical text (e.g. John 1:5) and missionaries deployed it everywhere, extravagantly and often. The Presbyterians in the New Hebrides shared appreciation of these same lights. They christened their various mission vessels *Dayspring*. They titled a jubilee history of the mission *Light in Dark Isles*[27] and otherwise celebrated the light in book titles like *Heralds of Dawn*.[28] Their books featured recurring graphics of white triumph over black. Colour contrast was both spiritual and racial and was further highlighted by missionary sartorial fondness for white garments (at least in book illustration, Figures 11 and 12).[29] John Paton's white raiment signified his bright heart and soul—white skin, white trousers, white heart. Mission photos pointedly emphasised tonal contrasts. Maurice Frater, who ministered on Paama and Epi islands, 1900–1939, included in his autobiography one study in contrast, 'natives admiring photographs of themselves'[30] wherein white suits juxtaposed dark nudity, and cummerbund reflected penis wrapper, in photograph and in life alike (Figure 13). When projected at night with a magic lantern, these images of white body and spirit were particularly powerful as they 'floated and shimmered' in the darkness.[31]

---

27   Alexander Don, 1918, *Light in Dark Isles: A Jubilee Record and Study of the New Hebrides Mission of the Presbyterian Church of New Zealand*, Dunedin: Foreign Missions Committee, Presbyterian Church of New Zealand.
28   William Gunn, 1924, *Heralds of Dawn: Early Converts in the New Hebrides*, London: Hodder and Stroughton.
29   Michael, *John Gibson Paton, DD*, p. 69.
30   Maurice Frater, 1922, *Midst Volcanic Fires: An Account of Missionary Tours among the Volcanic Islands of the New Hebrides*, London: James Clarke & Co, facing p. 72.
31   Landau, 'The illumination of Christ in the Kalahari Desert', p. 32.

Figure 12. Paton in white.
Source. Charles D. Michael, 1912, *John Gibson Paton, DD: The Missionary Hero of the New Hebrides*, London: S.W. Partridge, p. 69.

Figure 13. Light and dark.
Source. Maurice Frater, 1922, *Midst Volcanic Fires: An Account of Missionary Tours among the Volcanic Islands of the New Hebrides*, London: James Clarke, p. 73.

Figure 14. The missionary's 'gun'.

Source. Oscar Michelsen, 1893, *Cannibals Won for Christ: A Story of Missionary Perils and Triumphs in Tongoa, New Hebrides*, London: Morgan and Scott, p. 41.

Christian light must engulf heathen darkness in the end. Miaki's men on Tanna, after all, understandably desired and stole John Paton's white sheets and blankets. The Christian gospel vanquishes the darkness, the sacred pen mightier than the sword (or, rather, rifles and clubs in the New Hebrides). The Bible, in fact, was the missionary's 'gun' (Figures 14 and 15).[32] Mission imagination was also notably fond of before/after comparison—this second sort of juxtaposition the intrinsic consequence of initial darkness/light contrast. Transformed and enlightened islanders would enwhiten, and mission publication regularly illustrated this process in 'before and after' views of village scenes (Figures 16 and 17).[33] New churches and schools came to supplant old heathen structures, as another mission postcard (Figure 18) depicted—the school, here,

---

32   Oscar Michelsen, 1893, *Cannibals Won for Christ: A Story of Missionary Perils and Triumphs in Tongoa, New Hebrides*, London: Morgan and Scott, p. 41; Paton, *The Story of John G. Paton Told for Young Folks, or Thirty Years among South Sea Cannibals*, p. 81.

33   Emma H. Adams, 1890, *Two Cannibal Archipelagoes: New Hebrides and Solomon Groups*, Oakland, CA: Pacific Press Publishing Co., pp. 90–91.

a key institution in Christian education and enlightenment. Mission images also celebrated transformations in native demeanour, including, notably, their now clothed, newly spruced up bodies. Futuna Island missionary William Gunn's attempt at one such comparative portrayal (Figure 19) was spoiled, somewhat, by his heathen subject's move to cover over her traditional bark skirt with a dress ('heathen to the left, dressed in order to have her photo taken'),[34] although her wilder hair and bark underskirt contrast vividly with her Christian sister's long, white Mother Hubbard and elegant turban.

Figure 15. Bible vs rifle.
Source. John Paton, 1898, *The Story of John G. Paton Told for Young Folks, or Thirty Years among South Sea Cannibals*, London: Hodder and Stoughton, p. 81.

---

34   Gunn, *Heralds of Dawn*, facing p. 127.

A VILLAGE UNDER HEATHENISM—SUN-WORSHIP.

Figure 16. Heathen darkness, before.

Source. Emma H. Adams, 1890, *Two Cannibal Archipelagoes: New Hebrides and Solomon Groups*, Oakland, CA: Pacific Press Publishing, p. 90.

THE SAME VILLAGE, UNDER CHRISTIANITY.

Figure 17. Christian light, after.

Source. Emma H. Adams, 1890, *Two Cannibal Archipelagoes: New Hebrides and Solomon Groups*, Oakland, CA: Pacific Press Publishing Co., p. 91.

" Kava " House about to be destroyed, Village School on left.

Figure 18. School supplants kava houses.
Source. Anonymous; author's collection.

To portray possibility of Christian transformation, as Thomas has noted,[35] mission representation of islanders tilted towards metaphors of age more than of gender. Islanders were children but nonetheless could develop and mature if bathed in Christian light. Colonial administrators and settlers, conversely, tended more often to feminise islanders. Portrayed and fixed thusly as female, witless and weak, islanders would require long and firm tutoring by their white masculine masters, an interminable colonial administration. Mission imagery, however, portrayed a happier future. One could, in fact, hope for Christian maturity and an ultimate shared humanity as sibling children of God.

---

35   Thomas, 'Colonial conversations', pp. 377–78.

HEATHEN.   CHRISTIAN.
Heathen to the left, dressed in order to have her photo taken.

Figure 19. Heathen and Christian.
Source. William Gunn, 1924, *Heralds of Dawn: Early Converts in the New Hebrides*, London: Hodder and Stroughton, facing p. 127.

Mission images thus often played with the passing of the old, with their heathen idols, and their replacement by vigorous and healthy Christian youth, as did the frontispiece of missionary Robert Lamb's autobiography (Figure 20): 'The old men ... sit down together and weep'.[36] Taking their place, a new generation of Christian youth will remake their island homes. Mission imagery frequently portrayed local children, scrubbed and dressed in preparation to join global Christian civilisation, as does a postcard (Figure 21) of babies newly washed in the blood of Jesus, and in water, too. If unlikely ever to become British knights, cleansed island children would at least be educated in proper spirituality in mission schools and as the offspring of caring, convert fathers and mothers.[37] Christian families thus were another very common motif in missionary literature. Frank Paton, for example, included six family portraits in *Lomai of Lenakel*, including one of Titonga, Litsi, and their child Somo (Figure 22).[38]

Mission images, shaped to serve parochial goals, dominated representations of island life before mass tourism and before more diverse information sources developed. These pictures often were not always graphically reliable as many illustrators—who had never themselves met an actual islander—defaulted to drawing generic heathen or indeterminate native (see, for example, Figure 7). Generic imagery circulated from book to book—this also a form of travel as pictures were recycled and reused. The same illustration, for example (Figure 10), might appear in a series of mission journal articles and books, recaptioned for a variety of purposes. Emma Adams' 1890 tale of mission work in two 'cannibal archipelagoes', recycled the same depictions of transformed village life (Figures 16 and 17) that earlier had appeared in William Watt Gill's 1876 mission account: where they were captioned 'A village in Pukapuka, under heathenism' and 'The same village, under Christianity'.[39] God, the Gospel, and natives taken everywhere to be about the same, readers may not much have minded illustrative leaps from the Cook Islands into Melanesia as pictures made their rounds.

---

36   Robert Lamb, 1905, *Saints and Savages: The Story of Five Years in the New Hebrides*, Edinburgh and London: William Blackwood and Sons.

37   Weir, '"Deeply interested in these children whom you have not seen"', pp. 58–59.

38   Frank H.L. Paton, 1903, *Lomai of Lenakel: A Hero of the New Hebrides. A Fresh Chapter in the Triumph of the Gospel*, London: Hodder and Stoughton, facing p. 150.

39   William Watt Gill, 1876, *Life in the Southern Islands; or, Scenes and Incidents in the South Pacific and New Guinea*, London: Religious Tract Society, pp. 18–19.

"AMONG THE BROKEN GODS."

"THE OLD MEN . . . SIT DOWN TOGETHER AND WEEP."— PAGE 224.

Figure 20. Old men and their broken gods.

Source. Robert Lamb, 1905, *Saints and Savages: The Story of Five Years in the New Hebrides*, Edinburgh and London: William Blackwood and Sons, frontispiece.

The Order of the Bath.

Figure 21. The order of the bath.
Source. Anonymous; author's collection.

Other mission images, however, particularly photographs and those drawings based on photographs (Figure 23),[40] more accurately depicted island reality. These, although certainly posed, did capture some measure of ethnographic authenticity. Mission writers often also included drawings and photos of landscape to ground their texts. Maggie Paton's book, for example, featured her sketches of Tanna's Iasur volcano and an Erromango island beach scene,[41] and Agnes Watt's letters were illustrated by photographs also of Tanna's volcano and its nearby lake along with a mountain waterfall.[42]

40   Patterson, *Missionary Life among the Cannibals*, p. 498.
41   Paton, *Letters and Sketches from the New Hebrides*, pp. 339, 343.
42   Watt, *Twenty-five Years' Mission life on Tanna, New Hebrides*, pp. 69, 175, 347.

Figure 22. The new Christian family.
Source. Frank H.L. Paton, 1903, *Lomai of Lenakel: A Hero of the New Hebrides. A Fresh Chapter in the Triumph of the Gospel*, London: Hodder and Stoughton, p. 151.

Figure 23. *Dayspring's* island crew.
Source. George Patterson, 1882, *Missionary Life among the Cannibals: Being the life of the Rev. John Geddie, D.D., First Missionary to the New Hebrides*, Toronto: James Cample & Son, James Bain & Son, and Hart & Co, p. 498.

These mission landscapes and portraits in book, lantern slide, or postcard carried views of the islands forth into the outside world. Until the beginnings of mass tourism, print images moved more easily and freely than did people; the circulation of representative pictures as book illustration or postcard far eclipsed that of people themselves, although these too were on the move. Figure 23, for instance, which began as a photograph on board *Dayspring*, was transformed into an etching in Toronto, to be appreciated by Presbyterian faithful around the world. It depicts New Hebrideans who, along with their images, were then also travelling. Islanders like *Dayspring's* crew beginning in the 1860s journeyed abroad and sailed regularly into Sydney, Melbourne and Auckland, just as outsiders were increasingly arriving on island shores.

Although missionaries continue to arrive in Vanuatu today and metropolitan churches send hordes of youthful volunteers annually into these islands, mission views no longer dominate the global graphic archive. Still, these views for many years cultivated powerful expectations of island life, and the tropes that capture this, and they have sunk down deep into common knowledge of tropical people and places. The increasing numbers of tourists visiting Tanna today, for example, may not expect to have their bed linens stolen, but they do arrive with existing, directed if diffuse expectations of what they will find there.[43] Travelling mission images significantly framed and sparked much of the tourism to come.

References

Adams, Emma H. 1890. *Two Cannibal Archipelagoes: New Hebrides and Solomon Groups*. Oakland, CA: Pacific Press Publishing Co.

Adams, Ron. 1984. *In the Land of Strangers: A Century of European Contact with Tanna, 1774–1874*. Pacific Research Monograph. Canberra: Australian National University Press.

Ahrens, Prue, Lamont Lindstrom and Fiona Paisley. 2013. *Across the World with the Johnsons: Film, Photography, and American Empire*. Farnham: Ashgate.

Angleviel, Frédéric and Max Shekleton. 1997. '"Olfala pija blong Niuhebridis blong bifo": Old pictures of the early New Hebrides (Vanuatu).' *Pacific Studies* 20(4): 161–85.

Bryum, Bessie L. 1924. *John G. Paton: Hero of the South Seas*. Anderson, IN: Warner Press.

Connell, John and Prue Robinson. 2008. '"Everything is truthful here": Custom village tourism in Tanna, Vanuatu.' In *Tourism at the Grassroots: Villagers and Visitors in the Asia-Pacific*, ed. John Connell and Barbara Rugendyke, pp. 77–97. London: Routledge.

Connell, John and Barbara Rugendyke (eds). 2008. *Tourism at the Grassroots: Villagers and Visitors in the Asia-Pacific*. London: Routledge.

---

43 See John Connell and Prue Robinson, 2008, '"Everything is truthful here": Custom village tourism in Tanna, Vanuatu', in *Tourism at the Grassroots: Villagers and Visitors in the Asia-Pacific*, ed. John Connell and Barbara Rugendyke, pp. 77–97, London: Routledge. See also John Taylor, 'Pikinini in paradise: Photography, souvenirs and the fantasy of 'child native' in tourism', this volume, for discussion of contemporary tourist appreciation of island children.

Don, Alexander. 1918. *Light in Dark Isles: A Jubilee Record and Study of the New Hebrides Mission of the Presbyterian Church of New Zealand*. Dunedin: Foreign Missions Committee, Presbyterian Church of New Zealand.

Douglas, Ngaire. 1996. *They Came for Savages: 100 Years of Tourism in Melanesia*. Alstonville, NSW: Southern Cross University Press.

Ferguson, John Alexander. 1917–1943. *A Bibliography of the New Hebrides and a History of the Mission Press*, parts 1–3. Sydney: privately printed.

Frater, Maurice. 1922. *Midst Volcanic Fires: An Account of Missionary Tours among the Volcanic Islands of the New Hebrides*. London: James Clarke.

Gill, William Watt. 1876. *Life in the Southern Islands; or, Scenes and Incidents in the South Pacific and New Guinea*. London: Religious Tract Society.

Gunn, William. 1924. *Heralds of Dawn: Early Converts in the New Hebrides*. London: Hodder and Stroughton.

Kaplan, Daile. 1984. 'Enlightened women in darkened lands.' *Studies in Visual Communication* 10: 61–77.

Lamb, Robert. 1905. *Saints and Savages: The Story of Five Years in the New Hebrides*. Edinburgh and London: William Blackwood and Sons.

Landau, Paul. 1994. 'The illumination of Christ in the Kalahari Desert.' *Representations* 45: 26–40.

Langridge, A.K. and F.H.L. Paton. 1910. *John G. Paton: Later Years and Farewell*. London: Hodder and Stoughton.

Laracy, Eugénie and Hugh Laracy. 1977. 'Beatrice Grimshaw: Pride and prejudice in Papua.' *Journal of Pacific History* 12: 154–75.

Lübcke, Antje. 2012. 'Two New Hebrides Mission photograph albums: An object-story of story-objects.' *Journal of Pacific History* 47: 187–209.

Melanesian Mission. 1913. 'What helps to make successful meetings: Hints to Local secretaries.' *The Southern Cross Log* (December): 197–99.

Michael, Charles D. 1912. *John Gibson Paton, DD: The Missionary Hero of the New Hebrides*. London: S.W. Partridge & Co.

Michelsen, Oscar. 1893. *Cannibals Won for Christ: A Story of Missionary Perils and Triumphs in Tongoa, New Hebrides*. London: Morgan and Scott.

Paton, Frank H.L. 1903. *Lomai of Lenakel: A Hero of the New Hebrides. A Fresh Chapter in the Triumph of the Gospel*. London: Hodder and Stoughton.

Paton, John G. 1890. *An Autobiography*. London: Hodder and Stoughton.

Paton, John. 1898. *The Story of John G. Paton Told for Young Folks, or Thirty Years among South Sea Cannibals*. London: Hodder and Stoughton.

———. 1923. *The Story of John G. Paton's Thirty Years with South Sea Cannibals*, ed. Dr. James Paton, revised by A.K. Langridge. London: Hodder and Stoughton.

Paton, Maggie Whitecross. 1894. *Letters and Sketches from the New Hebrides*. London: Hodder and Stoughton.

Patterson, George. 1864. *Memoirs of the Rev. S.F. Johnston, the Rev. J.W. Matheson, and Mrs. Mary Johnston Matheson, Missionaries on Tanna*. Philadelphia: W.S. & A. Martien.

———. 1882. *Missionary Life among the Cannibals: Being the life of the Rev. John Geddie, D.D., First Missionary to the New Hebrides*. Toronto: James Cample & Son, James Bain & Son, and Hart & Co.

Robertson, H.A. 1903. *Erromanga: The Martyr Isle*. London: Hodder and Stroughton.

Shepard, Elizabeth. 1987. 'The magic lantern slide in entertainment and education, 1860–1920.' *History of Photography* 11: 91–108.

Taylor, John. n.d. 'Pikinini in paradise: Photography, souvenirs and the fantasy of 'child native' in tourism.' Unpublished paper.

Thomas, Nicholas. 1992. 'Colonial conversations: Difference, hierarchy, and history in early twentieth-century evangelical propaganda.' *Comparative Studies in Society and History* 34: 366–89.

Watt, Agnes Craig Patterson. 1896. *Twenty-five Years' Mission life on Tanna, New Hebrides*. Paisley: J. and R. Parlane.

Weir, Christine. 2013. '"Deeply interested in these children whom you have not seen": The Protestant Sunday School view of the Pacific.' *Journal of Pacific History* 48: 43–62.

4

Tourism

William C. Clarke

Idle now
the pier last night
was lit by a hundred suns,
portholes glaring down
from the cruise ship's wall of steel.

It was the Princess Something-or-Other
or the Islander Whatever—I forget—
moored into connection with our town.

Perhaps another name,
perhaps it never came at all
but something left
a stain of alien wealth
upon our ground.[1]

---

1   This poem first appeared in *A Momentary Stay* (2002) Pandanus Books, Canberra. It is reproduced with permission of the Estate of William C. Clarke.

5

The Cruise Ship

Frances Steel

The late nineteenth-century cruise ship was more than a mode of transport, ferrying white tourists to island shores; it was a destination in and of itself. In Michel Foucault's formulation, the ship might be conceived of as 'a floating piece of space, a place without a place that exists by itself, that is closed in on itself and at the same time is given over to the infinity of the sea'.[1] This assumes a deep-ocean location. A ship docked at the wharf or lying at anchor in harbour was a space where rituals of entry and exit took on particular significance. Attending to the flows from shore to ship, rather than following European passengers as they disembarked and toured port towns or wandered along native tracks and through villages, opens up new angles of vision on the sites and spaces of colonial tourism. Indigenous Islanders boarded the ship, also as mobile subjects and consumers of different sights, sounds and new encounters. These reversals direct us to the highly contextual and negotiated nature of colonial touring and, in so doing, raise new questions about the touristic value and meaning attached to the novel, exotic and unfamiliar.

***

---

1   Michel Foucault, 1986, 'Of other spaces', *Diacritics* 16(1): 22–27.

Cruise tourism developed on a commercial scale in the Pacific and elsewhere from the early 1880s as shipping companies began offering tours dedicated to leisure travel independent of their regular trade routes. The Union Steam Ship Company of New Zealand (USSCo.) played a key role, operating four island cruises before the turn of the century, pitched to wealthy settlers in the Australasian colonies. Two month-long tours in 1884 linked Sydney and Auckland with Fiji, Samoa and Tonga. Later, two six-week cruises offered more wide-ranging itineraries: in 1898 a tour extended into the eastern Pacific, touching at Rarotonga and French Polynesia and returning to Australia via Samoa and Tonga. In 1899 the cruise ship steamed west, linking Fiji, Tonga and Samoa with the New Hebrides and New Caledonia.[2] Cruising was marketed as a superior way to know the Pacific, even as the package tour locked passengers into a company-managed itinerary. Ordinary steamers with their more mundane concerns of cargo and mail only stayed in port long enough 'to enable the work to be done', as one 1898 brochure put it, while the cruise ship prioritised the interests of passengers not traders.[3]

As a space dedicated to leisure and consumption, the cruise ship appeared to skirt around contemporary colonial interventions in island life. On the passage between Auckland and Suva, it dawned upon one man as he ordered alcoholic beverages from the stewards that they were 'a party on pleasure bent, and not a missionary expedition carrying with us a cargo of tracts and flannel waistcoats for the little heathens'.[4] Tourists were understood to require levels of comfort and sophistication superior to other empire travellers, with one shipping official enthusing that the 3,000-ton vessel 'has been fitted up, equipped, and provisioned exactly as if the tourists had purchased her and themselves fitted her out as a private yacht'.[5] Neither steerage nor second-class tickets were issued; all passengers travelled first class, reinforcing the association of cruising with exclusivity and privilege. On the inaugural cruise in 1884, one tourist delighted in the fact that they were treated 'with the respect due to

---

2   This chapter draws on and extends some of the evidence and arguments discussed in Frances Steel, 2013, 'An ocean of leisure: Early cruise tours of the Pacific in an age of empire', *Journal of Colonialism and Colonial History* 14(2): 1–12.
3   USSCo., 1898, *Off To Tahiti! Trip to the South Seas Islands*, Dunedin: J. Wilkie & Co.
4   'The cruise of the Wairarapa', *Nelson Evening Mail*, 25 June 1884.
5   'A winter excursion', *Sydney Morning Herald*, 1 July 1898.

pioneers'.[6] This pioneering quality spoke to the sense of occasion in opening up a new traffic. Regardless of the attendant comforts and structured itinerary, this chronicler also fancied they were embarking on an 'expedition', following directly in the wake of prior voyages of 'discovery'.[7] But with its level of provisioning and especially the new technology of refrigeration, the cruise ship represented a turning point in the maritime history of the Pacific. It was now a question, one passenger quipped, 'whether Vanilla icecreams … were ever before eaten in a similar expedition, certainly not off the islands of Samoa'.[8]

The excursion steamer was not automatically hailed or recognised as such in island ports. Rather, its entry was linked to longer associations with ships as bearers of potentially harmful influences: alcohol, disease, new ideas, or 'unsavoury' characters. Passengers were informed prior to disembarking in Suva that they were liable to fines if offering Fijians alcohol or for 'striking a native', indicative of a sense of unease about the relative hedonism of the cruise. It was perhaps feared they were to enter a world in which the normal restraints did not apply. In any case, the very first cruise was disrupted by an outbreak of measles amongst the crew after leaving Fiji, which prevented passengers landing at either Samoa or Tonga. Here it was as if they arrived on a 'veritable plague ship'.[9] The tourists could not be assured of a welcome reception at destination ports as harmless, high-status pleasure seekers. In quarantine (their 'prison life') in Apia harbour, they performed their own *meke* (ceremonial dances) and kava ceremonies 'in clumsy Australian imitation of the Fijians'[10] (Figure 24). Their expectations of encounters with primitive Islanders were reduced to a one-sided enactment, with the cruise ship serving as a self-contained stage whereupon passengers played with boundaries of selfhood.

6   'Among the coral islands', *Sydney Morning Herald*, 10 June 1884.
7   Ibid.
8   'The Wairarapa's cruise in the Pacific', *Te Aroha News*, 9 August 1884.
9   'Among the coral islands', *Sydney Morning Herald*, 19 July 1884.
10   'Among the coral islands', *Sydney Morning Herald*, 17 July 1884. Another passenger recorded that this 'solemn meke' developed into 'imitations of a menagerie, with crowing of cocks, the barking of dogs, the howling of lost spirits in pain'. See 'Oceania: Steam-yachting in the Pacific', *Otago Witness*, 19 July 1884.

Figure 24. 'English Méké', *Wairarapa*, June 1884.
Source. Museum of New Zealand Te Papa Tongarewa, Burton Brothers Studio, O.000762.

In ports where disembarkation went smoothly, the ship did not simply lie at anchor, at the periphery of the tourism encounter. As the European passengers came streaming on shore and 'spread themselves over the place to see all that was worth seeing', so too did 'a moving mass of gaping natives' board the steamship, as a female passenger from Adelaide, M. Methuen, reported in Fiji, and 'even penetrated into the cabins, where they felt and examined the dresses and boxes of the absent occupants with greedy wonder'.[11] The scene on the decks 'was one long to be remembered', reflected Dunedin photographer Alfred Burton, with Islanders 'impelled by curiosity and wonder; some on trading thoughts intent, and others perhaps full of tenderer feelings'.[12] In both Fiji and Samoa, with an estimated 200 visitors at the latter, 'though the ship was crowded with them, and they poked into every hole and corner, yet nothing was missed by any passengers of the many attractions which lie about'.[13] On arrival at Pago Pago, however, 'the natives were disappointing after our previous experience. Many of them were as bad beggars as one would expect to find in a large city, and they were not all averse to playfully picking pockets of handkerchiefs and small articles.'[14]

'Invading' the ship was one of the immediate means available to Islanders to undermine or avoid the voyeuristic tourist gaze. The over-determined speculations about indigenous motivations and actions—as greedy, grasping or desiring—reflected a self-conscious awareness on the part of the European passengers that they were themselves objects of scrutiny and curiosity, and that the ship was not a space reserved solely for their 'play'. Here the passengers became spectacles: 'All of us will bear in our minds the many handsome faces framed in as many portholes, as they gazed on the *beauties* and the *beasts* feeding [emphasis in original]'.[15] This mild amusement at the indigenous response to their presence was not shared by everyone and it may have been a retrospective construct. An insistent Islander gaze was certainly discomforting for some. As one Australian passenger remarked with reference to their reception on shore, they were scrutinised by the Fijians 'till we felt quite embarrassed'.[16]

11   *Fiji Times*, 5 July 1884; M.M. 'A trip to Fiji in the Wairarapa', *South Australian Register*, 28 July 1884.
12   Alfred Burton, 1884, *The Camera in the Coral Islands*, Dunedin: Burton Brothers, p. 15.
13   C.G. de Betham, 1884, *The Wairarapa Wilderness: In which will be found the wanderings of the passengers on the second cruise of the S.S. Wairarapa from Auckland to the South Sea Islands and back during the month of July 1884*, Wellington, p. 17; 'The Wairarapa's cruise in the Pacific', *Te Aroha News*, 9 August 1884.
14   de Betham, *The Wairarapa Wilderness*, p. 17.
15   Ibid.
16   'Among the coral islands', *Sydney Morning Herald*, 1 July 1884.

Such attention and curiosity might also confirm in the minds of tourists the seeming 'innocence' and 'naivety' of the Islanders. The steamship carried extra lights to hoist into the rigging, with which, the captain had enthused in Sydney, 'we hope to be able to "astonish the natives"'.[17] Moments of 'techno-drama' where Europeans sought to elicit or evoke wonder from indigenous communities were a kind of 'set piece' in narratives of cross-cultural encounter.[18] The captain's remarks implied that a scripted demonstration was almost expected of them, the cruise intended as a spectacle of modern industrial efficacy. Once on board ship, some Islander visitors were 'sorely puzzled' by the electric lamps, 'the problem being to discover the pipe which supplies the kerosene'.[19] This apparent befuddlement denied that the indigenous observers inhabited a rational realm, inspecting these 'mysterious' objects on the basis of their existing knowledge. One young boy caught his reflection in a mirror hanging in the saloon. Captivated, he returned again and again 'when he fancied no one was watching'.[20] Later in the century, the gramophone on board the *Waikare* was an object of intrigue: 'the old men and women gazed open-mouthed at the talking devil, whilst the younger and more enlightened laughed as if they understood it all'.[21] This unwillingness to acknowledge Islanders as 'knowing subjects', to insist on their failure to recognise correctly how such objects worked, was to claim the power and authority of magic.[22]

The refrigerating equipment was a highlight, with passengers recording Fijians' confusion at the ice. A man 'dropped it in fright, as if it had been a hot coal'. A 'practical joke', another passenger related, 'is to clap a handful of snow on a Fijian's bare back and see him jump'.[23] This kind of mocking play with unsuspecting Islanders was also an assertion of power over the terms of encounter. As these exchanges occurred in a space controlled by Europeans, this seemed to encourage a certain physical licence. When some Samoan women sat on deck, they were quickly surrounded by 'an admiring group of

---

17 'Steam-yachting in the Pacific', *Otago Daily Times*, 15 July 1884.
18 Chris Ballard, 2010, 'Watching first contact', *Journal of Pacific History* 45(1): 21–36, p. 34.
19 'Steam yachting in the Pacific', *Otago Daily Times*, 15 July 1884.
20 M.M. 'A trip to Fiji in the Warirarapa', *South Australian Register*, 28 July 1884.
21 'With the Waikare', *Sydney Morning Herald*, 17 August 1899.
22 Gyan Prakash, 1999, *Another Reason: Science and the Imagination of Modern India*, Princeton: Princeton University Press, p. 48.
23 'Among the coral islands', *Sydney Morning Herald*, 14 July 1884; 'Oceania: Steam-yachting in the Pacific', *Otago Witness*, 19 July 1884.

young men and officers, all desirous of obtaining at least one glance from the beautiful wild dark eyes that gleamed'.[24] One crew member 'made himself specially conspicuous' by distributing cigarettes to the women and lighting them. 'The ladies smoked and flirted and laughed with the utmost grace and complacency', Methuen reported. But friendliness turned to familiarity: 'the young man produced and applied ice to their fair lips, they resented it so thoroughly that two of them pushed all the ice they could lay their hands on down the nape of his neck'.[25] Though still on board ship, the women took charge and asserted control, marking out their own boundaries of interpersonal contact.

White women were also placed in potentially inappropriate situations, notably with indigenous women. One 'beautiful girl' called 'Ruth' followed Methuen about deck. She 'stroked me all over, felt with her slender brown fingers if I was solid good material, and then said "Savonake"' [(sic); translated by her as 'very good']. Methuen 'answered her by feeling her loose blue robe, rubbing her hands, stroking her head, and by saying "Savonake"'.[26] This episode suggests a mutual fascination with the physical proximities afforded by the confines of the ship, a fleeting intimacy that collapsed the distance expressed through 'the tourist gaze'. It also worked to disrupt the dominant agential position of the voyeuristic white male, placing white and indigenous women in more active roles in these spaces of encounter. Same-sex intimacies, though not necessarily erotic or sexual, were also part of the cross-cultural mix, particularly as these cruises carried a significant proportion of women. Yet other passengers narrated the tour as privileging heterosexual male desire. The photographer Alfred Burton drew an on-/off-ship distinction to suggest more covert liaisons, such as the 'select circle' of male passengers who left the ship after dinner one evening, for they were 'in on a secret' that a 'proper' Samoan *meke* would be performed by women at a private house in Apia.[27]

These episodes show that even a single encounter could encapsulate rapid shifts in contextual relations of power. Such unstable boundaries were unsettling enough, it seems, to have prompted tighter regulations

---

24   M.M., 'A trip to Fiji in the Wairarapa', *South Australian Register*, 28 July 1884.
25   Ibid.
26   Ibid.
27   Burton, *The Camera in the Coral Islands*, p. 13.

over the flows from shore to ship. Even on the first cruise it was 'thought advisable' after leaving Suva en route to Levuka, 'not to berth alongside in these ports, because the anchorage is pleasanter and the ship not over-run by people from the shore'.[28] In finalising preparations for a cruise at the end of the century, the captain insisted on keeping the ship 'in hand' and placing checks on visitors, especially in Fiji. The island's 'principal magnates' could come to dinner on board ship, but only 'a few at a time'. He felt that 'the people will think the better of us for keeping our ships in order'.[29] 'The essence of shipboard life was boundary maintenance', Greg Dening observed. He depicted sailing ship captains keeping 'their ships at sea, as it were' when anchored in Pacific harbours, preventing crew from toing and froing freely, for ports 'were beyond the boundaries of the ship' where 'the rules did not apply'.[30] In the context of a tourist cruise the fears rested with incursions from shore, the crew (mostly invisible in these accounts) were tasked instead with mediating connections between passengers and Islanders, and in a sense schooling them in the way of the ship. Shutting out indigenous visitors also entailed a forced self-denial of pleasure given the fascination previously expressed with shipboard 'swamping'. But, again, these published travel narratives have not shed light on passengers' more private thoughts, including possible anxieties about or distaste for cross-cultural proximities. A stricter policing of flows may have been a welcome intervention.

In other ways the ship was embraced as a retreat from the islands, a space at a distance, from where one might safely reflect upon experiences ashore. The prospect of swimming in the seas off Mago Island in Fiji was enticing, but deemed too dangerous. 'More secure, if less romantic, is the saltwater bath available on board', related one man, where he could safely 'wash off the dust and sweat' from shore, the ship serving as a space of purification, even of ritual cleansing.[31] For others, too, time on board was important for physical restoration and recuperation, for 'we go the pace too hard on land', remarked one Scotsman.[32]

---

28   T.W. Leys, 1884, *The Cruise of the Wairarapa*, Auckland: Evening Star, p. 11.

29   Richardson to Mills, 3 July 1899, Hocken Collections, USSCo. Records, AG–292–005–001/057.

30   Greg Dening,1980, *Islands and Beaches: Discourse on a Silent Land, Marquesas 1774–1880*, Melbourne: Dorsey Press, pp. 158–59.

31   'Oceania: Steam-yachting in the Pacific', *Otago Witness*, 19 July 1884.

32   'Sailing in the South Seas', *Sydney Morning Herald*, 5 August 1899.

In keeping with the desired image of a disciplined, well-ordered vessel, the cruise ship was a space for selective diplomatic exchanges, conforming to a longer maritime tradition. The passenger lists included lawyers, shipping magnates and retired politicians, many of whom hosted island dignitaries on board, dispensing hospitality rather than receiving it. In Rarotonga, members of the royal family and a number of chiefs joined the passengers for dinner, and were made to feel 'quite at home'. Wandering freely over the 'mammoth yacht' they seemed 'greatly impressed', and after an evening of dancing, singing and speech-making they left at midnight, 'giving us many cheers'.[33] At Pape'ete, 250 leading members of the indigenous and French communities partook of a Sunday cruise on the *Waikare* to Moorea. It was reportedly 'a great treat, as it was an opportunity rarely afforded to the residents'.[34]

The cruise ship offered a stage for performing and enacting roles of contested hierarchies. The only recorded Māori passenger was the prominent Ngāti Kahungunu landowner Airini Tonore (Donnelly), who travelled with her daughter Maud. We only learn of their presence on the *Waikare* from the account of fellow passenger, journalist Forestina Ross, who was commissioned by the USSCo. to write up the tour for the Dunedin press. At Apia, Tonore invited the 18-year-old Samoan vice-King, Malietoa Tanumafili, on board. The likeness between the 'two natives of the highest rank' struck Ross as 'remarkable', and 'pointed plainly to these islands being the home of the Maori'. With his retinue on board as well as commissioners and officers of the competing imperial powers of Britain, United States and Germany, the saloon was 'filled with personages, naval, political, and regal'.[35] Given that the *Waikare* had steamed into the thick of political unrest in mid-1899 as negotiations over the imperial partition of the Samoan Islands continued, these shipboard intimacies were highly sensitive. As reported later, 'some unpleasantness' occurred during the week 'owing to the invitations to a dance given on board being chiefly confined to Germans'.[36] The ship appeared to be used as leverage in a

33   William Meeks Fehon, 1898, *Six Weeks' Excursion to the South Seas and Eastern Pacific Islands: Comprising Raratonga, Tahiti, Raiatea, Samoa and the Friendly Islands, by the new steamer "Waikare", 3,000 tons : (Union Steam Ship Company of N.Z., Ltd.) from Sydney, 30th June, 1898*, Sydney: S.D. Townsend & Co., p. 8.
34   'The Waikare's excursion', *Otago Daily Times*, 8 August 1898.
35   Mrs Malcolm Ross, 'In Southern Seas: The Waikare's excursion', *Evening Post*, 12 August 1899.
36   'Affairs in Samoa', *Launceston Examiner*, 7 August 1899.

performative role between imperial rivals, dispensing and according privilege. En route to Pago Pago the *Waikare* ferried a number of chiefs and their relatives back to their homes in Tutuila after a key meeting before the commissioners as part of the political negotiations. Ross remarked, 'It was judged safer to get them away from the simmering intrigue of Apia and they themselves were pleased to be granted a deck passage on so grand a boat'.[37]

* * *

While the promotional literature of the period orients us to the imagined appeal of the tropics to white settler audiences around the ocean's rim, focusing on the cruise ship points us instead to the meanings generated in the course of touring, to the action unfolding in specific encounters. Docked at island ports, the cruise ship was variously a space of wonder and display, diplomacy and hospitality, a symbol of civilisation and ties to a wider imperial community. Centring the ship as a tourist space shows the extent to which passengers hoped to make an impression on the people living in these 'exotic' locations, just as they desired similarly novel experiences ashore. The extent of the reversals from shore to ship were perhaps unanticipated and at times unsettling, but they also reveal colonial touring as an inherently open, negotiated and unstable practice, one of cross-cutting mobilities, improvisations, and multi-sensorial encounters.

References

Archival repository

Hocken Collections Uare Taoka o Hākena, University of Otago, Union Steam Ship Company of New Zealand Records.

Books, journals and articles

Ballard, Chris. 2010. 'Watching first contact.' *Journal of Pacific History* 45(1): 21–36.

---

37   Mrs Malcolm Ross, 'The Waikare's excursion', *Evening Post*, 19 August 1899.

Burton, Alfred. 1884. *The Camera in the Coral Islands.* Dunedin: Burton Brothers.

de Betham, C.G. 1884. *The Wairarapa Wilderness: In which will be found the wanderings of the passengers on the second cruise of the S.S. Wairarapa from Auckland to the South Sea Islands and back during the month of July 1884.* Wellington.

Dening, Greg. 1980. *Islands and Beaches: Discourse on a Silent Land, Marquesas 1774–1880.* Melbourne: Dorsey Press.

Fehon, William Meeks. 1898. *Six Weeks' Excursion to the South Seas and Eastern Pacific Islands: Comprising Raratonga, Tahiti, Raiatea, Samoa and the Friendly Islands, by the new steamer "Waikare", 3,000 tons : (Union Steam Ship Company of N.Z., Ltd.) from Sydney, 30th June, 1898,* Sydney: S.D. Townsend & Co.

Foucault, Michel. 1986. 'Of other spaces.' *Diacritics* 16(1): 22–27.

Leys, T.W. 1884. *The Cruise of the Wairarapa.* Auckland: Evening Star.

Prakash, Gyan. 1999. *Another Reason: Science and the Imagination of Modern India.* Princeton: Princeton University Press.

Steel, Frances. 2013. 'An ocean of leisure: Early cruise tours of the Pacific in an age of empire.' *Journal of Colonialism and Colonial History* 14(2 Summer): 1–12.

USSCo. 1898. *Off To Tahiti! Trip to the South Seas Islands.* Dunedin: J. Wilkie & Co.

Newspapers

Evening Post (Wellington)

Fiji Times

Launceston Examiner

Nelson Evening Mail

Otago Daily Times

Otago Witness

South Australian Register

Sydney Morning Herald

Te Aroha News (Waikato)

6

Pitcairn and the *Bounty* Story

Maria Amoamo

> It is Pitcairn's Island, the setting is 1790 for the final act of one of the
> greatest sea dramas of all time, the mutiny aboard His Majesty's Armed
> Transport Bounty on 28 April 1789. Inch for inch, it is the repository
> of more history – romantic history, bloody history, bogus history –
> than any other island in the Pacific.[1]

Islands have long held a central place in western cultures' mythical
geographies. The following narrative examines Pitcairn Island, the
last remaining British overseas territory in the Pacific and the unique
heritage that underlies its inception and image. Pitcairn was settled by
Bounty mutineers and Tahitians in 1790 and where, today, fewer than
50 *Bounty* descendants still reside. Discussion highlights key symbolic
referents that contribute to a sense of 'exclusivity' of Pitcairn culture
and posits 'myth-making' as a key determinant in helping build
a sustainable tourism industry for Pitcairn.

Few island peoples in the world could boast the body of literature
written about their history, happenings and unique lifestyle than
Pitcairn. It has been estimated some 1,200 books, 3,200 magazine and
uncounted newspaper articles, documentary films and three major
Hollywood movies produced relating to the mutiny on the *Bounty*

---

1   Ian M. Ball, 1973, *Pitcairn: Children of the Bounty*, London: Gollancz, p. 4.

have accounted for Pitcairn's iconic status.[2] The story is not myth but has served to mythologise Pitcairn.[3] Collectively, such texts formulate the gaze over landscape and reveal how place-myth is both shaped and organised through discourse. What becomes relevant to ascertaining the role of myth in relation to the *Bounty* story is its resilience and mutability. Robert Kirk states of Pitcairners: 'They are the heirs of Odyssean voyages, surging passions, of steamy romance … Pitcairn lies in the public imagination and the presence of the mutineer's pedigreed descendants perpetuates the island's status as an icon.'[4] Such musings help foster the *Bounty* image alongside the community's unique social and cultural inception, thus transferred to its present-day descendants, of whom several keenly exploit this connection as a tourist commodity.

Constructing place: Pitcairn's cultural landscape

Pitcairn is both marginal in the sense of its remote geographic location and also as a site of illicit action represented by the very act of mutiny. This act marks the island and its inhabitants on the periphery of cultural systems of space. Upon landing the mutineers burned the ship—an act that both ensured their isolation and containment, and some may argue their allegiance to British law. Of note, the ritual performance of 'burning the Bounty' on 23 January is an annual event re-enacted by descendants not only on Pitcairn but also by wider diaspora in Norfolk Island and New Zealand.[5] Such acts remind us that performances *of* place are not fixed in inert cartographically coordinated spaces but contingently *enacted* in an ongoing, complex process involving cultural production. The latter involve

---

2   Philip Hayward, 2006, *Bounty Chords: Music, Dance and Cultural Heritage on Norfolk and Pitcairn Islands*, Eastleigh: John Libbey Publishing.
3   As a result of the mutiny, nine mutineers together with 12 Tahitian women and six men landed on Pitcairn in January 1790. The island was not visited by outsiders until 1808, an indication of the remoteness that typifies Pitcairn. Pitcairn became a British possession in 1838.
4   Robert W. Kirk, 2008, *Pitcairn Island, The Bounty Mutineers and their Descendants, A History*, Jeffersen, NC: McFarland & Co, p. 232.
5   In 1856 the entire population was coerced to migrate to Norfolk Island some 3,700 miles to the west. However, some families returned to Pitcairn a few years later and there remain strong cultural ties with Norfolk Island. See Peter Clarke, 1986, *Hell and Paradise: The Norfolk, Bounty, Pitcairn Saga*, Ringwood: Viking.

performances of scripting, designing, building and storytelling.[6] The historical trajectory of settlement in the nineteenth century served to create a Pitcairn identity manifest in isolation, insularity and a sense of exclusivity.

Figure 25. Burning the *Bounty*.
Source. Photographed by Maria Amoamo, Pitcairn Island, 23 January 2009.

Over time the *Bounty* settlers would develop life skills particularly adapted to the environment; speak an exclusive 'Pitkern' language—a creole mixture of eighteenth-century English and Tahitian—and operate their own unique form of self-government. Today most residents are Seventh Day Adventists, having converted to the faith in 1886 following the visit of an American missionary of that persuasion. Critics have argued that places are more than simply geographic sites with definitive physical and textual characteristics; places are also settings (or locales) in which social relations and identities are constituted.[7] As such, we need to acknowledge the

6   Jonas Larsen, 2012, 'Performance, space and tourism', in *The Routledge Handbook of Tourism Geographies*, ed. Julie Wilson, pp. 67–73, Abingdon, Oxon: Routledge.
7   John Agnew, 1987, *Place and Politics: The Geographical Mediation of State and Society*, London: George Allen and Unwin.

complex intersection of the senses in people's encounters with places.[8] An example of this analogy is the culturally layered landscape of Pitcairn. Upon arrival the island was a blank slate on which to inscribe place names and suggest the mutineers and their descendants saw Pitcairn as a new independent world, not a replication of Britain or Tahiti. The cultural landscape of Pitcairn tells of the relationships between people and place.[9] Place names depict past events, reminders of people and actions. Lack of allusion to anything British found in other colonial outposts is notable, perhaps not surprising given the mutineers rebelled against such heritage in the very act of mutiny. Examples include 'Bang on iron', the site of the *Bounty*'s forge, and 'Isaac's Stone', an offshore rock claimed by mutineer Isaac Martin. A Polynesian male who arrived on the *Bounty* was murdered at a place called 'Timiti's Crack'. Many places recall accidents and death, 'Where Dan Fall', 'McCoy's Drop', 'Broken Hip' and 'Where Minnie Off', or descriptors of artificial structures like 'Big Fence', 'Down the Grave' and 'The Edge'. 'Christian's Cave' is perhaps the most iconic site situated high on the cliff-face overlooking Adamstown. Lead mutineer Fletcher Christian is reported to have spent many an hour 'brooding' over his rebellious actions and that the cave offered a hideaway in case of discovery.[10] Visitors to the island often ascend the steep and treacherous route to the cave. The latter affords not only spectacular views but represents how people's actions materially spatialise the myth of place by seeking out physical sites representative of myth. Similarly, the 'Hill of Difficulty', a steep half-kilometre incline from Bounty Bay to Adamstown, is an iconic landmark 'nearly unique as a literary allusion that has lent itself as a place name'.[11] This iconic landmark is a 'must' for most visitors whom often refuse the US$2 quad bike ride to the top. Visitors are often keen to experience the hill 'first-hand', seemingly to substantiate the myth with reality. 'I've waited forty years for this', an elderly British tourist stated on arrival in 2011, 'it's a boyhood dream come true'. Unbeknown to him, the names of all Pitcairners are engraved at intervals on the concrete

---

8   Larsen, 'Performance, space and tourism'.
9   Maria Amoamo, 2012, '(de)Constructing place-myth: Pitcairn Island and the "Bounty" story, tourism geographies', in *New Perspectives on Tropical Coastal and Island Tourism Development*, special issue of *An International Journal of Tourism Space, Place and Environment* 15(1): 107–24.
10   Glynn Christian, 1999, *Fragile Paradise: The Discovery of Fletcher Christian, Bounty Mutineer*, Sydney: Doubleday.
11   Robert W. Kirk, 2008, *Pitcairn Island, The Bounty Mutineers and their Descendants, A History*, Jeffersen, NC: McFarland & Co., p. 134.

sections of the hill, starting with the oldest resident's name at Bounty Bay Landing and ending with the youngest at the top. The road was only paved in 2005, previously being described as a 'gruelling slog up the rough track sliced out of the cliff face'.[12] Upon landing, Ian Ball stated, 'We stood at last on the little lip of rock and shingle that had been Fletcher Christian's first landfall on Pitcairn'.[13] We can, to some extent then, view tourists seeking a Pitcairn experience as those who chase myths.[14] The 'myth', bound to childhood dreams as in the aforementioned comment, and fuelled by the wealth of existent *Bounty* literature is reflected in the actual host/visitor experience. The relationship to myth as a mode of analysis is relevant to present-day Pitcairn society and the role tourism plays in its future development.

Figure 26. Christian's Cave.
Source. Photographed by Maria Amoamo, Pitcairn Island, 23 January 2009.

12   Ball, *Pitcairn*, p. 159.
13   Ball, *Pitcairn*, p. 158.
14   See Tom Selwyn's edited volume, 1996, *The Tourist Image Myths and Myth Making in Tourism*, Chichester: John Wiley & Sons.

Pitcairn is still, some would say, an island lost in time. Tourists who seek it out are often motivated by a strong will and desire to experience something of the Bounty story; to catch a glimpse of its romantic past and meet first-hand the descendants of these intrepid mutineers. For present-day Pitcairn, the pressing needs of economic development and re-population are the most critical issues for the island's future survival. The fragility of Pitcairn's economic base is recognised by the islanders, who have prioritised tourism as a new focus sector for attracting income to the island and building a sustainable future for this small Pacific Island community.

Pitcairn: The social and economic context

Figures 27 and 28. Pitcairn Island.
Source. Photographed by Maria Amoamo, Pitcairn Island, 23 February 2013.

Situated halfway between New Zealand and South America, Pitcairn is often referred to as one of the most isolated islands in the world. Its tiny size, rugged coastline and sheer cliffs offer no safe anchorage for ships that must lie a mile or two offshore.[15] Transport to the island is governed by the skill of local men and their longboats. Due to Pitcairn's remote location there is no air strip and access to the island is by ship, a journey of 36 hours from Mangareva, French Polynesia's far-flung archipelago of Gambier Islands. The current service operates only four times a year and has continually been a barrier to economic growth. A handful of cruise ships, charter vessels and yachts visit

---

15   Pitcairn is 3.2 km (2 miles) long by 1.6 km (1 mile) wide with an irregular shape of which only 8 per cent is flat and its highest point 347 metres (1,138 feet). The Pitcairn Island Group is a British Overseas Territory including Henderson, Ducie and Oeno Islands. Oeno and Ducie are small low atolls while Henderson is a much larger raised coral island and a UNESCO world heritage site.

the island annually. Today, Pitcairn's populace is dwindling. Out of necessity, cooperative work is more important at times than in more 'traditional' communities elsewhere.[16] According to Godfrey Baldacchino such resourcefulness and resilience counters the alleged structural vulnerabilities of such small island sites.[17]

Figure 29. Pitcairn longboat.
Source. Photographed by Maria Amoamo, Pitcairn Island, 31 August 2008.

Pitcairn's economy is heavily dependent on a small number of activities. Much of the islander's day to day life is committed to maintaining roads, building homes, upkeep of basic infrastructure, gardening, government jobs, fishing, trading on ships, taking care of the family and household duties.[18] The islanders support themselves by making handicrafts, which they sell primarily to cruise ship passengers or those who arrive on small chartered vessels. Pitcairn men produce fine wooden carvings including figures such as sharks, whales, dolphins,

16   John Connell, 1988, 'The end ever nigh: Contemporary population change on Pitcairn Island', *GeoJournal* 16(2): 193–200, p. 194.
17   Godfrey Baldacchino, 2005, 'The contribution of "social capital" to economic growth: Lessons from Island jurisdictions', *The Round Table* 94(1): 31–46.
18   Pitcairn Islands Administration, 1999, *Guide to Pitcairn*, Auckland: Government of the Islands of Pitcairn, Henderson, Ducie and Oeno.

turtles and walking sticks, whilst the women weave intricate baskets, fans, hats and mats, as well as painted dried 'hattie' leaves. Carved replicas of the *Bounty* and longboats are particular favourites with visitors and can fetch several hundred dollars each. Pitcairn's main economy has been derived from philately, but decline in the demand for stamps has resulted in a need to develop other sources of income. The promotion of the Pitcairn domain name (.pn) is proving to be one source of government income, along with the production and export of local honey.[19] The *Bounty* image is by far the strongest motivational factor that attracts visitors, but key challenges for the community include the need to diversify economic activity. Tourism studies have identified the main potential for tourism development on Pitcairn to be carefully managed cruise tourism, long-stay VFR/study/volunteer tourism, short-stay and special interest tourism (e.g. ecotourism) and yachting tourism.[20] Several locals offer homestay accommodation to visitors and the growth of this sector would significantly benefit local incomes.

In 2009, a government restructure devolved operational responsibility for local governance to the community and aims to develop a more self-sufficient local economic model giving attention to biosecurity, education, public health, agriculture and fisheries, culture and tourism. Outmigration, primarily to New Zealand, has thinned the population from a peak of 233 in 1937 to its present number of 49 and there is a crucial need for repopulation to meet these objectives. Pitcairn is heavily reliant on UK budgetary aid (planned to be £2.9 million for the year 2012/13) administered by the Department

19   Pitcairn Islands Administration, 2008, *Pitcairn Islands Governance Restructure Concept Document*, Auckland: Government of the Islands of Pitcairn, Henderson Ducie and Oeno.

20   See Tourism Resource Consultants, 2005, 'Pitcairn Island Tourism Development Feasibility Study', Wellington: FCO Overseas Territories Department and Pitcairn Island Administration; Tourism Resource Consultants, 2008, 'Pitcairn Island 2008 cruise ship survey', Auckland. One option currently under negotiation is the creation of a marine reserve in Pitcairn waters, an EEZ area of some 836,000 square kilometres (322,781 square miles). Lobbying by Pew Environmental Group supported by a four-week *National Geographic* expedition to the islands in 2012 revealed Pitcairn's marine ecosystem to be one of the most pristine in the world. See Eric A. Sala et al., 2012, *Pitcairn Islands Expedition Report*, National Geographic Society and Pew Environmental Group. The creation of a marine reserve and the existing world heritage designation of Henderson could help Pitcairn develop ecotourism products and build a stronger brand image in the global marketplace.

for International Development (DFID).[21] This provides the support and services of contracted professionals, including a doctor, school teacher, community advisor, NZ police officer and the UK Governor's Representative. Furthermore, European Union funds have been approved to build an alternative harbour to help increase tourists landed and to support the development of the tourism sectors in terms of infrastructure improvements, other services and marketing. These proposed projects hope to increase the flow of tourism to the island. Great Britain has until now subsidised Pitcairn but it is uncertain whether it will continue to underwrite the expenses of its tiny but costly colony.

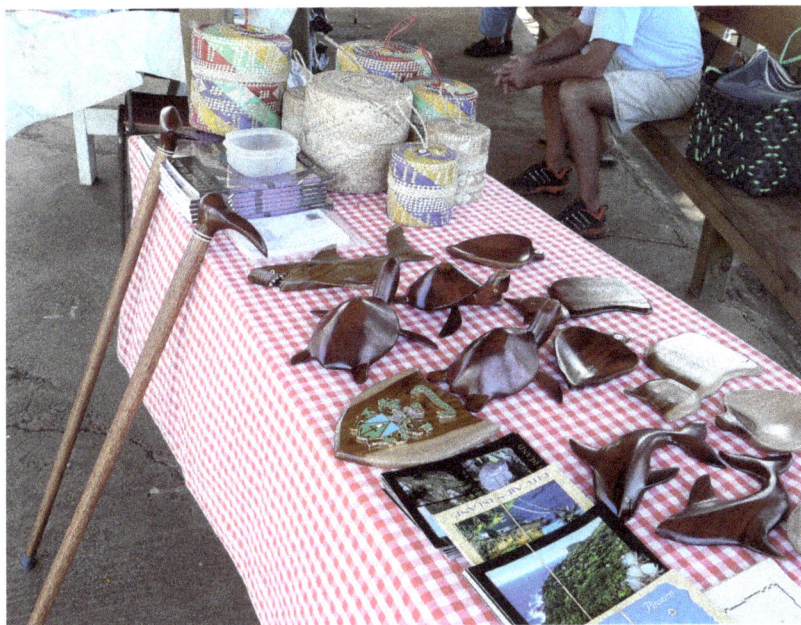

Figure 30. Pitcairn crafts.
Source. Photographed by Maria Amoamo, Pitcairn Island, 19 September 2008.

---

21 Ian Dickie, Guy Whiteley and Adam Dutton, 2012, *Revised Final Draft Report: Economic Analysis of Marine Reserve Designation in Pitcairn Islands' Waters*, London: Economics for the Environment Consultancy, August.

Performing place: Enacting myth

One example of the intersection of the senses in people's encounters with places is the tangible landscape of Pitcairn—which is also transferrable. That is, when islanders take their souvenirs and handicrafts to visiting cruise ships, it is not unusual for locals to 'bring' Pitcairn to visitors. That is, the tangible dimension of Pitcairn is transported in the form of Pitcairn soil; thus allowing cruise passengers to say they have 'walked on Pitcairn soil'. This *performance* establishes a connection with the physical (Pitcairn Island) and between host and guest in the touristic encounter. Many tourists actively seek out Pitcairners who are direct descendants of mutineers—the chance to be photographed with a local whose surname is 'Christian' holds resonance with, and gives evidence of, the literary connection. Some male islanders have also created a new type of image—that of the Pitcairn 'pirate', a figure replete with abundant jewellery (pierced and otherwise) as well as sporting the renowned 'tatow' (the term used by William Bligh when describing the Tahitian body tattoos). Female cruise passengers are especially keen to be photographed beside such male 'images'. Here is an example of the creation of 'new' myth (pirates were never part of the *Bounty* saga). Furthermore, John Urry links tourism and photography with constituting a self-reinforcing closed circle of representation, in which tourist photographs both reflect and inform destination images.[22] This also aligns with Roland Barthes' notion that myth is not just confined to oral speech; photography also serves to support mythical speech.[23] According to Jean-François Lyotard, such performance also links with creating a type of 'phantasy' through new motifs.[24] Such motifs highlight that locals engage with their audience using a particular image to provide a convincing vision. We might conclude that a level of commodification is perpetuated through such performative acts.

---

22   John Urry, 1990, *The Tourist Gaze: Leisure and Travel in Contemporary Societies*, London and New York: Routledge.

23   Roland Barthes, 1972, *Mythologies*, trans. Annette Lavers, New York: Hill and Wang.

24   Jean-François Lyotard, 1989, 'Figure foreclosed', trans. David Macey, in *The Lyotard Reader*, ed. Andrew Benjamin, pp. 69–110, Oxford: Basil Blackwell.

Figure 31. Cruise ship passengers arrive at Bounty Bay.
Source. Photographed by Maria Amoamo, Pitcairn Island, 19 September 2009.

When possible the transfer of cruise passengers onshore is undertaken by Pitcairn longboat—an 'attraction' that has, through historical imagery (literature, stamp issues), become an iconic symbol of Pitcairn culture. The symbolic is also reified in the ritual singing by islanders of the 'farewell song' as the longboat circles a departing ship. Passengers crowd the side of a ship to wave whilst transfixed on the visual and aural spectacle of both Pitcairner and longboat; an activity that embodies Tom Selwyn's notion of myth making.[25] Selwyn contextualises this type of setting or context in the cultural milieu in which contemporary tourism operates and the search for the authentic.[26] The ritual, performed less often today from longboat, has been transferred to on-board performance whereby Pitcairners often congregate together in a performative space and sing the many popular hymns and songs that epitomise the *Bounty* heritage. These performances connect to, and reflect, the past and present mythology of Pitcairn as the iconic 'utopia' created in the nineteenth century. The host/visitor

---

25   Tom Selwyn, 1996, 'Introduction', in *The Tourist Image Myths and Myth Making in Tourism*, ed. Tom Selwyn, pp. 1–32, Chichester: John Wiley & Sons, p. 28.
26   Selwyn, 'Introduction', p. 29.

interaction reflects to some extent how tourist destinations are places where fantasies and myth are superimposed on landscapes. Tourists arrive at their destination with their own agendas, prepared to make their tourist sites conform to their fantasies and gazes, recruiting their 'subjects' so to speak. In addition, such performances add to a certain understanding they (Pitkerners) have of themselves.

Concluding remarks

Chris Rojek and John Urry argue that 'myth and fantasy play an unusually large role in the social construction of all travel and tourist sights'.[27] The latter serves to organise, on the one hand, the tourist 'gaze', its expectations and observations, and on the other hand, the institutions, policies and workings of the community/place/space that is being gazed upon. The development of a greater diversity of economic activity is the key challenge for Pitcairn, with the current focus on reducing isolation, providing opportunities for economic growth and ensuring basic services. John Gillis reminds us, 'It is one of the great paradoxes of our times that the value of remoteness increases even as modern communications make all parts of the world more accessible'.[28] As this once isolated community, hidden from the world, emerged in the public imagination in the early nineteenth century, the 'myth' surrounding Pitcairn has grown ever larger. Today, remoteness offers both advantages and obstacles, however 'myth making' continues to contribute to how Pitcairn might endeavour to secure a sustainable future for its handful of inhabitants.

References

Agnew, John. 1987. *Place and Politics: The Geographical Mediation of State and Society*. London: George Allen and Unwin.

---

27 Chris Rojek, 1997, 'Indexing, dragging and the social construction of tourist sights', in *Touring Cultures: Transformations of Travel and Theory,* ed. Chris Rojek and John Urry, pp. 52–74, London: Routledge, p. 53.
28 John Gillis, 2004, *Islands of the Mind*, New York: Palgrave MacMillan, p. 152.

Amoamo, Maria. 2012. '(de)Constructing place-myth: Pitcairn Island and the "Bounty" story, tourism geographies.' In *New Perspectives on Tropical Coastal and Island Tourism Development*. Special issue of *An International Journal of Tourism Space, Place and Environment* 15(1): 107–124.

Baldacchino, Godfrey. 2005. 'The contribution of "social capital" to economic growth: Lessons from Island jurisdictions.' *The Round Table* 94(1): 31–46.

Ball, Ian M. 1973. *Pitcairn: Children of the Bounty*. London: Gollancz.

Barthes, Roland. 1972. *Mythologies*, trans. Annette Lavers. New York: Hill and Wang.

Benjamin, Andrew (ed.). 1989. *The Lyotard Reader*. Oxford: Basil Blackwell.

Christian, Glynn. 1999. *Fragile Paradise: The Discovery of Fletcher Christian, Bounty Mutineer*. Sydney: Doubleday.

Clarke, Peter. 1986. *Hell and Paradise: The Norfolk, Bounty, Pitcairn Saga*. Ringwood: Viking.

Connell, John. 1988. 'The end ever nigh: Contemporary population change on Pitcairn Island.' *GeoJournal* 16(2): 193–200.

Dickie, Ian, Guy Whiteley and Adam Dutton. 2012. *Revised Final Draft Report: Economic Analysis of Marine Reserve Designation in Pitcairn Islands' Waters*. London: Economics for the Environment Consultancy. August.

Fullerton, William Young. 1923. *The Romance of Pitcairn ... Illustrated*. London: Carey Press.

Gillis, John. 2004. *Islands of the Mind*. New York: Palgrave MacMillan.

Hayward, Philip. 2006. *Bounty Chords: Music, Dance and Cultural Heritage on Norfolk and Pitcairn Islands*. Eastleigh: John Libbey Publishing.

Kirk, Robert W. 2008. *Pitcairn Island, The Bounty Mutineers and their Descendants, A History*. Jeffersen, NC: McFarland & Co.

Larsen, Jonas. 2012. 'Performance, space and tourism.' In *The Routledge Handbook of Tourism Geographies*, ed. Julie Wilson, pp. 67–73. Abingdon, Oxon: Routledge.

Lyotard, Jean-François. 1989. 'Figure foreclosed.' Trans. David Macey. In *The Lyotard Reader*, ed. Andrew Benjamin, pp. 69–110. Oxford: Basil Blackwell.

Pitcairn Islands Administration. 1999. *Guide to Pitcairn*. Auckland: Government of the Islands of Pitcairn, Henderson Ducie and Oeno.

———. 2008. *Pitcairn Islands Governance Restructure Concept Document*. Auckland: Government of the Islands of Pitcairn, Henderson Ducie and Oeno.

Rojek, Chris. 1997. 'Indexing, dragging and the social construction of tourist sights.' In *Touring Cultures: Transformations of Travel and Theory*, ed. Chris Rojek and John Urry, pp. 52–74. London: Routledge.

Rojek, Chris and John Urry (eds). 1997. *Touring Cultures: Transformations of Travel and Theory*. London: Routledge.

Royle, Stephen A. 2001. *A Geography of Islands Small Island Insularity*. London: Routledge.

Sala, Eric, Alan M. Friedlander, Enric Ballesteros, Eric Brown, Heather Bradner, Jennifer Caselle, Michael Fay and Alan Turchik. 2012. *Pitcairn Islands Expedition Report*. National Geographic Society and Pew Environmental Group.

Selwyn, Tom (ed). 1996. *The Tourist Image Myths and Myth Making in Tourism*. Chichester: John Wiley & Sons.

Selwyn, Tom. 1996. 'Introduction.' In *The Tourist Image Myths and Myth Making in Tourism*, ed. Tom Selwyn, pp. 1–32. Chichester: John Wiley & Sons.

Tourism Resource Consultants. 2005. 'Pitcairn Island Tourism Development Feasibility Study.' Wellington: FCO Overseas Territories Department and Pitcairn Island Administration.

———. 2008. 'Pitcairn Island 2008 cruise ship survey.' Auckland.

Urry, John. 1990. *The Tourist Gaze: Leisure and Travel in Contemporary Societies*. London and New York: Routledge.

Wilson, Julie (ed.). 2012. '*The Routledge Handbook of Tourism Geographies*. Abingdon, Oxon: Routledge.

7

Guys like Gauguin

Selina Tusitala Marsh

I

thanks Bougainville
for desiring em young
so guys like Gauguin could dream
and dream
then take his syphilitic body
downstream to the tropics
to test his artistic hypothesis
about how the uncivilised
ripen like paw paw
are best slightly raw
delectably firm
dangling like golden prepubescent buds
seeding nymphomania
for guys like Gauguin

II

thanks Balboa
for crossing the Isthmus
of Panama
in 1513
and pronouncing our ocean
the South Seas

hey thanks, Vasco
for making us
your underbelly
the occidental opposite of all
your nightmares
your waking dreams
inversion of all your laws
your darkest fantasies

thanks for seeing the earth as a body
the North, its head
full of rationality
reasoned seasons
of meaning
cultivated gardens
of consciousness
sown in masculine
orderly fashion
a high evolution
toward the light

thanks for making the South
an erogenous zone
corporeal and sexual
emotive and natural
waiting in the shadows
of dark feminine instinct
populated by the Africas
the Orient, the Americas
and now us

8

Statued (stat you?) Traditions

Selina Tusitala Marsh

The 'Golden Past'
Is
Frozen Fast
In
anthro-pological
socio-logical
ethno-graphical
historio-graphical
feminist-epist-o-mological
bio-logical
psycho-logical
audio-logical
edu-cational
environ-mental
human-biological
pharma-co-logical
theo-logical
gyna-co-logical
crimin-o-logical
scientifically
geothermically
text-booked
documented

locked-fast
bound-cemented
rock-hard
she wears lei
  around Gauguinesque
    blossoming breasts
      sweeping brown
        round and around
        looping above
        firm flat belly button
          peeking over
            see-thru hula skirt
          (not from her island – but what does it hurt?)
she swings her hips
  with lips
    slightly parted
    lip-stick red
              with 'come-to-bed' eyes
                  highlighted by REVLON
                    black sheen of hair
                      sweeps the air
(come if you dare
to these mysterious islands)
frozen in glossy post-card form
  she is adorned
    with dreams
      ready for you / to
        fantasise
        romantisise
        over gorgeous big brown eyes
          gorging thighs
(gorged out eyes from forging lies!)
'Lovely hula hands'
always understands
  make good island wife – for life – no strife
  (no hy-phenated name!)
  always to sing
  island lullaby song
  petals caressing wind
  all night long

drowning in
frangipani scent
dreaming, seeming
hours spent
in islands aphrodisiac
  no lack
  no loss
  in these
'Lovely hula hands'
  always understands
  make good island wife - …
multiplying
 in silhouetted
  still-water of
   rippling
    text and
     image
      history unchallenged
       mystery 'solved'.
We have evolved
  from Noble Savagess
   to Tropical Princess
    moremore
     fantasise
      romanticise
     mesmerise
      metamorphosise your own image
       planted before we shed seeds of ourselves in the Pacific
(and not the seed of Margaret Mead nor the semen of Derek Freeman)
  Moremore
  Fantasise
  Romanticise
  Frankensize
   the monster of you
    into
    our flesh
stitching parts of islands together:
Solomon beads
 Hawaiian lei
  Kakala seeds

of perfume spray from Tonga
  Fijian salusalu
    Samoan ula
      Hawaiian hula
      skirt
(you don't wear it that way – but what does it hurt?)
Cook Islands head dress
 and coconut breasts
 from the Marquesas
  (just to please us / and the camera)
'So colourful the way they sit together!'
 stat you tradition?
 picture post-card / history diagram
 stat you tradition?
 stat me in you?
Who
 is that Pacific Princess?
 always waiting
  warm bare breasted
  anticipating
   between 'jungle' leaves
   waiting weighting
    looking out to sea
    fating the sight of you
    on the site of me
aaah – moment of 'discovery' –
stat you tradition?
the glossed publications
 of island salutations
  'Talofa!' 'Kia Ora!'
  'Bula Vanaka!' 'Malo e Lelei!'
  'Kia Ora Ana!' 'Aloha!' and
   'Have a *nice* day!'
forever static
forever still
 motion-less
 meaning-less
  not my past
  not my blessed
genealogical

'tis fantasy
& will freeze itself apart
as disciplines crack under heated pressure
of our golden rays
tropical sun melts the haze
  breezed island days
    blow away petrified images of
no-people
no-where
to-disappear
no need
no more
  to hypothesise
  theorise
  or
  romanticise
my tradition is here, within my eyes
  and those of my mother
For tradition
  Eludes
  Precludes
  Concludes
  stasis
tis 'anti-stasis'
  ever-moving
  ever-grooving
  to beaten drum of lali soothing
  voices in fagogo telling
  tales of old and new
ever-revolving
ever-solving
mysteries of itself
  by itself
ever-growing
ever-knowing
  of itself and other worlds
    incorporating
      investigating
        revitalising
          unto itself

indigenising
outside selves
Statued traditions
stun still water
swimming through
our son and daughter
break the surface
breach the haze
of cemented tradition
of Golden Age
till
looking with new eyes
nothing is left
she on the post-card
has Frozen to death.[1]

---

1   Previously published in *Wasafiri* 25 (1997): 52–54.

9

Detouring Kwajalein: At Home Between Coral and Concrete in the Marshall Islands

Greg Dvorak

Kwaj Kid[1]

Not too many people know about Kwajalein, a small island in the Marshall Islands. Of course I do, or I wouldn't be writing this essay. The reason I know about it is because I lived there until I was nine years old. When we moved from our home in New Jersey, our predictions were to stay for a year ... then it became another, then another, and finally almost seven years.

◀◀ Here I am in sixth grade in 1984 trying to make sense out of myself and my situation: a little 11-year-old boy sitting at his desk in New Jersey, enduring the third winter ever of his life, up past his bedtime, doing English homework at the last minute—dreaming of sunshine while writing his very first essay about the island home he once took for granted. It has been nearly two years since he moved away from Kwajalein in the Marshall Islands with his family, and the initial chaos has past. In the rapid and turbulent transition from small island tropics to landlocked autumn, the boy believes he has learned to put it all in perspective. He has learned three lessons:

---

1   I use this two-column style with homage to Teresia Teaiwa, who used a similar layout to narrate her academic and personal journey, and the history of Native Pacific Studies, in her article 'L(o)osing the Edge', *The Contemporary Pacific* 13(2) (2001): 343–57. Here, I use this format to narrate my own ambivalence about my personal relationship to occupied Marshallese land as 'home'.

What many people think about Kwaj besides, 'What's that?' usually sounds like this: 'It's too small.' Everyone says that. I think, no, it's not, because in my view it was a little paradise to me. Since it is a missile range, everyone imagines a barren battlefield with a runway and rocket smoke in the air. No way, it's a beautiful, one-square-mile island with palm trees and hibiscus flowers everywhere!

I really should start telling about Kwajalein itself. Homes were supplied by the Army and electricity, phone calls, and water were all free. Homes consisted of trailers and houses. Trailers were nice little homes that most people were used to living in. No, they weren't trailers like you see travelling on the highway, they weren't even like our school's trailers. These were big, well-built, silver trailers! One slight problem we had were cockroaches, big brown cockroaches.

The transportation of Kwaj is an interesting topic. Everyone rode on bikes! Everything was so close to our homes, all you had to do was hop on a bike and ride for two minutes at the most!

One of the most fascinating topics of Kwaj is the ocean. It was very beautiful. Our trailer was located right next to it, so the view out of our dining room window was remarkable. The activities we did were swimming, snorkelling, scuba diving and fishing. Let's not forget sailboating and other numerous activities.

Kwaj is very far away, Kwaj is in the middle of nowhere, and Kwaj is virtually everything New Jersey isn't—sort of. With the exception of the rows and rows of tidy houses, the gated community-feel, the American faces, American food, and *Sesame Street*, Kwaj might as well be in a completely different universe altogether.

Though he proclaims to know the legend of how 'we' moved to Kwajalein and stayed for seven years, he actually has no recollection of what came before that, or even why we lived there. Nor does he relate to the nostalgia of cold autumn nights and spiced apple cider. But his parents do, and he has begun to cultivate these memories and this identity for his own survival and comfort. For the boy, there actually was never anything *but* Kwajalein, except for brief summertime sojourns with relatives 'backinthestates'. Backinthestates: the word used to describe the world where Grandmom lived—an alternative reality reached only through a series of flights on trans-Pacific and trans-continental airships.

Physically living backinthestates, however, is another matter: In this other dimension, one must pretend to belong and know, and being as 'grown-up' as he is, the boy has finally begun to learn the ropes. It is a process of putting things in context, framing them like a Waikiki postcard so that everyone understands, making up stories about fishing and surfing for good measure.

After all, 'Kwaj' is in the past. It *was* temporary. It *was* just a decade-long vacation in the tropics. It *was* never really home, he discovers; the biggest joke of his life, like Dorothy waking up from her crazy dreams of Oz—there's no place like home. And home isn't in the Marshall Islands. Is it? We're Americans, anyway. All just a dream, just a paradise island, just a moment frozen in time, in between Reality and Reality. There are no palm trees in Reality. No baby coconuts to take to the Marshallese maintenance man at the pool for him to custom spraypaint in bright colours. Yes, just a dream, just a place to be. Sort of.

Even though I didn't fish much, fishing was interesting to watch. Deep sea fishing was most popular. People would go out on boats and ride for hours. Of all the little sailboats that a few people rode on, there was one big grey fishing boat. Today I like to refer to this boat as the big diesel. First of all, it was very huge. Second of all, it was very nauseating and it rocked rapidly. Some fish we caught were mahi-mahi, a very rich and juicy fish, tuna, flounder, and sunfish.

The people that lived on Kwaj were mostly people from all over the world, usually from the United States. There were also the original inhabitants, the Marshallese. During World War II, they were sort of forced off the island. A few of them even had radiation. After that, they moved out of Kwaj and made their home on an island north of Kwaj called Ebeye.

So all together Kwajalein in the Marshall Islands was and still is a really nice place to live.

And what of 'the Marshallese' who were 'sort of forced' off their islands? What really happened to them, he wonders. Why was Kwaj for Americans, and Ebeye for Marshallese? They smiled and sang and 'had radiation', whatever that meant. All he knew was that Ebeye, a few islands down the chain, was a hideous and fantastic place—it haunted and excited him all at once. It was a treeless place that smelled at once of seafood and fried chicken and sewage and burning trash and birthday cake, and his mother warned him not to touch the broken glass. But it was also the place where children ran freely and laughed, a place of wondrous freedom and camaraderie, where the music blasted and everyone played ball games in the street.

If Kwaj wasn't *really* home, what, then, is that cozy feeling he remembers of coming back to Kwaj after a long month of summer vacation on the mainland—that snuggly sensation on the way back from the air terminal at night? Soothed by the silent warmth of the island, by the trade winds and the thick smell of flowers and reef barnacles sweating in the damp air, he remembers a sleepy calm as comforting as getting tucked into bed at night, and secretly wishes that he could just go home.

Kwajalein in the Marshall Islands: Almost the first decade of my life. A perfect lagoon to rival the greatest tropical paradises of the world. A testing ground where unarmed missiles fell from the sky. Stolen Marshallese land? Rented Marshallese land? A Really Nice Place to Live.

Crossings

It is with this childhood essay[2] that I welcome you to Kwajalein Atoll in the Marshall Islands, one of the largest inhabited atolls on earth, a vast boomerang-shaped string of roughly 100 slender coral islands encompassing a lagoon of over 2,000 square kilometres. It is a place that has been significant to Islander voyagers and settlers for thousands of years, and also to the Spanish, German, Japanese, and especially American colonial and military communities who claimed or used it over the past centuries to the present.

Welcome to Kwajalein

Figure 32. Cover image from the orientation materials my parents received in 1975.
Source. Bell Laboratories, 1972, 'Kwajalein Orientation Guide', Pamphlet.

History at Kwajalein, as with most Pacific places, is like its reefs, the stories of countless human beings amalgamated like the layers of coral whose tiny polyps migrated from afar, settled, sedimented, and spread further in all directions and dimensions over tens of thousands of years in deep time. Pacific histories, as so many navigators, elders, scholars and artists tell us, are genealogies that connect people

---

2   For an earlier version of this essay and its interpretation, see my master's thesis, where my focus was on exploring American notions of 'home'. See Greg Dvorak, 2004, 'Remapping home: Touring the betweenness of Kwajalein', MA thesis, University of Hawai'i at Mānoa, Honolulu, 2004. This chapter also draws extensively on my doctoral work about competing Marshallese, Japanese, and American histories at Kwajalein Atoll over the past century. Greg Dvorak, 2008, 'Seeds from afar, flowers from the reef, re-membering the coral and concrete of Kwajalein Atoll', PhD thesis, The Australian National University, Canberra.

across and through the ocean. They are often contradictory linkages, fraught with pleasure and peril, memory and forgetting, pain and perseverance, and legacies of injustice.

In summer of 1975, not long after the fall of Saigon, a young and eager couple shipped their belongings to the Central Pacific and moved from New Jersey with their baby son to Kwajalein Atoll. My father, a civilian systems engineer at a major aerospace defence company, was invited on a family contract to work in the north of the atoll at the radar installations on Roi-Namur as part of the intercontinental ballistic missile Cold War target practice that was being conducted at the time by the US military.[3] Commuting daily by small aircraft, he would cross the giant atoll each morning and evening while my mother and I (and later my brother) would spend our days going to school, working, and playing in an idyllic small-town community that looked somewhat like 1950s American suburbia, enhanced by its brilliant turquoise lagoon, coconut palms and tropical flowers. Relocating to 'Kwaj' was, for my parents, a short opportunity to live on a Pacific island for a few years, experience a new environment, have their second child and save money. For me, it was the foundation of my life, the beginning of my own awkward and ambivalent link to a particular Pacific genealogy of war and settlement, when I formed my roots in the reef of that immense and mysterious lagoon.

My family's heritage was, in fact, already comprised of many trans-oceanic crossings before we crossed the Pacific to the Marshall Islands. My mother's grandmother was still a baby at the turn of the twentieth century when her Jewish family made their Atlantic crossing from Galatz, Romania, to Philadelphia. The man she would marry came from a Roman Catholic family that had crossed a generation earlier from the Abruzzo region of Italy. My mother's paternal grandparents had crossed from the borderlands of Russia and Poland. My father's

---

3   This 'target practice' continues today, though far more sporadically, having evolved into Ronald Reagan's Strategic Defense Initiative 'Star Wars' programs in the 1980s and later variations that tested the interception of incoming missiles before they impacted earth. In recent decades, the testing site at US Army Garrison Kwajalein Atoll (USAGKA), facilitated by the United States Army but managed by a consortium of corporations, is a location for NASA and private spaceflight testing such as Elon Musk's SpaceX Program, along with a number of other research and space surveillance programs.

grandfather was a Czech tailor in Manhattan; his grandmother, a brave woman who was only 16 when she crossed from Bratislava seeking her brother who had made his own crossing to find work in the United States. These crossings were plagued with the seasickness of culture shock and the turbulence of change.

Figure 33. With my father and mother on Kwajalein, 1976.
Source. Family archive, photographer unknown.

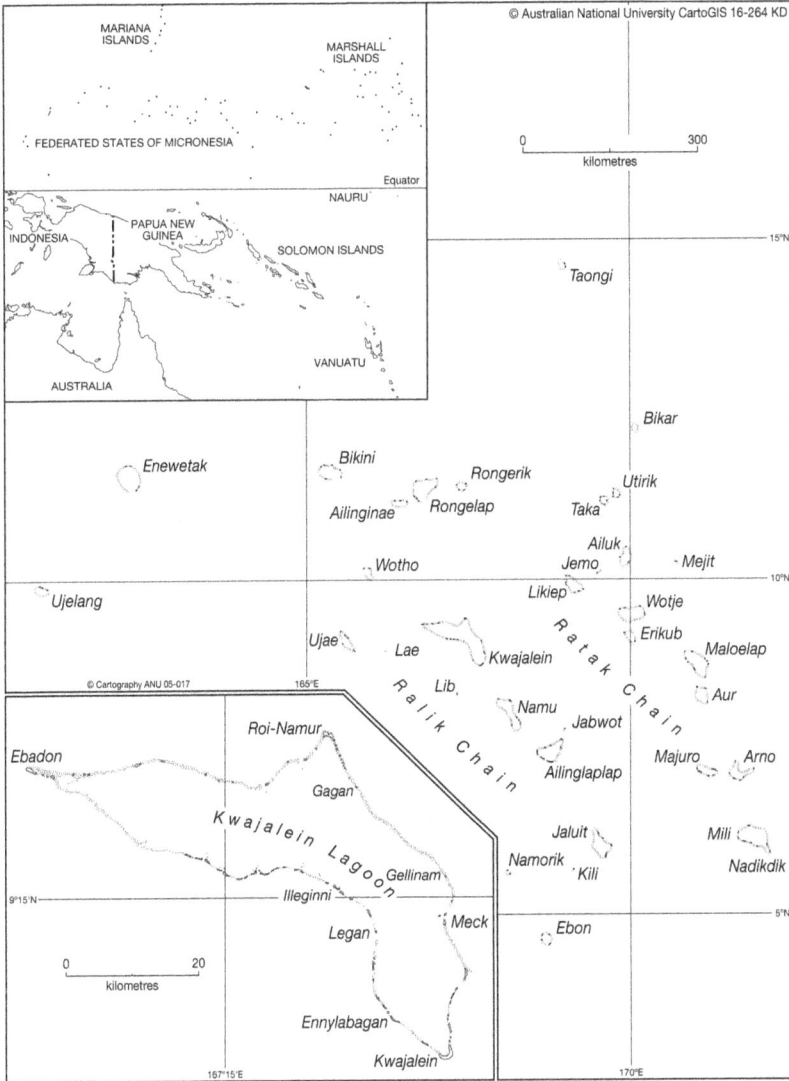

Map 1. Kwajalein Atoll. Kwajalein is the southernmost islet of Kwajalein Atoll, shown here in the lower-left inset.

Source. © Australian National University Cartography, CartoGIS 16 264 KD. Used with permission.

When my parents carried that hard-to-pronounce Czech name further across another ocean, however, the American mission of national security facilitated and smoothed their sailing. It was a job, a 'tour of duty', and little else. This coaxed them and other American families into an ambivalent ignorance about the peacelessness of the Pacific world they entered and the tremendous changes that were taking place throughout Oceania. The year 1975 was one in which 5,000 Māori marched to fight for their land claims in Aotearoa-New Zealand, and when East Timor declared its independence. American history classes and newspapers had not taught my parents the horrific histories of nuclear weapons testing and displacement that Marshall Islanders had already endured for so many decades. They had no idea about the frustration of Kwajalein landowners or their desire to reoccupy the islands Japan and then the United States military had forcefully taken from them—including the land where our American suburbia was located. And they did not realise that even 30 years after the Pacific War had ended, the remains of over 8,000 Japanese and Koreans who died in the Pacific War were still buried beneath the concrete and asphalt where we lived, or that the bereaved family members of those war dead had still not received permission to visit the graves of their loved ones.

Only a tour

To this day, employees and their families on the Kwajalein base (a group that increasingly includes a small number of Marshallese residents who have higher status jobs on the base) live in a residential zone that was fashioned after a middle-class American community of yesteryear; it was deliberately designed to evoke home-away-from-home and to reassure its constituents that they had never actually left the United States. As historian Lauren Hirshberg writes, 'During the 1960s, the army transformed this Marshallese island into small-town suburban America. Army officials designed Kwajalein as a space that captured one paradoxical narrative of 1950s Cold War America: anxiety over nuclear insecurity eased by the illusion of greater nuclear-family security through the suburban refuge.'[4]

My family's life in the American 'suburban refuge' of Kwajalein was less than a decade, but after we left, I experienced an intense homesickness that was only exacerbated by the shocking realisation that life for Americans on Kwajalein was only supposed to be a mere

---

4   Lauren Hirshberg, 2012, 'Nuclear families: (Re)producing 1950s suburban America in the Marshall Islands', *Organization of American Historians Magazine of History* 26(4): 39–43, p. 39.

'tour of duty' and not a permanent place to settle. 'Tour' was the word that even American civilian contractors and their families, like mine, used to describe our existence in the Marshall Islands. And considering that civilians and their dependents have always outnumbered soldiers since the beginning of the missile-testing range (in the 1970s, there were nearly 5,000 American civilians living on Kwajalein versus a mere 20 employees of the US Army), 'touring' was a pun that was more suggestive of our leisurely lifestyle than it was an active defence assignment.

When I would hear kids at school on Kwaj talk about coming back for another tour, or my own parents speak about the end of our own tour, I presumed that we were talking about the idea that we were all on an extended holiday. Despite the smallness of our island we did, for instance, have two movie theatres, two swimming pools, yacht and country clubs, several pristine beaches, a golf course and multiple playing fields for every sport imaginable, a fully stocked supermarket, free snorkelling and scuba diving, sailing, water-skiing, and so on— all on a tiny island in the centre of the Pacific Ocean.[5] Every evening, couples holding hands and families with cameras would congregate in front of our lagoonside home to watch the sunset. We would even gather with popcorn and lemonade to watch the missile tests at night. We lived in comfortable, air-conditioned homes and rode around slowly on rusty bicycles. We had barbecues down by the beach. It *was* a tour, but we weren't exactly tourists. Or at least we took our tourism seriously.

Even if no actual tourist industry exists in Kwajalein Atoll, aside from the recreation services provided for personnel and their families, the dynamics of militarism and tourism mutually create and justify each other's existence there. This is rather like Teresia Teaiwa's idea of 'militourism', which she describes as 'a phenomenon by which military or paramilitary force ensures the smooth running of a tourist industry, and that same tourist industry masks the military force behind it'.[6]

---

5   In recent years, the base also has its own Burger King and Subway fast food restaurants, which seem particularly out of place considering Kwajalein's tiny population and distance from the United States.

6   Teresia Teaiwa, 1999, 'Reading Gauguin's *Noa Noa* with Epeli Hau'ofa's *Kisses in the Nederends*: Militourism, Feminism, and the Polynesian Body', in *Inside Out: Literature, Cultural Politics, and Identity in the New Pacific*, ed. Vilsoni Hereniko and Rob Wilson, pp. 249–63, Lanham: Rowman & Littlefield, p. 251.

The touristic comforts of living on a beautiful Pacific Island, together with above-average remuneration and minimal cost of living, has always been a large part of what has sustained the American labour force there since the 1960s and given incentive for civilians—not only aerospace contract engineers from Raytheon, Lockheed-Martin, Boeing, McDonnell-Douglas, NASA, and other corporations, but also schoolteachers, architects, mechanics, department store clerks, cooks or lifeguards—to collaborate in supporting and shaping the military mission of weapons testing.

It has arguably also been the potential revocation of those pleasures and rewards that has silenced many Americans from speaking up about countless injustices against indigenous people over the decades, or even noticing any injustice to begin with. The ongoing tour of Americans at Kwaj marginalises Marshallese to the exotic fringes of US national security, all the while reinforcing American hegemony in the Pacific as natural and unquestionable. Even as a small boy, it was quite obvious to me that Marshallese people were not being accorded the same dignity that I enjoyed, nor were they seen for who they really were. Thinly veiled, racist discourses about Micronesians undercut the ideology of our world.

This is not to say that the reality of Kwajalein was in fact so clear-cut and racist. Rather, ours was actually a rather diverse community, including a significant population of Japanese Americans and Native Hawaiians who had come to work from Hawai'i for the main contractor in the atoll. Our community included many African Americans and had a very open-minded attitude toward sexual minorities. Most of the adult population had a higher degree. Though there were some elements of segregation, this was not apartheid-era South Africa or the US South in the pre–civil rights era. There were also Marshall Islanders who lived on the island in higher-paid professional positions and had a deep rapport with the rest of the community, as were there some Americans who worked or volunteered directly in nuclear-affected Marshallese communities, some who spoke Marshallese fluently. Still, official American narratives and public discourses about Marshall Islanders rendered the fluidity and complexity of Kwajalein Atoll in stark black-and-whiteness, cultivating an attitude of apathy and endorsing orientalism.

Figure 34. Aerial photo of Kwajalein Atoll.
Source. Photographed by official photographer, Sue Rosoff, 2000.

Marginalised and objectified by American discourses of science, development, politics, and racial difference, 'The Marshallese' were kept at a safe distance. Despite there being over 1,000 islands and 24 atolls in the vast archipelagoes of the Marshall Islands, to many Americans, all Marshall Islanders seemed to live 30 minutes away by ferry in the labour community that serviced our base, the crowded, tiny Ebeye Islet, just to the north of Kwajalein. It was within sight of Kwaj, on the same reef, reachable even by walking at low tide. It is the third island up the chain; it appears white on this aerial photograph because of its urban concrete sprawl. Marshallese on Ebeye were far enough away not to be threatening, but close enough to come and work for cheap pay. In casual banter, it was always 'The Marshallese' who were blamed for mismanaging their money—'feudal' landowners who did not share the wealth they gleaned from US rental payments with commoners or Marshallese workers who squandered their salaries. It was always 'The Marshallese' who had an alcohol problem, despite the high rate of alcoholism in the American population and the enormous quantities of alcohol the base stocked for its residents. It was always the Americans who had what 'The Marshallese' lacked.

Strangers on their own land, the Marshallese I encountered as a child represented to me gaps in the green-lawn-picket-fence suburban vision the United States Army had painted onto the landscape of my childhood. I peered through that gap and saw those contradictions, even if I didn't understand them at the time. My mother participated in cultural exchanges with Marshallese women from time to time and also conducted research on Marshallese childbirth practices. My own visits to Ebeye were very rare, such as when we attended the *kemem* (one-year-old birthday celebration) of the son of a man who worked at the checkout counter in Surfway supermarket, or when we attended the annual Marshallese Christmas festivities. On such excursions, my parents would grasp my hand firmly as we disembarked the *Tarlang* ferry into the streets of Ebeye, cautioning me against touching anything dirty and lamenting that they hadn't made me wear closed shoes, lest I step in broken glass. But for me, Ebeye was vibrant, exciting, brimming with youth and overflowing with kids my age, unlike the eerie silence of Kwaj. I wanted to play with these children, and they looked back at me, sometimes beckoning me to join in their games, but we always had to hurry back to our ferry before nightfall. Their world was off-limits to me and obscured from view.

There were encounters on a daily basis, too. There was, for instance, the Marshallese man that worked as a janitor by the swimming pool, who would paint baby coconuts for me in colours of my choosing. Or there was our housekeeper Neitari, whom I would later consider to be my Bubu (grandmother). When I was six, I told her I would marry her.

Figure 35. Neitari Pound in 1978 on Kwajalein.
Source. Photographed by Christine Dvorak; from the family archive.

Wandering around the island on my bicycle like most Kwaj Kids, I would veer off the beaten paths and make my own sense of the landscape. In practice, I may have lived the life of a tourist-settler child on a paradise island, seduced by our resort-like reality; in spirit, however, I was restless and burning with curiosity like many of my peers. I naturally saw beyond the contradictory utopia of our cement and grassy lawns to the deeper coral roots below, and I felt a visceral sense of belonging there, in spite of the military metanarratives of temporariness and distance from the American homeland. The breezes across the lagoon from other islets in the atoll haunted me with the perfumes of mythical flowers, the ghostly musk of death and buried memories, or the rotting stench of 'development' and broken promises. I played on forlorn Japanese wartime concrete bunkers that remained after the American amphibious invasion of 1944, bicycled between shiny new white radar globes and rusty atomic-age junk, and wondered often about the Marshallese workers who passed in and out of our American civilian community to toil by day as our carpenters, painters, maids and custodians and return by ferry every evening to the shantytown on Ebeye.

As a Kwaj Kid, these realities and rhythms, however unsettling or colonial they may seem, were associated with the idea of home in my mind, but they also conjured in me a yearning to know more. As geographer Yi-Fu Tuan argued, 'space' is something that *becomes* place, that 'what begins as undifferentiated space becomes place as we get to know it better and endow it with value'.[7] 'The city or land is viewed as mother, and it nourishes; place is an archive of fond memories and splendid achievements that inspire the present; place is permanent and hence reassuring.'[8] Though bugged by my intuition to dig deeper and eventually return home to Kwajalein, it would take decades before I consciously became aware that my little hometown, so quiet and 'innocent' in its seemingly homespun goodness, was but a tiny speck precariously perched atop the unfathomably profound reefs of history in the Marshall Islands, and that it was a place that had different meanings to different people. My detours have only begun to scratch the surface.

---

7   Yi-Fu Tuan, 2003, *Space and Place: The Perspective of Experience*, Minneapolis: University of Minnesota Press, p. 6.

8   Ibid., p. 154.

The missile

Figure 36. Kwajalein Missile Monument in 1977.
Source. Photographed by Walter Dvorak; from the family archive.

My father took the photo in 1977, probably early in the morning on his way to work. It is of a missile rising proudly against the sky, as if launching out of the sunrise, above the coconut palms and the fence of the softball field. This inactive rocket, neutered of its nuclear payload, stood watch over the little league baseball teams playing each other under the bright lights, and the Kwaj Karnival that happened in its shadow every year—a fair that included even a carousel and a ferris wheel. People would sit on its concrete steps watching sports, playing music by the Eagles or John Denver, drinking Olympia Beer as the sun set and the stars came out.

It was so ordinary and natural in its existence there on our ball field that we never questioned it. I remember hugging that missile to see if my arms would reach around it (they didn't), and how hot its white metallic skin felt in the midday sun, how its paint smelled. We would lean against it and pose for photos in our school yearbook. And at the same time, it was awesome, monumental, phallic, reassuringly pointing skyward to heroically defend us against The Enemy. It was a friend, a mascot, and an icon, and it bespoke the seamlessness with which our suburban Americana blurred into the Cold War. It symbolised, in many ways, the raison d'être of our existence on Kwaj and yet it was so central that we barely thought twice about it. According to an extensive Facebook page for former Kwaj residents, this missile was installed around 1965 and dismantled in 1991 after succumbing to severe corrosion that caused its fins to fall off and resulted in an overall safety hazard. Were it not for rust, this ubiquitous elephant in our living room would probably still be standing today.

Take this map from 1972 published by Bell Laboratories for newcomers to the island. 'Places to Go and Things to Do on Kwajalein' is a compact and easy-to-access guide to orient its users in a whimsical and carefree way to the pleasures and conveniences of our island home. It depicts Surfway Grocery Store (35), the barber shop (25), Coral Sands Beach (54), Emon Beach (47, appropriated from the Marshallese word *emman*, meaning 'good'), the Small Boat Marina (49), the scout camp (4), tennis courts (34), the Richardson outdoor movie theatre (9), and my elementary school (37). Aside from Launch Hill (1), which was also known as 'Mt Olympus', the numerous testing and tracking facilities sited on the other end of the airstrip are not mentioned at all in this map, nor are any of the Japanese structures remaining from the war, the mass graves of the fallen soldiers, or Marshallese sacred cultural sites. And as always, our friendly missile here is such a natural part of the landscape that it is drawn on the map but not even labelled. There it is, just to the left of the Grace Sherwood Library and the bowling alley (10).

PLACES TO GO AND THINGS TO DO ON KWAJALEIN

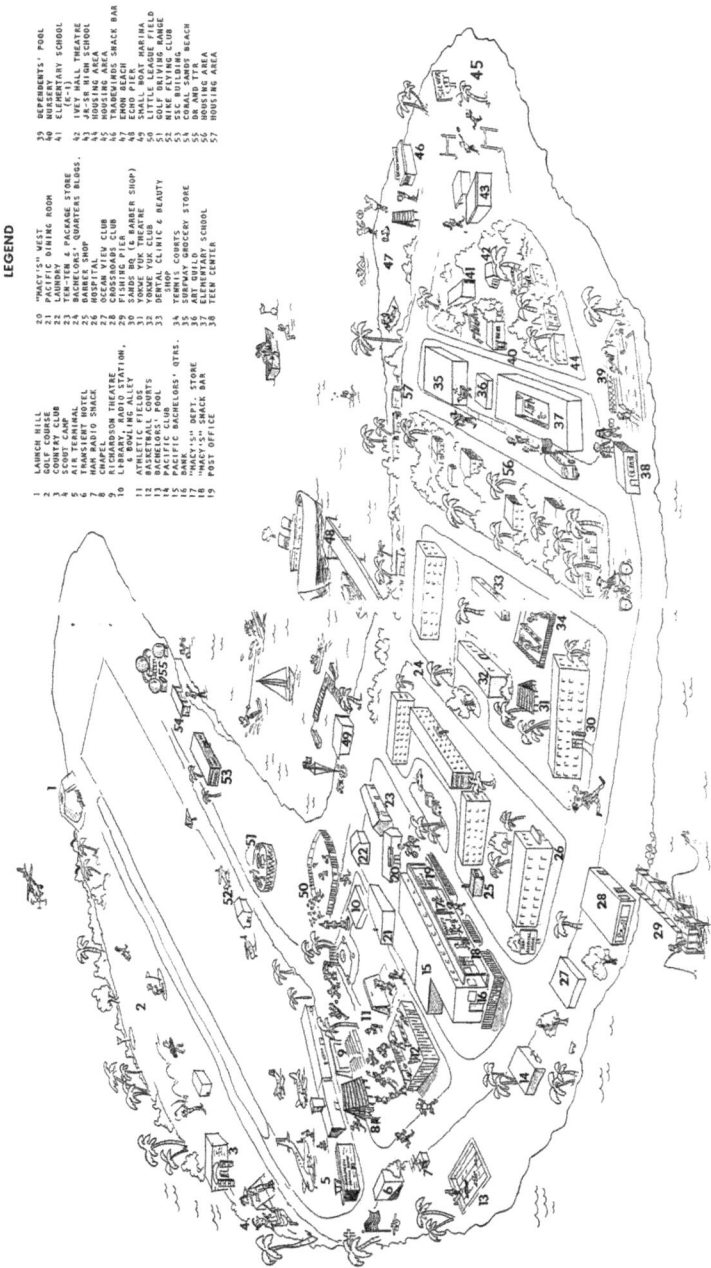

LEGEND

1 LAUNCH HILL
2 GOLF COURSE
3 COUNTRY CLUB
4 SCUBA CAMP
5 AIR TERMINAL
6 TRANSIENT HOTEL
7 HAM RADIO SHACK
8 CHAPEL
9 RICHARDSON THEATRE
10 LIBRARY, RADIO STATION, & BOWLING ALLEY
11 ATHLETIC FIELDS
12 BASKETBALL COURTS
13 BACHELORS' POOL
14 PACIFIC CLUB
15 PACIFIC BACHELORS' QTRS.
16 BANK
17 "MACY'S" DEPT. STORE
18 "MACY'S" SNACK BAR
19 POST OFFICE

20 "MACY'S" WEST
21 PACIFIC DINING ROOM
22 LAUNDRY
23 TEN-TEN & PACKAGE STORE
24 BACHELORS' QUARTERS BLDGS.
25 BARBER SHOP
26 HOSPITAL
27 OCEAN VIEW CLUB
28 CROSSROADS CLUB
29 FISHING PIER
30 SANDS BQ (& BARBER SHOP)
31 YOKWE YUK THEATRE
32 YOKWE YUK CLUB
33 DENTAL CLINIC & BEAUTY SHOP
34 TENNIS COURTS
35 SURFWAY GROCERY STORE
36 ART GUILD
37 ELEMENTARY SCHOOL
38 TEEN CENTER

39 DEPENDENTS' POOL
40 NURSERY
41 ELEMENTARY SCHOOL (K-6)
42 IVEY HALL THEATRE
43 JR-SR HIGH SCHOOL
44 HOUSING AREA
45 HOUSING AREA
46 TRADEWINDS SNACK BAR
47 EMON BEACH
48 ECHO PIER
49 SMALL BOAT MARINA
50 LITTLE LEAGUE FIELD
51 GOLF DRIVING RANGE
52 NIKE FLYING CLUB
53 SSC BUILDING
54 CORAL SANDS BEACH
55 BR AND TTR
56 HOUSING AREA
57 HOUSING AREA

Figure 37. 'Places to Go and Things to Do on Kwajalein'.

Source. Bell Laboratories, 'Kwajalein Orientation Guide'.

Like this map, the Kwajalein telephone directory is another sort of banal, everyday guide that relegates missile testing to the background. The *2001 Telephone Directory*, for example, contains several pages of regulations and safety notices interwoven with cultural or recreational information; it is described as 'recommended reading', according to the base commander in his greeting letter published on the inside cover. He writes, 'Today, as in the past, the men and women of the US Army Kwajalein Atoll/Kwajalein Missile Range are performing an important mission, essential to the security of our country. I am pleased to have you join us, and I am confident that you will find your stay enjoyable.'[9] The recruitment to an important mission of missile testing and space operations is thus fused with expectations for an 'enjoyable stay' on the island, words that might be spoken by a hotel manager or cruise director. He orders the American Kwajalein employee both to work hard *and* to play, to devote themselves to the security of the United States, and to ignore whatever contradictions arise.

Throughout the text of the phonebook, various safety notices are printed that warn of the many perils of life on island and the importance of adhering to operational protocols, such as not discussing classified information over the phone. Repetitive in their clip-art banality, most users probably would not ponder these messages deeply, but stepping back and detouring the margins, one notices how the ideologies of national security naturalise weapons of mass destruction into everyday life. At the bottom of the same page that contains office listings for the Federal Aviation Association, National Missile Defense Agency, and Lockheed Martin, there appears a 'Safety Note', which warns of the hazards of gathering seashells on the reef and features a cartoon of a straw hat, sunglasses, boots, and tongs.[10]

---

9   US Army Kwajalein Atoll, 2001, *2001 Telephone Directory*.
10   US Army Kwajalein Atoll, *2001 Telephone Directory*, p. 40.

♪ Safety Note

Reefing

For your protection and comfort while reefing you should take a few simple precautions.

Wear a hat, sunglasses, and use sun screen to protect yourself from the sun.

Use tongs or wear gloves to protect your hands.

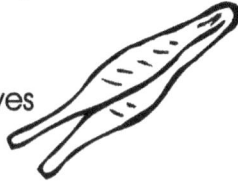

Wear sturdy shoes and socks to protect your feet against sharp coral, sea urchins, and jellyfish.

Figure 38. 'Safety Note'.
Source. US Army Kwajalein Atoll, 2001, *2001 Telephone Directory*, p. 40.

It is in this style that the official tour of Kwajalein emphasises leisure as serious business, fraught with its own peculiar dangers. 'For your protection and comfort while reefing you should take a few simple precautions', the note nags. True to typical discursive practice regarding the 'mission' of the base, the contradictory activities of missile testing and reefing are thus packaged together as a matter of everyday domesticity. Defence-related offices are listed in small Helvetica print among food services and other ordinary items, boringly, not worthy of mention. Yet the danger (and thrill) of exploring the reef is advertised with much embellishment, illustration, and a significantly larger typeface, filling up two-thirds of the page. Like the missile monument on the playing fields, the directory thereby visually offsets and obscures the real perils of life on a high-security testing range and a former World War II battlefield in favour of more benign and tropical (albeit somewhat 'dangerous') pastimes, which it simultaneously flaunts and exaggerates to draw attention away from missile defence.

Not only does the official discourse of US power at Kwajalein maintain the double-edged tour of duty/pleasure at Kwajalein, it also elides Marshallese people from the picture and removes the American community from its geographical context in the Marshall Islands. Beginning with its establishment in 1964, the missile testing range even succeeded for nearly 40 years in ignoring the international dateline so that it could synchronise Kwajalein Atoll with the work schedule of the continental United States, a logistical tactic that the Republic of the Marshall Islands finally overrode in 1993 when it required the test site to standardise itself with the rest of the country.[11] It has since rescheduled the work week within the US-leased islands to run from Tuesdays to Saturdays, but this time/place dislocation continues to disrupt the lives of Marshall Islander commuters, who are unable to prepare adequately for Sunday church services or take care of their families on Saturdays when their children are not in school.

The phone directory likewise dislocates residents of the American community into a special space that is removed from the Marshall Islands altogether. Personnel are listed, and thereby enlisted, to the official American tour by their name and company, with numbers that can be dialled by a local extension. There are extensive listings about how to call the continental United States and various military bases worldwide through military exchanges. Yet, despite their proximity, the telephone directory does not list any numbers or any instructions for calling any of the islands in the Marshall Islands beyond the military installation, not even Ebeye and the islands right next door.

Homecoming

It is 1982. My mother, baby brother, and I are on our way to the air terminal to say farewell to a friend who is leaving the island. We push our bicycles over the broad grassy field between that towering missile and the racketball courts, past the water silo and the baseball diamond. Assembled in the hot sun in all directions around the giant

---

11 'In Marshall Islands, Friday is followed by Sunday', 1993, *New York Times*, 22 August.

shade tree by the chapel are hundreds of Marshallese people, mostly women—sitting, talking, weaving baskets, singing songs. There is a strange tension in the air, a feeling that there is something I don't quite understand here. My mother looks flustered, bothered by something.

'Why are all of these Marshallese people sitting here?' I ask.

'I'm not sure, but I think it's because they're unhappy about their land,' she answers.

'What do you mean?'

'I'm not really sure,' she answers.

We walk carefully around the edge of the crowd. I do not know what to say to them or how to react, but they feel familiar to me. Some of the women look up and smile at me. They remind me of the many women my mother has introduced to me, including the housekeepers who have taken care of me.

Coming by boat and camping at the south end of the island at Camp Hamilton, the place where my Cub Scouts troop holds its annual picnics, most of the protesters are women and children. Most men are afraid of losing their jobs or even being killed; it is the women who bravely stand up for the sake of their land and their children's future.[12] American residents of Kwajalein know very little of what is happening even on the same island, but perhaps this is why my mother's expression looks so uneasy. The military guards are multiplying—they have been sent in from Hawai'i. They are cold, inflexible. The cashiers now ask for our badges in *Ten-Ten* Store. I've never had a badge. The guards stop even the American women who try to bring homemade food to the Marshallese protesters. What to make of this break in the narrative of our happy piece of paradise? What does this mean?

I had witnessed the beginning of Operation Homecoming, the biggest peaceful protest of the indigenous people of Kwajalein against the military occupation of their land without proper compensation. Under the blessing of Iroojlaplap (Paramount Chief) Lejolan Kabua, protest leader Handel Dribo, together with Irooj Imata Kabua, Ataji Balos and other leaders, almost 1,000 protestors would converge on Kwajalein and other islets, continuing a series of 'sail-ins' that had been increasing

---

12   This is according to landowner Ataji Balos, one of the leaders of the movement, whom I interviewed on 14 March 2005.

in size since the 1960s. Many Marshallese in Kwajalein came to call these peaceful protests *jodiks*, cleverly dubbed after the Japanese word *jōriku,* meaning 'land invasion'. Making their own amphibious arrivals just as the Americans did in 1944 and peacefully reclaiming their land, Operation Homecoming was true civil disobedience, not unlike Martin Luther King's march on the lawns of the American capital in 1963.

These 'landowners'[13] were protesting the United States government's 35-year military use agreement with the new national government of the Republic of the Marshall Islands, angry about having been removed from their small islands and forced to suffer miserable living conditions on Ebeye for far too long. They had already staged a major sail-in in 1979, when they disrupted the MX missile-testing schedule and demanded that the United States compensate them for having used their land since 1944 without their consent, a request that US negotiators furiously dismissed as a 'dead issue'.[14] Anxious about the impending implementation of the Compact of Free Association with the United States, they were worried that their voices would be silenced by the new alliance between their government and Washington. Operation Homecoming was a massive mobilisation that asked for higher land payments under another shorter interim land use agreement that would enable landowners to have more control over the terms of this military lease.

Though Kwajalein Marshallese were immensely frustrated by four decades of American negligence and military occupation, theirs was a good-spirited and remarkably nonviolent protest that reflected the grace and patience with which they had endured their plight. Yet, the US Army response to their civil disobedience was one of reactionary and absurd paranoia. Marshallese activist Darlene Keju and her journalist husband Giff Johnson travelled to Kwajalein by speedboat from Ebeye during the military lockdown and press blackout in July 1982 to observe the situation. Johnson took a photo of protestors on

---

13   'Landowner' is a term that suits a western ideology more than an indigenous one in terms of Marshallese lend tenure, given the fact that vast extended families—between *irooj* chiefs, *alap* clan heads, and *rijerbal* commoners (literally 'workers') all are considered to share the land rights and each group is entitled to a respective third of the fruits of that land, whether it be crops, fish, or military lease payments.

14   Giff Johnson, 2013, *Don't Ever Whisper: Darlene Keju—Pacific Health Pioneer, Champion for Nuclear Survivors*, p. 397.

the beach from the lagoon, knowing that any non-landowners would be arrested if they were to enter the military installation.[15] It is an image of children happily playing in the crystalline blue waters of the beach while adults chat quietly behind them; but in the middle of the photo, an American police officer earnestly takes notes about inbound and outbound Islanders and perhaps also about the 'child protesters'.[16]

Figure 39. Operation Homecoming in 1982.
Source. Photographed by Giff Johnson, Micronesian Seminar Collection.

Keju would later speak about this at an international gathering of the World Council of Churches in 1983:

They took their women and children and they sat on their islands. Now you must remember, the US government has taken two thirds of our islands. It means we cannot go fishing. We cannot go to visit our islands and get more food for the [population of Ebeye] ... it means we're stuck into what we call a jail. Can you imagine? The United States government is only leasing our islands. And we have to have passes to go onto our own islands?[17]

---

15   Personal correspondence with Giff Johnson, 12 May 2014.
16   Johnson, *Don't Ever Whisper*, p. 107.
17   Ibid., p. 143.

The protesters managed to sustain their presence on their ancestral lands until that October, in spite of the aggressive military response. In the months after the protest began, the US Army arrested leaders, prohibited 200 maids and groundskeepers from doing their jobs, conducted rigorous security inspections of, and confiscations from, all people entering and leaving the base, prevented all Marshallese from accessing their only bank (which was located on Kwajalein), and shut off toilets at Camp Hamilton, resulting not only in pollution for the campers, who used the beach instead, but for American residents as well.[18]

Under pressure to resolve these land disputes and activate the Compact of Free Association, which ultimately went into effect in 1986, First President Amata Kabua enacted his power as president to put all of Kwajalein lands under eminent domain, effectively foreclosing them in the public interest and forcing the new land use agreement to go through.[19] This agreement would, in part, ensure major US infrastructure support to the new Republic of the Marshall Islands in exchange for permission to use the islands (especially Kwajalein) for strategic purposes on an ongoing basis. It was the beginning of what American and Marshallese leaders to this day call their 'special relationship', and the beginning of more discontent for the people of Kwajalein.[20]

My family's 'tour' at Kwajalein ended in June 1982, only a month before Operation Homecoming was fully under way and Giff Johnson's photograph was taken. We left not because of civil unrest; in fact, my family knew very little about what was unfolding. Our tour ended simply because my parents were ready to settle back in the States, to live close to our relatives. But even though I never quite felt at

---

18   Ibid., pp. 105–106.
19   David L. Hanlon, 1998, *Remaking Micronesia: Discourses over Development in a Pacific Territory, 1944–1982*, Honolulu: University of Hawai'i Press, p. 212.
20   These wounds would be reopened when the Compact was renegotiated in 2003, once again without full consensus from the landowners, who were offered only less than half the amount of compensation they proposed after a thorough land appraisal and assessment of their risks and long-term needs to sustain Ebeye. After threatening for eight years to deny further American use of the atoll and return to their islands, in 2011, Paramount Chief Imata Kabua and other landowners signed a 50-year land use agreement through to 2086, thus formally ending the stalemate and ensuring that suspended land payments held in escrow would not be returned to the US government. As President Christopher Loeak (then senator and spokesman for the Kwajalein landowners) said of the agreement, 'The tide is not too high but it's not too shallow either. Where we are at today is a compromise which we've agreed upon to safeguard our future.' See Suzanne Chutaro, 2011, 'LUA signed after 8 years', *Marshall Islands Journal*, 13 May.

home in the States, at least my parents had the option to make our 'homecoming' to New Jersey any time they wanted. The displaced landowners of Kwajalein Atoll have never had that luxury.

Jambo

It is January 2001, and heavy rains have engulfed the atoll of Arno. Having lived in the States and Japan, I have come back to the Marshalls after nearly 20 years away and am trying to learn more about the country beyond the fringes of Kwajalein. My friend has introduced me to his relatives, who kindly have welcomed me to stay with them. I wake up to the sound of chickens crying out as they escape the rain. Nine-year-old Robill comes in to call me to breakfast, rice with boiled chicken and grated coconut. When the rains subside, Robill and his friends pull at my arm to take me out for my daily Marshallese lesson, '*Kwoj jambo*—wanna take a walk?' they ask. *Jambo* comes from the Japanese word *sanpō*, to stroll around, but it has an even broader usage in Marshallese—sometimes to take a trip, a random journey without any clear destination, a detour, perhaps.

I walk with the boys along the beach. The plants are all familiar to me—even if I do not know their names, I remember how their leaves feel, how their sap would taste if I were to chew on those twigs. Like these kids, I know how to blow on the hermit crabs to tease them out of their shells. And of course there are millions of things I don't know. They are all the same age that I was when I left Kwajalein, and all of them are as confident in their world as I was in mine. I have never played with Marshallese kids, I realise, not even when I was a kid myself. As we walk, they point at different objects and quiz me, '*Ta e*—What's this?' I learn various words for coral sand in different stages of wetness and coarseness, *baru* for crab, *bob* for pandanus, *mā* for breadfruit. I learn to count from *juon* (one) to *jibukwi* (100).

It begins to downpour again and I chase the boys into the jungle where there is more cover. We find shelter briefly under the leaves of a banana tree and then race across the open yard of an old wooden house where rows of burlap sacks filled with copra are laid out for the next ship. We run up onto the porch where an old, skinny man is sitting in a rocking chair. He nods at Robill to grab me a seat, and we sit facing each other. He starts to speak to me in Marshallese at length, smiling animatedly and pointing at the lagoon. Then, realising I have barely any idea what he's saying, he knits his eyebrows and focuses on the Japanese characters on the t-shirt I happen to be wearing. '*Nihongo dekimasuka*—Can you speak Japanese?' he asks, in flawless Japanese.

We proceed to speak in Japanese for several hours. He tells me about the crazy weather patterns, about schooldays during the Japanese times. He hesitates as he tries to tell me about his family and confesses that he does not know the word for 'grandchild' in Japanese, because he was too young to ever hear anyone use that word in the Marshall Islands. At this point it becomes clear to me that even though my new friend is probably in his 80s, he speaks the Japanese of a child, because that is how old he was when the war broke out, when the Japanese era effectively ended.

> 'I grew up on Kwajalein', I explain to him. He squints, trying to make out what I am saying until I enunciate *Kuwajleen*, the Marshallese pronunciation.
>
> 'Ah, so many people died in that atoll in the war, so sad,' he says. 'I had family there too. *Sensō wa dame*—War is bad.'

I look down at the 10 boys who have gathered curiously around us on the porch to watch as we speak in Japanese, not understanding a word we have spoken. They giggle as our eyes meet.

Postcards and pilgrimages

This Japanese postcard is from the 1930s, depicting the atoll of Jaluit in the Marshall Islands, which was once an integral part of the Japanese Empire, part of the Nanyō Guntō South Seas mandated territories that Japan was awarded in 1922 by the League of Nations.[21] The Marshalls were, in fact, the first islands officially declared Japanese territory after Japan wrested Micronesia from Germany during World War I in 1914. Jaluit, which had been a major hub of German economic activity from the late nineteenth century, became the farthest eastern edge of the Japanese Pacific.

---

21   This postcard is an example of the ephemera I have found by scouring online auction sites in Japan. Few materials like this are available in archives or libraries, and most come from private collections.

Figure 40. Postcard of Jaluit Atoll, Nanyō Guntō Mandated Islands of Japan, pandanus trees and Islanders, cancelled with Jaluit Post Office stamp, c. 1935.

Source. From the author's personal collection.

Postcards like these were printed for destinations all over Micronesia and depicted a wide range of island scenes, typically with Islanders posed in traditional dress. In this image, three girls sit on a beach, probably in the capital of Jabor Islet. The caption of the postcard reads 'Jaluit, Marshall Islands: pandanus tree and *tōmin* (Islanders)'. Touristic scenes like these were quite common projections that held currency in the Japanese public imaginary of the 1920s to 1930s. The Marshall Islands were, not unlike Hawai'i for Americans and Tahiti for French, also a site of wanderlust and desire. The trope of the available, virgin *shūchō no musume* (chieftain's daughter) was popularised by a satirical song of the same title, a romantic but racist musical tale of a Japanese man who falls in love with an island princess and tries to marry her but needs to learn local dances in order to win her hand.[22] This image was propagated further by various versions of the song and different 'South Seas dances' or *Nanyō odori* performed all over Japan and later in the islands themselves.

---

22   Dvorak, 'Seeds from afar, flowers from the reef, re-membering the coral and concrete of Kwajalein Atoll'.

Colonial desire for the South (not only the Japanese territories of Micronesia but all of Southeast Asia as well) was represented in boys' comics and games as well. A Japanese board game of *sugoroku* drawn by children's book illustrator Hara Yasuo and published in 1941 demonstrates this perfectly. Shown here (Figure 41), *Nanyō Meguri Sugoroku*[23] is a game of conquest and adventure in which players trace the journey of a 'white' Japanese boy who departs Yokohama on a seaplane (1), passing volcanic Urracas Island in the Northern Mariana Islands (2), climbing pandanus trees (3), examining stone money in Yap (10), cooking with breadfruit (15), looking at a Palauan meeting *bai* or meeting house (19), and visiting a Japanese school for 'natives' (*dojin*, a word that was already politically incorrect at the time this game was made). Ultimately, a player wins by rolling the dice to arrive first at the epicentre of Japanese civilisation in the Nanyō Guntō, the Nanyō Shrine of Koror, Palau, a massive site that was dedicated in 1940.[24]

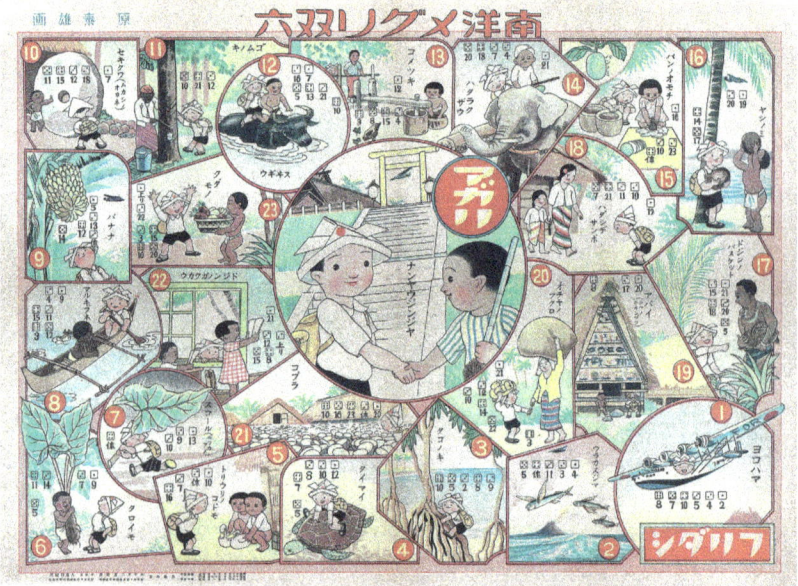

Figure 41. *Nanyō Meguri Sugoroku* board game.
Source. Illustrated by Hara Yasuo, published by Futaba Shobō, Tokyo 1941.

---

23   I found this board game quite by accident in an antique shop in Kyoto, where it had been preserved in a plastic wrapper and taped to the ceiling. As it is quite large, I had it professionally scanned at a high resolution.

24   Donald R. Shuster, 1982, 'State Shinto in Micronesia during Japanese rule, 1914–1945', *Pacific Studies* 5(2): 20–43, p. 27.

Visions like these inscribed the Nanyō Guntō territories as carefree sites of leisure, adventure, and pleasure, and more importantly as safe, comfortable sites to which one could relocate one's family and start a new life. They were compelling enough to draw up to 96,000 migrants to the region from Japan by 1942—mostly to the major populations of Saipan and Palau.[25] Even in the Marshall Islands, the number of Japanese civilians was reported as nearly 530 individuals living in Jaluit in 1939, a number that certainly was small compared to over 10,000 Marshallese living in the atoll that same year but significant enough to be felt in the small main island of Jabor.[26]

Not only in Jaluit but all throughout the Marshall Islands, Marshallese who grew up before the 1940s make a clear distinction between the war years and the civilian Japanese times that preceded them.[27] Those 30 years before 1944 are remembered with a sense of bittersweet nostalgia, not only for good schooling, health care, and opportunities for economic advancement, but also for the nostalgia of new products and foods like rice, canned food, or shaved ice, and a whole new wave of popular culture, from samurai films and music to sumo wrestling and baseball, which is still referred to in Marshallese by its Japanese name, *yakyū*.

Kwajalein Atoll had only a handful of civilian Japanese residents prior to its transformation into a military base, but with its schoolhouse, a number of shops, and frequent visits by copra ships, Islanders were already very exposed to Japanese people. In 1939, however, the Nanyō command headquarters initiated construction in Kwajalein Atoll, with the intention of transforming it from a rural copra-trading outpost into one of the most important naval air bases in Eastern Micronesia.[28] The civilian government, including the school and its teachers, and all of the students, were relocated to Namu Atoll. This dramatic change was the first time that the people of Kwajalein were displaced from their land, but many were also offered jobs working for the military throughout the atoll.

25   Brij Lal and Kate Fortune, 1999, *The Pacific Islands: An Encyclopedia*, Honolulu: University of Hawai'i Press, p. 238.
26   United States Chief of Naval Operations (USCNO), 1943, *Military Government Handbook OPNAV P22–1: Marshall Islands*, Government Publication, p. 19.
27   Lin Poyer, Suzanne Falgout and Laurence Marshall Carucci, 2001, *The Typhoon of War: Micronesian Experiences of the Pacific War*, Honolulu: University of Hawai'i Press.
28   Mark Peattie, 1988, *Nan'yō: The Rise and Fall of the Japanese in Micronesia, 1885–1945*, Honolulu: University of Hawai'i Press, pp. 250–51.

As Kwajalein and Roi-Namur in the north of the atoll were fortified, the Japanese military population swelled to several thousand men, most of whom—unlike the settlers who came before them—knew nothing about life in the Marshall Islands, let alone how to survive on a tropical island. Not unlike the American soldiers who would follow in their footsteps after their defeat, they had little interaction with indigenous people in general, and like the American community I grew up in during the 1970s, they also lived in their own sequestered world, drank sake, and bathed in Japanese-style communal hot baths. Some of these soldiers would eventually be transferred to other tours of duty, but as the war began and the Marshall Islands heated up as the front lines of defence for the entire Japanese Empire, many soldiers started to see their tour at Kwajalein as a mission of no return.

***

It is 2005, and I am back on Kwajalein as a doctoral student, together with 20 Japanese elders from the Marshall Islands Bereaved Families Association of Japan. We have come to the atoll for one of the group's regular pilgrimages of *ireisai*, memorial ceremonies for the souls of the fallen Japanese soldiers who died in the American invasion of Kwajalein in 1944. This is yet another kind of tour, I soon realise.

After breakfast in the cafeteria where Marshallese servers at the buffet counter dutifully heap our plates with scrambled eggs, we board a white bus labelled 'US ARMY' and depart the Kwaj Lodge transient hotel. Some of the elders are dressed in funereal attire; others wear khaki adventure outdoor clothes and vests, as if on safari. After everyone has found a seat, their professional guide from a Tokyo travel company bows to the group with the conciliatory smile of a funeral director. Over the roar of the bus engine, he uses very polite Japanese to announce to us that today's itinerary will begin with a formal ceremony followed by a bus tour of the 1944 battlefield upon which the group's loved ones perished.

We ride to the southern edge of the airstrip, past the pond where I used to feed the sea turtles and down toward the hilly landfill I used to climb with my father and pretend it was a mountain. Passing the big missile-tracking radars and antennas, we reach the memorial, which is labelled 'Japanese Cemetery'. For these families, however, the remains of the soldiers and sailors who died in Operation Flintlock are in various places on different islands, and in the sunken ships at the bottom of the lagoon. Only a fraction of unidentified remains have been repatriated to Japan. For the bereaved Japanese families of Kwajalein war dead, the entire atoll is a cemetery, and our memorial tour is not one of mere war commemoration but rather an opportunity to commune with and console the spirits who have been here ever since the war.

A slender old woman with white hair and dark sunglasses taps me on the shoulder. 'See those trees?' Satake Esu asks me, pointing to two enormous Japanese pine trees towering over the bland off-white Kwajalein Range Services Photo Lab and the small memorial. Of course I know those trees—I used to ride past this memorial on my bicycle as a little boy.

Figure 42. Satake Esu visiting Kwajalein Japanese Cemetery in 2005.
Source. Photographed by Greg Dvorak, 6 October 2012.

'Well, I was the one who planted those in 1975 when they were just seedlings, the first time we ever got to get off the plane here on the base and came here to mourn. You must have been two then … and— can you help me with this?' She holds onto her hat as she lassoes a loop of twine over the red *torii* gate of the Japanese Cemetery. She ties it to a large yellow paper lantern that reads, *Māsharu-hōmen Izokukai*, 'Marshall Islands Bereaved Families Association'. Other members string American, Marshallese, and Japanese flags across the cemetery site.

'I'm in my 80s now but I was only married two months, you know,' Esu continues, 'and back in those days you had to be a "good wife" and just listen while the men did all the talking, and my husband was in the Imperial Army and he'd come and go all the time and never quite tell me what he was up to, even if I asked. All I knew was that he was a pilot. And being a good *okusan* (wife) I told him that if he ever got captured by the enemy, well ...', she makes a fist and grins stiffly, 'you'd better blow yourself up with a grenade or otherwise make sure you die before they kill you first.'

'Ima da to shinjirarenai koto dakedo ne—I couldn't believe I said all those things back then', she sighs and props up her dark sunglasses,

> but several years after he was killed here in this atoll, I regretted it so much ... and so I found myself wanting to do something for life. So I became a doctor, and I started going around the world campaigning for peace. I've been everywhere. I was just in Iraq a couple years ago. You know, we have to remember how bad war is. We have to remember how all these boys died out here. Most people have forgotten, you know.

Esu grabs a large handful of incense sticks and plugs them into a pot, and several others lay out family photographs in front of the memorial to show to the spirits. There are also letters and notes, children's artwork—the kinds of things one might send to a loved one living far away. Esu takes a plastic branch of artificial maple leaves and places them on the altar as well, explaining that it is fall in Japan and the soldiers must miss the cool weather.

'And some flowers,' Esu says, placing a bouquet of plumerias that she has just picked from a nearby tree, 'to represent all the pretty girlfriends you boys never got to have.'

Figure 43. Offerings from bereaved families at the Japanese War Dead Memorial in 2005, Kwajalein.

Source. Photographed by Greg Dvorak, 6 October 2005.

The families begin their ceremony by singing the Japanese national anthem and a series of songs like 'Umi Yukaba' (If I Go Away to Sea) and 'Sayonara, Yashi no Shima' (Goodbye, Island of Palms), both melancholic melodies with lyrics about leaving home and never returning. Many of the mourners cry as they sing together, facing the memorial as if they were looking into the faces of the lost soldiers.

This is followed by a long Buddhist chant, after which the other 20 bereaved individuals come up one by one, entering the small white picket fence, passing through the *torii* gate, and approaching the granite memorial as if it were a gravestone.

'*Oyaji*—Dad!' one man shouts as he stands, trembling as he holds out a letter with two hands. It is apparently his first visit to Kwajalein. 'Father, I have finally come to the place where you died, this place where they made you come all by yourself, leaving your children and your wife behind. You must have been so scared, father, but you came here to this island of palms so bravely!' he shouts, his voice breaking. 'Thank you for everything, Dad—*Oyaji, arigatō*!'

Figure 44. Japanese and Korean military construction corps workers building the base at Kwajalein, 1944.

Source. Image from Hitotsubashi University Archives, unknown origin.

After the ceremony, our battlefield tour begins near the memorial, where the group assembles under the palm trees. The guide gestures toward the impressive sight of cargo planes lined up on the tarmac far in the distance. 'Japanese engineers built this runway before the war', he explains, 'and they designed it so that it would act as a freshwater lens to supply water to the soldiers who were posted here.' The elderly pilgrims all nod their heads and make sounds of approval. They are probably unaware that prior to the building of this airstrip this area was once a wooded area that contained an important chief's house, a Marshallese cemetery, and the Japanese schoolhouse. But they do not see these things, for their eyes are set only upon a tragic landscape of battle and loss. They also probably do not realise that the bulk of the work done to build this airstrip and many of the fortifications around the atoll was conducted by hundreds of Korean laborers who were forcefully drafted by the Japanese military from the countryside near Busan and other regions and brought by ship to Kwajalein to work in the blazing sun. The *setsueibutai*, or construction corps, were mainly made up of these workers, seen here (Figure 44) on Kwajalein in January 1944, the month that the American invasion would take place. Here they push supplies along a narrow-gauge railroad, one of the techniques used to haul heavy materials across rough terrain or even across the coral reef between islands.

The road where we stand, the guide explains, was once the beach where American marines made landfall on the island when they launched their assault from neighbouring Carlson (Enubuj) Islet. He unfolds a pamphlet written in English, marked up with highlighter pen and Japanese notes. It is the 'World War Battlefield Tour' brochure published by the US Army Kwajalein Atoll. It begins with a block of text that describes 'Kwajalein Before World War Two', which charts a narrative that begins not with thousands of years of Marshallese navigation and settlement but with Spanish exploration in 1542 and German conquest of the Marshall Islands, followed by a very brief mention of Japanese capture of the islands. Japan's extensive 30-year civilian involvement in the islands is barely addressed:

> Germany's commercial interest in the Marshalls led to their purchase from Spain in 1885. Imperial Japan, as a member of the Allied powers during World War I, quickly seized the islands from Germany in 1914. Japanese control of the islands, despite a strong protest from the United States, was formalized by the League of Nations in 1920, whose members permitted Imperial Japan to retain the islands under a class 'C' mandate which allowed no naval or military installations.

The Japanese presence in the Marshalls was of grave concern to American military officials, because the islands provided sheltered bases from which Japanese ships and planes could interdict the American supply lines to the Philippines, at that time an American colony.[29]

The pamphlet justifies the overwhelming American attack on Kwajalein by explaining that Japanese colonialism was a nuisance to American links between the West Coast, Hawai'i, Guam and the Philippines—portraying American hegemony as the only rightful form of colonialism in the Pacific. It describes the amphibious invasion of Kwajalein Atoll and the rest of the Marshalls as nothing more than 'a textbook operation' for American cadets to study and celebrate. It is this 'liberation story' of Kwajalein that dismisses Japan's prewar decades of peace and prosperity in Micronesia, at the same time it buries the narratives of Japanese, Korean and Marshallese survivors or memories of war dead. The battlefield tour pamphlet leads us seamlessly from reef to reef, from the landing at one end of the island to a nondescript mound of dirt covering a Japanese concrete emplacement, known as 'Bunker Hill' at the other end, where the 7th Infantry Division finally defeated Japanese forces in the south of the atoll and where we used to play hide-and-seek as children. It is a story in which the Americans are the heroes, the Japanese the villains, and Koreans or Marshallese nothing more than silent bystanders caught in the crossfire.

Standing on the golf course near a concrete pillbox, one of the elders asks, 'So how did my brother die, exactly? Do you think he even knew what was coming?'

The guide keeps his professional composure and, pausing momentarily, answers politely, 'We will never know that, I suppose, but this pamphlet says that the Japanese were expecting the Americans to strike elsewhere in the Marshall Islands, and so they were caught off-guard when they were overwhelmed by such a massive invasion. But I'm sure they put up quite a fight.' He flinches briefly at the sound of a golf club hitting a ball nearby, but his well-practised sympathetic smile lingers for awhile, as if to emphasise these are questions best left unasked.

29   US Army Kwajalein Atoll (USAKA), 2005, 'Kwajalein Battlefield Tour'.

The elderly visitors get back onboard and stare out the windows quietly as the bus chugs back around the island, passing the airport and the island chapel, the church where our good old family friend used to be pastor. There is a stained glass memorial there that depicts an American soldier earnestly bent on one knee, his head raised to the US flag and heaven, hand over his heart, his back to the Marshallese flag. We pass George Seitz Elementary School, where I once learned reading and arithmetic; the commander's house; the Kwajalein Junior-Senior High School; the rows of 'new housing' at the northern tip of the island from which one can see Ebeye; and back past Emon Beach, where I used to swim every day after school.

As we walk from the dining hall after dinner that evening and the sun leaves streaks of salmon pink in its setting wake, the Southern Cross rises above the playing fields—the same fields where the Kwaj Karnival happened each year, where that missile once stood, and where Operation Homecoming began. The Japanese visitors excitedly remember how their husbands, brothers and fathers used to write home about the constellation in their letters and postcards from the Marshall Islands; even the logo of their organisation is the Southern Cross, *minamijūjisei,* on a turquoise background. As the group members try to hold still to take photographs in the dark, the guide explains, 'This area was close to the Japanese Imperial Admiralty. It's where most of the soldiers and the top-rank officers of this base lived and worked. Perhaps it is also where many of them left this world.'

It is surreal to hear these familiar elements of my military-engineered childhood suburbia described as part of the saccharine monologue of a professional Japanese tour guide, as if we were visiting the major sights of Kyoto. It is stranger, however, to hear the landscape described as if neither its American crust nor Marshallese roots even existed. And imagining it all as if it were frozen in 1944, I, too, can see the ghostly layer of the island through the eyes of these pilgrims, and smell the smoke and the death blowing on the night breezes. It is as if over 60 years have not passed and the Battle of Kwajalein took place only yesterday.

The special place

My detours of Kwajalein always seem to end in the same place, as they do today in 2016, in a small picnic area on the ocean side of the island where my father and I shared a basket of sandwiches together on a windy day when I was seven years old. My father, the sole reason for our original crossing to Kwajalein Atoll, died in 1999 of cancer. His battle against his devastating disease, like the fight of the Japanese defenders of the atoll, was short but unwavering. Even though I said goodbye to him in New Jersey it was in part his death that precipitated my journey back to uncover the unanswered questions of my formative years. In the 10 or so times I have returned, and in the course of my research, I have realised how little I knew about Kwajalein and how little I even knew about my own father or what he did there.

Figures 45 and 46. The special place.
Source. Photographed by my father in 1979 (left) and by me in 2001 (right).

We called it our 'Special Place'. It is a small shady enclave alongside the runway, with a rusty old picnic table in a grove of palms, and a breathtaking view of the reef, the drop-off, and the open ocean. The decaying mouldy air terminal is within view in one direction, as is the old country club that still hosts parties today. The Special Place is not far from the site of the legendary *utilomar* flowering tree in Marshallese cosmology that symbolises the abundance of the islet and the reason why so many voyagers came from around the world to harvest the atoll's many flowers.[30] Since the deep time past it has also been part of the land parcel (*w to*) known as Lo-pat, where heavenly bodies land, which is why elders say it eventually became the landing

---

30   Laurence M. Carucci, 1997, *In Anxious Anticipation of Kuwajleen's Uneven Fruits: A Cultural History of the Significant Locations and Important Resources of Kuwajleen Atoll*, Huntsville, AL: United States Army Space and Strategic Defense Command, p. 50.

point for airplanes.[31] During the war it was where Japanese soldiers would hide during the bombardment; later, it was from its offshore reef where Americans would mine coral gravel to rebuild and expand the Japanese airstrip for onward invasions. After the war, it was the edge of the Marshallese labour camp that was later removed in 1951 from the island during the atomic testing program at Bikini and Enewetak. This removal was in part because American authorities saw this Marshallese presence as an 'eyesore'.[32] Later, this precious Marshallese land became the first American boy scout camp and the entrance to the golf course.

Coming back is never easy. It involves asking friends on island to sponsor me and waiting for military approval, flying for two days and spending large amounts of money. Each time I return, although the atoll itself is its same familiar self, the atmosphere on Kwaj is always different. In 2016, it is tense and strange in the airport, as the military police brief us on new rules and regulations to comply with their latest perception of danger in the world. Now all non-American visitors to the atoll, even if merely transiting briefly from the only airport (which happens to be on the base) to Ebeye or other islands in the sovereign Republic of the Marshall Islands, must be scrutinised, their names and biometric data—fingerprints and iris scans—recorded in a database. Though the US only leases parts of the atoll, for all extensive purposes, this is America now.

After crossing through the discomfort of the checkpoints at the airport and dock, I come back here to this picnic place to be with my father. I sit on the grass and watch the ants walk over my feet, feel the trade winds pummel my body, and I sense his presence. I imagine him waiting for me in the Special Place, wearing that sweaty bright orange mesh 'Kwajalein Missile Range' cap, his nostrils flaring as he eagerly breathes the fresh air, as fascinated with the sea as he is with the aeroplanes that take off nearby, imbuing in me his reverence for both nature and technology, both the coral and the concrete. My father teaches me to open up to the contradictions, to see them squarely, to ask questions, and to teach my students to do the same.

---

31 Ibid., p. 195.
32 Jack A. Tobin, 1954, *Ebeye Village: An Atypical Marshallese Community. Majuro, Marshall Islands*, photocopied report in University of Hawai'i Library Pacific Collection, p. 3.

Surely, my father knew very little about these histories, but he had great respect for the Marshallese people he knew, many who immediately remember him fondly when they see me and notice our resemblance. As an engineer, he loved the mysteries of the machinery with which he worked, and he did his job with the commitment of defending our family and our country. The engineers of Kwajalein who test these weapons and work with space surveillance are mostly people like my dad was—men and women who earnestly believe in what they do as a vital part of securing global stability. Landowners and other leaders in the atoll also assert their own agency in this relationship by asserting that the biggest export of the Marshall Islands is indeed world peace. But the flip side of this is that the legacy of war, nuclear weapons, and missiles—together with all the trauma they caused—are what made our presence at Kwajalein possible in the first place. And the perpetual paranoia and vigilance about unseen foes that has lasted from the Cold War to the War on Terror is, by its very nature, the antithesis of peace. As former protestor, teacher, and minister Julian Riklon once said of the ongoing military use of Kwajalein, 'The Americans were among the first to bring the word of God and [to teach us] how to love one another. It's funny, because today they are telling me that I should have enemies, something totally different from what they first taught me.'[33]

The curse and potential gift for me in being a Kwaj Kid has been wondering how to reconcile the genuine love for my father and my memory of home with the deep, dark contradictions of the past and present. I have had to learn that the nostalgic story of my childhood landscape is intertwined with a silent kind of violence that persists into the present day. As Vincent Crapanzano wrote of white memory in South Africa:

> We play with our stories in ways we cannot with the *violence* itself. We cast ourselves as heroes or anti-heroes, men and women of delicacy and sensitivity or crudeness and insensitivity. We participate in our stories, identify with the protagonists we create, or disengage ourselves from them ... For the listener and the storyteller the stories and tales of violence are a kind of rehearsal for stories and tales of the future, which may have to be lived as well as told. They give cover to the terrifying silence of the pure act.[34]

33   Adam Horowitz, 1990, *Home on the Range*, Equatorial Films.
34   Vincent Crapanzano, 1985, *Waiting: The Whites of South Africa*, New York: Random House, p. 238.

Detouring Kwajalein is difficult work that demands I listen to that 'terrifying silence' of that violence—to bear witness to the harsh contradictions that unfold before my very eyes. It demands a sensitivity to what lies beyond the breathtaking sunset and the turquoise lagoon, the manicured lawns and beaches and palms, to see what Mark Gevisser calls 'the history of pain in beauty'.[35] Unlike Gevisser, however, who writes triumphantly of being able to marry another man of another race in post-apartheid, post–marriage equality South Africa, I cannot go back home and revel in a sense of reconciliation. Our detours as Kwaj Kids require vulnerability, humility and the realisation that perhaps true reconciliation may never be possible, at least when so many of these contradictions persist.

My returns to Kwajalein in mind and body fill me with ambivalence, but they are not tragic visitations of sadness and regret like those of bereaved Japanese pilgrims; they are, rather, demarcations in my own growing and learning process. But my visits are fraught with the uncertainty about whether the military will even grant me access, filled with nostalgic delight, and frustration over the continuing problems I witness and my own inability to fix anything. There is also still immense joy, the laughter of children and the dancing and singing of Christmas time on Ebaye—the celebration of life itself.[36]

I wonder, too, would my father be angry with me for asking the questions I have asked, for criticising the work he did so earnestly, for daring to implicate our family in the drama of war and empire? Does it matter?

My visits are also plagued by ambivalence and increasing disillusionment with my candy-coated past. On my last trip I discovered that the trailer home where my family had lived in the 1970s was, like many of the trailers that had once been installed by the military, thrown out in a dump at the south end of the island. There it sat rotting, infested with rats, its windows broken, graffiti sprayed on the walls. Like the rusty missile, it too was just a part of the ephemeral American suburban dreamscape. Like the Japanese sunken ships

---

35   Mark Gevisser, 2006, 'Inheritance', in *Beautiful/Ugly: African and Diaspora Aesthetics*, ed. Sarah Nuttall, pp. 204–223, Durham: Duke University Press, p. 223.

36   Monica LaBriola, 2006, '*Iien Ippān Doon*: Celebrating survival in an "atypical Marshallese community"', unpublished MA thesis, University of Hawai'i at Mānoa, Honolulu.

at the bottom of the lagoon and the Cold War paraphernalia strewn throughout the atoll, my childhood landscape, too, is swiftly turning into an archaeological site.

I take some solace in that thought, knowing that eventually the footprints of our trespasses may fade, but I worry that America will also forget what has happened here. Unlike the generations of Marshall Islander families who have lived in Kwajalein Atoll all along and remember these histories vividly, Americans come and go, and with them goes the institutional memory, the learning, the wisdom, and often the compassion for Marshallese neighbours and all they have endured.

And what of the rising waters of our warming earth that threaten to swallow *all* of these islands by the end of the twenty-first century? What will happen to the brave, generous and patient people of the Marshall Islands then?

Here in this special place, at home between the coral and concrete of Kwajalein, I remember that I have little choice but to surrender to the hugeness of it all. Everything continues to change, and silently and slowly the reef creeps outwards as it expands decade by decade. I feel deeply mournful, on the verge of tears; and simultaneously I feel overjoyed and awed by the largeness of this all. It is so much bigger than me, than any of us. I am grateful to know this reef, to listen to and tell its stories, and to continue this detour further.

Acknowledgements

I want to thank my parents, Walter and Christine, and my brother, Tim, for all of that they have taught me through our family's relationship to Kwajalein. I also want to express deep gratitude to my many teachers and mentors all throughout Oceania who continue to support me. In Japan I thank the Marshall Islands Bereaved Families Association for welcoming me to join them in honouring the atoll's war dead, especially Satake Esu, who passed away in 2010 after a long life devoted to peace. Finally, I thank my sixth grade teacher Miss Kasse, who urged me to save the essay I wrote for her class.

References

Bell Laboratories. 1972. 'Kwajalein Orientation Guide.' Pamphlet.

Carucci, Laurence M. 1997. *In Anxious Anticipation of Kuwajleen's Uneven Fruits: A Cultural History of the Significant Locations and Important Resources of Kuwajleen Atoll.* Huntsville, AL: United States Army Space and Strategic Defense Command.

Chutaro, Suzanne. 2011. 'LUA signed after 8 years.' *Marshall Islands Journal*, 13 May.

Crapanzano, Vincent. 1985. *Waiting: The Whites of South Africa.* New York: Random House.

Dvorak, Greg. 2004. 'Remapping home: Touring the betweenness of Kwajalein.' MA thesis. University of Hawai'i at Mānoa, Honolulu, 2004.

———. 2008. 'Seeds from afar, flowers from the reef, re-membering the coral and concrete of Kwajalein Atoll.' PhD thesis. The Australian National University, Canberra.

Gevisser, Mark. 2006. 'Inheritance.' In *Beautiful/Ugly: African and Diaspora Aesthetics*, ed. Sarah Nuttall, pp. 204–23. Durham: Duke University Press.

Hanlon, David L. 1998. *Remaking Micronesia: Discourses over Development in a Pacific Territory, 1944–1982.* Honolulu: University of Hawai'i Press.

Hirshberg, Lauren. 2012. 'Nuclear families: (Re)producing 1950s suburban America in the Marshall Islands.' *Organization of American Historians Magazine of History* 26(4): 39–43.

Horowitz, Adam. 1990. *Home on the Range*, Equatorial Films.

Johnson, Giff. 2013. *Don't Ever Whisper: Darlene Keju—Pacific Health Pioneer, Champion for Nuclear Survivors*: n.p.

LaBriola, Monica. 2006. '*Iien Ippān Doon*: Celebrating survival in an "atypical Marshallese community".' Unpublished MA thesis, University of Hawai'i at Mānoa, Honolulu.

Lal, Brij and Kate Fortune. 1999. *The Pacific Islands: An Encyclopedia*. Honolulu: University of Hawai'i Press.

Nuttall, Sarah. 2006. *Beautiful/Ugly: African and Diaspora Aesthetics*. Durham: Duke University Press.

Peattie, Mark. 1988. *Nan'yō: The Rise and Fall of the Japanese in Micronesia, 1885–1945*. Honolulu: University of Hawai'i Press.

Poyer, Lin, Suzanne Falgout and Laurence Marshall Carucci. 2001. *The Typhoon of War: Micronesian Experiences of the Pacific War*. Honolulu: University of Hawai'i Press.

Shuster, Donald R. 1982. 'State Shinto in Micronesia during Japanese rule, 1914–1945.' *Pacific Studies* 5(2): 20–43.

Teaiwa, Teresia. 1999. 'Reading Gauguin's *Noa Noa* with Epeli Hau'ofa's *Kisses in the Nederends*: Militourism, Feminism, and the Polynesian Body.' In *Inside Out: Literature, Cultural Politics, and Identity in the New Pacific*, ed. Vilsoni Hereniko and Rob Wilson, pp. 249–63. Lanham: Rowman & Littlefield.

———. 2001. 'L(o)osing the edge.' *The Contemporary Pacific* 13(2): 343–57.

Tobin, Jack A. 1954. *Ebeye Village: An Atypical Marshallese Community. Majuro, Marshall Islands*. Photocopied report in University of Hawai'i Library Pacific Collection.

Tuan, Yi-Fu. 2003. *Space and Place: The Perspective of Experience*. Minneapolis: University of Minnesota Press.

United States Chief of Naval Operations (USCNO) (1943) *Military Government Handbook OPNAV P22–1: Marshall Islands*, Government Publication.

US Army Kwajalein Atoll (USAKA). 2001. *2001 Telephone Directory*.

US Army Kwajalein Atoll (USAKA). 2005. 'Kwajalein Battlefield Tour.'

10

Yuki Kihara's *Culture for Sale* and the History of Pacific Cultural Performance

Mandy Treagus

One or more dancers in traditional Samoan dress are located on raised platforms; in a darkened adjacent area there is a row of slot machines. The performers, and slot machines, are static unless a viewer interacts with them. In the case of the machines, placing 20 cents in the slot activates a short film loop, featuring one of the performers doing a particular Samoan dance. Similarly, each live performer has a bowl at his or her feet. When a viewer drops money into the bowl, the dancer delivers a short rendering—about 45 seconds—of a dance, each one performing a different traditional form. This is *Culture for Sale*, a video, installation and performance work, first staged in its full realisation at the Campbelltown Arts Centre for the Sydney Festival in 2012.[1] It was part of the New Zealand Arts Festival in February 2014 at City Gallery, Wellington, New Zealand, and also featured at Rautenstrauch Joest Museum, Cologne, in January of the same year. *Culture for Sale* has been explicitly connected by artist Yuki Kihara to the German administration of Samoa and the 'exotic' entertainments provided by

---

1   *Culture for Sale*, 2012, short film of the staging of *Culture for Sale*, dir. Yuki Kihara. It had been staged in performance only, without the slot machines, at the National Gallery of Victoria in 2010.

Samoans in German *Völkerschau* around that period,[2] during which Samoans functioned as living objects in both performance and onsite villages.[3] Samoans also featured in other colonial exhibitions, notably the Chicago World's Fair in 1893, at which a group of them, along with other Pacific Islanders, performed and lived. What Kihara evokes so effectively in *Culture for Sale* is the set of viewing relations and discourses surrounding these original tours, thereby raising wider questions about what happens when culture goes on tour. Viewer pleasure, and potentially discomfort at the contemporary performances cannot be divorced from notions of 'savagery' and 'the primitive' as they circulated in the original colonial tours. The installation also interrogates the distinction between 'the gift' and 'the commodity'; what happens when performances that have been part of 'gift' societies move into capitalist arenas?

Figure 47. Performer. Ali Korey Vaifale. *Culture for Sale*. City Gallery, Wellington, 21 February 2014.

Source. Photographed by Sarah Hunter, 21 February 2014, and used with permission.

---

2   Yuki Kihara and Mandy Treagus, 2014, Forum on *Culture for Sale*, City Gallery, Wellington, 22 February.

3   Hilke Thode-Arora, 2014, '"Our new fellow countrymen": The Samoa show of 1900–01', in *From Samoa with Love? Samoan Travellers in Germany 1895–1911. Retracing the Footsteps*, ed. Hilke Thode-Arora, pp. 117–37, Munich: Museum Fünf Kontinente.

Figure 48. Performer. Ali Korey Vaifale. *Culture for Sale*. City Gallery, Wellington, 21 February 2014.

Source. Photographed by Sarah Hunter, 21 February 2014, and used with permission.

Should we conceive of the performers who went to Chicago as cultural ambassadors, sharing the culture of their homelands with new audiences, or were they ethnographic objects, on display to illustrate the racial theories of the West and the power of a developing empire that could assemble such curiosities in one place? This is not an idle question, only to be considered in relation to the past. Kihara's work forces us to consider the cost and meaning of contemporary cultural displays in our own time and place. What does it mean to 'sell' culture? Can it be done? Is there always something unequal about the exchange that occurs in cultural performances put on for entertainment? The dances seen in *Culture for Sale* have a place in traditional life, but up until now that place was not in the gallery. The dances are part of everyday life. Sometimes that place is in formal ceremony; at others it is at events like fundraisers, where dancers are rewarded with money—lafo—for their efforts (and where, significantly, that money is studiously ignored by the performers while in performance). Is there something fundamentally different about dancing to raise funds within a community and dancing for palagi (foreigners) who have paid to be entertained? Cultures are not fixed; they change and indeed they must if they are to continue. But if one's cultural products are primarily seen as commercial, does this make them culturally less valuable, and less authentic? And if this is the case, what do we make of the use of cultural performances in the tourist industry? Are some aspects of culture now mainly involved in commercial exchange?

The history of exhibitions and contemporary tourism in the Pacific might seem distant from each other, but in fact they have illuminating links. This chapter seeks to draw out these connections, which are apparent from the early days of the modern phenomena of exhibition practice in the nineteenth century. I specifically explore this relation through the Chicago World's Fair, and consider the ways in which Kihara's *Culture for Sale* engages with these histories. While challenging the power relations inherent in nineteenth-century tours and celebrating the islander participants who made them possible, *Culture for Sale* also evokes a range of viewing positions and responses that reproduce such relations. It is this ambivalence that nuances the work and gives it great strength.

While a variety of exhibition forms occurred in Europe over several centuries, including various displays of 'native peoples', modern exhibition culture dates primarily from the Great Exhibition of 1851. As the centre of the largest empire ever seen, London of 1851 set the tone for the multiplicity of Expositions, World's Fairs and Exhibitions that followed over the next century. The tastes of Londoners—'an ever unstable mixture, in which an insatiable appetite for novelty contended with a perennial loyalty to staple attractions such as waxworks and freaks'[4]—produced a particular kind of exhibition that always involved entertainment, even when the stated motivations for the Great Exhibition were to demonstrate 'commercial utility, recreation, and instruction'.[5] The 'curiosity' of Londoners, and the fact that all classes were engaged,[6] resulted in displays that could be meaningful to the illiterate as well as the educated. Part of this appeal, especially in the ongoing life of the Crystal Palace, was predicated on the perception that its 'exhibits appeared to transcend place and time, to make possible "virtual tourism" to foreign lands

4   Richard Altick, 1978, *The Shows of London*, Cambridge, Massachusetts: Harvard University Press, p. 3.
5   Alexander Chase-Levinson, 2012, 'Annihilating time and space: Eclecticism and virtual tourism at the Sydenham Crystal Palace', *Nineteenth-Century Contexts* 34(5): 461–75, p. 462.
6   Altick, *The Shows of London*, p. 3.

and distant epochs'.[7] This form of tourism became an inherent part of exhibition planning, execution and appeal. Curtis Hinsley links the gaze employed by those wandering through the Chicago exhibition to the *flâneur*: 'The eyes of the Midway are those of the *flâneur*, the stroller through the street arcade of human differences, whose experience is not the holistic, integrated ideal of the anthropologist but the segmented, seriatim fleetingness of the modern tourist "just passing through".'[8] He goes on to suggest that 'at Chicago in 1893, public curiosity about other peoples, mediated by the terms of the marketplace, produced an early form of touristic consumption'[9] that was immeasurably enhanced by the presence of 'native' performers and workers.

Following the Great Exhibition, the Paris Exposition of 1889 consolidated the practice of displaying humans as objects of interest in its 'The History of Human Habitation'.[10] These displays became *de rigueur* in exhibitions over the next 50 years, and were often the most noted features of them. They seemed to offer an experience of parts and peoples of the world not otherwise available before the age of mass tourism. Of the original in Paris, 'The exhibit was in the form of a street of thirty-nine houses, stretching from the Champ de Mars to the Trocadéro, each one representing a culture and a stage in world housing from prehistoric times to the present'.[11] The effect of such displays is well-captured by the French writer Paul Morand, who, as a child, experienced the Paris Exhibition of 1900:

> I made a thousand extraordinary journeys almost without moving; under the Eiffel Tower, near the little lake, was hidden the Tonkinese village with its junks and its women chewing betel; sometimes I watched the old Cambodian elephant sent by Doumer and called 'Chérie' drinking there ... The entire hill was nothing but perfumes, incense, vanilla, the aromatic fumes of the seraglio; one could hear the scraping of the Chinese violins, the sounds of the castanets,

7   Chase-Levinson, 'Annihilating time and space', p. 463.
8   Curtis Hinsley, 1991, 'The World as marketplace: Commodification of the exotic at the World's Columbian Exposition, Chicago, 1893', in *Exhibition Cultures: The Poetics and Politics of Museum Display*, ed. Ivan Karp and Steven D. Lavine, pp. 344–65, Washington and London: Smithsonian Institution Press, p. 356.
9   Hinsley, 'The World as marketplace', p. 363.
10   Paul Greenhalgh, 1988, *Ephemeral Vistas: The Expositions Universelles, Great Exhibitions and World's Fair, 1851–1939*, Manchester: Manchester University Press, p. 4.
11   Greenhalgh, *Ephemeral Vistas*, p. 20.

the wailing flutes of the Arab bands, the mystical howling of the Aissawas more heavily painted than De Max, the cries of the Ouled Naïl with their mobile bellies; I followed this opiate mixture, this perfume of Javanese dancing girls, sherbets and rahat-lakoum, as far as the Dahomean village.[12]

It was into such realms of curiosity and virtual tourism that the party from Samoa ventured in 1893. Chicago World's Fair was officially named 'The Columbian Exposition' to celebrate the 'discovery' of the Americas by Columbus 400 years earlier, though its lengthy preparations meant that it occurred a year after the actual quadricentenary. It ran over six months, on grounds covering some 250 hectares.[13] Numerically, one in four Americans saw the Fair, and it was the subject of many features in the press. The Fair was consciously designed to show how much progress the nation had made; it now represented itself as a world leader in technology, industry and know-how. The fact that the Fair also contained 'native' displays, shops and villages only served to contrast a vision of modernity on the one hand, and a past of 'primitive' stagnation on the other. While some downplayed the importance of 'native' entertainments, the contrast between their apparent frivolity and the serious technological development in the other displays meant that the notion of progress took on a racialised meaning. Human displays provided the contrast needed in order for visitors to fully apprehend how advanced the halls of industry were.

This was enhanced, if anything, by the fact that the large part of the Fair celebrating industry and modern achievements was called the White City. Its name came from the temporary coating on the buildings: staff, 'a mixture of powdered gypsum, alumina, glycerine, and dextrine mixed with fibers to create a plaster' that was effective temporarily but barely lasted the length of the Fair.[14] Despite its apparently neutral origins, this name persisted in later exhibitions, seeming to serve the

---

12   Philippe Jullian, 1974, *The Triumph of Art Nouveau: Paris Exhibition 1900*, London: Phaidon, pp. 158–59.
13   Julian Ralph, 1893, *Harper's Chicago and the World's Fair: The Chapters on the Exposition being Collected from Official Sources and Approved by the Department of Publicity and Promotion of the World's Columbian Exposition*, New York: Harper and Brothers, p. 235.
14   Judith Adams, 1996, 'The American dream actualized: The glistening "white city" and the lurking shadows of the World's Columbian Exhibition', *The World's Columbian Exposition: A Centennial Bibliographic Guide*, ed. David J. Bertuca, Donald K. Hartman and Susan M. Neumesiter, pp. xix–xxix, Westport: Greenwood, p. xxiii.

message of progress well, and with it an understanding about race, technology and advancement. Julian Hawthorne, the journalist son of writer Nathaniel, wrote that 'No one pair of eyes can even see it all in six months: as to digesting what you see, that is out of the question. For here are amassed examples of everything that the civilized world produces.'[15] Around 27 million visitors, many from rural USA, came to the Fair via the new railway networks, and they were exposed to inventions that seemed to signal the true advent of Modernity: 'elevators, cash registers, calculating machines, massive search lights, automatic door openers, ironing machines, dishwashers, carpet sweepers, doorbells, phonographs, clocks, industrial motors, an electric dentist's drill, even an electric cigar lighter!'[16] Such displays ushered in modern consumerism, along with promoting the prowess and industrious ingenuity of the nation that produced them.[17] It also proved to be in marked contrast with the so-called 'primitives and savages' on the Midway. The Ferris Wheel, at 264 feet high, weighing over 45 tons and built of the largest piece of steel thus far forged,[18] seemed to speak of the Fair's joint industrial and entertainment functions.

This setting, especially its contrast between the modernity of the White City and the 'primitive' nature of the Midway, provided a highly specific lens through which the South Pacific islanders on tour would be viewed by the general public. *Culture for Sale* also has a very definite frame that evokes specific readings for viewers. Its most distinguishing context is its gallery setting. Not only does this take the performances out of an everyday environment, but it moves them into the arena of fine arts, an unusual one for traditional dance. Who, then, is/are the artist/s here? Is it the performers themselves, whether on film or in the flesh, or is it Kihara, the *auteur* of the work? Certain factors lead viewers to objectify the performers in similar ways to those in the colonial tours. Performers filmed in the slot machines are inherently objectified; the medium itself offers those portrayed within it to the cinematic gaze of the viewer. Viewers' control of the display via the use of coins enhances this. Similarly, the act of initiating live

---

15   Julian Hawthorne, 1893, 'The Lady of the Lake (at the Fair)', *Lippincott's* August: 240–47, p. 241.
16   Adams, 'The American dream actualized', p. xxi.
17   Ibid., p. xx.
18   Ibid., p. xv.

dances though putting coins in a bowl empowers viewers, but it is the positioning of performers on plinths that invites the most direct objectification. They are inherently placed as statues, static unless activated, and hence under the control of those who gaze at them. Their method of enlistment into the project may not be dissimilar to that of some of the original tourists though, especially those who travelled to the US.

In response to the overtures of Leigh S. Lynch, 'Special Commissioner of the World's Fair for the South Sea Islands',[19] Harry J. Moors formed a group to perform at the World's Fair. Moors, or Misimoa as he was known to Samoans, was an American businessman who had married Nimo, a Samoan woman, and lived in Apia for almost 20 years, acquiring plantations and businesses. As an American, he also took a very clear position on the civil conflict that gripped Samoa over the final two decades of the nineteenth century, when it was under combined colonial rule. Moors and his previous business partner, William Blacklock, by now the US Consul in Samoa, had had a falling out over the Malietoa-Mata'afa conflict,[20] and this conflict continued in all their dealings with each other.[21] Blacklock had officially asked the Samoan Government to provide an exhibit at the Fair but they did not take up the offer;[22] it was perhaps this failure to initiate a display that antagonised Blacklock when Moors produced his own private arrangement for an exhibit on the Midway. The Samoan press expressed

19   'From the South Sea Islands', 1892, *Chicago Daily Tribune*, 6 February, p. 12.
20   John Alexander Clinton Gray, 1960, *Amerika Samoa: A History of American Samoa and its United States Naval Administration*, Annapolis, MD: US Naval Institute, p. 135.
21   While Samoa was not in fact under the sovereign control of a colonial power, it was still largely controlled by the consuls of three nations with interests in the region: Germany, Britain and the United States. This proved to be unworkable: the 'three powers', as they were known in Apia, with their European understandings of royalty and inability or unwillingness to comprehend the Samoan chiefly system, supported one chiefly titleholder as 'king' over the islands. See Malama Meleisea, Penelope Schoeffel Meleisea and Gatoloai Pesta S. Sio, 1987, 'The struggle for monarchy', in *Lagaga: A Short History of Western Samoa*, ed. Malama Meleisea and Penelope Schoeffel Meleisea, pp. 89–101, Suva: South Pacific Books, p. 99. This was the holder of the Malietoa title of the time. Most Samoans, though, supported the claims of Mata'afa over those of Malietoa. Along with his friend Robert Louis Stevenson, Moors provided both material and moral support to Mata'afa, as the British Consul, Cusack-Smith, complained to Lord Roseberry. See Gerald Horne, 2007, *The White Pacific: U.S. Imperialism and Black Slavery in the South Seas after the Civil War*, Honolulu: University of Hawai'i Press, p. 218. Stevenson wrote extensively about this conflict and its poor handling by foreign powers, for both *The Times of London* and in his *A Footnote to History*. See Robert Louis Stevenson, 1892, *A Footnote to History: Eight Years of Trouble in Samoa*, London: Cassell.
22   William Blacklock, 1892, Letter to Secretary of State, 8 September, National Archives, USA, Records of the Foreign Service Posts of the Department of State, 84.3.

doubts about what kind of impression visitors to Moors' exhibit might gain.[23] Apparently because of Moors' support for Mata'afa, the official ruler, Malietoa, banned Samoans from travelling to Chicago. Blacklock confirms this: 'The real reason why the Government will not allow any Samoans to go with Moors is because of his continued opposition to Malietoa and his Government.'[24] The government refused to support Moors' group when he publicly requested their help, claiming, with an edge of bitterness, that it would have sent its own group if it had the means. Moors responded in the press by outlining his plan for the Fair:

> I have to say that I fear an entirely erroneous idea as to the object of the proposed visit to Chicago and the employment of the people while there seems to have got abroad, and has no doubt somewhat influenced the Government in their decision … Our people would only be on exhibition in the same way as are the people of China, Japan, Java, Lahore, India, and numerous other places. They will be expected during certain hours of the day to dress in their native way, to paddle canoes, build canoes, cook 'Faa Samoa', and give native songs and dances, sell fans and other things, just in the same way as they will see many other people doing … It is my object to present in Chicago a perfect picture of Samoan life under favorable circumstances, showing all that is good and attractive and leaving out all that is bad.[25]

Blacklock responded by writing to the captains of the SS *Alameda* and the SS *Mariposa*, reminding them of the ban on Samoans travelling overseas without permission, warning them that the Samoan Government 'has reason to believe an attempt will be made to take Samoans away from here to the United States without its consent' and pointing out that Samoans needed a permit to leave the country.[26] He also informed the US Assistant Secretary of State of the permit law, and of the fact that no Samoans had been given permission to leave the country for the Fair.[27] The Samoan Government sent a ship to check one of the steamers, in case anyone joined them at sea. As the *Samoa Times* reported, a Samoan girl, Tua'a, 'an excellent Siva dancer … tried to stow away in the Upolu last trip', in order to get to

23   Harry J. Moors, 1893, Letter to T. Maben, 1 March, *Samoa Weekly Herald*, 4 March.
24   Blacklock, Letter to Secretary of State, 8 September.
25   Moors, Letter to T. Maben.
26   William Blacklock, 1893, Letter to Captain Morse, 27 February, National Archives, USA, Records of the Foreign Service Posts of the Department of State, 84.3.
27   Blacklock, 1892, Letter to Secretary of State, 8 September.

Chicago to join the group.[28] Later, on the next arrival of the *Mariposa* into San Francisco, four men and a woman were found who were clearly on their way to Chicago to join the group. Despite denials in Samoa, once the performers had arrived in Chicago, it seemed that a number of them were prepared to admit to being Samoan, given their statements to the press. Other islanders made up the rest of the party, including some from Fiji, Wallis, Rotuma and Tonga, along with 'afakasi (literally half-castes). Some of these may have been in indenture prior to the trip. Six Samoan women and two small Moors children made up the group.[29] There were also a number of artefacts for display and sale, including a traditionally made 70-foot reversible canoe (taumualua).[30]

While it is impossible to say whether all of these travelled voluntarily, is seems clear that many of them did, as indicated by the enthusiasm for the following year's tour to the Mid-Winter Fair in San Francisco. The ship Moors had chartered, the *Vine*, arrived back in Apia from the Chicago trip on 6 January. On 18 January, a fresh group sailed out to return to Fair life, going via Wallis Island in order to recruit more performers. They had a small adventure while there: at Wallis Island Moors was served with a notice from the French Resident prohibiting him from taking islanders and police were put on the ship to see that the order was obeyed. The ship sailed, the police left, and then three canoes came alongside. When one was swamped, the occupants of the other two—eight persons—were taken on board. They headed for Futuna, followed by a French warship, which had the intention of 'seizing the Vine and arresting her owners'.[31] Moors was tipped off while on Futuna though, and 'hastened off to his vessel with five Futuna boys. All sail was made, and when the warship came round the island the Vine, which is a capital sailor, was hull down on the horizon.'[32] While this is something of an adventure tale, it also indicates that many islanders were keen to be part of these tours, and took risks to join them. When Moors was back in Chicago in 1894, he claimed that

---

28 *Samoa Times*, 10 June 1893.
29 *Honolulu Weekly Bulletin*, 11 April 1893, in *Samoa Weekly Herald*, 20 May 1893.
30 Hubert Howe Bancroft, 1893, *The Book of the Fair*, Chicago and San Francisco: Bancroft Company, p. 859.
31 *Samoa Weekly Herald*, 14 April 1894.
32 Ibid.

the group were all 'delighted with their Chicago experience'.[33] This cannot be said with the same degree of certainty about the German tours, as outlined by Hilke Thode-Arora.[34]

Performers in *Culture for Sale*, on the other hand, were engaged through expatriate community connections, and their involvement in the performances and filming were personally guided by the artist. Before the opening of the show at City Gallery, Wellington, Kihara personally oversaw preparations by the dancers, both in terms of performance, costume and mental preparedness. She also spent some time debriefing with them after the show, as this proved to be a time of conflicting thoughts and emotions. The effort of standing motionless (when not prompted to dance) and disengaged from viewers appears to have required a different mental approach to that needed for other public performances of traditional dancing. The delicate balance between employing them to highlight the objectification of their ancestors while maintaining their dignity as holders of cultural 'possessions'[35] and respected skilled members of their communities needed some negotiation on Kihara's part. At the same time, the critique of objectification that is embodied in *Culture for Sale* has to be measured with the sense of agency held by many who participated in the original colonial tours.

Human displays in colonial exhibitions developed two dominant kinds of performance: 'staged recreations of cultural performances … and the drama of the quotidian'.[36] In its presence on the Midway in Chicago, the South Seas exhibit typified both of these styles. There was a village, built in Samoan style from materials shipped with them, in which stood five traditional fale, including one in the centre 'which stood for ten years in the village of King Mata'afa, and which was sent to the exhibit by him'.[37] The village was open each day, and visitors could see demonstrations of 'mat weaving, fire making

33   'Eli liked his trip', 1894, *Chicago Daily Tribune*, 7 June, p. 9.
34   Hilke Thode-Arora, 2014, '"The belles of Samoa": The Samoa Show of 1895–97', in *From Samoa with Love? Samoan Travellers in Germany 1895–1911. Retracing the Footsteps*, Munich: Museum Fünf Kontinente, p. 106.
35   Nicholas Thomas, 1999, *Possessions: Indigenous Art, Colonial Culture*, New York: Thames and Hudson.
36   Barbara Kirshenblatt-Gimblett, 1991, 'Objects of ethnography', in *Exhibition Cultures: The Poetics and Politics of Museum Display*, ed. Ivan Karp and Steven D. Lavine, pp. 386–443, Washington and London: Smithsonian Institution Press, p. 405.
37   *Samoa Weekly Herald*, 21 October 1893.

and kava preparation'.[38] Villagers 'played, sang and drank kava'[39] and gave apparently impromptu musical performances. The verisimilitude of the quotidian was convincing enough to convey a sense that actual Samoan life was being observed in a 'staged authenticity' to use Dean MacCannell's term.[40] The fact that at 'times, visitors told of seeing the villagers napping in corners of the structure',[41] only emphasised this. One visitor wrote that 'their manners and customs and ways of living are a source of never-ending wonder to the visitors and they always have attentive audiences whether engaged in making fires by rubbing two sticks together or in making their favorite brew' (presumably 'ava (kava)).[42] Items of Samoan material culture, including a range of weapons as well as smaller canoes, added to this sense of authenticity. Many of these artefacts from the Fair were bought by the Field Museum when the Fair ended.[43] Authenticity was a potent form of currency even when its paradoxically constructed nature was acknowledged by all involved.

An incident early in their tour showed both the group's attempts to adapt to US culture, and the steadfast demand by both public and their management that they refuse to do so. When they arrived their hair had reportedly stood out a foot from their heads, in the manner of the day.[44] Seeing that the locals had short hair, the Samoan men cut their own in an attempt to look the same. They were also wearing western dress, which they were advised to exchange for traditional Samoan garb.[45] It is likely that they were 'comfortable in both modes of dress' as the performers had attended mission schools.[46] As they were living onsite until late Fall, wearing scant and light Samoan clothing in order to maintain an aura of 'native' authenticity would have created a real degree of hardship; the islanders were 'anxious to get to a sunnier clime' as the *Chicago Daily Tribune* reported when they

38   Gertrude M. Scott, 1992, 'Village performance: Villages at the Chicago World's Columbian Exposition 1893', PhD thesis, New York University, p. 273.
39   Scott, 'Village performance', p. 274.
40   Kirshenblatt-Gimblett, 'Objects of ethnography', p. 408.
41   Scott, 'Village performance', p. 272.
42   *The Dream City: A Portfolio of Photographic Views of the World's Columbian Exhibition*, 1893, St Louis: The World's Columbian Exhibition.
43   Accession File No. 11, Field Museum, Chicago.
44   *The Dream City*.
45   Wayne quoted in Paige Raibmon, 2005, *Authentic Indians: Episodes of Encounter from the Late-Nineteenth Century Northwest Coast*, Durham: Duke University Press, p. 223.
46   Scott, 'Village performance', p. 279.

left on 3 November.[47] According to press reports, haircutting ceased soon after arrival in the US and 'the Samoans are making a heroic and laudable effort to resume their natural state of barbarism'.[48] This comment indicates that both management and press were aware that 'the primitive' was a construct serving the purposes of the Fair; it was not something intrinsic in itself. And it is perhaps this notion that clings to all cultural performances when they are presented as entertainment. It also invites interrogation about what is being offered. It seems clear that audiences wanted the *sense* of authenticity however constructed that might be known to be.

The theatre was a more obviously western affair than the village, built as it was for the comfort of audiences and therefore more clearly concerned with entertainment. The shows included dances, songs and chants from the various islands and cultures represented by group members, but it also involved their modification for the theatre environment. The South Seas Theatre was painted by Joe Strong (former stepson-in-law of Robert Louis Stevenson). Julian Hawthorne described it as 'a comfortable little theatre, seating four hundred, with a stage and drop curtain'.[49] He suggests that he attended it daily, so clearly it held immense appeal for some. Before each show, performers would parade, chanting with a drum in order to attract a crowd, 'while the audience waited, and when a sufficient "house" was obtained, the performance would begin'.[50] War dances were especially thrilling for audiences, and were a large feature of the show, as they were in many others along the Midway. They also suited the environment of the theatre, as they were by 'nature a crafted, stylised exhibition designed precisely for impressing enemies and strangers with what the performers wanted them to see'.[51] and hence could shift from the original cultural setting with little adaptation. Their shows also included paddle dances, sitting dances and the suitably shocking 'cannibal dance', which must have been convincing: 'many of these

---

47   'Going! Going! Gone!' 1893, *Chicago Daily Tribune*, 4 November, p. 2.
48   Robert W. Rydell, 1984, *All the World's a Fair: Visions of Empire at American International Expositions, 1876–1916*, Chicago: Chicago University Press, p. 66.
49   Scott, 'Village performance', p. 271.
50   *The Dream City.*
51   Jane R. Goodall, 2002, *Performance and Evolution in the Age of Darwinism: Out of the Natural Order*, London: Routledge, p. 103.

are but little removed from their period of complete savagery',[52] an observer reported, without any of the irony of other press reports. A history of cannibalism was often evoked in 'native' performances, and it was a useful marketing tool for attracting audiences, another mark of authentic primitivism. Entry prices were typical for the Midway: the South Sea Island Village was 10 cents and the South Sea Island Theater was 25 cents.[53]

Many commentators rated the village and theatre performances very highly. In *The 'Time Saver': A Book which Names and Locates 5,000 things at the World's Fair that Visitors should not fail to see*, a Key rates attractions according to the following scale: '1. Interesting, 2. Very Interesting and 3. Remarkably Interesting'.[54] Most entries, out of 5,000, are rated at 1. On the Midway, the 'Samoan village' joins only the Javanese, German, Chinese & Hagenbeck's Zoological Arena in being rated at 2.[55] The only attraction to be awarded 3 is the highlight of the Fair, the Ferris Wheel.[56] Hinsley claims that 'by 1890 two traditions of human display were established: the Hagenbeck-type-tour, which occasionally made some claim to ethnographic authenticity and sobriety, and the Barnum-type sideshow of human freaks and oddities. Both were already being incorporated into World's Fairs for the public, and each usually had elements of the other.'[57] Theatre and village manage to incorporate both elements, along with that sense of authenticity, and on the Midway, authenticity lay in evoking the primitive: humanity being experienced in an earlier and more 'natural' state. The constructed nature of this primitivism, and the knowingness with which it was maintained, comes through in both the behaviour of the touring group and in the press reports about them.

When audiences enter the gallery space in which *Culture for Sale* is being staged, the presence of living performers can seem to breach the conventions around what is appropriate for such spaces (though human participants are increasingly being found in gallery installations).

---

52   *The Vanished City: The World's Columbian Exposition in Pen and Picture*, n.d., Chicago: Werner.
53   John Flinn, 1893, *Official Guide to the Midway Plaisance: The Authorized Official Guide to the World's Columbian Exposition*, Chicago: Columbian Guide Company, no. 50.
54   *The 'Time Saver': A Book which Names and Locates 5,000 things at the World's Fair that Visitors should not Fail to See*, 1893, Chicago: W.E. Hamilton.
55   *The 'Time Saver'*, p. 101.
56   *The 'Time Saver'*.
57   Hinsley, 'The World as marketplace', p. 346.

Costuming and difference invite a colonial eye, even if one is aware that one is observing a staged version of 'the native', 'the primitive' or even of the 'Samoan'. The sense of engaging with an actual person counteracts, somewhat, the staged authenticity of such interactions. Similarly, and despite ethnographers taking a role in the organising regimes of the Midway, the very presence of living native performers meant that the range of meanings possible for visitors could not be prescribed in the ways they could in the new museums of the time. The possibility that 'exhibits' could step out of their roles as 'primitive' forebears and function as cosmopolitan contemporaries was something that ethnologists at the Fair attempted to limit. When the Samoans cut their hair and wore American clothes, they had the potential to appear as equal correspondents in modernity, entertainers rather than illustrations of Social Darwinism. Though to see the islanders wearing very little enhanced the primitivist illusion, when it became cold in Chicago the touring group was less inclined to play along with the performance and were keen to get into western dress again. Likewise, in *Culture for Sale*, performers finish their performances, leave their plinths, and return wearing their usual forms of dress, thereby potentially shattering the illusion of their status as human objects.

The apparent message of the Fair—suggested in its division between the White City and the Midway and via its guidebooks—was that humanity existed in lesser and higher forms. This no doubt helped to justify the expansion into the Pacific of US interests, seen in the annexation of the Philippines, Hawai'i and the eastern islands of Samoa. American businessmen secured the deposition of Queen Lili'uokalani in Hawai'i just prior to the Fair, and the US, along with Great Britain and Germany, had controlled Samoa for some time through the condominium arrangement of three consuls largely manipulating the Malietoa. There was, of course, resistance to this, as seen in the outbreak of war while the group was away at the Fair. The fact that the South Sea Islanders concluded their shows by singing 'America' in Samoan must have been reassuring, though it is probable that many Americans knew little about the expansion westward beyond the Pacific coast.[58] However they might have been described, in both press and guidebooks, the touring group of Samoans and other islanders did not see themselves as illustrations of humanity's savage

---

58   'The International Ball at the Fair', 1893, *Chicago Daily Tribune*, 17 August, p. 1.

past. It seems much more likely that they saw themselves as working performers at the Fair, travelling, and encountering different cultures and experiences. As Damon Salesa has noted:

> The islanders who went with Moors agreed to rigid terms – strict limits on behavior and dress, and work on Sundays – all for $12 a month. But Samoans seemed eager to accept those terms for a chance to *tafao* (wander about) overseas. The Samoans who went with him to San Francisco, Moors promised ... will return to Samoa happy with the strange things they have seen in distant lands, and the things they have brought with them.[59]

Famous travel writer Paul du Chaillu, signing himself simply 'Chaillu', gives an account of a feast given in his honour in the village after Fair hours. It provides some insight into the islanders, and their position in relation to others at the Fair. Before the feast, 'ava (kava) was shared, and the visitor, as a high-status guest, was given the first cup.[60] This makes it clear that they were welcoming Chaillu as their own guest, not as paid performers in their roles as 'native objects'. The feast was marked by an abundance of food, including a pig, ducks, chicken, fish and other items.[61] As reported in James Campbell's *Illustrated History of the World's Columbian Exposition* (1894), when visitors came to the village during work hours, observers noted that they 'tried to give visitors a correct idea of their home life and customs'.[62] This conveys their sense of themselves as cultural ambassadors, not ethnographic objects. Performers in *Culture for Sale*, on the other hand, were questioned after their performances as to whether they were representing themselves as objects. After the Campbelltown installation, for example, one dancer described feeling 'claustrophobic' while waiting on the plinth; both being ignored or observed by viewers could induce a sense of diminution by the role and situation.[63] Another spoke of feeling 'betrayed, exploited, because

59   Damon Salesa, 2005, 'Misimoa: An American on the beach', *Common-Place* 5(2): n.p.
60   Chaillu, 1893, *Samoa Weekly Herald*, 30 December.
61   Bancroft, *The Book of the Fair*, p. 859.
62   James B. Campbell, 1894, *Campbell's Illustrated History of the World's Columbian Exposition* quoted in Scott, 'Village performance', p. 275.
63   *Culture for Sale*, 2012, Short film of the staging of *Culture for Sale*, Dir. Yuki Kihara.

I had to dance for money'.[64] This is accentuated because performers within the space of the installation have no opportunity to interact with viewers, and because money is the signal to perform. They are inherently objectified, and this is part of the power relations Kihara has evoked in the work. How different this might be from being observed performing the quotidian of village life on the Midway is difficult to say, but the villagers were fundamentally made objects by their status as educational entertainment; both situations produce and reproduce the power relations of colonialism.

Though most often framed through the stereotypes of savagery and cannibalism in the press, the Chicago group was also greatly admired, and praised for their exceptional physiques, especially the men. Casts of both women and men were taken by the Smithsonian as representations of the ideal,[65] with the stereotype of the 'Noble Savage' clearly at play. Commentators, especially in the press, offered commentary on the bodies of the group, without apparent self-consciousness. One of these, appearing in the San Francisco *Examiner* as 'Lady Writer', describes the men enthusiastically: 'great, big strong, muscular fellows, with dark, shining skins and black eyes – [they] dress very scantily indeed'.[66] Another writer claimed they 'were the best physical specimens of manhood offered by the World's Fair'.[67] The guidebook *Midway Types* provides a photo caption that reads: 'A Samoan warrior. A magnificent specimen of the men of the Samoan Village. Their shiny skins, looking like burnished copper, the muscles standing out like ropes, and the quiet manners of these people, made their display one of the most attractive of the Fair.'[68] *Midway Types* is typical of the many guides and souvenir books that sought to provide racial classifications for any and all of the performers on the Midway.

---

64   Ibid.
65   See Graphics Collection, Chicago History Museum.
66   Lady writer, 1893, *Samoa Weekly Herald*, 19 August.
67   *The Dream City*, n.p.
68   *Midway Types: A Book of Illustrated Lessons about The People of the Midway Plaisance – World's Fair 1893*, 1894, Chicago: American Engraving Company, no page.

Figure 49. Photographs of men from the Samoan Village taken at the Columbian Exhibition, Chicago, 1893.

Source. Photographed by Thomas Arnold and held in the Chicago Public Library.

Figure 50. Photograph of women from the Samoan Village taken at the Columbian Exhibition, Chicago, 1893.

Source. Photographed by Thomas Arnold, and held in the Chicago Public Library.

Similarly, female performers were also eroticised, as in descriptions such as this from the Chicago press: 'Lola, Siva, Fetoai and Mele, the four handsome Samoan girls, whose bare, shining, brown skins, are not among the least attractions of the village.'[69] Mildly erotic photos were taken of them and other women from the Midway. This was, after all, the Fair that popularised the erotic dancing of Little Egypt in the US. One article in the press reported on their attendance of the Fair ball. It is written in an amusing, if patronising, tone and the writer seems pleased with his description of the fashions. In a list of A to Z are reports on the various outfits worn:

Fetoai (South Sea Islander) – Costume of bark cloth, skirt cut short, bodice low, ornaments, shells and seed necklace of bright red.

Lola (South Sea Islander) – Native costume of bark cloth covering about half the body, with low cut and sleeveless bodice. Ornaments sea shells, seed bracelets and necklace.

Mele, Miss (Samoan) – One square yard of bark cloth, fringed at the lower edges and held on by a bodice of white muslin cut without sleeves, trimmed with seashells; necklace of grass and weeds; no shoes, no hair ornaments.[70]

The dancers in *Culture for Sale* are also set apart in the gallery space by their customary dress, including items very similar in description to those listed above, including fine mats, tapa, feathers and *tuiga* (ceremonial headdresses). These can be read in various ways, as the above press report indicates. The fact that they are still in contemporary use for specific events and celebrations indicates their currency in Samoan life, but it is also possible to read them as items of the exotic other, and hence as an indication of the primitive. Some performers, such as Ali Korey Vaifale in the Wellington *Culture for Sale*, were also adorned with traditional tattoos, in his case the pe'a. Such body adornments can invite their own specific viewing relations, leading to a further eroticised objectification.

This question of the role of the performers is also raised by *Culture for Sale*. Viewers can enter the gallery space, and look at the pictures of performers, but involvement is required in order to see a performance. The host of responses the work evokes in the audience is a major

---

69   *Samoa Times*, 9 December 1893.
70   'The International Ball at the Fair'.

part of the way the piece works. Its interactivity means that viewers are not passive in the exchange; they are co-opted into triggering performances and their individual actions in doing this make the exchange much more personal than it would be if they were anonymous members of an audience. The two different parts of the performance evoke a differing range of potential responses. The constant part of the exhibition, the slot machines, provide a much clearer monetary transaction. For each 20 cents, the viewer sees one short film of a dance. The environment, which has been slightly darkened, resonates strongly with overtones of voyeurism. Slot machines only accentuate this, with the specific aesthetics of the peep show coming into play. Despite the fact that the dancers on film are not performing in an erotic manner, the environment in which they are viewed has connotations of erotic performance as part of monetary exchange. This, in turn, has echoes of the original performances in Chicago and Germany, during which a certain amount of sexualised voyeurism was a clear element. Performers were objectified, not just sexually, but also as humans with reduced subjectivity, on display to satisfy racial theories and ethnic curiosity as well as to fulfill preconceived notions of the primitive. These overtones cling to *Culture for Sale*, and to the slot machine part of the exhibition. More overtly eroticised images were taken the year following Chicago when members of the group attended the Mid-Winter Fair in San Francisco in 1894. These invite an eroticised viewing, with the models posed to evoke the male gaze, even though they were not seen in performance wearing so little or in such poses. Even without an erotic element such as was present in representations of nineteenth-century performers, the slot machine aspect of the piece is empowering to viewers, who remain in control.

This does not shut down other meanings of the slot machines; the skill, balance and beauty of the dancing is significant, and it is also seen in the live performances, which evoke a new set of interactions and power relations. Observing a dancer becoming tired and sore, especially in the case of the slap dance, is a very close and personal experience for viewers, and makes the power relations very stark. Throw money in the bowl, make the dancer dance. The sounds of coins in a china bowl is a strong reminder of the economics of what is occurring; it cannot, however, wholly account for the viewer's response to the dancer's skill, nor does it necessarily contain the dancer's participation in traditional dance.

Figure 51. 'Samoan Belles'. Mid-Winter Fair, San Francisco, 1894.
Source. Courtesy of The Bancroft Library, University of California, Berkeley.
Call number: I0015235.

Figure 52. 'Samoan Girls Polonga and Olonga'. Mid-Winter Fair,
San Francisco, 1894.
Source. Courtesy of The Bancroft Library, University of California, Berkeley.
Call number: I0015232.

I return to the questions posed early in this chapter. *Culture for Sale* not only critiques and draws attention to the nineteenth-century tours it speaks back to, but it also questions the power relations inherent in contemporary tourism. It asks whether any exchange of cultural performance for money shifts the meaning of that cultural possession from gift to commodity, thereby abandoning the 'reciprocal dependence and inalienability' of that gift by taking it out of its original culture and placing it in a western market system.[71] It also complicates the binary, which sees cultural possessions such as dances as 'inalienable' gifts, by forcing viewers to engage with them as 'commodities'.[72] In addition to this, as Teresia Teaiwa asked during a *Culture for Sale* forum, is Kihara functioning as a modern-day Mr Moors, perpetuating the same set of relations as existed in colonial exhibitions?[73] Viewers of the installation and performance are forced to examine their own relations with performers when they 'buy' culture in this way, and Kihara deliberately skates close to reinforcing the viewing relations of colonialism in staging this work. The provocation of riding this knife edge between colonising and decolonising discourses makes *Culture for Sale* powerful, disturbing and arresting, both as a piece that allows for the unpredictability of performance and interaction, and as one that simultaneously evokes the power relations it seeks to critique.

References

Archival repositories

Chicago Field Museum.

Chicago History Museum, Graphics Collection.

National Archives, USA, Records of the Foreign Service Posts of the Department of State.

71   Chris A. Gregory, 1982, *Gifts and Commodities*, New York: Academic Press, p. 24.
72   Nicholas Thomas, 1991, *Entangled Objects: Exchange, Material Culture, and Colonialism in the Pacific*, Cambridge MA: Harvard University Press, p. 15.
73   Kihara and Treagus, forum on *Culture for Sale*.

Books, articles and chapters

Adams, Judith A. 1996. 'The American dream actualized: The Glistening "white city" and the lurking shadows of the World's Columbian Exhibition.' In *The World's Columbian Exposition: a Centennial Bibliographic Guide*, ed. David J. Bertuca, Donald K. Hartman and Susan M. Neumesiter, pp. xix–xxix. Westport: Greenwood.

Altick, Richard. 1978. *The Shows of London*. Cambridge, Massachusetts: Harvard University Press.

Bancroft, Hubert Howe. 1893. *The Book of the Fair*. Chicago and San Francisco: Bancroft Company.

Blacklock, William. 1892. Letter to Secretary of State. 8 September. National Archives, USA, Records of the Foreign Service Posts of the Department of State, 84.3.

——. 1893. Letter to Captain Morse. 27 February. National Archives, USA, Records of the Foreign Service Posts of the Department of State, 84.3.

Chase-Levinson, Alexander. 2012. 'Annihilating time and space: Eclecticism and virtual tourism at the Sydenham Crystal Palace.' *Nineteenth-Century Contexts* 34(5): 461–75.

Culture for Sale. 2012. Short film of the staging of *Culture for Sale*. Dir. Yuki Kihara.

Flinn, John. 1893. *Official Guide to the Midway Plaisance: The Authorized Official Guide to the World's Columbian Exposition*. Chicago: Columbian Guide Company.

Goodall, Jane R. 2002. *Performance and Evolution in the Age of Darwinism: Out of the Natural Order*. London: Routledge.

Gray, John Alexander Clinton. 1960. *Amerika Samoa: A History of American Samoa and its United States Naval Administration*. Annapolis, MD: US Naval Institute.

Greenhalgh, Paul. 1988. *Ephemeral Vistas: The Expositions Universelles, Great Exhibitions and World's Fair, 1851–1939*. Manchester: Manchester University Press.

Gregory, Chris A. 1982. *Gifts and Commodities*, New York: Academic Press.

Hawthorne, Julian. 1893. 'The Lady of the Lake (at the Fair).' *Lippincott's* August: 240–47.

Hinsley, Curtis. 1991. 'The World as marketplace: Commodification of the exotic at the World's Columbian Exposition, Chicago, 1893.' In *Exhibition Cultures: The Poetics and Politics of Museum Display*, ed. Ivan Karp and Steven D. Lavine, pp. 344–65. Washington and London: Smithsonian Institution Press.

Horne, Gerald. 2007. *The White Pacific: U.S. Imperialism and Black Slavery in the South Seas after the Civil War*. Honolulu: University of Hawai'i Press.

Jullian, Philippe. 1974. *The Triumph of Art Nouveau: Paris Exhibition 1900*. London: Phaidon.

Karp, Ivan and Steven D. Lavine (eds). 1991. *Exhibition Cultures: The Poetics and Politics of Museum Display*. Washington and London: Smithsonian Institution Press.

Kihara, Yuki, 2012–15. *Culture for Sale*. Installation, performance and video work.

Kihara, Yuki and Mandy Treagus. 2014. Forum on *Culture for Sale*. City Gallery, Wellington, 22 February.

Kirshenblatt-Gimblett, Barbara. 1991. 'Objects of ethnography.' In *Exhibition Cultures: The Poetics and Politics of Museum Display*, ed. Ivan Karp and Steven D. Lavine, pp. 386–443. Washington and London: Smithsonian Institution Press.

Meleisea Malama and Penelope Schoeffel Meleisea (eds). 1987. *Lagaga: A Short History of Western Samoa*. Suva: South Pacific Books.

Meleisea Malama, Penelope Schoeffel Meleisea and Gatoloai Pesta S. Sio. 1987. 'The struggle for monarchy.' In *Lagaga: A Short History of Western Samoa*, ed. Malama Meleisea and Penelope Schoeffel Meleisea, pp. 89–101. Suva: South Pacific Books.

Midway Types: A Book of Illustrated Lessons about The People of the Midway Plaisance – World's Fair 1893. 1894. Chicago: American Engraving Company.

Raibmon, Paige. 2005. *Authentic Indians: Episodes of Encounter from the Late-Nineteenth Century Northwest Coast*. Durham: Duke University Press.

Ralph, Julian. 1893. *Harper's Chicago and the World's Fair: The Chapters on the Exposition being collected from Official Sources and Approved by the Department of Publicity and Promotion of the World's Columbian Exposition*. New York: Harper and Brothers.

Rydell, Robert W. 1984. *All the World's a Fair: Visions of Empire at American International Expositions, 1876–1916*. Chicago: Chicago University Press.

Salesa, Damon. 2005. 'Misimoa: An American on the beach.' *Common-Place* 5(2): n.p.

Scott, Gertrude M. 1992. 'Village performance: Villages at the Chicago World's Columbian Exposition 1893.' PhD thesis. New York University.

Stevenson, Robert Louis. 1892. *A Footnote to History: Eight Years of Trouble in Samoa*. London: Cassell.

The Dream City: A Portfolio of Photographic Views of the World's Columbian Exhibition. 1893. St Louis: The World's Columbian Exhibition.

The 'Time Saver': A Book which Names and Locates 5,000 things at the World's Fair that Visitors should not Fail to See. 1893. Chicago: W.E. Hamilton.

The Vanished City: The World's Columbian Exposition in Pen and Picture (n.d.). Chicago: Werner.

Thode-Arora, Hilke, 2014. '"The Belles of Samoa": The Samoa Show of 1895–97.' In *From Samoa with Love? Samoan Travellers in Germany 1895–1911. Retracing the Footsteps*, ed. Hilke Thode-Arora, pp. 93–116. Munich: Museum Fünf Kontinente.

———. 2014. '"Our new fellow countrymen": The Samoa show of 1900–01.' In *From Samoa with Love? Samoan Travellers in Germany 1895–1911. Retracing the Footsteps*, ed. Hilke Thode-Arora, pp. 117–37. Munich: Museum Fünf Kontinente.

Thode-Arora, Hilke (ed.). 2014. *From Samoa with Love? Samoan Travellers in Germany 1895–1911. Retracing the Footsteps*. Munich: Museum Fünf Kontinente.

Thomas, Nicholas. 1991. *Entangled Objects: Exchange, Material Culture, and Colonialism in the Pacific*. Cambridge MA: Harvard University Press.

Thomas, Nicholas. 1999. *Possessions: Indigenous Art, Colonial Culture*. New York: Thames and Hudson.

Newspapers

Chicago Daily Tribune

Honolulu Weekly Bulletin

Samoa Times

Samoa Weekly Herald

Samoa Weekly Herald

San Francisco Examiner

11

Native Realities in an Imaginary World: Contemporary Kanaka Maoli Art at Aulani, A Disney Resort & Spa

A. Marata Tamaira

Pixie dust over Hawai'i

On 22 September 2011, after three years of planning and construction and an expenditure of US$850 million, Aulani, A Disney Resort & Spa opened its doors to Hawai'i's public with a twilight ceremony that included a theatrical extravaganza of oli (Hawaiian chant),[1] hula, a performance by Hawaiian singer/songwriter Keali'i Reichel, and the presentation of a ceremonial 'umeke (bowl), into which the Chairman and CEO of Walt Disney Company Bob Iger and the Chairman of Walt Disney Parks and Resorts Tom Staggs poured sand and pixie dust to symbolise the joining of two cultures, Hawai'i and Disney, respectively.

---

1   Aulani is the latest addition to the Ko Olina Resort Community and Marina complex, a consortium of tourist accommodation and leisure-time facilities located in Kapolei on the leeward coast of O'ahu, Hawai'i.

Before the vessel was formally transferred to the Vice President and Managing Director of Aulani for their stewardship, Iger proclaimed, 'We are now and for all time 'ohana, one family'.[2]

Two months after the grand opening, I had the opportunity to stay at Aulani with my family and experience it first-hand. I came away from that encounter deeply ambivalent about Aulani's place in Hawai'i and skeptical of its use of Native culture as part of Disney's corporate strategy to attract tourists to the Islands. In her landmark publication, *From a Native Daughter: Colonialism and Sovereignty in Hawai'i*, Kanaka Maoli scholar Haunani-Kay Trask equates tourism in Hawai'i with the exploitation of Kānaka Maoli,[3] declaring: 'To most Americans … Hawai'i is *theirs*: to use, to take, and, above all, to fantasize about long after the experience [emphasis in original].'[4] The deleterious impact of tourism on Native lives is, of course, not unique to Hawai'i but equally evident in other Pacific homelands. In her own critique of tourism, Tongan scholar Konai Helu Thaman refers to it as a 'process of cultural invasion' with links to colonialism.[5] The parallel Thaman draws between tourism and colonialism is especially salient for Hawai'i, a land colonised and occupied by the United States. Having myself lived in the Islands for over a decade now, it is often difficult to see where tourism begins and American colonialism ends because they are so tightly intertwined. What is also difficult to discern is where indigenous engagement with the tourist industry constitutes complicity with the broader hegemonic power structure and where it functions as a form of strategic intervention. In this instance, the situation at the Aulani Resort is a noteworthy case to consider given that dozens of Kānaka Maoli were involved in its conceptualisation and development. Here, the participation of Kanaka Maoli consultants, practitioners and artists in the Aulani project could potentially be perceived as an endorsement of the tourist enterprise, which has had a devastating impact on Kanaka Maoli culture and lands. On the other

---

2   A video of the opening ceremony is available at: 'Aulani Grand Opening Ceremony Pt. 1', 2011, *YouTube*, 22 September. Online: www.youtube.com/watch?v=UnINYe1jfC8 (accessed 19 February 2016).
3   I include the macron (i.e. Kānaka Maoli) to indicate its use as a plural noun, but when used as a singular noun and adjective, I omit the macron.
4   Haunani-Kay Trask, 1999, *From a Native Daughter: Colonialism and Sovereignty in Hawai'i*, Honolulu: University of Hawai'i Press, p. 136.
5   Konai Helu-Thaman, 1993, 'Beyond hula, hotels, and handicrafts: A Pacific Islander's perspective of tourism development', *The Contemporary Pacific* 5(1): 104–11, p. 104.

hand, their involvement could be seen as a powerful assertion of Native agency to intervene in a colonial space. Focusing on my experience at Aulani as a point of reference offers an opportunity for considering some of the broader issues relating to how Kānaka Maoli negotiated this ambivalent co-presence of collusion and agency.

As a master of storytelling and fantasy creation, Disney has been a major contributor to the cinematic packaging of Hawai'i for American consumption with films like *Hawaiian Holiday* (1937), *The Parent Trap: Hawaiian Honeymoon* (1989), *Johnny Tsunami* (1999), *Rip Girls* (2000), and the animated feature *Lilo and Stitch* (2002). Of significant note concerning the latter production, Disney provoked the ire of Kānaka Maoli with its misappropriation of two mele inoa (sacred name chants)—composed to honour the last two monarchs of the Hawaiian Kingdom, King David Kalākaua and Queen Lili'uokalani—that were rearranged to create a song for the lead protagonist, Lilo.[6]

Such thefts of cultural heritage together with the flagrant misrepresentation of the land and the people are present in many of the Disney films mentioned above. Stereotypes of Hawai'i and Kanaka Maoli culture are designed to spark in the American imagination a sense of what is 'theirs' to experience in the 'Aloha State': sun, sand, surfing, Aloha shirts, 'ukulele-strumming Natives, swaying hula girls, and the ever-present welcoming Hawaiian host ready to bestow a lei on the inbound guest: all to the strains of a slack-key guitar.

However, in 2008, when Aulani was first being conceptualised by Disney's team of Imagineers ('designers' in the Disney lexicon), the question of how to responsibly and respectfully incorporate a Kanaka Maoli worldview into the fabricated, imaginary world of Disney became a pressing concern. Rather than relying on its own authority to weave a story around Aulani, Disney took a different approach: to draw from already present Native perspectives of culture and place. In one of many interviews he gave to promote the resort, Senior Vice President of Walt Disney Imagineering Joe Rohde stated, 'The look and feel of Aulani is inspired directly by Hawaiian culture itself.

---

6   Nina Mantilla, 2011, 'The new Hawaiian model: The native Hawaiian cultural trademark movement and the quest for intellectual property rights to protect and preserve Native Hawaiian Culture', *Intellectual Property Brief* 3(2): 26–41, p. 26.

People come to these islands and what gives Hawai'i its identity except the Hawaiians. So we went directly to Hawaiian art, Hawaiian tradition, and Hawaiian story.'[7]

The strategy to foreground Native culture to forward corporate tourist business agendas is nothing new. In *Reimagining the American Pacific*, Rob Wilson notes: 'Tourism, for Hawai'i if not for Pacific sites more generally, depends on the globalization-of-the-local into a marketable image with lasting appeal, with enduring charm and mysterious *claim to uniqueness* [emphasis added].'[8] But while a focus on the transformation of Native heritage into tourist commodity is critically important for illuminating the exploitative nature of tourism—and there is a large body of scholarship that deals with this—of equal value is the acknowledgement of indigenous involvement in this complex and negotiable process of exchange.

Displaying native realities at Aulani

Experiencing Aulani in the flesh, as I did shortly after it opened, it is hard not to be impressed by the grand scope of the place. Driving up to the main porte cochére, visitors encounter a lo'i (irrigated terrace) stocked with kalo, a plant that holds significant cultural value for Kānaka Maoli and which has sustained them for millennia. In designing Aulani—the name meaning 'messenger of the chief'—Disney worked closely with indigenous stakeholders, cultural consultants and artists to tell Hawai'i's story. One of the most notable features of the resort is its rich display of contemporary Kanaka Maoli art. With the guidance of Kanaka Maoli businesswoman and entrepreneur Maile Meyer, Disney commissioned more than 60 indigenous artists to produce works ranging from paintings, sculptures, murals, to customary pieces such as 'umeke, poi pounders and kapa implements. One of the artists, painter Meala Bishop, noted the underlying significance of the works of art being displayed in the resort: 'You're gonna have a glimpse through the Native Hawaiian person's eye of the epic story of Hawai'i. What we see our history as. And it's so different from the commercial,

7   Jeanenne Tornatore, 2011, Orbitz exclusive interview with Joe Rohde, Senior Vice President of Walt Disney Imagineering, *YouTube*, 23 September.
8   Rob Wilson, 2000, *Reimagining the American Pacific: From South Pacific to Bamboo Ridge and Beyond*, Durham, NC: Duke University Press, p. xv.

kitschy Hawai'i that we're all used to.'[9] Through the involvement of Meyer, Bishop, and other indigenous contributors, a Kanaka Maoli–centric story of the Islands is borne out at Aulani in a compelling way.

Figure 53. Exterior view of Aulani, A Disney Resort & Spa with the lo'i kalo in the foreground.

Source. Photo by Marata Tamaira, 3 November 2011.

The largest works in the collection—eight 15-storey-high bas-reliefs, which furnish the exteriors of the two principle towers of the Aulani complex—were created by Carl F.K. Pao and Harinani Orme. In four of the bas-reliefs, Pao employed his own unique graphic writing style to render oli composed by artist and musician Doug Tolentino (who also served as a cultural consultant on the Aulani project). In the first two bas-reliefs, the Kanaka Maoli concept of balance between the male (Kū) and female (Hina) principles is invoked through the story of the rising and setting of the masculine sun and feminine moon. In following the recommendation of the artist and cultural consultants, Disney positioned the works in an east (male)–west (female) orientation to reflect the gender-encoded cardinal points of reference observed in Kanaka Maoli culture. The remaining two works by Pao—which face toward the mountains—pay tribute to two important individuals

9   *Aulani, a Disney Resort & Spa: Artist Interviews* [video], n.d.

of the area, respected kupuna (elder) Kamokila Campbell and famous seventeenth-century Oʻahu chief Kākuhihewa. Orme's bas-reliefs, which look out toward the ocean and the mountains, are graphic representations of the story of Hina the moon goddess, the famous Polynesian trickster Maui and Hawaiian ocean voyaging.

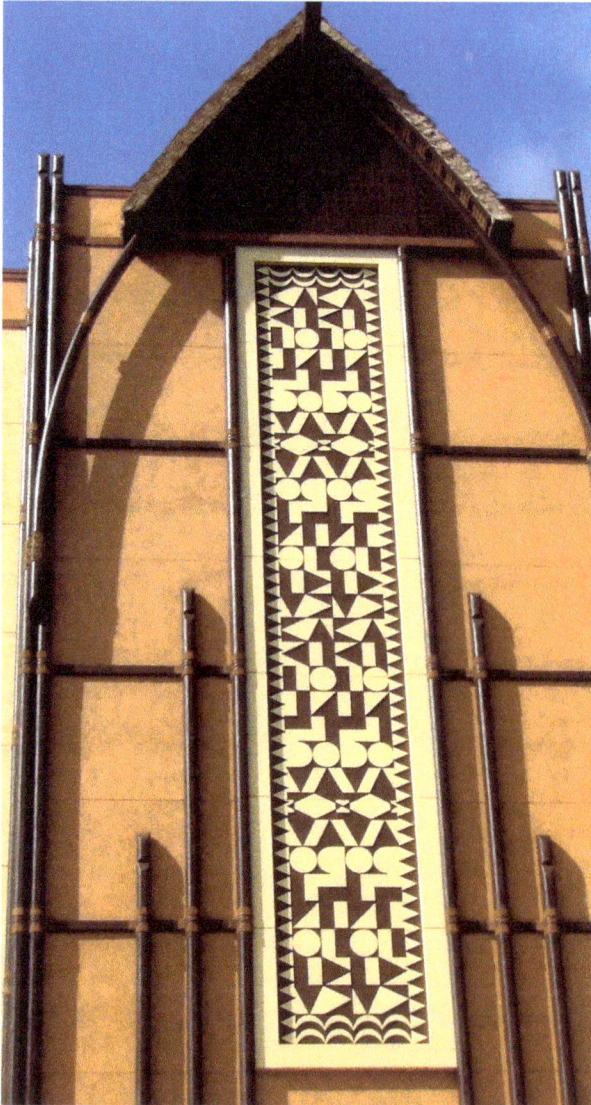

Figure 54. Untitled bas-relief based on a chant composed by Doug Tolentino in honour of the Oʻahu chief Kākuhihewa, by Carl F.K. Pao, 2011.
Source. Photo by Marata Tamaira, 3 November 2011.

Figure 55. Untitled bas-relief based on the story of the demi-god Maui, by Harinani Orme, 2011.

Source. Photo by Marata Tamaira, 3 November 2011.

Flanking the driveway that winds up to the entrance of Aulani, ki'i (sculpted images) by Rocky Jensen, Pat Pine and Jordan Souza stand like sentinels, their carved features a blend of customary and contemporary styles. They are not of the same order as the mass-produced kitsch 'tikis' found in airports, bars, and tourist stores all over Hawai'i and in other parts of the Pacific. Rather, the inspiration behind these works is rooted in the artists having a genealogical connection to the land and a deep understanding and commitment to their cultural heritage. This is what makes these ki'i mana-filled representations of contemporary Kanaka Maoli identity as opposed to rootless imitations. After being welcomed into Aulani's lobby by male and female 'Cultural Greeters'—some Kanaka Maoli, others local non–Kanaka Maoli—attired in beautifully patterned kīhei (cape-like garments worn over one shoulder), the visitor encounters Dalani Tanahy's kapa mural, a series of prints that symbolise the mutual principles of Kū and Hina. In one section of the work, Tanahy depicts Hina through three of the goddess' kinolau (physical manifestations). The top tier represents the different phases of the moon, the tier below represents the feet of the alae (the Hawaiian moorhen, a native bird of the Islands), and the bottom tier represents wana or sea urchin. At the apex of the lobby's cathedral-like transverse arches, Doug Tolentino's acrylic creations relay the epic stories of Pele (goddess of fire) and her sister Hi'iaka (goddess of hula), Kanaloa (god of the sea), and Kāne (god of procreation). Kanaka Maoli artworks are not confined to the resort's central area but also feature in private guest rooms, in the resort's restaurants, in public hallways, and at elevator alcoves. Aulani currently holds one of the largest collections of contemporary Maoli art in the world.

Figure 56. Kapa prints representing the goddess Hina,
by Dalani Tanahy, 2011.

Source. Photo by Marata Tamaira, 3 November 2011.

The complexities of claiming space

In Hawai'i, where Kanaka Maoli artists struggle to find gallery space
in which to exhibit their work, the display of such a large assemblage
of indigenous art at Aulani might be seen as a positive development.
Further, that a Kanaka Maoli perspective suffuses the conceptual and
physical design of the resort is evidence of Disney's willingness to
collaborate with the Native community, something that is lacking
in other tourist venues. But that does not mean that Kanaka Maoli
culture completely avoids being caught in 'a play of illusions and
phantasms'.[10] The lo'i mentioned earlier, for instance, is a simulacrum
in that the kalo plants, while undeniably real, are restricted to plastic
pots rather than being planted in the ground. They grow, but not in
any way that is sustainable—their roots have nowhere to go. A sign

---

10   Jean Baudrillard, 1994, *Simulation and Simulacra*, Ann Arbor: University of Michigan
Press, p. 12.

blocking the path to the loʻi further announces the illusion: 'Cast Members Only'. Further, menehune—a legendary people who are credited with building fishponds and temples throughout Hawaiʻi— are trivialised by the display of small, plastic effigies of them, which are hidden all over Aulani's expansive grounds for guests to find. As for the beach on which Aulani is located, the fine sand is not natural to the area but rather has been imported from Australia to create the lagoon—one of four artificial ones in the Ko Olina complex—which was blasted and dug out in the 1980s when Ko Olina was first being developed. Indeed, Disney's invitation to guests to 'Relax on white sands, delight in gentle ocean breezes and play in peaceful ocean waters' met with the odiferous whiff of reality in April 2013 when Aulani was forced to close its lagoon after 1,000 gallons of raw sewerage spilled into the ocean near Ko Olina.[11] In many ways, within this fog of fantasy, the ability of Kānaka Maoli to lay claim to Aulani as a space in which they can represent themselves is mediated by Disney's biased selection of stories and culture-reducing tropes that correspond with its own tourist selling point of Hawaiʻi as a place of charm and beauty. As a result, other Kanaka Maoli narratives are obscured.

From the hotel room I stayed in at Aulani, I had an unencumbered view of the Leeward Coast from my lanai. A short 16 kilometres (10 miles) away, I could see the communities of Nānākuli and Waiʻanae. Predominantly Kanaka Maoli in terms of demography, both places are socially vibrant and rich in Hawaiian culture. However, they are also sites of economic hardship. The stretch of beach on which they are located has in parts been transformed into a string of 'tent cities' with families of homeless, many of whom are Kānaka Maoli, struggling to survive in a homeland where they can no longer afford housing. Further in the distance I could see Mākua Valley, a place that holds significant symbolic and cultural value for Kānaka Maoli and is the habitat of several endangered Native plants and animals. Since the 1930s, this important cultural site has been used as a target range for US military live-fire training exercises, resulting in the destruction of numerous sacred sites as well as biota found nowhere else on the planet. It goes without saying that these troubling realities are out of joint with the Aulani narrative that, as it says on the resort's official website, invites guests to immerse themselves in 'the legends of the

---

11   *Aulani, a Disney Resort & Spa*, n.d.

islands' so they 'can experience the true enchantment of Hawai'i'.[12] Aulani is just a few miles from Nānākuli, Wai'anae, and Mākua Valley, but once within the walls of the resort, tourists and local visitors alike are transported to an imaginary world far away.

Does this imply, then, that the Kanaka Maoli artists who were commissioned to help tell Hawai'i's story have been co-opted into a Disney rendition of the Islands, one that uses indigenous culture, history and tradition to sell the idea of a paradise that does not exist in reality? Indeed, does the participation of the artists—and the other Kānaka Maoli who collaborated on the project—help naturalise US colonialism in the Islands and neutralise the troubling realities faced by Kānaka Maoli every day? As Haunani-Kay Trask has so acutely observed, 'The political, economic, and cultural reality for most Hawaiians is hard, ugly, and cruel'.[13] On the surface, it could potentially be seen that way, and certainly such readings cannot be discounted. In fact, the participation of Native artists in the Aulani project was the topic of critique in the 2013 Maoli Arts Month exhibition '"a" mini retort', held at the Arts at Mark's Garage in Honolulu. Curated by April Drexel, the aim of the show—which comprised an all–Kanaka Maoli lineup of artists—was to examine the 'existing implications and nuances associated with "imaging" and "imagined" constructs' in specific relation to the characterisation of Hawaiian culture at the Aulani.[14] One artist in particular, celebrated photographer Kapulani Landgraf, produced a strong retort in her installation titled 'Ka Maunu Pololoi? (The Right Bait?)'. The piece itself included over 40 spring-mounted rat traps located on the floor and attached to an entire single wall. Some of the traps were primed with faux money, while others had inkjet photographs of the commissioned Kanaka Maoli artworks at the Aulani fixed in the 'snap'. The printed text on the traps, 'LANI'—which in Hawaiian means heavens, sky, elite, or spiritual—constituted a truncated version of the resort's name. The artist incorporated a stylised arch in the letter 'A' in the text, a visual echo of Aulani's signature marketing logo.

---

12 'The Aulani Story', n.d., *Aulani, Disney Resort and Spa*. Online: resorts.disney.go.com/aulani-hawaii-resort/about-aulani/story/ (accessed 18 February 2016).

13 Trask, *From a Native Daughter*, p. 137.

14 '"a" mini retort', 2013, Arts at Mark's Garage, Honolulu, Hawai'I, 30 April – 1 June.

While the work revealed the bitter ideological divides extant in the Kanaka Maoli arts community regarding Native artistic engagement in the tourist industry in general and resorts in particular, Carl F.K. Pao views the inclusion of Native art at Aulani not as co-option or entrapment but as an articulation of Native agency in which Kānaka Maoli are empowered to tell their own stories and have a say in how their people and culture are represented. Pao notes, too, that although the Aulani artists might have been commissioned to produce works that were commensurate with Disney's vision, it did not prevent them from embedding in the works their own kaona, or hidden meaning. For example, in a series of painted panels he produced for one of Aulani's corridors, Pao depicted the god Kū's many kinolau. One of the motifs he used was a stylised phallus. The artist states, 'It represents one of the manifestations of Kū, but I also use it to symbolize Kanaka Maoli strength and potential in the face of colonialism'.[15] From Pao's perspective, his concealed mo'olelo (story/history) is a strategic intervention in the larger story told by Disney, a Native reality that he believes has potency.

Figure 57. Makahiki mural, by Solomon Enos, 2011.
Source. Photo courtesy of the artist.

---

15   Carl F.K. Pao in interview with author, Honolulu, Hawai'i, 5 August 2012.

Other Kānaka Maoli who participated in the project share Pao's empowering perspective. Fellow artist Solomon Enos created a vibrant mural for the Makahiki restaurant, which depicts the Makahiki ceremony in Mākua Valley.[16] For Enos, the mural manifests a more empowering reality for Mākua than what currently exists: 'So you look at [Mākua] being a military reserve and the health and well-being of cultural and environmental ecosystems are threatened in this environment … [By] drawing it as a thriving community, it becomes that much closer to being a thriving community again.'[17] In speaking about Aulani, Maile Meyer likens it to a loko iʻa (fishpond), a traditional means by which Kānaka Maoli raised fish for food:

> For me, I view those people [i.e., Aulani] as fish in a fishpond feeding our people … That's my metaphor to survive. I think they can be fattened up and feed our people. As long as they stay contained. And, Aulani is a containment to me. As long as they don't make a left out the gate, to me I'm happy. Because they can stay contained, they can bring their dollars, they can help support our people by working the fishpond and by feeding our families with wages. They helped sustain and grow the arts community because as a result of those commissions at least 20 people in this town made enough money in a year or two to be able to choose to do more art if they wanted to … I know that it's reordered the universe because more people are making art.[18]

For Meyer, partnering with corporate entities like Disney is part of a larger strategy not only to feed Kānaka Maoli but also to give them an affirmative presence in their own homeland by showcasing their culture through a rich body of visual artistic expression.

Back to reality

On the final day of my stay at Aulani, I sit in the lobby waiting for my husband to check us out of our suite. It is the early afternoon and I am looking forward to escaping the world of imagination and getting back to reality. We would never in a million years have thought to come to this place for a vacation, but my husband—Carl F.K. Pao, who is featured in this writing—along with several other Kanaka Maoli

---

16   The Makahiki is the Hawaiian New Year that is marked by festivities and peace.
17   Solomon Enos in interview with author, Honolulu, Hawaiʻi, 16 January 2013.
18   Maile Meyer in interview with author, Honolulu, Hawaiʻi, 24 September 2012.

artists received a free three-night stay at the resort. While I wait, I take the opportunity to jot down some more notes about this perplexing place, where pixie dust and Native sand are brought together in seemingly artificial combination. As I write, a young man approaches me and introduces himself. He is one of several Kanaka Maoli hosts who welcome guests as they enter the resort. After chatting with him for several minutes I begin to feel comfortable enough to share my own opinions about the resort, touching on the positive aspects as well as the seeming contradictions. In response, the young man leans in, lowers his voice, and murmurs: 'There's a script [here], but no one's following it.'

At the time, the statement struck me as somewhat incendiary, mutinous even. Thinking about it now, I believe it illustrates one of several agentic ways Kānaka Maoli navigate the tourism milieu in which they find themselves. Whether through not following 'the script', inserting hidden meanings into a visual creation, or 'fishing' out resources to feed the people, this kind of agency and enterprise is part of a Native reality that is currently being played out in places like Aulani. At this point in time, the corporate tourism machine seems to have a permanent foothold in Hawai'i (some might say it is less a foothold and more a stranglehold). Nevertheless, as with all foreign things that have come up on these shores, Kānaka Maoli have found ways to turn flotsam like Aulani into a tool of self-empowerment by using the resort as a space in which to tell the story of Hawai'i from their own perspective, significantly through the visual arts. It remains to be seen, however, just how long they are able to contain the exotic 'fish' that has swum into their waters, before it escapes the enclosure and, as Meyer states, 'make[s] a left out the gate'.

References

'"a" mini retort'. 2013. Arts at Mark's Garage. Honolulu, Hawai'i. 30 April – 1 June.

Aulani, a Disney Resort & Spa: Artist Interviews [video]. n.d. Online: www.popscreen.com/v/5W6Tx/Aulani-a-Disney-Resort-Spa-Artist-Interviews (accessed 11 March 2013, link subsequently removed).

Aulani, a Disney Resort & Spa. n.d. Online: resorts.disney.go.com/aulani-hawaii-resort/activities-amenities/pools-beach/beach/ (accessed 13 August 2013).

Baudrillard, Jean. 1994. *Simulation and Simulacra*. Ann Arbor: University of Michigan Press.

Helu-Thaman, Konai. 1993. 'Beyond hula, hotels, and handicrafts: A Pacific Islander's perspective of tourism development.' *The Contemporary Pacific* 5(1): 104–111.

Mantilla, Nina. 2011. 'The new Hawaiian model: The native Hawaiian cultural trademark movement and the quest for intellectual property rights to protect and preserve Native Hawaiian Culture.' *Intellectual Property Brief* 3(2): 26–41.

'The Aulani Story.' n.d. *Aulani, Disney Resort and Spa*. Online: resorts.disney.go.com/aulani-hawaii-resort/about-aulani/story/ (accessed 18 February 2016).

'The Grand Opening Ceremony for Disney's Aulani Resort & Spa in Ko Olina, Hawaii.' 2011. *YouTube*. 22 September. Online: www.youtube.com/watch?v=UnINYe1jfC8 (accessed 19 February 2016).

Tornatore, Jeanenne. 2011. Orbitz exclusive interview with Joe Rohde, Senior Vice President of Walt Disney Imagineering. *YouTube*. 23 September. Online: www.youtube.com/watch?v=O2stKOSSRF 4&feature=player_detailpage (13 August 2013).

Trask, Haunani-Kay. 1999. *From a Native Daughter: Colonialism and Sovereignty in Hawai'i*. Honolulu: University of Hawai'i Press.

Wilson, Rob. 2000. *Reimagining the American Pacific: From South Pacific to Bamboo Ridge and Beyond*. Durham, NC: Duke University Press.

12

Moving Towers: Worlding the Spectacle of Masculinities Between South Pentecost and Munich

Margaret Jolly

A small *gol* in Germany

On 10 June 2009, outside the austere stone façade of the State Museum of Ethnology in Munich, an unusual construction began to emerge: a latticed wooden tower, tethered with vines, and tapering to the top. Commissioned by anthropologist and filmmaker Thorolf Lipp, this was a quarter-size replica of a land-diving tower, or *gol*.[1] It was fashioned by three men, Betu Watas, Tolak Telkon and Mathias Wataskon, who had been flown from South Pentecost, Vanuatu, to build it for the opening of an exhibition of Lipp's photographs, entitled *UrSprung in der Südsee: An Encounter with the Pentecost Landivers*.[2] They had already spent some weeks in Obergünzburg, a small town in Bavaria, where they had reassembled an *im*, a bamboo and thatch house, replete with bamboo beds and kitchen artefacts, shipped from Vanuatu to complement the South Seas collection in a local museum.

---

1   *Gol* refers both to the tower and event. In Bislama it is called *nanngol*.
2   Thorolf Lipp, 2009, *UrSprung in der Südsee: Begugnung mit den Turmspringurm von Pentecost*.

Figure 58. Betu Watas, Tolak Telkon, and Mathias Watskon building the one-quarter-size model of a land-diving tower in front of the State Museum for Ethnography in Munich, June 2009.

Source. Photographed by Jacob Kapere and used with permission.

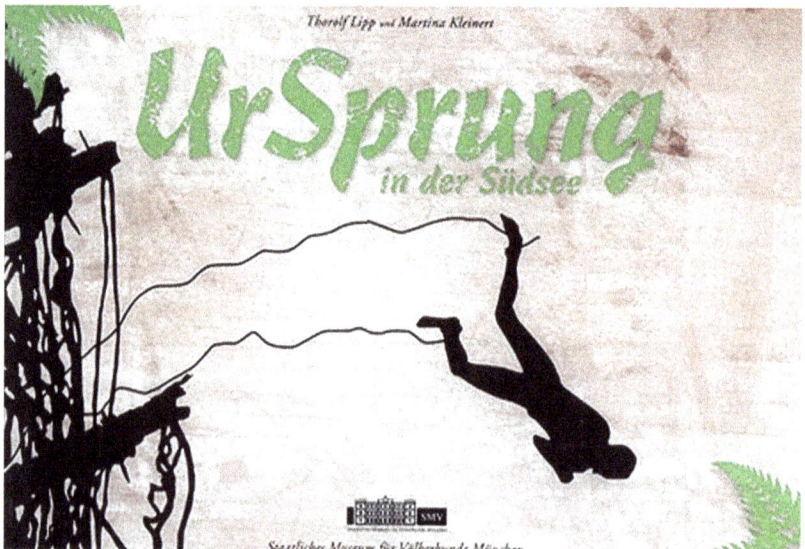

Figure 59. *UrSprung* brochure.

Source. Brochure in author's library.

I met the three men there, and talking in Bislama and a smattering of Sa[3] (the *tok ples* that I learnt during several sojourns in South Pentecost from 1970), heard that they had relished the deep green Bavarian landscape, the pristine streams and the local rural hospitality with its abundance of German bread and beer. On 4 June, they had also attended the closing of an exhibition of Pentecost Island *jubwan* masks from Lipp's collection, at Iwalewa-Haus in Bayreuth. We then moved on to Munich where, while the tower was being constructed, Thorolf had arranged for the men to camp in a small caravan at the back of the museum. Every night kava sessions preceded takeaway meals from pizza bars and Asian restaurants. On their days off from building the tower, we toured the city thronged with holiday crowds, climbed up bell towers and on Sunday joined the packed congregation in the opulent central Catholic cathedral. These three men were not world travellers; only one of them had left Vanuatu before, as a seasonal worker to New Zealand. They spoke neither German nor English, only Bislama and Sa. Though looked after well by Lipp and his partner Martina Kleinert, and accompanied and supported on their travels by Jif Jacob Kapere, Head of the Film Unit at the Vanuatu Cultural Centre (VKS), they were sometimes visibly apprehensive. This was not just because they were inexperienced travellers, but because of events back in South Pentecost in the months before their departure. Some of the details were divulged and fleshed out over lunch one day in a beer hall.

3   Bislama is the lingua franca of Vanuatu, a variant of Melanesian Pidgin. Sa is the language spoken in South Pentecost by approximately 2,700 speakers today. According to Murray Garde, it has five distinct dialects, thus manifesting great internal diversity. It is the subject of ongoing research by Murray Garde, Nicholas Evans and another scholar under an ARC Laureate Fellowship awarded to Nicholas Evans, 'Wellsprings of Linguistic Diversity', which commenced in July 2014.

Figure 60. The caravan behind the museum in Munich.
Photographed by Lamont Lindstrom, 9 June 2009.

Thorolf Lipp's main interlocutor and confidante in Bunlap village, Bebe Malegel, a middle-aged, healthy man, had died suddenly in March 2009. Some thought he was killed by sorcery; some suggested this was at the behest of his uncle, Jif Telkon Watas.[4] (Others later told us that Bebe had exceeded his authority and had been killed by an *armwat ensanga*, a malevolent ancestral spirit, angered by Bebe's plan to export both the *im* and the *gol*.)[5] The descriptions of his death and burial offered by the trio of men in Munich were circumspect if gruesome. They said Bebe Malegel was buried very quickly after his death and, oddly, that blood was seeping through the pandanus textiles (*baji*) in which his body was wrapped, suggestive of foul play or sorcery.

---

4   Jif Telkon Watas is also known by his last title, Liusbangbang.

5   This was the dominant explanation I was offered during a visit to Bunlap in April 2013, admittedly by close kin of Jif Telkon Watas. Still some of them were critical of his long residence away from Pentecost, in Erakor near the capital Port Vila, and his presumption of a monopoly on custodianship and brokerage of the *gol*. Lipp refrains from repeating such allegations, stating only apropos the death of Bebe Malegel, his dear friend and Jif Telkon's opponent, that 'all circumstances indicate that it did not have a natural cause'. See Guido Carlo Pigliasco and Thorolf Lipp, 2011, 'The islands have memory: Reflections on two collaborative projects in contemporary Oceania', *The Contemporary Pacific* 23(2): 371–410, p. 397. As this chapter goes to press I have just become aware of a recent book edited by Martina Kleinert and Thorolf Lipp in German, entitled *Auf Augenhöhe? Von Begegnungen mit der Südsee und angewandter Ethnologie* but have not been able to consider this here.

Figure 61. Kava preparation.
Photographed by Lamont Lindstrom, 9 June 2009.

Figure 62. Lunch at the beer hall.
Photographed by Lamont Lindstrom, 9 June 2009.

Bebe Malegel, together with several other high-ranking men in Bunlap, had agreed to collaborate with Lipp to build a *gol* in Munich to celebrate this iconic spectacle of *kastom* from Pentecost and Vanuatu, and to help promote exhibitions of Lipp's films and photographs and his collection of *jubwan* masks. This plan to build a small tower in Munich had been violently opposed by Jif Telkon Watas, in Lipp's words, 'still the most influential and feared man of Bunlap',[6] even though he had been living since 1995 in the peri-urban village of Erakor Haf Road on the outskirts of Port Vila. When the men originally scheduled for the trip to Munich arrived in Port Vila in January 2009 to secure passports and visas, Telkon informed the police, the Vanuatu Cultural Centre and the Malvatumauri (the National Council of Chiefs) to try to prevent them departing. He made angry comments to the press and on television that alleged both theft of national heritage, and of his own cultural property, since he claimed control of the *kastom* of the *gol* and did not approve of this model tower being built overseas. Lipp suggests a majority of men at a village meeting in Bunlap decided

---

6   Pigliasco and Lipp, 'The islands have memory', p. 393.

the Munich project should proceed,[7] but, cowed by Telkon's violent public opposition and perhaps fearing that they may suffer the same fate as Bebe Malegel, several high-ranking men who were due to depart for Germany withdrew.

And so alternative arrangements proceeded in secret; the three men who did dare venture to Munich were from South Pentecost but then resident in Port Vila, and were rather younger, and not influential *kastom* leaders. After consultations with Ralph Regenvanu, then Director of the Vanuatu Cultural Council, and with Jacob Kapere of the Vanuatu Cultural Centre (VKS) Film Unit, Lipp decided to risk continuing with the German visit. Arrangements were well advanced, Lipp had the support of the VKS and the Malvatumauri and it seemed mutually advantageous to confront Telkon's threats and erode his monopolistic control over the export of the *gol*. This was despite many cautions from critics in Germany: that Lipp was promoting a 'cultural zoo', exploiting an exotic, eroticised spectacle[8] and that his aims of 'reverse anthropology' and reciprocal empowerment were vitiated by unequal relations with illiterate, unworldly men. Some even suggested that the punning title of the exhibition *UrSprung* (origin, jump into life) resonated with dubious German notions of a 'mythic consciousness'.[9] Many warned that continuing with the project risked further conflict, even death. But he decided after much soul-searching to continue: 'This was not the moment to stop, it was the moment to continue',[10] in order to break what he saw as Telkon's presumptuous chiefly authority, a desire he also imputes to those three men who dared to go to Munich, who were, he suggests, 'outraged by what had happened in Bunlap'.[11] After some personal anguish about the ethics and the politics of this tragic situation, Lamont Lindstrom and I, who were both attached to CREDO[12] in Marseille at the time, decided to join the group to offer sympathy and moral support, and to witness the worlding of this spectacular masculine performance.

---

7   Ibid., p. 397; email from Thorolf Lipp to author, 22 May 2009.
8   Pigliasco and Lipp, 'The islands have memory', p. 386.
9   Ibid., p. 385.
10   Ibid., p. 398.
11   Ibid.
12   This is the acronym for Centre de Recherche et Documentation sur l'Océanie based at the Université de Provence and funded by both Centre National de le Recherche Scientifique (CNRS) and L'ecole des Hautes Etudes en Sciences Sociales (EHESS).

There was an extraordinary paradox at the heart of this bitter conflict since Jif Telkon Watas himself had already been involved in exporting the *gol,* not as a small replica but in full scale, complete with divers, to places overseas (to Australia and to Japan) and to other islands in the archipelago. He had arranged for many men and women to travel to the island of Espiritu Santo and to construct a model village and *gol* tower during the making of the execrable B-grade movie *Till There Was You* in 1990.[13] Many people from Bunlap village were employed to act as extras, but since the producers did not pay extra money for the right to photograph the land dive, the tower was torn down on Telkon's instructions. The Pentecost Island Council of Chiefs had vigorously opposed this relocation of the *gol.* Later, in 1995, Jif Luke Fargo from Londot village (near Wali) on the west coast of Pentecost built a tower in Santo but was opposed by the Kaonsel blong Turism blong Saot Pentikos (Tourism Council of South Pentecost, which ironically he had set up) and by Jif Telkon, his erstwhile collaborator and business partner. That case occasioned a dispute about intellectual property rights put to the Malvatumauri and Luke Fargo was ordered to pay 100,000 vatu (US$1,058)[14] and several pandanus textiles for attempting this internal export of the *gol.*[15]

Since tourist land dives performed by people from the *kastom* villages of the southeast were first initiated in the early 1970s, Jif Telkon was one of the main beneficiaries of the revenue from such performances and payments from foreign filmmakers during the annual season between April and June. Lipp suggests that he was demanding US$25,000 for filming a single land dive in the southeast, a more remote, 'exotic' and thus more expensive location than the west coast.[16] But he was not the only one. There were and are many rival male entrepreneurs in Christian villages, especially on the more accessible west coast, as Lipp documents in detail,[17] and as I witnessed

---

13   John Seale (director), 1990, *Till There was you,* written by Michael Thomas.
14   All conversions are as at 26 January 2014, rather than contemporaneous.
15   Miranda Forsyth, 2012, 'Lifting the lid on "the community": Who has the right to control access to traditional knowledge and cultural expression', *International Journal of Cultural Property* 19: 1–31.
16   Pigliasco and Lipp, 'The islands have memory', p. 393. He also observes that Jif Telkon was the major recipient of 600,000 vatu for the making of the documentary soapie *The Bunlaps.*
17   Thorolf Lipp, 2008, *Gol. Turmspingen auf der Insel Pentecost in Vanuatu. Beschreibung und Analyse eines riskanten Spektakels* (Gol: Land Diving on the Island of Pentecost in Vanuatu: A Description and Analysis of a Risky Spectacle), Berlin: Lit Verlag, p. 266 ff.

on a visit to Pentecost in April 2013: near the airport at Lonorore, at Panngi, Panlimsi, Randoa, etc. Some say Jif Telkon passed the knowledge of the land dive originating in the sacred site of Rebrion near Bunlap village to Luke Fargo.[18] But there is also evidence of far earlier entrepreneurial activity from the 1950s to sell the spectacle as a commodity for foreigners and tourists on the part of influential men from the Anglican and Church of Christ villages from the south and west coasts.[19]

The extraordinary sequence of events in 2009 surrounding the Munich *gol* followed the untimely death of ni-Vanuatu cameraman Hardy Ligo, filming the *gol* in South Pentecost for *National Geographic* in 2008. On that occasion, the tower collapsed under the weight of the film crew and heavy equipment and three other South Pentecost men were killed or seriously injured.[20] This happened despite a moratorium imposed on such filming of the *gol* by the Vanuatu Cultural Centre (VKS) in 2006; it seems this was regularly ignored or circumvented.[21] So, performing the land dive has become a very risky business, in both Pentecost and foreign locales. Although the element of male risk-taking and youthful daring has long been an integral aspect of the ritual, its reconfiguration as a tourist commodity and as contested intellectual and cultural property has amplified those risks enormously, through a spiralling vertigo of contesting masculinities.

---

18   Forsyth, 'Lifting the lid on "the community"', p. 18; Murray Garde, 2015, '"Stories of long ago" and the forces of modernity in South Pentecost', in *Narrative Practices and Identity Constructions in the Pacific Islands*, ed. Farzana Gounder, pp. 133–52, Amsterdam: John Benjamins, Studies in Narrative series.
19   Lipp, *Gol. Turmpsingen auf der Insel Pentecost in Vanuatu*, p. 266.
20   Margaret Jolly, fieldwork notes, April 2013.
21   As Tabani reports since Ligo was a ni-Vanuatu TV cameraman, the VKS moratorium did not apply to him. He reports, allegations that Ligo was bribed to film the *gol* by the Australian production company Beyond Productions acting on behalf of the National Geographic Society. See Marc Tabani, 2010, 'The carnival of custom: Land dives, millenarian parades and other spectacular ritualizations in Vanuatu', *Oceania* 80(3): 309–28, p. 326n15.

Map 2. Vanuatu and inset in relation to Australia.
Source. © Australian National University Cartography, CartoGIS 08-087.

Map 3. Pentecost Island showing villages.

Source. Patricia Siméoni, 2009, *Atlas du Vanouatou* (Vanuatu), Port Vila: Éditions Géo-consulte, p. 49 and used with permission.

Ambivalences

I must confess to a deep-seated ambivalence about the *gol*. This ambivalence has its origins deep in my formation as a feminist anthropologist. As a young woman conducting doctoral research in the *kastom* communities of the southeast from the early 1970s, I relished living with these feisty, anti-colonial and anti-Christian folk.[22] But at first I was humiliated by the contrast powerful male leaders such as Telkon's late elder brother Bumangari Kaon, better known as Bong, made between myself, seemingly a young, weak, white woman from Australia, and Kal Muller, a strong, mature man and filmmaker from that mythical country, America, who had lived in Bunlap for some months just before my arrival in 1970. He had not only made a film (the profits of which were promised to be locally shared, yet proved elusive) but he was the first white man to jump from the tower, wearing the *pipis*, the pandanus penis wrapper, a sign of strong men of *kastom*. That spectacle was revealed in his article in *National Geographic*.[23]

When I walked with scores of *kastom* people from several villages in the southeast for the erection of one of the first towers for tourists near Lonorore airport in 1972, like all local women I was forbidden to see the tower being constructed (a ban that I noticed did not extend to short-haired female tourist agents from Port Vila). But, in a classic backhander, I was assured by my adopted father that this was because, speaking the language so well, I was now an *êsên na ôt lo*, a woman of the place. 'How would you feel Margaret if your brother fell from the tower?'[24] Given these rather sensitive gender dynamics during my doctoral research, and my disquiet about the early impacts of commoditisation of the *gol* as a tourist spectacle, it is perhaps understandable that I did not share the ebullient enthusiasm of some male observers: tourists, filmmakers, anthropologists.[25]

---

22   Relations have changed since to a more ecumenical ethos and *kastom* people might now be better described as non-Christian rather than anti-Christian.
23   Kal Muller, 1970, 'Land diving with the Pentecost Islanders', *National Geographic* 1138(6): 796–817.
24   See Margaret Jolly, 1994, '*Kastom* as commodity: The land dive as indigenous rite and tourist spectacle in Vanuatu', in *Culture – Kastom – Tradition. Developing Cultural Policy in Melanesia*, ed. Lamont Lindstrom and Geoffrey White, pp. 131–44. Suva: Institute of Pacific Studies, University of the South Pacific, p. 143n5.
25   See Margaret Jolly, 1994, *Women of the Place*: Kastom, *Colonialism, and Gender in Vanuatu*, Philadelphia: Harwood Academic Publishers; Jolly, '*Kastom* as commodity'.

Most of my knowledge about how the tower is constructed is thus derived not from observation or participation, which is possible only for men, but from conversations with local men and women and from several foreign men who were able to witness it: François Le Fur in 1902,[26] Elie Tattevin,[27] a Marist priest of the early twentieth century, Kal Muller in the 1960s,[28] and most recently in extraordinary detail Thorolf Lipp, in his book *Gol das Turmspringen auf der Insel Pentecost in Vanuatu*.[29] I will not attempt here to offer the details of how the *gol* has changed historically, nor the complexities of Lipp's rather provocative exegeses and critiques of all those who have interpreted the *gol* in the past and his own uncertain conclusion that it is primarily a risky spectacle, a game more than a ritual.[30] However, I agree with him that the *gol* is a multi-layered phenomenon that defies facile interpretations of it as a compulsory initiation rite or a necessary display of youthful masculinity. Here I rather pursue some earlier thoughts apropos how performances of the land dive evince relational masculinities,[31] historically changing and contested, among indigenous men and between indigenous men and foreign men. This is inseparable from how *kastom* has become commodified and converted into 'property', intellectual or cultural, and the fact that custodianship is increasingly seen less as a collective heritage, and more as the 'ownership' of individual powerful men, who promote their chiefly rights to control.[32]

---

26   Paul Monnier, 1991, *L'eglise catholique au Vanuatu*. Port Vila: Mission Mariste, p. 15.

27   Élie Tattevin, 1927, 'Sur les bords de la mer sauvage', *Revue d'Histoire des Missions* 4: 82–97, 407–429, 557–59; Élie Tattevin, 1929, 'Mythes et Légendes du Sud de I'île Pentecôte', *Anthropos* 24: 983–1004; Élie Tattevin, 1931, 'Mythes et Légendes du Sud de I'île Pentecôte', *Anthropos* 26: 489–512, 863–81.

28   Kal Muller, 1970, 'Land diving with the Pentecost Islanders', *National Geographic* 1138(6): 796–817; and Kal Muller, 1971, 'Le Saut du Gaul dans le sud de l'île de la Pentecôte, Nouvelles-Hébrides', *Journal de la Societe des Oceanistes* 32: 219–234.

29   Thorolf, *Gol. Turmpsingen auf der Insel Pentecost in Vanuatu*. I am indebted to Sabine Hess who completed an abbreviated translation and a distillation of the main content of this book in 2012.

30   I simply observe that in his tables summarising previous approaches it is hard to reconcile his telegraphic exegeses with the arguments presented by the authors. See Lipp, *Gol. Turmpsingen auf der Insel Pentecost in Vanuatu*, pp. 36 and 396.

31   Jolly, '*Kastom* as commodity'; Margaret Jolly, 2008, 'Introduction. Moving masculinities: Memories and bodies across Oceania in Re-membering Oceanic Masculinities', *The Contemporary Pacific* 20(1): 1–24.

32   See Siobhan McDonnell, 2013, 'Exploring the cultural power of land law in Vanuatu: Law as a performance that creates meaning and identities', in *Grounding Travelling Concepts: Dialogues with Sally Engle Merry about Gender and Justice*, ed. Hilary Charlesworth and Margaret Jolly, *Intersections: Gender and Sexuality in Asia and the Pacific*, issue 33; Siobhan McDonnell, 2016, 'My land my life: Power, property and identity in land transformations in Vanuatu', PhD thesis, The Australian National University.

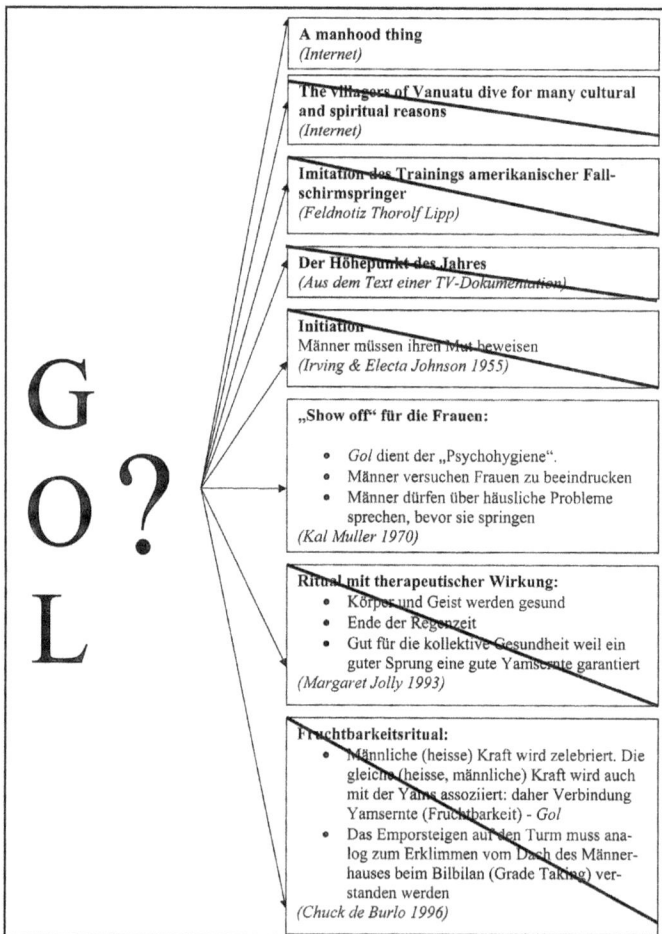

Figure 63. Lipp's table expounding and critiquing earlier approaches.
Source. Lipp, 2008, *Gol. Turmpsingen auf der Insel Pentecost in Vanuatu*, table 30, p. 396.

Dun na ngamômô: The origin of *gol*

To explain most *kastom* practices in South Pentecost—the origin of life and of death, of sexual difference, the separation of the household dwelling and the men's house—outsiders and anthropologists, like young children, are usually told a *dun na ngamômô* a 'story of long ago'.[33] These stories are typically performed by older people,

---

33   Garde, '"Stories of long ago" and the forces of modernity in South Pentecost'.

men and women, and are usually punctuated with poignant songs, in both everyday and archaic exotic/language, led by the main storyteller who is then joined in chorus by the surrounding audience. These are both didactic and immensely pleasurable shared aesthetic experiences.[34] A pivotal story in the rich Sa corpus of verbal arts is the *dun na gol*: the story of land diving, which explains why men engage in such an arduous construction every year and jump from its dizzying heights with only lianas tied to their ankles.

As Lipp records[35] and Garde consummately analyses,[36] there is not one story but several versions, indeed several competing stories of the origin of the land dive.[37] Yet the gendered dynamics of the land dive are palpable in all versions. Here is a telegraphic summary of a short, simple version:

---

34 See Margaret Jolly, 1999, 'Another time, another place', *Oceania* 69(4): 282–99; Margaret Jolly, 2003, 'Spouses and siblings in Sa stories', *The Australian Journal of Anthropology* 14(2): 188–208. Let me here briefly lament that Lipp fails to acknowledge either of these papers, in which I consider not just the diversity of versions of *dun* but historical transformations in origin stories collected by Tattevin and myself. See Lipp, *Gol. Turmpsingen auf der Insel Pentecost in Vanuatu*. For excellent studies from PNG see Alan Rumsey and Don Niles (eds), 2011, *Sung Tales from the Papua New Guinea Highlands: Studies in Form, Meaning, and Sociocultural Context*, Canberra: ANU E Press.

35 Lipp, *Gol. Turmpsingen auf der Insel Pentecost in Vanuatu*, p. 303ff.

36 Garde, '"Stories of long ago" and the forces of modernity in South Pentecost'.

37 Murray Garde discerns the following elements in all versions of *dun na gol*:
1. a husband and wife were in an unsatisfactory relationship
2. after much disputation the wife flees
3. the husband pursues the wife and she climbs up a tall tree
4. the husband follows her up the tree
5. the woman ties vines/aerial roots/coconut palm leaf fibre around her ankles
6. when the husband lurches to grab her she jumps out of the tree
7. the husband falls and with nothing to restrain him, he hits the ground and dies but the woman is saved by her vines
8. others reflect on how the woman was saved and they copy her.

See Garde, '"Stories of long ago" and the forces of modernity in South Pentecost', pp. 3–4. There are also many variations based on region and on the speaker. See Garde, '"Stories of long ago" and the forces of modernity in South Pentecost'; Lipp, *Gol. Turmpsingen auf der Insel Pentecost in Vanuatu*. Some specify that the wife feels pain in sex, is held against her will or beaten by the husband; some specify that the husband is lazy or deformed. Some versions detail a banyan tree and liana restraints; others a coconut tree and palm leaf ties. In condensed versions the husband simply falls and dies; in other fuller versions (often told in *kastom* villages in the southeast, as in Telkon's long version of September 2012), the wife brings him back to life to satisfy her desires, whipping each successive part of his body in turn, and singing a song that revives him even, in some versions, reanimating his penis, ensuring a more fulfilling domestic life. The concluding credo varies too: sometimes men usurp control so that women do not expose their genitals jumping in grass skirts, which fly upwards; sometimes it is claimed that having outwitted men, women rather handed over this clever ploy. In the version told by Jif Telkon Watas, he declared that women insisted that the sign of its female origins should remain in the 'lips of the vagina', which is a crucial part of the supporting wooden struts for each platform.

A woman was living with her husband Tamlie but found his sexual desires excessive and violent. She decided to leave him and climbed a banyan tree to escape. He zealously pursued her up the tree. She tied lianas around her ankles and, as he reached out to grab her, she jumped and saved herself. He jumped after her but, with no restraints, he hit the ground and died. Men telling this version often conclude, 'Since then things have been the right way up, men jump from the tower and women dance in adoration underneath.'

Figure 64. *Gol*—tapering to the top or 'head' of tower.
Source. Photographed by Murray Garde, Wali, south-west Pentecost, 5 June 2004.

Gol refers to both the tower itself and the performance of the dive. The tower is usually between 20–30 metres high, made of logs in a lattice construction and, as constructed in Bunlap (*gol abri*), tapering at the top. Lipp argues that the dominant form in the past as recorded by Tattevin was built around the trunk of a large tree.[38] The ground around the tower should be sloping and is cleared and sifted scrupulously of hard objects, readying it for the tower to grow, and men to dive, just as the ground is sifted for the planting of long yams. Diving platforms are added at successive heights.

---

38   Lipp, *Gol. Turmpsingen auf der Insel Pentecost in Vanuatu*, pp. 234–35.

The tower is conceived of as a human body (although *gol* is not the word commonly used for the body, which is rather *tarben*; the whole tower can be called *tarbe gol*).[39] The tower has legs and knees, a belly, breasts, neck, shoulders, armpits and a head. I was told by several men that it embodied the spirit of an ancestor. Some said it was Tamlie, that hapless first male diver. Others said it was Sêngêt from whose body different kinds of yams emerged: long yams from his back, protuberant yams from his fingers, red yams from his blood.[40] Yet despite a resident male spirit, sensed in the crackling noises of the tower and tinglings on the skin of the divers, the *gol* is manifestly a bisexual body. The different parts of its several diving platforms are sexually differentiated: the central log is the shaft of the penis, the surrounding supports, the lips of the vagina.

Young boys and younger men dive from the tower at successive heights. There is no compulsion for men to perform the land dive, it is a matter of personal preference and, as both Lipp and I attest,[41] many high-ranking and powerful men have not. In my experience, there is no shame in not jumping, even if the diver comes to the end of the platform and then decides not to jump (although more recently other observers have noted some tough persuasion if not coercion of young boys). But the jump should be a graceful swallow dive, head first and with arms held tight to the chest and body well clear of the tower. On the higher levels, other men can help the diver by ensuring his ropes are not caught, impeding a smooth dive. The divers are freed from their hanging lianas by older men, often fathers or brothers, who check to see they are not hurt, embrace them and celebrate a successful leap.

---

39   A linguistic note from Murray Garde. 'It is interesting that in the case of the *gol* tower, you can use the human third person singular possessor *tarbe-n* "its body" because the tower is given human-like status.' If it were thought of as a tree it would rather be: *tenlê bôtôa* 'trunk of a tree'. Email to author 16 February 2015.

40   Jolly, *Women of the Place*, p. 66; see Telkon Watas and Murray Garde, 2012, *Dun na gol*, transcribed and translated by Murray Garde, filmed by Kim McKenzie, September. In Jif Telkon Watas's story, *senget* is not a proper name of a male ancestor but the generic word for a person covered in sores with rotting fingernails (perhaps a reference to the skin condition psoriasis or, my editor Jack Taylor suggests, an old decaying yam?).

41   Lipp, *Gol. Turmpsingen auf der Insel Pentecost in Vanuatu*; Jolly, *Women of the Place*, p. 242.

Figure 65. *Gol*—a diver poised to jump from the middle of the tower.
Source. Photographed by Murray Garde, Wali, South Pentecost, 5 June 2004.

Figure 66. *Gol*—a diver in full flight.
Source. Photographed by Murray Garde, Wali, South Pentecost, 5 June 2004.

This is a spectacle primarily directed at the men and especially the women who are dancing underneath. Women are forbidden to see the tower until its construction is complete and the spirit inhabits its body. Men must refrain from sexual relations with wives or lovers before they dive, or risk their platform breaking and their lianas snapping. But the presence of women is crucial to the final spectacle:

dressed in their best white grass skirts made of banana spathe rather than pandanus, with perfumed leaves adorning their bodies, they perform dances of celebration after each successful dive, sometimes mothers and sisters (but never wives), embracing divers as they touch the ground, cradling croton leaves and towels as if they were surrogate babies, chanting and whistling loudly, in a piercing style, uncannily like a wolf whistle. These are beautiful black male bodies on display, and diving evinces not just their athletic power and courage but their sexual appeal to women, their virility and fertility.

Despite Lipp's attempt to disarticulate the land dive and the yam harvest,[42] I am persuaded that there is a crucial link between the two, at least for *kastom* people. Indeed, this was stressed by all my interlocutors and is a central motif in the long epic version of the *dun na gol*, as performed by Jif Telkon Watas for Murray Garde and the late filmmaker Kim McKenzie in September 2012. In this instance, clutching a yam as a prop, Jif Telkon Watas declared and then repeated that, 'the land dive was created in relation to yams'.[43] The yam cycle still structures the Sa calendar in South Pentecost (even now when the dry seems to be starting later; as people told us during a very wet April in 2013—*klaemet i jenis* (the 'climate is changing')). The tower is built when the yams are ready to harvest and the lianas are drying out. This ensures that the vines have the right springy tensility to hold the diver and ensure he does not rebound too far and hit the body of the tower. Indeed *kastom* people in the southeast are to this day critical of their Christian kin on the west coast who start tourist land dives too early, before yams have been ritually harvested, and blame the increase in injuries and accidents on reckless disregard of these rules and the pursuit of profit.[44]

---

42 Lipp, *Gol. Turmpsingen auf der Insel Pentecost in Vanuatu*, p. 396.
43 Garde, '"Stories of long ago" and the forces of modernity in South Pentecost'; Watas and Garde, *Dun na gol*.
44 This is highlighted in Telkon's epic version: 'If you do not respect the part that the yams play, you will be injured.' This seems to suggest that the yams themselves are animated agents that can harm. As Garde notes, this means waiting to harvest the yams first. This is usually done by the *loas na dam*, the yam specialist who has the expertise to initiate the harvest with spells and magical techniques. For five days after this no one can leave or enter the village. Murray and I were subject to this stricture on our visit to Bunlap in April 2013, and waited on the west coast at Baie Homo till we could safely walk in. Then the cutting of the timber for the towers should follow, 10 days after the new moon in April. These strictures are not followed so closely by Christian people and thus the critical link to yams is not made. See Garde, '"Stories of long ago" and the forces of modernity in South Pentecost', p. 10.

During my doctoral research I was told that, despite the obvious real risks of concussion, injury and death, diving was masculine bodily therapy after the aches of the rainy season. The yam is the canonical symbol of the male body and especially the penis in the competitive cultivation of the long yam, *dam bis*. There is an intimate connection in myths and this ritual between long, strong yams and men's fertile bodies. Like the grade-taking rituals in which both men and women can rise in rank, assuming higher titles, it is a prime occasion for young men to impress young women with their beauty and strength. Some men in pursuit of particular lovers whisper love magic before they dive and drop special leaves that they hope their desired partners will catch.

But, the spectacle of masculinity that is on display in *gol* is a fiery, hot, youthful masculinity, evincing the muscular athleticism and the power to take risks that was epitomised in the past by young warriors or *bwari*. The frequent internecine raids and battles that prevailed in South Pentecost up until the 1920s were ended by that process of colonial conquest paradoxically called 'pacification'. Without suggesting a functionalist hydraulics of male fluids,[45] I suggest that some of the energies and values of masculinity associated with warfare in the past have flowed into the *gol*. But this is not the most privileged or hegemonic form of masculinity.[46] That was and is associated rather with the cool wisdom of the peacemaker, the *warsangul*, the high-ranking man, or the *jif* (chief) who can mediate and settle disputes. These opposed but hierarchically structured figures—'men of war' and 'men of peace'[47]—were in the past linked with seasonal cycles (while taking titles there should be no wars and vice versa), echoing the alternating powers of the God of War (Kū) and the God of Peace (Lono) in Hawai'i. In South Pentecost, men of peace typically eclipsed men of war.

---

45   See Margaret Jolly, 2001, 'Damming the rivers of milk? Fertility, sexuality, and modernity in Melanesia and Amazonia', in *Gender in Amazonia and Melanesia: An Exploration of the Comparative Method*, ed. Thomas A. Gregor and Donald Tuzin, pp. 175–206, Berkeley: University of California Press.

46   See R.W. Connell and James W. Messerschmidt, 2005, 'Hegemonic masculinity: Rethinking the concept', *Gender and Society* 19(6): 829–59.

47   See Margaret Jolly, 1991, 'Gifts, commodities and corporeality: Food and gender in South Pentecost', *Canberra Anthropology* 14(1): 45–66; Jolly, *Women of the Place*; and Margaret Jolly, 2016, 'Men of war, men of peace: Changing masculinities in Vanuatu', in *Emerging Masculinities in the Pacific*, ed. Aletta Biersack and Martha Macintyre. *The Asia Pacific Journal of Anthropology*, 17(3–4): 306–323.

Figure 67. A young man wearing a penis wrapper and bark belt about to dive, epitomising hot, youthful masculinity

Source. Photographed by John Taylor, Pentecost, 9 June 2007.

Colonial reconfigurations: The French Resident Commissioner and Queen Elizabeth II

Clearly the indigenous significance of the *gol* has radically changed over the century or more from when it was first witnessed by the Marist priests like Elie Tattevin in the early twentieth century.[48] But the most profound transformations derive from its performance as a tourist spectacle from the early 1970s. In the past only a few towers were built each year, the *gol* was produced for internal consumption and then destroyed and used for firewood. Today, despite attempts both by the VKS and local authorities to restrict the number of *gol* to a few per season, there may be 20 or 30 performed at several rival sites during the dry season from April through June, where the audience is primarily paying tourists, filmmakers and anthropologists, and where the tower is sometimes recycled for later performances. I have earlier traced the origins of this commoditisation of *kastom* to two critical events in the colonial period, both of which reveal crucial gender dynamics at work.[49]

The first is described both in oral history and documents in the colonial government archives. In 1952, there was a rumour spread by a Church of Christ convert that a 'cargo cult' was spreading amongst the *kastom* adherents of Bunlap and adjacent villages.[50] The conjoint colonial authorities were so fearful of a violent anti-colonial revolt that they dispatched both British and French troops who made a nocturnal raid on Bunlap. They thought they saw signs of preparation for war but rather witnessed arrangements for a major grade-taking

---

48   Following Lipp, Tabani, notes the transformation over several decades from the form described by Tattevin where branches of a banyan tree served as diving platforms to the construction of a tower in *gol abwal*. See Lipp, *Gol. Turmpsingen auf der Insel Pentecost in Vanuatu*; and Tabini, 'The carnival of custom', p. 321. Tabini speculates that the towers constructed by the American forces to train parachutists in World War II may have been a model for the latter form. Though Lipp rejects this hypothesis as tourist gossip (pp. 395–96), Tabani insists that the speculation needs to be seriously considered. Certainly Lindstrom and Tabani have both shown how ritual spectacles now indigenous to Tanna have been dramatically shaped by external influences and especially the American presence, most notably the pervasive drilling, the red cross and the telegraph wires of the John Frum movement in its several manifestations.

49   Jolly, '*Kastom* as commodity'.

50   Jolly, *Women of the Place*, pp. 45–48.

ritual.[51] They arrested several old men, including Meleun Tamat, the father of Bumangari Kaon (Bong) and Liusbangbang (Telkon Watas), and imprisoned them in a copra dock at the Catholic mission station of Baie Barrier. Several younger men offered themselves in lieu of their fathers, and were later imprisoned in Port Vila. Some say that the man who spread the rumour confessed that he did so in order to get *kastom* people to convert and the young men were thus freed and he was rather imprisoned. Others say the then French Resident Commissioner Pierre Anthonioz offered that their sentences be commuted if these young men organised a land dive for him to watch.[52] A *gol* was built and performed and the divers were paid three blocks of stick tobacco in recompense. This important historical event was recalled in a chant I heard sung in the 1970s at land dives, the words of which celebrated the power of black men over white men.

The second is a story circulated locally and on the internet about the performance of the *gol* for Queen Elizabeth II on 16 February 1974.[53] At the urging of the British colonial administration, the people of Point Cross, a village of Anglican adherents of the Melanesian Mission, agreed to perform the *gol* for the royal visit. This was organised by Kiliman, who in this instance refused to allow a performance in Port Vila and required the Queen to come to Pentecost. Despite this insistence, it was still the wet season, and the lianas were too slack. One diver from Point Cross was desperately unlucky; both his lianas broke, he fell and broke his back and later died in hospital. There was intense speculation about the causes of this tragic occurrence. Some said the diver had slept with his girlfriend the night before, and was thus cursed. The dominant explanation in Bunlap, however, was that this was a sign of the incapacity of weak Christian men to perform

---

51   In his report of this event, Tabani observes, based on a conversation with me, that it was a 'Warsangul initiatory ceremony during which very large quantities of goods are ostentatiously accumulated'. See Tabani, 'The carnival of custom', p. 313. I would, however, like to clarify this issue, as this is a curious representation of what I said; *warsangul* ceremonies are not initiations but rather entail men and women taking titles and though they involve display and exchanges of taro and tams, pigs and pandanus titles, they do not occasion 'ostentatious accumulation'. For a detailed description of such ceremonies, see Jolly, *Women of the Place*, p. 173ff.

52   See Pierre Anthonioz, 1953, 'La danse du Gaul dans le sud de l'île de Pentecôte', *Mission des isles* 46: 6–7; Pierre Anthonioz, 1954, 'La danse du Gaul, céremonie rituelle de l'île Pentecôte', *Etudes Mélanésiennes* 8: 92–95.

53   I must apologise for an error in the date in earlier publications: Jolly, *Women of the Place* and '*Kastom* as commodity'. Heartfelt thanks to my colleague Gregory Rawlings for pointing this out. The official record of Queen Elizabeth's visit to the New Hebrides is 15–16 February 1974.

the *gol*: they said it was dangerously mistimed in the middle of the wet season and the men constructing the tower lacked the knowledge and technical expertise to build it properly, and to select appropriate lianas. This infamous incident therefore fuelled the already existing divisions between *kastom* and Christian peoples in the early 1970s. When I returned to Pentecost in 1977, following this incident, Bumangari Kaon shared his outrage with me, suggesting that it made the men diving appear like 'circus animals'.

Cosmetic *kastom* and commodities

But as I intimated in my paper '*Kastom* as commodity'[54] and Lipp records in fine detail,[55] the history of Christians performing the *gol* is far more complex and varied than that suggested by oral historians in Bunlap. In fact, Oskar Newman, the Australian planter based at Malakula, hearing of the *gol* performed for Pierre Anthonioz by Bunlap men in 1952, commissioned a *gol* by men of Point Cross about 1955. In that instance, several New Zealand and Australian guests paid £300 each. Following the success of that event, around 1957 Newman commissioned a second when 40 Americans paid £500 each. Around the same time, in 1954, the American adventurers Electra and Irving Johnson filmed a land dive performed at Lonorore near the airport and Thevenin's plantation. In this instance, contrary to the current aesthetic of 'full *kastom*', the men can be seen wearing shorts.[56] They also took about 1,600 still photographs. Some years later, in 1971, men from Point Cross performed a *gol* at Aligo in North Pentecost to raise funds for building a Melanesian Mission (Anglican) church in the south. This was three years before the notorious and tragic performance for Queen Elizabeth II.

The prior examples given above demonstrate that the *gol* was already being thoroughly 'worlded' in the immediate post–World War II period. The involvement of Christian and *kastom* villagers in *gol* oriented to outside guests and commercial purposes spread far more widely following the organisation and filming of a *gol* by Kal Muller

54 Jolly, '*Kastom* as commodity'.
55 Lipp, *Gol. Turmpsingen auf der Insel Pentecost in Vanuatu.*
56 See Irving Johnson and Electra Johnson, 1955, 'South Seas incredible land divers', *National Geographic* January: 77–92.

in Bunlap village in 1969. His film and a related *National Geographic* article converted the land dive into an international media spectacle,[57] soliciting the involvement of tour companies, and the large upmarket hotel in Port Vila, Le Meridien. But there was a crucial difference in the land dive filmed by Muller.[58] It not only involved a white man diving in a *pipis*, it also entailed the cosmetic recreation of an exotic, authentic *kastom*. No more shorts; men must wear only the *pipis* or penis wrapper with bark belts and women only their best *ra is* or grass skirts. Locals say he forbad women to carry towels or manufactured cloth (with which they often dance) and even tried to prevent women wearing safety pin earrings, a feminine fashion preference in South Pentecost long before the punk style fashionable in the US, UK and Australia in the 1970s. This cosmetic recreation of *kastom* was also adopted by those in Christian villages. They either hired people from the *kastom* villages to perform the dives, songs and dances, or else swapped their shirts and shorts and *aelan dres* for those iconic signs of *kastom*: the penis wrapper and the grass skirt.[59] This is not without a sense of discomfort and even shame on the part of Christian villagers. In Bunlap in the 1970s, corrugated iron roofs (*im kap*) were forbidden and when such structures were later built in *kastom* villages they were often covered up with thatch or palm leaves for the eye of the tourist and the eye of the camera.[60]

In the decades since, complex patterns of both collaboration and rivalry have emerged between those in *kastom* and Christian villages. *Kastom* men from Bunlap led by Jif Telkon Watas reinstructed Christian men in the practice but also sought to hold their own *gol* in Christian villages on the west coast, which were far more accessible to tourists coming by boat or air. There was concern about Christians 'stealing' *kastom*

---

57   Muller, 1970, 'Land diving with the Pentecost Islanders'.

58   Tabani notes that Muller acknowledges he was looking for cultures scarcely touched by European civilisation, but fails to note the tension between the exclusion of all visible European influences and the fact of Muller himself participating in the rite, an enactment of going native that Tabani dubs 'a Hollywood fantasy worthy of Tarzan films'. See Tabani, 'The carnival of custom', p. 314.

59   See Margaret Jolly, 2014, 'A saturated history of Christianity and cloth', in *Divine Domesticities: Christian Paradoxes in Asia and the Pacific*, ed. Hyaeweol Choi and Margaret Jolly, pp. 429–54, Canberra: ANU Press.

60   On a French film team in Bunlap in 2002, see Lipp, *Gol. Turmpsingen auf der Insel Pentecost in Vanuatu*, p. 81; and on 'photogenic authenticity', see John Taylor, 2010, 'Photogenic authenticity and the spectacular in tourism', *La Ricerca Folkorica*, special issue *Indigenous Tourism and the Intricacies of Cross-Cultural Understanding* 61: 33–40.

and having to share the profits, but the advantages were also clear. The collaboration between Jif Telkon Watas and Luke Fargo of Londot resulted in *gol* being performed at Panlimsi, Londot and Wali and near Panas on the west coast between 1976 and 1990. They collaborated but regularly fell out over money. Fargo established the Kaonsel blong Turism Blong Saot Pentikos in 1983, and was successively involved with several tourist agencies: Tour Vanuatu, Island Holidays and Island Safaris. There was also a revival of *gol* by Catholic villagers at Wanur in the south and in the villages north of Baie Barrier. Their remote location on a turbulent coast made tourist accessibility even more difficult than Bunlap, so they shifted to Rangusuksu on the west coast. But in many of these west coast land dives, *kastom* people were still hired for diving, dancing and singing.

In the early 2000s, when Lipp and Martina Kleinert spent five months in Bunlap, there were about 30 land dives per season, with several being performed at one site in successive weeks. There have been attempts both by the state through the VKS and by local associations to regulate the number of land dives per year. In 2011 there was a widely publicised dispute between the Kaonsel blong Turism Blong Saot Pentikos (South Pentecost Tourism Council), which planned 26 dives that year, and the Council of Chiefs of South Pentecost, who decided there should be just four. At this point Jif Telkon Watas was the chairman of the Council of Chiefs and claimed that only it had the customary authority in the matter. There are also material reasons for restricting the number of dives: in many locales the *gol* is only performed if there are sufficient bookings. The interests of filmmakers have also spiralled and many film crews have made movies both before and after the VKS moratorium of 2006.[61]

---

61 The moratorium was justified on the grounds of conserving the natural resources used for the dive, preserving the traditional knowledge and transmitting it to younger generations and promoting a co-ordinated plan whereby revenues generated by commercial activities were 'properly channelled into sustainable development appropriate to the needs of the communities of this region'. Vanuatu Cultural Centre website, www.vanuatuculture.org (accessed 4 May 2006).

The *gol* has today become a lucrative and burgeoning business. Tourists pay a different price depending on context; some passengers on large cruise ships pay only about 2800 vatu (about US$30) per person. But the shipping companies have had to pay millions of vatu for jetties, landing rights and the right to watch and film. Package deals for tourists travelling from Port Vila with return flights and an overnight stay cost 33,900 vatu (US$359) in 2002, 38,900 vatu (US$412) in 2004 and 47,600 vatu (US$504) in 2006.[62] Filmmakers pay far more, for example a French team of seven filming in 2004 paid 1 million vatu (US$10,526) for a two-week stay. Lipp and his partner Martina Kleinert paid 600,000 vatu (US$6,316) to live in Bunlap and to film and photograph in 2002 and 2004.[63] There are regularly disputes and scandals about the proportional distribution of this money between all participants: those who are the custodians of the land where the dive is held, the divers and the entrepreneurial organisers, like Jif Telekon Watas. The latter regularly commandeered the largest amount, although there have been attempts to change this and to direct the funds into projects of sustainable development such as water tanks and building projects. An association called PonWaHa was set up in Wanur with this in mind and ostensibly Bebe Malegel and his collaborators in Bunlap were striving for something similar. Another association 'Holding Nagol na Wawan Association' emerged from a meeting at Salap village in October 2008. This was expressly to debate issues about 'ownership' of the *gol*.[64] Significantly, whereas in the period of my doctoral research the tower was usually named for the man who dived from its *bôtôn/bwôtôn*, or head (e.g. *gol na Iya, gol na Watas*), today the tower is more usually known by the name of the male entrepreneur who is the main organiser or 'boss' of the tower.

---

62 Lipp, *Gol. Turmpsingen auf der Insel Pentecost in Vanuatu*, pp. 294–95.
63 Ibid., p. 295.
64 Garde, '"Stories of long ago" and the forces of modernity in South Pentecost', p. 11.

Figure 68. Tourists witnessing a *gol* on the west coast of Pentecost.
Source. Photographed by John Taylor, Pentecost, 9 June 2007.

A carnival of commodities? Cultural custodianship, intellectual property and emergent male individualism

The *gol* is now absolutely entangled with money, as tightly as the vines are lashed onto its logs. For some this entanglement is a sign of a 'carnival of *kastom*';[65] of how culture has become reified as *kastom* and how commoditisation promotes emergent inequalities. There is no doubt that what was likely a ritualised indigenous spectacle in the past has become an aestheticised commodity spectacle performed primarily, if not exclusively, for tourists. But to see this as 'inauthentic', or as cultural degeneration, presumes a view of culture as a timeless, pure whole.[66] It suggests a romantic view of culture as eternal, beyond the worlding of historical change and ultimately reinscribes a vision of culture as unsullied by time or external influences, in a way uncannily akin to the rhetoric and visual lures of much tourist promotion.

Moreover, in this case the emergent inequalities deriving from the commoditisation of *kastom* provokes contesting masculinities in newly risky and sometimes deadly ways. And this again is not just local but worlded. This engages ni-Vanuatu men emerging as individualist entrepreneurs aspiring to control their 'intellectual' or 'cultural property' on Pentecost Island in the context of new national and global regimes of heritage and of copyright. It also involves those who are attempting to control and sometimes suppress the business and perceived corruption from Port Vila, or even as far away as Munich. It engages those white men who have become fascinated from a distance, those who have witnessed it as a spectacle in the flesh or on the screen and have imitated the performance either in its indigenous form (like Kal Muller or Karl Pilkington in a hilarious satire as *An Idiot Abroad* on YouTube, viewed over 75,000 times). Or those who have participated in the extreme global sport of bungee jumping. This congregation includes more distant culture brokers who have facilitated and fuelled its status as an iconic national and global spectacle and those who have criticised and attempted to corral it. My own work, including this text, is surely an integral part of

---

65 Tabani, 'The carnival of custom'.
66 Margaret Jolly, 1992, 'Specters of inauthenticity', *The Contemporary Pacific* 4(1): 49–72; Tabani, 'The carnival of custom', p. 310.

such a process of worlding. But I suggest the gendered nature of the *gol* itself exerts a dynamic and dangerous allure that remains fundamentally masculine.

So, in conclusion, let me elaborate my arguments in the light of recent appraisals of the *gol* by Marc Tabani, Miranda Forsyth and John Taylor. I agree with Tabani that there has been an aestheticisation of an 'authentic' *kastom* at work here and that there are crucial contests since the *gol* is iconic not just of Pentecost but of Vanuatu and its tourist branding.[67] As Tabani insists the *gol* is promoted by diverse governments in Vanuatu as a symbol par excellence of 'traditional knowledge and expressions of culture' (TKEC), as formulated by UNESCO.[68] This was clear in dealings with Alan Hackett, who although he long acknowledged the inspiration of *gol* in bungee jumping, insisted that his technical innovations warranted intellectual property patents.[69] The worth of his business is now estimated at about US$80 million. A legal case of breach of intellectual property rights against Alan Hackett, was not just a claim for compensation by people from Pentecost but became a national concern articulated by the Vanuatu Prime Minister and the Attorney General in 1995. These contests both within the archipelago and with overseas entrepreneurs likewise have a markedly masculine character: they are contests between men for control over a supremely masculine spectacle.

I also agree with Forsyth that there are incredible tensions between competing approaches to intellectual and cultural property.[70] These contests are complex and intense, engaging national, regional and global regulation, especially since the formation of the World Intellectual Property Organization (WIPO) in 1999 as a United Nations instrument and the recognition of both traditional knowledge (TK) and Traditional Cultural Expressions (TEC) as a basis for UN Conventions, regional treaties and charters and national legislation in

---

67 Tabani, 'The carnival of custom'.
68 Ibid., p. 316.
69 Alan Hackett a New Zealander entrepreneur, long interested in extreme sports popularised bungee (or bungy) jumping, first by jumping off bridges in his native country in 1986 and then by a jump from the Eiffel Tower in 1987. He first used a parachute harness but later developed an ankle harness with an extremely elastic cord. He established bungee jumping sites in Queenstown, NZ, and later Australia, France, Germany, Indonesia and the US. His autobiography chronicles his contributions to adventure tourism. See John Alan Hackett, 2006, *Jump Start. The Autobiography of Bungy Pioneer A.J. Hackett*, Auckland: Random House.
70 Forsyth, 'Lifting the lid on "the community"'.

the Pacific.[71] Forsyth warns against the assumption that recognising TK perforce means recognising property rights. She argues that reified ideas of *kastom* and 'community' occlude the political contests and disputes going on within and between peoples in this diverse cultural region. As we have seen, this is palpable in recent contests about the *gol* within and beyond Pentecost. We have also witnessed how these local contests are articulated with contests involving state and global agencies: 'Indigenous people are not immune from seeking to capitalize on control over traditional knowledge in order to commodify it and profit from it, and state laws and foreign purses can become very effective tools in manipulating claims by one individual against another.'[72]

Moreover, the local use of the language of 'property' for the *gol* is akin to the property claims and use of state legal powers with the commoditisation of indigenous land as real estate by powerful male leaders and *jifs*, especially on the island of Efate.[73] It names a novel power asserted by individual male entrepreneurs who claim the authority, often as chiefs to own and control the *gol* as theirs. Witness the strenuous claims by Jif Telkon Watas to protect not just his financial but his cultural capital invested in the *gol* as a right derived from his pre-eminent authority as a chief. Even as agents of the state portrayed him as an avaricious even unworthy *jif*, they had to acknowledge the pervasive legitimacy of chiefs in the post-colonial state and the growing legitimacy of the concepts of intellectual and cultural property, ever since the debate about a national Copyright

---

71 See Tabani, 'The carnival of custom'; and Forsyth, 'Lifting the lid on "the community"', for details of these. Forsyth, discerns three distinct initiatives apropos the TK of the *gol*: the *sui generis* initiative adopted in Vanuatu's Copyright Act formulated in 2000 but not gazetted till 2011; the cultural industries initiative; and that grounded in the ICH Convention, which aims to safeguard intangible cultural heritage for the benefit of all humanity. These diverse approaches have different implications for the locus of ultimate control and the concentration and spread of financial benefits. Forsyth summarises their divergent emphases thus: the *sui generis* legislation that presumes no defining characteristics is aimed to prevent misappropriation and commercialisation, the cultural industries approach is focused on commercialisation and the ICH convention is predominantly about preservation. She discerns crucial tensions between them in how they deal with political and practical issues in the fraught relation between commerce and culture, and who they empower at local, national and regional levels.

72 Forsyth, 'Lifting the lid on "the community"', p. 3.

73 See McDonnell, 'Exploring the cultural power of land law in Vanuatu: Law as a performance that creates meaning and identities'; McDonnell, 'My land my life: Power, property and identity in land transformations in Vanuatu'. I thank Siobhan McDonnell for crucial insights here. I have had the benefit of reading her published and forthcoming papers as well as chapters from her fine PhD thesis, recently awarded.

Act from 2000. The debate was rather about who had the power to control and regulate and on what basis. All of the contenders were men, from local and regional *jifs* to national judges, cultural custodians and politicians.

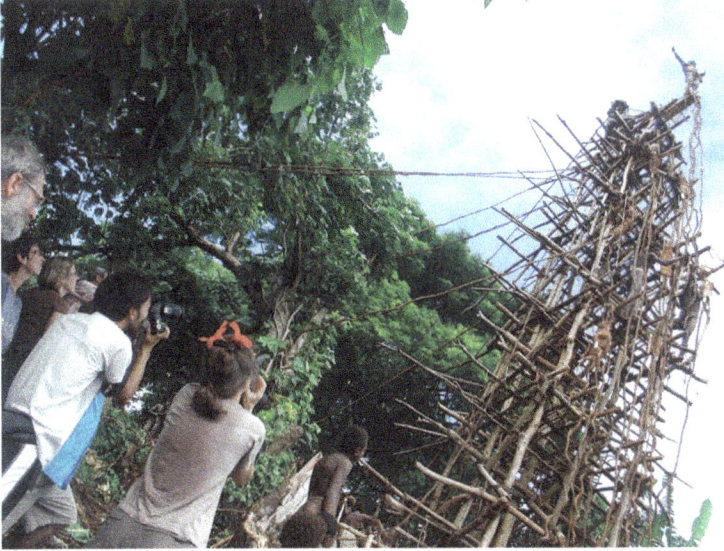

Figure 69. Spectators, necks craning upwards, and feeling 'uncannily disempowered' or 'small' underneath the tower.

Source. Photographed by John Taylor, Pentecost, 9 June 2007.

John Taylor has, in an innovative article, rather looked at the intersubjective character of the performance of *gol* based on his first-hand experiences between 2000 and 2008.[74] He suggests that it is more than just an exotic spectacle or 'staged authenticity', whereby locals and tourists are 'unwilling puppets performing a gaudy dance on the fingertips of some nebulously conceived "'tourism industry"'.[75] I agree. Such a view is demeaning of both and fails to take into account the extraordinary corporeal energy and emotions experienced by divers and spectators alike, with pulses racing and, from the viewpoint of scopophiliac spectators, necks craning upwards, and feeling 'uncannily disempowered' or 'small' underneath

---

74   John Taylor, 2010, 'Photogenic authenticity and the spectacular in tourism', *La Ricerca Folkorica*, special issue *Indigenous Tourism and the Intricacies of Cross-cultural Understanding* 61: 33–40.

75   Ibid., p. 38.

the tower (in the words of a fellow male tourist).[76] He highlights his sense not just of exotic difference but of human sameness in the shared experience of risk, of fragility, impermanence and ultimate transcendence. He celebrates this sense of connection *with* rather than of racial and cultural difference *from* the male divers as he stands being photographed with them after the event they mutually experienced. But, crucially, both the sense of sameness and difference is here again experienced in a canonically masculine mode.

But finally I return to Jif Telkon and to that bitter dispute with Thorolf Lipp about his right to control the *gol* and its worlding. In the pages of *The Contemporary Pacific*, Lipp published a dialogue with Guido Pigliasco on their twin projects of 'collaboration' in contemporary Oceania.[77] Here Lipp reflects on the events of 2009 and how his connection with the Bunlap community was hampered by Jif Telkon's presumptuous, violent authority. Here Lipp portrays Jif Telkon as mythologising and exploiting his chiefly ancestry as a natural right, observing that his promises to use profits for communal development on the island had rarely eventuated. He stresses that Jif Telkon Watas left the island of Pentecost long ago, and 'returns only sporadically to Bunlap'.[78] There is no doubt that even close kin of Telkon in Bunlap chafed at his continuing chiefly authority over them; on our visit to Bunlap in April 2013 some labelled him 'man Efate'. Yet, as a man making money from *kastom*, he seemed to attract more opprobrium than his Christian kin, rival custodians of the *gol*. Engagement with the commodity economy seems to fit more comfortably with being a Christian man, for whom cashcropping and small business have long been a valued way of making a living, and does not seem to compromise their legitimacy as ni-Vanuatu men or as chiefs in a way similar to men of *kastom*. Moreover, Lipp acknowledges the moral peril of condemning Jif Telkon Watas for 'having attitudes on which our own society is largely built'.[79]

---

76 Ibid., p. 36.
77 Pigliasco and Lipp, 'The islands have memory'.
78 Ibid., p. 393.
79 Ibid., p. 394.

But in the pages of that scholarly journal (which Telkon could not read), Lipp went rather further to discredit his authority:

> Telkon clearly was the 'local custodian' of the *gol*, but his knowledge about it, compared to that of other *kastom* Sa, was not very elaborate. Nor did learning more about this heritage, its history and its diverse meanings – for the sake of just knowing and potentially preserving it – occur to him as something positive or necessary.[80]

This suggests the moral superiority of those who learn about and preserve *kastom* as a value in itself (ni-Vanuatu *filwokas*, foreign anthropologists?) as against those for whom there is a practical even a pecuniary interest.[81] As far as I know, Telkon was not aware of this published critique but it is intriguing that with failing health and the prospect of his own imminent mortality, he chose to perform and record for posterity his own epic version of the *dun na gol*.

A small *gol* at Erakor Haf Rod

This extraordinary epic was performed at Erakor Haf Rod, and recorded by Murray Garde and the late filmmaker Kim McKenzie, on 28 September 2012. Murray and Kim arrived to find Telkon and his son, Warisus, dressed in their best penis sheaths and bark belts with pigs' tusks glistening on their breasts, palpable signs of their high rank. They had erected a small replica of the *gol* about three metres high, not unlike that which was erected outside the museum in Munich. This tower was meticulous in its use of materials, its geometry, and in the details of its platforms and struts. As he spoke, Telkon clutched a yam to stress the intimate imbrication of growing yams and making towers, visibly moving those who jumped and those who watched with the thrill of a masculine spectacle. He then proceeded to tell a very long story, which artfully linked other *dun na ngamômô* to the *gol*. The transcript of those words in Sa, and English translation runs to 48 pages.[82] It was not only a long but a very elaborate epic.

---

80 Ibid., p. 393.
81 Ibid., p. 394. This seems to neglect the material and personal career benefits of doing anthropology and making films.
82 Watas and Garde, *Dun na gol*.

Figure 70. Jif Telkon Watas clutching a yam and his son Waris Sus.
Source. Still from film of Kim McKenzie, 28 September 2012, courtesy of Murray Garde.

Following Garde's consummate analysis we can distil some of the crucial features of this telling.[83] Telkon linked the site of the original tower to Rebrion, the place where the first human beings (all men) emerged and where one was converted to a woman, Sermop, through the agency of hot chestnuts.[84] He tied this story to that of Singit, a man whose body was the origin of yams of all kinds. The sacred site of Rebrion is one over which his *buluim* (place-based descent group) claims custodianship and control.[85] Telling the story or the history of the origin in this way was also a claim to precedence or even originary ownership, not just of that place but the practice of the *gol*. Telkon concluded his epic with the words: '*nê ae nê bos natê, nê mbe bos na gol Vanuatu*' (I, I am the boss of it; I am the boss of the *gol* of Vanuatu).

In other contexts where different versions of the *dun na gol* have been told there has been much discussion over which one is 'true'. At a community meeting of the Wawan Association of South Pentecost in 2011 where five versions of *dun na gol* were told, the version told by

---

83   Garde, '"Stories of long ago" and the forces of modernity in South Pentecost'.
84   See Jolly, *Women of the Place*, pp. 141–43; Jolly, 'Spouses and siblings in Sa stories'.
85   Garde also notes a link between this claim to origin and that of Luke Fargo of Londot, but since this is restricted knowledge that cannot be detailed here.

Jif Telkon was seemingly supported by most of the 26 communities represented.[86] The idea of 'truth' or authenticity here seems to combine both the idea of a spatio-temporal origin and of a compelling telling. But, as Garde shows, the conversion of oral narratives into texts also imparts an air of 'authenticity' detached from the original contexts. Telkon's version, which was over 4,000 words, had been typed up and circulated at that meeting in 2011. And in the version filmed by Garde and Mackenzie in September 2012, Telkon frequently cited that written text of his own prior telling, to give more details that he did not choose to repeat and were thereby imbued with undisputed authority. As Garde astutely observes for Telkon's narrative, the Sa word for 'we' changes: the exclusive form *gema* is used when he references close kin and the truth of the story is seen as contestable; the all inclusive form *kêt* is used to refer to 'all of us' when an uncontestable truth is articulated.[87]

In my own experience and that of Murray Garde, Sa-speaking people young and old, have been keen to get copies of Elie Tattevin's texts published in the early twentieth century (1915, 1929, 1931) as seemingly dispassionate, disembodied evidence that might be valued not just as heritage or cultural capital but rhetorical weapons in disputes.[88] After I recorded contemporary versions of *dun na ngamômô* during my doctoral research, I circulated copies of Tattevin's texts locally. More recently we gave copies of these texts to Bong Désiré, a talented Francophone interlocutor from Baie Barrier who has worked closely with Murray Garde over many years. The other main genre of stories, *dun na buluim*, are far more restricted in their telling and circulation and are crucial in contests over custodianship and use of land till today. The varieties of telling of origin stories of long ago, such as the origin of life or sexual difference are not nearly so consequential although they may serve individual strategic interests.[89] But contests about how to best tell the story of the land dive are now we see

---

86   Garde, '"Stories of long ago" and the forces of modernity in South Pentecost', p. 11.

87   I discerned a similar pattern in recordings of dispute meetings in Sa in the 1970s as litigants moved from expressing disputes based on contestable grounds (*gema*, an exclusive 'we') to expressing an all inclusive consensus (*kêt*, the inclusive 'we') emerging with a successful conclusion to a meeting.

88   Élie Tattevin, 1915, 'A l'ombre des ignames. Mythes et légendes de l'île Pentecôte', *Les Missionnes Catholiques* 47: 213, 226–27, 236–37; Tattevin, 'Mythes et Légendes du Sud de I'île Pentecôte'; Tattevin, 'Mythes et Légendes du Sud de I'île Pentecôte'.

89   See Jolly, 'Spouses and siblings in Sa stories'.

potentially a deadly combat. This combat is not just between local men as individualist entrepreneurs but articulates these contests with broader national and global relations.

His performance of a novel epic of the *gol* was a claim to pre-eminent custodianship and control by Jif Telkon Watas. He says as much. In the 18 months after this film was made his health deteriorated rapidly and, since neither the medicine of *kastom* nor the hospital in Port Vila had delivered a cure or indeed much relief, we heard late in 2013 that he had gone home to Pentecost, to Bunlap, close to Rebrion, where his life and indeed all life began. He died there on 8 January 2014. The world he had imagined and fashioned through the travels of *gol* thus returned home too.

Acknowledgements

My heartfelt thanks to the people of South Pentecost for welcoming me with such hospitality, familarity, and good humour, first as a young woman in the 1970s and more recently as an old woman or *jiwit*. Particular thanks to the late Jif Telkon Watas for his epic recording of the *dun na gol* with Murray Garde and the late Kim McKenzie. Murray has been an exceptional colleague and I thank him greatly for his rigour, empathy, generosity and wit on our travels together between Canberra, Vila and Pentecost. A huge thanks to Sabine Hess for the excellent distillation and translation of Lipp's German text. Thanks are also due to several colleagues for close readings and suggestions on this essay in various iterations, including Chris Ballard, Miranda Forsyth, Murray Garde, Siobhan McDonnell, Greg Rawlings, Lamont (Monty) Lindstrom and John (Jack) Taylor, my editor. Thanks to Murray, Monty and Jack for permission to use their photographs in this volume and to the copyright holders of other images. I also benefited greatly from discussions of this paper in the Reading and Writing Group of our Laureate Project, and when I presented it at the Australian Anthropological Society meetings in Canberra, 6–8 November 2013, in The Australian National University Anthropology series on 5 March 2014, and in a much shorter version at the European Society for Oceanists in Brussels in July 2015. All errors and infelicities remaining are mine. This research was generously funded by The Australian National University and the Australian

Research Council Laureate Fellowship 'Engendering Persons, Transforming Things: Christianities, Commodities and Individualism in Oceania' (FL100100196).

References

'An Lianen in die Tiefe.' 2009. *Süddeutsche Zeitung*, June. Online: www. sueddeutsche.de/muenchen/voelkerkundemuseum-muenchen-an-lianen-in-die-tiefe-1.97914 (accessed 4 March 2016).

Anthonioz, Pierre. 1953. 'La danse du Gaul dans le sud de l'île de Pentecôte.' *Mission des isles* 46: 6–7.

———. 1954. 'La danse du Gaul, cérémonie rituelle de l'île Pentecôte.' *Etudes Mélanésiennes* 8: 92–95.

Connell, R.W. and James W. Messerschmidt. 2005. 'Hegemonic masculinity: Rethinking the concept.' *Gender and Society* 19(6): 829–59.

Forsyth, Miranda. 2012. 'Lifting the lid on "the community": Who has the right to control access to traditional knowledge and cultural expression.' *International Journal of Cultural Property* 19: 1–31.

Garde, Murray. 2015. '"Stories of long ago" and the forces of modernity in South Pentecost.' In *Narrative Practices and Identity Constructions in the Pacific Islands*, ed. Farzana Gounder, pp. 133–52. Amsterdam: John Benjamins, Studies in Narrative series.

Hackett, Alan John. 2006. *Jump Start. The Autobiography of Bungy Pioneer A.J. Hackett*. Auckland: Random House.

Jolly, Margaret. 1981. 'People and their products in South Pentecost.' In *Vanuatu: Politics, Economics and Ritual in Island Melanesia*, ed. Michael Allen, pp. 269–93. Sydney and New York: Academic Press.

———. 1991. 'Gifts, commodities and corporeality: Food and gender in South Pentecost.' *Canberra Anthropology* 14(1): 45–66.

———. 1992. 'Specters of inauthenticity.' *The Contemporary Pacific* 4(1): 49–72.

——. 1994. *Women of the Place:* Kastom, *Colonialism, and Gender in Vanuatu.* Philadelphia: Harwood Academic Publishers.

——. 1994. '*Kastom* as commodity: The land dive as indigenous rite and tourist spectacle in Vanuatu.' In *Culture – Kastom – Tradition. Developing Cultural Policy in Melanesia,* ed. Lamont Lindstrom and Geoffrey White, pp. 131–44. Suva: Institute of Pacific Studies, University of the South Pacific.

——. 1999. 'Another time, another place.' *Oceania* 69(4):282–99.

——. 2001. 'Damming the rivers of milk? Fertility, sexuality, and modernity in Melanesia and Amazonia.' In *Gender in Amazonia and Melanesia: An Exploration of the Comparative Method,* ed. Thomas A. Gregor and Donald Tuzin, pp. 175–206. Berkeley: University of California Press.

——. 2003. 'Spouses and siblings in Sa stories.' *The Australian Journal of Anthropology* 14(2): 188–208.

——. 2008. 'Introduction. Moving masculinities: Memories and bodies across Oceania in *Re-membering Oceanic Masculinities.*' *The Contemporary Pacific* 20(1): 1–24.

——. 2014. 'A saturated history of Christianity and cloth.' In *Divine Domesticities: Christian Paradoxes in Asia and the Pacific,* ed. Hyaeweol Choi and Margaret Jolly, pp. 429–54. Canberra: ANU Press. Online: press.anu.edu.au/publications/divine-domesticities (accessed 4 March 2016).

——. 2016. 'Men of war, men of peace: Changing masculinities in Vanuatu.' In *Emerging Masculinities in the Pacific,* ed. Aletta Biersack and Martha Macintyre. *The Asia Pacific Journal of Anthropology,* 17(3–4): 306–323.

Johnson, Irving and Electra Johnson. 1955. 'South Seas incredible land divers.' *National Geographic* January: 77–92.

Kleinert, Martina and Thorolf Lipp (eds). 2015. *Auf Augenhöhe? Von Begegnungen mit der Südsee und angewandter Ethnologie.* Berlin: Reimer.

Lipp, Thorolf. 2008. *Gol. Turmpsingen auf der Insel Pentecost in Vanuatu. Beschreibung und Analyse eines riskanten Spektakels* (Gol: Land Diving on the Island of Pentecost in Vanuatu: A Description and Analysis of a Risky Spectacle). Berlin: Lit Verlag.

——. 2009. *UrSprung in der Südsee: Begugnung mit den Turmspringurm von Pentecost.* Online: www.ursprung-in-der-suedsee.de (accessed 24 February 2015).

——. n.d. *Immaterielle Kulture im Museum. Die Turmspringen von Pentecost besuchen Indstrom Deutschland.* Berlin: Reimer.

McDonnell, Siobhan. 2013. 'Exploring the cultural power of land law in Vanuatu: Law as a performance that creates meaning and identities.' In *Grounding Travelling Concepts: Dialogues with Sally Engle Merry about Gender and Justice,* ed. Hilary Charlesworth and Margaret Jolly. *Intersections*: *Gender and Sexuality in Asia and the Pacific,* issue 33. Online: intersections.anu.edu.au/issue33/forsyth. htm (accessed 4 March 2016).

——. 2016. 'My land my life: Power, property and identity in land transformations in Vanuatu.' PhD thesis. The Australian National University.

Monnier, Paul. 1991. *L'eglise catholique au Vanuatu.* Port Vila: Mission Mariste.

Muller, Kal. 1970. 'Land diving with the Pentecost Islanders.' *National Geographic* 1138(6): 796–817.

——. 1971. 'Le Saut du Gaul dans le sud de l'île de la Pentecôte, Nouvelles-Hébrides.' *Journal de la Société–des Océanistes* 32: 219–234.

Pigliasco, Guido Carlo and Thorolf Lipp. 2011. 'The islands have memory: Reflections on two collaborative projects in contemporary Oceania.' *The Contemporary Pacific* 23(2): 371–410.

Rumsey, Alan and Don Niles (eds). 2011. *Sung Tales from the Papua New Guinea Highlands: Studies in Form, Meaning, and Sociocultural Context.* Canberra: ANU E Press. Online: press.anu. edu.au/publications/sung-tales-papua-new-guinea-highlands (accessed 23 April 2016).

Siméoni, Patricia. 2009. *Atlas du Vanouatou* (Vanuatu). Port Vila: Éditions Géo-consulte.

Tabani, Marc. 2008. *Une pirogue pour le paradis. Le culte de John Frum à Tanna* (Vanuatu). Paris: Editions de la Maison des Sciences de l'Homme.

——. 2010. 'The carnival of custom: Land dives, millenarian parades and other spectacular ritualizations in Vanuatu.' *Oceania* 80(3): 309–28.

Tattevin, Élie. 1915. 'A l'ombre des ignames. Mythes et légendes de l'île Pentecôte.' *Les Missionnes Catholiques* 47: 213, 226–27, 236–37.

——. 1927. 'Sur les bords de la mer sauvage.' *Revue d'Histoire des Missions* 4: 82–97, 407–429, 557–59.

——. 1929. 'Mythes et Légendes du Sud de I'île Pentecôte.' *Anthropos* 24: 983–1004.

——. 1931. 'Mythes et Légendes du Sud de I'île Pentecôte.' *Anthropos* 26: 489–512, 863–81.

Taylor, John. 2010. 'Photogenic authenticity and the spectacular in tourism.' *La Ricerca Folkorica*. Special issue *Indigenous Tourism and the Intricacies of Cross-cultural Understanding* 61: 33–40.

Vanuatu Cultural Centre website. n.d. Online: www.vanuatuculture.org (accessed 4 May 2006, link subsequently removed).

Watas, Telkon and Murray Garde. 2012. *Dun na gol*, transcribed and translated by Murray Garde, filmed by Kim McKenzie, September.

Visual and online sources

Gray, M. OMalley. 2010. *Tribal Life Bunlap*. 2010. Online: www.youtube.com/watch?v=F7rUrCBQzY4 (accessed 4 March 2016).

Merchant, Stephen, Karl Pilkington, Ricky Gervais. 2010. *An Idiot Abroad: Karl Pilkington*. British Sky Broadcasting.

Muller, Kal. 1972. *Land Divers of Melanesia* (with Robert Gardner for Film Study Centre, Harvard University). Distributed by Documentary Educational Resources. Online: www.der.org/films/landdivers-of-melanesia.html (accessed 4 March 2016).

Primal Vision Productions. 2006. *Meet the Bunlaps.* Televison series released in United States. Described as 'funky six part series on people who prefer penis sheaths to clothes and pigs to money'. Online: primalvision.com.au (accessed 4 March 2016).

Seale, John (director). 1990. *Till there was you.* Written by Michael Thomas.

13

Writing Home on the Pari and Touring in Pacific Studies

Jo Diamond

Editors' Note: Jo Diamond's paper presented at the Australian Association of Pacific Studies conference, Wollongong, Australia, April 2012, in our session 'Touring Pacific Cultures' was an extraordinary scholarly performance piece framed as a mystery tour. Textual content comprised a collection of notes to herself, postcards, exchanges with her dissertation supervisor, family and friends. This essay/performance is a pointed reminder of the many types of relations that make up the research and writing process as well as the pressing issues of cultural recognition and ownership, the ethics of cross-cultural curiosity and the politics of history and collecting.

Kia ora koutou, greetings everyone. Ko te mihi tuatahi, ko te mihi aroha mo o matou tupuna katoa I tua o te arai, takoto, takoto, takoto. ... I firstly acknowledge all those people, belonging to all of us, who have gone before us and without whom, we would not be here. This acknowledgement is in keeping with many cultural protocols of the world, including those associated with Māori people like me, who pay respects to ancestors.

Also in keeping with those protocols, I pay special tribute to tangata whenua—those living and deceased of this land where we have gathered now, no matter how temporarily. Nga mihi nunui ki te mana whenua, o te wahi nei, o te wa nei, o te po me te ao kikokiko hoki. Greetings to one and all!

Dear fellow conference delegates,

I am a traveller, a visitor; yes even a tourist when I take direction from C. Michael Hall, a fellow University of Canterbury, New Zealand scholar and his colleagues who addressed fieldwork in tourism.[1] He offers valuable insights regarding the following:

- variables afoot in tourism-based research such as positioning of the researcher and those being researched
- questions of the extent and paradigms of the so-called 'field' referred to by the term 'fieldwork'
- debates surrounding 'belonging' in amongst and quite apart from ethnographic foci
- and definitely not last or least, those vexed questions regarding cultural identity, performance and politics that sometimes seep in and at other times 'thump' with dramatic impact upon conceptual frameworks and elements of any kind of study, including definitions of 'touring' and 'tourism'.

These insights are valid, ongoing and helpful contributions for engagement with the very important notion or, more accurately, sets of notions surrounding touring in and of the/a Pacific region. The sets are the life-blood as, no matter how loosely or tightly they are interpreted as a 'field', they are invaluable to the advancement of Pacific Studies.

I have elected to create my contribution in somewhat l-i-t-e (borrowing from diet food labels) fashion. In doing so, I offer an engagement with the pari, a Māori bodice worn by cultural performance groups, that is not so based on a conventional or traditional model of an academic paper.

---

1   C. Michael Hall, 2011, 'Fieldwork in tourism/touring fields: Where does tourism end and fieldwork begin', in *Fieldwork in Tourism: Methods, Issues and Reflections*, ed. C. Michael Hall, pp. 7–18, Oxon, Routledge, p. 7ff.

Instead, I offer postcard, diary entry, letter-home and email-like snippets associated with a set of images. Some of these snippets are 'posted' here to you as if I am away overseas, writing home to you. Others are records of correspondence I actually have had or would have had with others who are not here. I may tend towards vagueness or inadequate explanations with this style and do encourage your questions or comments during or following this reading.

Please use these two images as a Tour Introduction of a big wide world of enquiry, no less, which for me began in earnest some 14 years ago whilst researching for my PhD.[2] A huge shout-out to my former fellow ANU instructors and students of that time, present here today. Images such as those in Figures 71 and 72 conjure in our minds stereotypical ideas about Māori culture. Tourist-attracting Māori women are glamorous, warm, welcoming and available, are they not? A veritable 'meal' they are, for discussing gender-related cultural identity and representation, including the staging with props of an ideal, attractive destination, ripe for the picking. Especially created for postcard, pamphlet, poster and coffee-table book viewing if not actual physical touring—don't you think? But, please do remember to focus on the bodice that each of these beautiful women is wearing. It is this pari that grabs hold of me (and, I assert, all of you) in the process of me telling some of its stories. Arohanui Jo

---

2   Jo Diamond, 2004, 'Revaluing Raranga: Weaving and women in trans-Tasman Māori cultural discourses', PhD thesis, The Australian National University.

Figure 71. Image of the welcoming and available Māori women.

Source. Mitchell, Leonard Cornwall, 1901–1971. Mitchell, Leonard Cornwall, 1901–1971: New Zealand for your next holiday. Issued by the New Zealand Government Publicity Office. Wholly printed in New Zealand by Coulls Somerville Wilkie Limited, Dunedin, Christchurch, Wellington, Auckland [ca 1925–1929]. Ref: Eph-E-TOURISM-1920s-02. With permission, Alexander Turnbull Library, Wellington, New Zealand. Online: natlib.govt. nz/records/23188666 (accessed 23 May 2016).

Figure 72. Image of the welcoming and available Māori women.

Source. New Zealand. Tourist and Publicity Department. New Zealand Tourist and Publicity Department: Here's a new wonderland! New Zealand. It's closer than you think! [1950s]. Ref: Eph-A-TOURISM-NZ-1950s-01. Alexander Turnbull Library, Wellington, New Zealand. With permission, Tourism New Zealand. Online: natlib.govt.nz/records/22863971 (accessed 23 May 2016).

Figure 73. As yet unidentified Māori woman weaving in taniko method.

Source. Māori woman weaving taniko. Birch, A E: Scenic negatives and prints taken by Thomas Pringle. Ref: 1/1-007019-G. With permission, Alexander Turnbull Library, Wellington, New Zealand. Online: natlib.govt.nz/records/22630497 (accessed 23 May 2016).

Note to Sylvia (my PhD supervisor),

There's got to be a connection between pari and photographic records such as these readily available for purchase from the Alexander Turnbull Library. As yet unidentified women, some weaving and others wearing, all capturing the fascination of photographers in the late nineteenth – early twentieth centuries. Such images entice me into the enquiry based on a rapidly forming curiosity about how, why and when the pari emerged. It was not there in the nineteenth century. It is, as you know, very much here in the twenty-first century. I am writing at least one chapter about what could be called a micro-history of the pari, especially since very little engagement with its 100 or so years of its existence, has yet to meet a published page. Best regards as always, Jo

Figure 74. Unidentified Māori women with poi, piupiu and white dresses accompanied by two men.

Source. Group with poi at Putiki. *Auckland Star*: Negatives. Ref: 1/1-003145-G. With permission, Alexander Turnbull Library, Wellington, New Zealand. Online: natlib.govt.nz/records/23087250 (accessed 23 May 2016).

Quick note to self,

White blouses, Victorian in character, poi and piupiu, not to mention feathers, say at least 2 things: Christianity had a role to play in the pari's forerunner for female cultural performers, replacing so-called 'native' dress or 'undress' with high-necked purity despite retaining some Māori trappings. A constrained cultural representation connoting the 'civilisation' of Māori performers into quaint poi-twirlers, women and men included, in starched white clothing. No sign here yet of the seductive pari that comes later. Perhaps this is a regionally based idea of moral appropriateness or religious conviction that whiteness is godliness; some fantasy based on civilising so-called savages. A precursor to the pari is this? Or, is it antithesis? Watch out for historicentric conclusions based on boiling (angry) blood in my veins. Softly, softly catchy pari.

Dear Sue,

Thanks for your advice on ordering copies of images from the National Library collection. Thanks also for your interest in my topic for the book. I'll pick the images up on my way to Te Papa next week. I'm convinced that the pictures dated in the 1920s are an historical link that I am looking for, between the trend of the late nineteenth century of wearing cloaks and piupiu around the shoulders and torso, and the later performance 'costume' (not the best name for it) that we are familiar with nowadays. Until we meet on Wednesday, best regards, Jo

Figure 75. Young Māori woman wearing piupiu as 'traditional' Māori dress, early twentieth century.

Source. Young Māori woman with poi. Tesla Studios: Negatives of Wanganui and district taken by Alfred Martin, Frank Denton and Mark Lampe (Tesla Studios). Ref: 1/1-020797-G. With permission, Alexander Turnbull Library, Wellington, New Zealand. Online: natlib. govt.nz/records/22492552 (accessed 23 May 2016).

Tena koe Ta Hirini Mead,

Please allow me to republish this image from your invaluable book on Taniko. I note the helpful one and a half page reference to the pari in amongst your beautiful discussion of our taonga rongonui (well-known treasure) taniko weaving. I aim to build upon your work with a whole book on the subject of pari where the respectful acknowledgement you gave these women in the photo in your book continues in mine. Ma te wa, nga mihi nui matua.

Figure 76. A variety of pari depicted in a monograph on the subject of taniko weaving. Performers from Ngati Porou of the East Coast of the North Island Aotearoa.

Source. Hirini Moko Mead, 1999, *Te Whatu Taniko: Taniko Weaving Techniques and Tradition*, Auckland: Reed, p. 12. Originally published in *The Weekly News* 1947.

Figure 77. Unidentified Māori women in dance performance wearing a variety of pari. Pickwick Club, Sydney, 1962.

Source. Māori dancers at a cocktail party at the Pickwick Club to celebrate New Zealand Day 1962, digital order no. d7_12060. With permission State Library of New South Wales.

Dear Joan,

Sending you an image I picked up during my recent trip to Sydney and the Mitchell Library. I don't know anything yet about the Pickwick Club let alone these women who are wearing all kinds of pari—one for each individual. Why am I still surprised that I can't find anything published or archived about these women? Will try the club angle. ... Thanks so much for encouraging me to explore the subject further. Love Jo

Dear Mum,

Sending you by email the photo we talked briefly about on the phone. Auntu Lottie most generously lent me the original when I last visited her. The pari you're wearing in the photo is unlike any I'd seen before but I am so pleased you recall it being made of kuta—a fibre I'm familiar with now, having woven with it for the past few months. Kuta is now mostly linked with the North, including Maraeroa near were Granpa [your father] was brought up, as you know. I'd love to know more about kuta's relationship with pari as well as Granpa. Since our phone call I found the other image in the Alexander Turnbull Library. As you can see its date is around the same time of your photo and has the only pari I know of that's similar to yours. I'll call you on the weekend to talk more about it. Do you know anyone in it? Love you, Jo

Left: Figure 78. My mother the late Te Mihinga Eileen Diamond in her early teens wearing a kuta pari.

Source. Photograph courtesy Tarati Waetford.

Right: Figure 79. Kuta pari worn by children of a winning kapa haka team, Maraeroa, c. 16 April 1947.

Source. New Zealand Free Lance. Photographic prints and negatives Studio De Luxe. Maori girls and boys of a winning haka team, Maraeroa. New Zealand Free Lance : Photographic prints and negatives. Ref: PAColl-6303-14. Alexander Turnbull Library, Wellington, New Zealand. Online: natlib.govt.nz/records/22607274 (accessed 23 June 2016).

Kia ora cousin Jo,

Here's a picture of my pari designed by my mum and my Aunty Lottie in the late 1970s. Its reference to our homeland up north is mainly on the left though the black bordered part refer to nga hau e wha—my place is at home and in all four corners of the world, it says. We made this pari while I was at Waikato University; each of us in the kapa haka (culture group) had our own unique one and another black and gold uniform one. Both were made with needlepoint on purchased canvas. Maybe one day I'll transfer the red, black and white one's design into taniko. Thanks for reassuring me that its design is safe with you. I am thinking though of making a point about my mother's and your concerns regarding cultural property and protecting it from theft—of itself and its design. So, we struggle on towards justice and respect. Whawhai tonu … Arohanui Jo

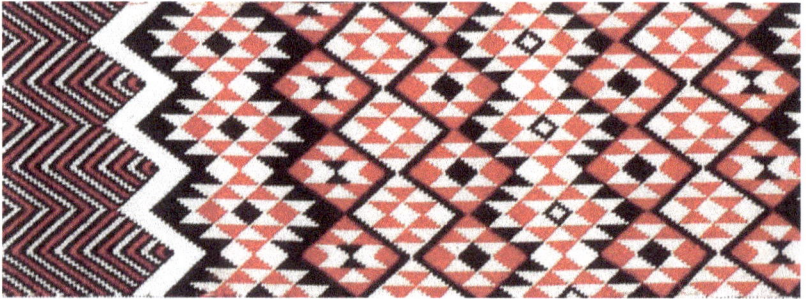

Figure 80. My pari made of wool cross-stitch designed by my mother Te Mihinga Eileen Diamond and her sister Tarati Waetford.
Source. Author's private collection.

Dear Nat,

Thank you for giving me permission to include this image of you in my thesis and book. The uniform of your group Te Rere o te Tarakakao of Canberra was first brought to my attention by my cousin Jo and has, to my knowledge, the only green and gold coloured pari anywhere in the world. Very appropriate for us Aussie Māori. All the best with your B. Enviro Science studies at Wollongong. Noho ora mai, Jo

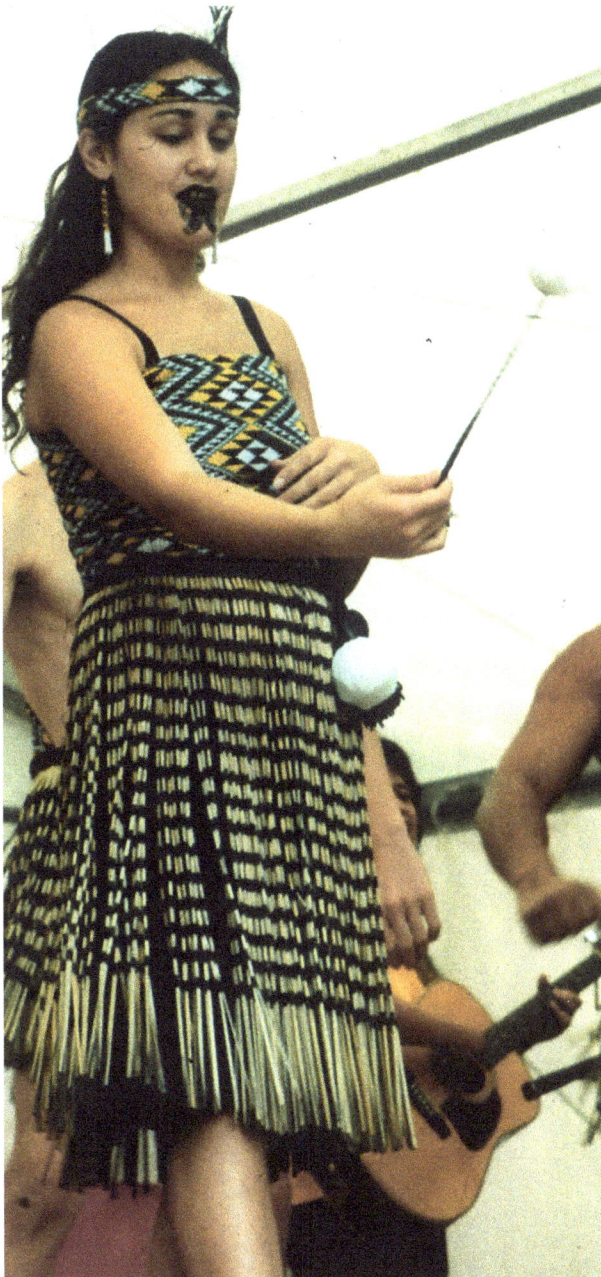

Figure 81. Nat Sullivan of Canberra-based Māori kapa haka, Te Rere o te Tarakakao wearing their distinctive green and gold pari based on Australian uniform colours.

Source. Reproduced from author's private collection and used with Nat Sullivan's permission.

Journal Entry,

Was randomly wandering around the Opera House when I came across this show with brochure and obliging group of Te Kotuku performers included. Wowee what a pari! Need to contact them again for more details as they had to leave soon after I took the photo. Design looks over the top but the creativity afoot in Australia is amazing. I wonder about this innovation too as it seems to fly in the face of cultural correctness and conservatism required for tourism displays and some Māori cultural groups here and back home in NZ.

Figure 82. Members of Te Kotuku Māori kapa haka, Sydney, wearing their distinctive uniform, including pari.

Source. Photographed with permission by author.

Dear Margaret

In reply to your enquiry, yes, my investigation continues into the history of the pari. I'm even more motivated by readily available images like those that appear on the internet with little description or analysis, including no identification of who the women are, let alone why and when their pari came about. In these images there is so much variety, including a colourful departure from usual designs and an extraordinary diversity of materials. 'What do they mean?' is still a constant question and apart from my dear, concerned mother who once cautioned me that some people may find the subject of pari tapu (sacred) due to its proximity to breasts and mute it accordingly, many people are impressed by my curiosity and willing to help. With best regards and appreciation, Jo

---

Tena koutou o te ropu Hakahula, nga mihi mahana … I am currently writing a book about pari and was delighted to find your photo online. I wish to come and talk with you about your uniform. Please let me know if and when that's possible. Heoi ano, naku noa na, Jo Diamond

---

Dear Roseanna

I'm so glad we're Facebook friends. Thanks for your skype details. It's certainly more economical talk to you that way especially about 'Ngati Ranana' and your distinctive pari. I hope to come to London soon though the uni here is facing huge financial struggles post-earthquakes. So I'll catch you on skype. Looking forward to learning about your pari—where it came from and where it might go along with the women who wear it so well over there on the other side of the world. Ma te aroha me te matauranga matou e manaaki, Jo

---

Dear Ambassador,

Further to my earlier letter, thank you for your kind willingness to participate in discussions with me and the 'Māori Manaia' group members regarding the World Tour last year (2011), their striking uniform, including the pari. As I arrive in London the day before, I see no problem in finding the venue for our scheduled meeting next month. Thank you for your concern and I look forward to meeting you in person. Very best regards, Jo

Figure 83. Keren Ruki, 1999, Māori girl (a kākahu) 120 x 90 cm.
Cotton, tape, cane, iron-on transfers.
Source. Photograph, courtesy of the artist.

E te wahine toa, my dear friend Keren,

The world has come full-circle for me and the pari and now I seek your permission once again to use this image for my book and exhibition. I know you appreciate that your self-portrait's pari is a significant expression of Māori identity and please know, if you don't already, that I've always respected the various layers of cultural meaning you address in your work. I'm assured that we are both in the business of commenting upon and bringing to light the richness of Māori experience, including those features not published or exhibited publicly except on our marae and in staged festivals and concerts. I look forward to our continued conversation on these and many other matters. An official invitation to the book launch and exhibition is on its way. Aroha pumau tonu, Jo

One more snippet.

So much remains to be said, written, sang and danced within the 'field' of pari and the wider 'field' of Pacific Studies. I am likely to continue critical analyses based on feminist and post-colonial discourses, those dominant and those marginalised. Not intending definitive conclusion, but offering a robust and substantial basis for critical engagement with pari, my work progresses. This endeavour has been and continues to be a tour of touring pari that finds comparison, if not equivalence with other Pacific items of clothing and the people of the past, present and future that design, make and wear them. That tour, this tour has begun …

References

Alexander Turnbull Library Photographic Collection. Online: natlib. govt.nz/collections/a-z/photographic-archive (accessed 25 February 2016).

Bigwood, Kenneth and Jean Bigwood. 1970. *New Zealand in Pictures: The Māoris: A Selection of Colour Plates*. Auckland and Wellington: A.H. and A.W. Reed.

Diamond, Jo. 2004. 'Revaluing Raranga: Weaving and women in Trans-Tasman Māori cultural discourses.' PhD thesis, The Australian National University.

Diamond, Jo. 2014. 'Pari: Narratives of a Māori bodice.' Unpublished manuscript.

Hall, C. Michael. 2011. 'Fieldwork in tourism/touring fields: Where does tourism end and fieldwork begin.' In *Fieldwork in Tourism: Methods, Issues and Reflections*, ed. C. Michael Hall, pp. 7–18. Oxon, Routledge.

Hall, C. Michael (ed.). 2011. *'Fieldwork in Tourism: Methods, Issues and Reflections*. Oxon, Routledge.

Mead, Hirini Moko. 1999. *Te Whatu Taniko: Taniko Weaving Techniques and Tradition*. Auckland: Reed.

14

Performing Indigenous Sovereignties across the Pacific

Peter Phipps

This chapter is a 'writing-performance'; reflecting the spirit of festivals as transient, dynamic, performative, meaning-making engagements. It is located on the increasingly ubiquitous 'ground' of festivals and performances on which Indigenous peoples publicly stage their identities both for themselves and for tourists and other visitors to experience, interpret and value. This performative ground is shaped by the intersection of post-colonial dynamics of places and their peoples, and the forces of commodification, which extend increasingly to culture and identity. Upon this festival 'ground', one core argument repeats the underlying rhythm: Indigenous cultural expression and sovereignty politics are deeply intertwined. They are intertwined in such a way as to open and enable spaces for distinctively Indigenous expressions of agency in the overlapping domains of culture and politics. This is a claim that culture and the performance of culture are deeply political acts.

Overlaying this argument are two very differently situated Pacific festival case studies (from Hilo and Port Moresby), much like dancers embodying and embellishing a rhythmic beat. These trans-Pacific sites provide empirical evidence of the intersection of politics and culture at the core of this argument. The research was undertaken in the spirit of a translocal, comparative ethnographic study of festivals; a touring methodology of observation, interviews and some participant observation. As observed in many places, anthropologists and tourists have a great deal in common,[1] in particular their attempts to create value from their conspicuous mobilities through the accumulation of carefully curated souvenirs, images, field notes, stories, anecdotes and experiences. Anthropologists generally do not like to be confused for tourists, despite the obvious similarities. The short duration of most of my fieldwork for this research made the resemblance not just likely, but an integral part of my method as tourist-researcher.

This identity conflation was made patently obvious to me in one awkward touristic research moment at the Ho'olaule'a (community hula celebration event) prior to the Merrie Monarch Festival in Hilo on the big island of Hawai'i. I was pulled up on stage to dance by a member of the Tahitian dance troupe, and in the process I became an amusing part of the show, 'Look, Haole (white man) dancing!' This classic, even clichéd, trope reversing the touristic gaze back onto the audience is still an effective power inversion strategy used by performers at tourist events. The awkward dances of tourists pulled on stage are a humorous and potent reminder of the cultural expertise of the real performers, born from long-term training within an ancestral performative tradition. It is my hope that each 'tourist snapshot' in this chapter-performance exceeds simple reinscription into a colonising touristic or anthropological value production system. The 'snap shots' are intended to carry an excess beyond writing; a sense of the performative effervescence that makes cultural performance traditions so engaging; the 'shining' quality as Yolngu Aboriginal aesthetics would have it, or perhaps even its Pacifica mana.[2]

---

1   James Clifford, 1997, *Routes: Travel and Translation in the Late Twentieth Century*, Cambridge, MA: Harvard University Press; John Hutnyk and Raminder Kaur (eds), 1999, *Travel Worlds: Journeys in Contemporary Cultural Politics*, London, Zed Books; John Hutnyk, 2000, *Critique of Exotica*, London: Pluto Press; Peter Phipps, 2006, 'Tourism and terrorism: An intimate equivalence', in *Tourists and Tourism: A Reader*, ed. Sharon Bohn Gmelch, pp. 71–90, Illinois: Waveland Press.

2   Howard Morphy, 1991, *Ancestral Connections: Art and an Aboriginal System of Knowledge*, Chicago: University of Chicago Press; Howard Morphy, 2008, *Becoming Art: Exploring Cross-cultural Categories*, Coogee: University of New South Wales Press.

Figure 84. The author dancing awkwardly at the community day.
Source. Photographed by Jason Kimberley, 31 March 2008. Used with permission.

Constrained as we are by both the limits of writing, and an academic heritage that grapples with a divide between intellectual critical practice and performative traditions,[3] this chapter is a performative production of value, but necessarily distinct from the brilliant performance traditions to which it seeks to pay due respect.[4] The gourd rhythm, stamping feet, swaying bodies and chant of Hawaiian hula kuhiko could accompany, enhance and implicitly critique this text. Play the sound track of your choice now; get up and dance.

3   Jacques Derrida, 1982, *Margins of Philosophy*, Chicago, University of Chicago Press; Katerina Martina Teaiwa, 2012, 'Choreographing difference: The (body) politics of Banaban dance', *The Contemporary Pacific* 24(1) Spring: 65–94.
4   This research is indebted to the generosity of cultural specialists in Australia, Hawai'i, Papua New Guinea and Kham. It is, among other things, an attempt to reciprocate that generosity by acknowledging these cultural treasures and their ancestral connections in continuity with current struggles.

The claims I make in this touring research agenda are grounded in fieldwork-based case studies of a number of Australian Indigenous festivals, particularly Garma in northeast Arnhem Land,[5] festivals in Tibetan Amdo, and the two festivals described in this chapter. These two annual festivals are Hiri Moale held in the Papua New Guinea capital Port Moresby, and the Merrie Monarch Festival in Hilo, Hawai'i; the latter contrasted with the experience of a thoroughly commercial Hawaiian cultural performance. The circumstances of these Indigenous peoples vary enormously: from Kanaka Maoli mourning the transformation of their independent Kingdom of Hawai'i into a US military, plantation and recreation outpost, contrasted with the situation of land encroachment experienced by the Motu-Koita people as customary owners of the land and waters in and around Port Moresby as the capital city of an independent post-colonial state.

Ritualised cultural performance has been an integral part of Indigenous encounters with colonising cultures from earliest contacts to the present day. The historical record suggests a broad pattern whereby these performances become more significant in periods when colonial relations are more strongly contested or are shifting into new terrain. Edward Said foregrounds the centrality of anti-colonial, national cultural practice in *Culture and Imperialism*, where the narrativisation of the nation through literature is understood as central to the struggle over sovereignty.[6] The Subaltern Studies school of Indian historiographers brings this same Foucauldian idea of the ubiquity of power to the performative politics of Indian peasants and tribals resisting colonial authority.[7] Historians of Pacific colonial encounters such as Inga Clendinnen, Greg Dening, Marshall Sahlins and others, emphasise an acute colonial sensitivity to these performances as a theatre of power integral to the earliest phases of colonisation.[8] They argue for taking these cultural performances seriously from both sides of the colonial encounter; lifting them out of the historical footnotes

5   Peter Phipps, 2010, 'Performances of power: Indigenous cultural festivals as globally engaged cultural strategy', *Alternatives: Global, Local, Political* 35(3): 217–40.
6   Edward W. Said, 1993, *Culture and Imperialism*, London: Chatto and Windus.
7   Ranajit Guha and Gayatri Chakravorty Spivak, 1988, *Selected Subaltern Studies*, New York: Oxford University Press.
8   Inga Clendinnen, 2003, *Dancing with Strangers*, Melbourne, Text Publishing; Greg Dening, 1993, *Mr Bligh's Bad Language: Passion, Power, and Theatre on the Bounty*, Cambridge: Cambridge University Press; Marshall Sahlins, 1995, *How 'Natives' Think: About Captain Cook, for Example*, Chicago: University of Chicago Press.

and onto centre-stage of the colonial process—whether it be Captain Cook's finally fatal encounters with Hawaiian ritual and politics,[9] or the New South Wales convict colony's first Governor Arthur Phillip's misrecognition of his own ritual spearing orchestrated by his adopted kin, Bennelong.[10]

I argue that this performative reading of the colonial experience applies equally to other phases of the colonial–post-colonial–decolonial process. The missionary process, for example, has its requisite ritual performances of Christian conversion and adherence, cleanliness and order, while failure to conform with these expectations are read as the inevitable signs of recidivism into a state of savagery requiring constant vigilance, punishment, repentance and reform; all confirming the genocidal logic underpinning imperial-missionary colonialism. The nation-building version of colonialism sets up similar impossible binaries of Indigenous subjectivity, both invoking and rejecting the incorporation of the 'native' into the national narrative. It demands ritual performances of enacted good citizenship and exemplary national subjectivity both through performances of Indigenous alterity for and within the nation, and conformity with the norms of national productive labour and reproductive order. Paradoxically those very performances of Indigenous alterity being demanded for the nation (folk dance, corrobboree, national-foundational historical re-enactment, 'traditional' festival) are symbolic evidence of the inevitable failure to live up to the national-modern ideal, thereby justifying their exclusion through racism and other forms of discrimination. Our 'good/bad citizen/native' fails to reach the impossible national ideal even though the colonising-national 'we' tried so very hard to include them in this overdetermined colonial theatre of power. This is the closed logic of colonial exclusion critiqued so powerfully in Richard Bell's artwork and essay, 'Aboriginal Art – It's a white thing'.[11]

---

9   Gananath Obeyesekere, 1992, *The Apotheosis of Captain Cook: European Mythmaking in the Pacific*, Princeton, NJ: Princeton University Press.

10   Clendinnen, *Dancing with Strangers*.

11   And related artwork, *Scientia E Metaphysica (Bell's Theorum)*, more commonly known by the text written across it, 'Aboriginal Art – It's a white thing', which won the 2003 Telstra National Aboriginal & Torres Strait Islander Art Award. Richard Bell, 2002. 'Bells theorum: Aboriginal art – It's a white thing', *The Koori History Website Project*. See also Richard Bell, *Australian Art It's An Aboriginal Thing*, synthetic polymer paint on canvas, TarraWarra Museum of Art collection, 2006.

At every stage of these colonising processes Indigenous peoples have performed serious, often urgent ritual displays and responses to cultural, political, spiritual and ethical domination, and transform or repair social relations through an Indigenous theatre of power. These performances have sometimes been the best strategy available to call colonisers into reciprocal intellectual recognition with Indigenous performative gifts of knowledge and ritual; in effect a realm of Indigenous sovereignty.[12] Tragically, these performances are often misunderstood and trivialised; if they are valued, it is most often for their ability to be commodified as tourist performances, or to enhance the settler-colonial or national narrative. Where their cultural-political significance has been recognised, particularly in more repressive colonial phases or where these Indigenous rituals made overt sovereign claims, they have been answered in further acts of cultural repression and violence. Examples of this dynamic abound, from missionary repression of Hawaiian hula and Aboriginal corroborees (for example, the Mulunga cult of the Kalkadoon resistance), to state repression of Sioux ghost dance rituals or the repeated banning (since 2008) of contemporary Khampa Tibetan horse festivals. Sometimes they have been understood and deeply resonated with individuals and specific groups from the colonising culture, while failing to make inroads at the institutional-social level.

Politics and culture: Indigenous sovereignties

For all this diversity of historical experience and current circumstance, peoples from all these settings hold regular festivals and cultural performances, all treat them as a significant part of their cultural life, and all of them are concerned in different ways, with the question of Indigenous sovereignty; what that means, how to express it, and how to enact and enforce it. It should be no great surprise then that questions of Indigenous sovereign expression are present at Indigenous festivals; sometimes overtly, more often obliquely, and of course in very different ways in these different circumstances, but strongly present nonetheless. For the purpose of this argument, it is

---

12 Stephen Muecke, 2004, *Ancient & Modern: Time, Culture and Indigenous Philosophy*, Sydney: University of New South Wales Press. See particularly Muecke's references to the 'ghost dance' style *Mulunga* cult of late-nineteenth-century Queensland. Similarly the 'adjustment movement' of north east Arnhem Land described in Morphy, *Ancestral Connections*, 1991.

sufficient to understand Indigenous sovereignties, in contradistinction from classical Westphalian nation-state sovereignty, as varied, uneven and frequently overlaying other forms of sovereignty.[13] For example, some Australian Indigenous groups have various forms of judicially recognised or state legislated native title or gazetted reserves (such as Yolngu in Arnhem Land), with certain rights that follow this recognition, in many cases co-existing with other rights such as leasehold title or mineral rights. In the Pacific, this overlapping or partial sovereignty can be found in the idea of free association of micro-nations such as Cook Islands or Marshall Islands with larger states such as New Zealand or the USA respectively.

More complex, and more challenging still for conventional political science understandings of sovereignty as absolute and singular, is the co-existence of contesting models of sovereignty. In these circumstances the dominant, colonising entity will very often refuse or fail to acknowledge the separate or co-existing sovereign claim of colonised or sub-nationally distinct Indigenous peoples to their full sovereignty (the absolute challenge of separatism), or certain kinds of partial, autonomous sovereign expression. While these concepts are not entirely foreign to post-colonial jurisprudence, it is not surprising that Indigenous notions of partial and overlaying sovereignties are the most substantial conceptual challenge to colonising systems, which see sovereign power as singular domination and any contrary claim as rebellion to be crushed. Indigenous sovereignties can be much more tolerant of ambiguity and multiplicity both for strategic imperatives (colonisers have the guns/police/welfare/law, etc.) as well as generally more open epistemological dispositions based in histories of overlapping and interdependent cultural and territorial domains (sovereignties).

This more complex expression of contested sovereignty, particularly in the massively asymmetrical circumstances of Indigenous groups facing modernising states, is particularly well suited to expression through culture, and in performative cultural expressions. Festivals

---

13   Aileen M. Moreton-Robinson, 2011, 'Virtuous racial states: The possessive logic of patriarchal white sovereignty and the United Nations Declaration on the Rights of Indigenous Peoples', *Griffith Law Review* 20(3): 641–58; John Bern and Susan Dodds, 2000, 'On the plurality of interests: Aboriginal self-government and land rights', in *Political Theory and the Rights of Indigenous Peoples*, ed. Duncan Ivison, Paul Patton and Will Sanders, pp. 163–65, Cambridge: Cambridge University Press.

and related performances are condensation events; those theatres of power mentioned earlier, imbued with concentrated symbolic meanings, rich in deliberate communicative acts expressing identity, where forms of lived or aspirational cultural difference are more self-consciously and deliberately curated and performed than in most daily life.[14] Communities' and individuals' cultural purposes in conducting and participating in festivals can include expression of collective identity and solidarity, cultural aspiration and forward projection, cultural nostalgia and reclamation, cultural assertion against other groups and their (sovereign) claims, and of course through all this, the cultivation of pleasure.

The intersection of colonial with capitalist epistemologies has tended to brutally trivialise or commercialise (frequently both) cultural enjoyments unevenly across social space. This burden falls most particularly on colonised and other dominated social groups, and the commercialised display of dominated cultures and bodies for the entertainment and reinscription of the power of the dominant cultures and groups. Jane Desmond traces this process of 'staging tourism' in Hawai'i through the commodification of leisure that has grown exponentially since the late nineteenth century.[15]

For Indigenous communities, festivals can be a brilliant strategic vehicle for staging, performing and asserting culture in the context of this dominant capitalist ethos (selling tickets, handicrafts, food, etc.). There need be no contradiction between making commercial uses of culture as a tourist service (though this is frequently a source of internal community tension) while at the same time projecting and renewing it for non-commercial, collective purposes. As Kalissa Alexeyeff has argued in *Dancing from the Heart*, cultural performance has a crucial place in the formation of Cook Islands identities and meaningful, expressive lives that far exceeds the limited utility of the tourist economy.[16] Enjoyment can also be an act of resistance against the dominant global culture and its preferences for productivity and commodified pleasures. Pleasure in the experience of specific, collective cultural difference really matters to people—most urgently

---

14   Arnold Van Gennep, 1960 [1909], *The Rites of Passage*, Chicago: University of Chicago Press.
15   Jane Desmond, 1999, *Staging Tourism: Bodies on Display from Waikiki to Sea World*, Chicago: University of Chicago Press.
16   Kalissa Alexeyeff, 2009, *Dancing from the Heart: Movement, Gender and Sociality in the Cook Islands*, Honolulu: University of Hawai'i Press.

to groups facing adversity. This is a serious point given the profound existential crisis the experience of (post)colonisation forces on Indigenous peoples.

From Merrie Monarch to tourist Lu'au

This struggle for cultural survival in the face of colonial cultures of domination and commodification is dramatically illustrated in Hawai'i. Hula has been a long-standing, ubiquitous presence in the Hawaiian tourism industry,[17] but also has a deep history as a profound cultural practice of spiritual and political significance.[18] Having been repressed by early missionaries in the Hawaiian kingdom, it has had various stages of revival, intimately associated with revivals of Hawaiian identity and claims to sovereignty. The most important of these revivals was in the second half of the nineteenth century when King David Kalākaua brought a modified form of hula back into the official life of the court and thus the international public sphere at his carefully staged Poni Mō'ī (coronation) event, which was attended by international monarchs and government officials.

Today the US occupation of Hawai'i is founded on an illegal coup against this Kingdom of Hawai'i a little over 100 years ago,[19] ostensibly legitimised through the 1959 act of statehood by plebiscite. In this context, cultural performance is no longer seen as any kind of threat to the established (post)colonial order. United States' hegemonic power at the cultural level is based on the rough settler-colonial equation as follows: massive military presence + performative liberal democracy + demographic dominance + (limited) economic opportunity = settler-colonial legitimacy. Hawaiian sovereignty activists' continuing cultural challenges to the legitimacy of the colonising state order therefore largely face official indifference, while more overtly political actions such as homeland reoccupations or blockades of military or civil development over sacred sites are brutally repressed.

---

17   Desmond, *Staging Tourism*.
18   Haunani-Kay Trask, 1999, *From a Native Daughter: Colonialism and Sovereignty in Hawai'i*, Honolulu, University of Hawai'i Press; Amy K. Stillman, 1998, *Sacred Hula: The Historical Hula 'Āla'apapa*, Honolulu: Bishop Museum Press; Noenoe K. Silva, 2004, *Aloha Betrayed: Native Hawaiian Resistance to American Colonialism*, Durham, NC: Duke University Press.
19   The 1993 US Congress 'Apology Resolution' (US Public Law 103–150) signed into law by Bill Clinton recognises US involvement in this overthrow.

Nearly 100 years after Kalākaua's initiatives to revive hula and sustain Hawaiian cultural and political sovereignty, another hula revival was underway, epitomised by a festival named in his honour. According to a key figure in this rennaissance, and festival founder, Uncle George Na'ope, the Merrie Monarch Festival was initially a state-sponsored tourism initiative in the early 1960s.[20] Held annually in Hilo, on Hawai'i Island, by 1971 it had incorporated a hula competition as its core activity, and rapidly became the centrepiece of another revival of the hula tradition. The competition draws in hālau (hula schools) from across the Hawaiian islands and North America, the Hawaiian diaspora in the USA (California, Nevada, Utah and elsewhere), and hula enthusiasts from around the world, particularly Japan.

From its very inception, the Merrie Monarch Festival was organised around the playful device that presumed the festival to be happening under the rule of the last Hawaiian King.[21] The competition within the Merrie Monarch Festival is overseen by a 'Hawaiian Royal Court' (selected to perform in this role for the duration of the festival) enthroned on an enormous float drawn by a truck. By honouring this Hawaiian monarch, the festival plays with the notion of the continuing sovereignty of the Hawaiian Kingdom, which was overthrown in a coup by American sugar planters in 1893.

This festival, with all its attendent Americanised modernity of a televised competition, ticket sales and t-shirts, has become a key institution in the revival and strengthening of the hula tradition; setting standards and managing innovations in the tradition. The festival is a key institutional element of hula as the living expression of an ancient practice reconfigured to the requirements of international modernity under the Hawaiian Kingdom, and reconfigured again in the face of the onslaught of twentieth-century American military, plantation and tourist capitalism. In her discussion of hula, Hunani-Kay Trask says, 'The cultural revitalization that Hawaiians are now experiencing and transmitting to their children is as much a repudiation of colonization by so-called Western civilization in its American form as it is a reclamation of our own past and our own

---

20   George Na'ope, 2006, 'The early years of the Merrie Monarch Festival', *Humu Mo'olelo, Journal of the Hula Arts* 1(1): 72–89.
21   Ibid.

ways of life … its political effect is decolonization of the mind'.[22] As a prominent expression of that 'revitalization' Trask describes, and despite being framed by the colonial artifice of 'competition', the festival is a cultural political act towards this 'decolonization of the mind'.

The lu'au as social practice

In stark contrast to the Merrie Monarch festival, as a performance of sovereignty the place of hula (and related Hawaiian cultural forms) in the commercial lu'au is considerably more ambivalent as a performance of sovereignty. 'Germaine's Luau' is a commercial operation owned and managed by a Japanese tourist company on the west coast of Oahu, and is a classic example of the commercialisation of Hawaiian culture into a massified tourist theme park–style experience.

A lu'au is a Hawaiian feast with a long cross-cultural history, which has become a popular, almost obligatory, tourist experience of a commercialised form of Hawaiian culture. I attended Germaine's Luau as part of an academic conference on cultural diversity, and with my fellow academics-become-tourists reacted with varying degrees of self-conscious horror and delight. The experience began as our group was bused from Waikiki along a busy freeway in the southwestern corner of Oahu, past many miles of military bases and the rundown industrial and residential infrastructure that maintains them. All along the way the bus hosts kept up a repartee of good humour, perhaps to distract us from the traffic jams and industrial wastelands we were part of. The bus hosts created a fictive kinship of cousinhood between us, interspersed with friendly jokes about Australian degeneracy, demanding audience participation from reluctant academics on board.

Arriving at Kapolei, the buses came to a stop beside the Campbell Industrial Estate, with a prominent oil refinery immediately in front of us. I arrived with Owens Wiwa, brother of the murdered Nigerian Ogoni delta human rights activist Ken Saro-Wiwa. Owens knows the smell of oil all too well from his Ogoni Nigerian homeland, and he confirmed the acrid smell of oil processing and its associated petro-chemical wastes burning our nostrils. This was the site of Germaine's

---

22 Trask, '"Lovely hula hands": Corporate tourism and the prostitution of Hawaiian culture'. in *From a Native Daughter*, p. 142.

Luau, where we were unloaded, factory style, to line up and be 'traditionally greeted by a Hawaiian host' with the gift of a lei of shells manufactured in the Philippines, and to pose for a photo against the backdrop of the sun setting over the sea and a couple of surviving but sick-looking coconut palms (which were planted by and signify Germaine's Luau's original owners). Conference participants, being quick to appreciate the irony of their surroundings, quickly turned their cameras on the aging industrial infrastructure that had been remarkably selected as the setting for this lu'au.

Figure 85. Conference participants and others at Germaine's Lu'au with refinery in background.
Source. Photo courtesy of Common Ground Conferences, 13 February 2003.

In an echo of the Merrie Monarch festival's recreation of a temporary performative Hawaiian monarch, we were invited to witness 'the King and Queen' of Hawai'i preside over the ceremonial opening of the earth oven (set in concrete), and removal of the cooked pig from within. Unlike the Merrie Monarch festival performance, this ersatz monarch, styled after the first king to unite the Hawaiian islands (Kamehameha I) had the limited duty to perform this one spectacle, and then be gone to leave us undisturbed to our industrial-scale consumption. We were sent by the table to line up and receive our 'authentic Hawaiian meal' of rice, poi, pork, chicken, fish and so on, on a disposable polystyrene platter.

Our large group sat with many many others at benches and tables, eating our lu'au foods as a floor show of 'Polynesian culture', mostly Tahitian-style dance and fire twirling, was performed on stage and broadcast over loudspeakers. This was interrupted by visits to the bar for our '3 complimentary exotic cocktails' of brightly coloured drinks, which by their very names signal the link between American imperialism and its leisure culture: 'Blue Hawaiian' and 'Pina Colada'.

Despite an Adorno-style academic predisposition for anomie when subject to mass-culture consumption experiences,[23] the conference participants made the most of the evening and most tried to enjoy themselves. One academic (not me this time) was enticed to join the 'audience participation' segment of the floor show, being dressed with a few other male visitors in grass skirts and coconut brassieres for a transcultural 'drag show', where the audience voted by voice for the best dancer. The Germaine's Luau staff appeared habituated to this performative parody of their cultures, being seen enjoying a meal and conversation, laughing relaxed together off to the side of the main scene. Afterwards, as we were reloading on to our buses, some of the 'professional Polynesian' protagonists of the floor show were practicing their fire-stick skills, and appearing to coach each other in slight improvements in performance, which along with some of the dancing showed moments of real virtuosity. These small moments of normal behaviour in the 'behind-the-scenes' narrative are a reminder of the everydayness of the flattening out of social and community life into forms available for easy commodification. Trask describes the process by which young Hawaiians are drawn into this normalised world of cultural commodification,

> Hawaiians, meanwhile, have little choice in all this. We can fill up the unemployment lines, enter the military, work in the tourist industry, or leave Hawai'i. Increasingly, Hawaiians are leaving, not by choice but out of economic necessity.

> Our people who work in the industry-dancers, waiters, singers, valets, gardeners, housekeepers, bartenders, and even a few managers-make between $10,000 and $25,000 a year, an impossible salary for a family

---

23   Hutnyk, *Critique of Exotica*.

in Hawai'i. Psychologically, our young people have begun to think of tourism as the only employment opportunity, trapped as they are by the lack of alternatives.[24]

Germaine's Luau positions Hawaiians and the other Polynesians who work there as relatively passive cultural ciphers, serving 'happily' in the tourism industry as cultural performers and catering staff. On learning conference delegates were being sent to Germaine's Luau, Hawaiian sovereignty activist Mililani Trask, a keynote speaker at the conference, had insisted we should attend precisely because of these experiences of grotesque commodification of Hawaiian culture. As tourist-academics, the experience also provoked the possibility that none of us is immune from the alienating experience of self-commodification; academics can also become paid performers of commodified parodies of our deeper cultures and selves.

Hiri Moale, urban space and resource royalties

The Hiri Moale festival is a celebration of Motu-Koita identity, the Papuan traditional owners of land and sea in and around Port Moresby, the capital of Papua New Guinea. The festival is also a complex local strategy for reasserting this Indigenous sovereignty within the city, renewing local traditions, while also providing the centrepiece of nation-day celebrations in the capital. Port Moresby faces many of the same challenges as other rapidly growing cities in the resource-rich developing world. With a mostly rural population living in subsistence-based tribal communities, the 35-year-old post-colonial state has only ever had a very shallow penetration into the social fabric. Increasingly, this remarkably diverse rural population is coming to the city for services and opportunities, and changing both local and national politics in the process. For the Motu-Koita landowners this shift puts them at the centre of national urban development with all its attendant risks and opportunities, and inevitable cultural anxieties.

24   Trask, '"Lovely hula hands": Corporate tourism and the prostitution of Hawaiian culture', in *From a Native Daughter*, p. 145.

Essentially, the Hiri Moale festival revolves around commemorating and preserving memory of the historic Motuan hiri trade of epic voyages and their related cultural practices, and has become a major event in the life of Motu-Koita people living in and around Port Moresby, as well as a significant event for many other residents of the city. Held annually in Port Moresby, it has been timed to coincide with the PNG independence day celebrations in mid-September every year (except 2008). This timing is strategic, as it justifies and attracts local government and other funding for the festival, but it also links the festival into complex dynamics as a local Indigenous event embedded within the multi-ethnic, capital-city celebrations of national independence.

In a program extending over six days, the Hiri Moale festival has a number of key elements and events. Two key elements lie at its centre: the construction and sailing of two lagatoi (large, multi-hulled Motu vessels specific to the hiri trade) and the Hiri Hanenamo, or 'Hiri maiden' selection. Structured as a competition, the Hiri Hanenamo panel of judges assesses young women already selected by their community to represent each of the 16 Motu-Koita villages on the performance of traditional dance, a test of Motu cultural knowledge and language and, in the spirit of beauty contests, the ability to present and converse with dignity in formal western evening wear.

The signature event of the festival, and most popular, is held at specially built elevated huts and shade shelters at Ela Beach. The lagatoi sail into Ela Beach packed with singing villagers from the villages selected to build them from scratch over eight weeks. The singers on the lagatoi are answered by the crowd massed on the beach to greet them. After speeches and the exchange of gifts by the lagatoi captains to Assembly and local government officials, the Hiri Hanenamo emerge from the huts in grass skirts and naked 'tattooed' torsos, calling out and swaying in time, under the watchful eye of the judges, and a large crowd bolstered partly by men motivated by the relative novelty of seeing *kastom* (hence topless) female dancers in increasingly modern Port Moresby.

The Hiri Hanenamo tattoo designs are drawn on the young women's bodies by their mothers and grandmothers using marker pens in place of traditional permanent tattoos. This layering of traditional designs on the skin as a temporary performance of customary ways of being associated with hiri, and hence deep Motu cultural traditions, involves a complicated set of negotiations for the community and for the young women themselves. The first of these is shedding normal city clothes for the customary costume described above, but also immersion in archaic language, songs and knowledge related to the hiri tradition. Another layer of complexity is added by the fact that hiri is a seafaring Motu tradition, but the competition is open to contestants from traditionally inland-dwelling Koitabu communities, since the two identities are now practically and politically intertwined in the structure and politics of everyday life in and around Port Moresby. Some other of these negotiations are not unrelated to the tensions inherent in 'beauty pageants' everywhere, which fetishise traditional, somewhat archaic ideas of female beauty and gender-specific cultural competence, while repressing other aspects of young women's actual experience of their place in the world. This is a dialectic that requires them to be both emblems or paragons of community traditions and virtues, while also being effective, competent social actors in the increasingly globally connected modern city. The overlay of these dual identities is captured symbolically in the image below: the traditional pattern drawn on in temporary marker pen, while a popular icon of global feminine identity, the blooming rose, is tattooed permanently beside it.

The festival culminates in a big cultural event that includes a street parade and performances by neighbouring and related cultural groups resident in mosbi at the Hubert Murray stadium (headquarters of the Motu-Koita Assembly), by extension an acknowledgement by those groups of the special status of Motu-Koita in the city. The event closes with more performances by the Hiri Hanenamo, speeches and the awarding of the Hiri Hanenamo title and sash to the winner. The winner has the benefit of a paid office position with the Assembly for a year, in addition to the personal, family and village prestige brought by her victory.

Figure 86. Hiri Hanenamo tattooed lower leg.

Source. Photographed by Peter Phipps, 17 September 2010.

While all this annual activity reinforces the presence and a certain cultural authority of Motu-Koita in mosbi, it is not uncontested. In 2006, a clan leader from Boera village (just outside the National Capital District area) applied for a court injunction to prevent the Hiri Moale festival from proceeding. Boera village has a special status as the origin site of the hiri legend, knowledge and tradition, being shared with other Motu villages from there. This legal action was motivated by a sense that the special status of the customary authorities in Boera were not being properly acknowledged by the provincial government authorities who ran the festival at that time. While unsuccessful, the court action reasserted Boera's place in the hiri tradition, a contestation of internal Motu authority motivated substantially by resource royalty politics that has become a major disruptive force in Motu-Koita internal dynamics for most of the past decade. The rights to stage a cultural performance tradition such as this can just as easily intersect with the overwhelming dynamics of the global resource extraction industry as in this case study from Papua New Guinea.

Conclusion—indigenous theatres of power

The case studies discussed briefly in this chapter illustrate the potent connections between contemporary cultural performance and claims to Indigenous power in two very different Pacific contexts. These Indigenous theatres of power draw on strong local cultural roots, but are the product of highly adaptive, mobile cultural forms. In this chapter I have tried to illustrate that hula, lu'au and hiri are variously Hawaiian and Motuan cultural traditions, but their contemporary staging is through hybrid, mobile cultural forms derived from colonial experience and the available global palette of performative modes, in these cases respectively: a dance competition, a tourist dinner show and a beauty pageant–style format. The first and last of these being embedded in the thoroughly globalised form of 'the festival', which is well established as both a commercial and cultural form throughout the Pacific and beyond. While the more overtly touristic 'dinner show' format of the lu'au experience may provide fewer opportunities to articulate Indigenous sovereignties, indeed they may have more of a tendency to reinscribe stereotypes of the happily subaltern 'native', even these thoroughly commercial stagings have subversive elements and opportunities for at least staging ambivalence towards the (post)colonial order. Whether it be under the oppressive authority of missions, other colonising state agencies, or the independent nation-state and the related pressures on land and resources from vastly powerful interests as in Papua New Guinea, festivals and other staged cultural performances have been spaces for mobility, contesting power, reforming identities and asserting Indigenous differences across the Pacific.

Despite, and sometimes even enabled by, the increasing mobility and commodification of identity and culture, these performances continue to contest the idea of a single sovereign power or cultural value. Instead, performances of these Pacific cultures are deployed to disrupt and reorient dominant national and sub-national social formations and insist on the co-existing Indigenous sovereignties discussed at the outset of this chapter. This doesn't mean these performances of power will prevail over other social forces, but they are a significant component in the contested dialogue between Indigenous communities and other social actors, institutions and forces. To perform and celebrate culture, despite its marginalisation and distortion by dominant cultures, the colonising state or processes of commodification, is an expression of the will to continue to exist in difference despite those cultures of domination which trivialise, degrade or reify Indigenous cultural difference. That stubborn insistence to survive and persist is in itself an act of resistance and a sovereign expression of the most existential kind.

References

Alexeyeff, Kalissa. 2009. *Dancing from the Heart: Movement, Gender and Sociality in the Cook Islands*. Honolulu: University of Hawai'i Press.

Bell, Richard. 2002. 'Bells theorum: Aboriginal art – It's a white thing.' *The Koori History Website Project*. Online: www.kooriweb.org/foley/great/art/bell.html (accessed 26 February 2016).

Bell, Richard. 2003. *Scientia E Metaphysica (Bell's Theorum)*, or 'Aboriginal Art – It's a white thing.' Online: www.milanigallery.com.au/artwork/scientia-e-metaphysica-bells-theorem (accessed 26 February 2016).

Bell, Richard. 2006. *Australian Art It's An Aboriginal Thing*, synthetic polymer paint on canvas, TarraWarra Museum of Art collection. Online nga.gov.au/Exhibition/NIAT07/Detail.cfm?IRN=163588&ViewID=2&MnuID=1 (accessed 26 February 2016).

Bern, John and Susan Dodds. 2000. 'On the plurality of interests: Aboriginal self-government and land rights.' In *Political Theory and the Rights of Indigenous Peoples*, ed. Duncan Ivison, Paul Patton and Will Sanders, pp. 163–79. Cambridge: Cambridge University Press.

Clendinnen, Inga. 2003. *Dancing with Strangers*. Melbourne, Text Publishing.

Clifford, James. 1997. *Routes: Travel and Translation in the Late Twentieth Century*. Cambridge, MA: Harvard University Press.

Dening, Greg. 1993. *Mr Bligh's Bad Language: Passion, Power, and Theatre on the Bounty*. Cambridge, Cambridge University Press.

Derrida, Jacques. 1982. *Margins of Philosophy*. Chicago, University of Chicago Press.

Desmond, Jane. 1999. *Staging Tourism: Bodies on Display from Waikiki to Sea World*. Chicago: University of Chicago Press.

Guha, Ranajit and Gayatri Chakravorty Spivak. 1988. *Selected Subaltern Studies*. New York: Oxford University Press.

Hutnyk, John. 2000. *Critique of Exotica*. London: Pluto Press.

Hutnyk, John and Raminder Kaur (eds). 1999. *Travel Worlds: Journeys in Contemporary Cultural Politics*. London, Zed Books.

Morphy, Howard. 1991. *Ancestral Connections: Art and an Aboriginal System of Knowledge*. Chicago: University of Chicago Press.

Morphy, Howard. 2008. *Becoming Art: Exploring Cross-cultural Categories*. Coogee: University of New South Wales Press.

Moreton-Robinson, Aileen M. 2011. 'Virtuous racial states: The possessive logic of patriarchal white sovereignty and the United Nations Declaration on the Rights of Indigenous Peoples.' *Griffith Law Review* 20(3): 641–58.

Muecke, Stephen. 2004. *Ancient & Modern: Time, Culture and Indigenous Philosophy*. Sydney: University of New South Wales Press.

Na'ope, George. 2006. 'The early years of the Merrie Monarch Festival.' *Humu Mo'olelo, Journal of the Hula Arts* 1(1): 72–89.

Obeyesekere, Gananath. 1992. *The Apotheosis of Captain Cook: European Mythmaking in the Pacific*. Princeton, NJ: Princeton University Press.

Phipps, Peter. 2006. 'Tourism and terrorism: An intimate equivalence.' In *Tourists and Tourism: A Reader*, ed. Sharon Bohn Gmelch, pp. 71–90. Illinois: Waveland Press.

Phipps, Peter. 2010. 'Performances of power: Indigenous cultural festivals as globally engaged cultural strategy.' *Alternatives: Global, Local, Political* 35(3): 217–40.

Sahlins, Marshall. 1995. *How 'Natives' Think : About Captain Cook, for Example*. Chicago: University of Chicago Press.

Said, Edward W. 1993. *Culture and Imperialism*. London: Chatto and Windus.

Silva, Noenoe K. 2004. *Aloha Betrayed: Native Hawaiian Resistance to American Colonialism*. Durham, NC: Duke University Press.

Stillman, Amy K. 1998. *Sacred Hula: The Historical Hula ʻĀlaʻapapa*. Honolulu: Bishop Museum Press.

Teaiwa, Katerina Martina. 2012. 'Choreographing difference: The (body) politics of Banaban dance.' *The Contemporary Pacific* 24(1) Spring: 65–94.

Trask, Haunani-Kay. 1999. *From a Native Daughter: Colonialism and Sovereignty in Hawaiʻi*. Honolulu, University of Hawaiʻi Press.

Van Gennep, Arnold. (1909) 1960 *The Rites of Passage*. London: Routledge.

15

New Pacific Portraits: Voices from the 11th Festival of Pacific Arts

Curated by Katerina Teaiwa and Joseph Vile

Introduction

This essay is a montage of reflections and portraits drawing on the work of Pacific Studies students from The Australian National University at the 2012 Festival of Pacific Arts in the Solomon Islands. The festival is a unique quadrennial regional event organised by Pacific peoples *for* Pacific peoples rather than for a tourist or other visitors' market. In 1972 the South Pacific Commission (now Secretariat of the Pacific Community or SPC) established the Festival of Pacific Arts (FOPA) to promote, develop and safeguard indigenous expressions of culture in Oceania. Forty years on the event is still going strong with thousands of local and visiting participants and artists gathering every four years to share a wide range of cultural practices. These include dance, music, painting, carving, tattooing, filmmaking, architecture, healing arts, ceremonial arts, literary arts, navigation and canoeing, culinary arts, fashion design and much more. Since 1996 the event has rotated between a Polynesian, Melanesian and Micronesian host country and has played a significant role in not just safeguarding but transforming arts and cultural practices across the region.[1]

---

1   Katerina Martina Teaiwa, 2014, 'Culture moves? The Festival of Pacific Arts and Dance Remix in Oceania', *Dance Research Aotearoa* 2: 2–19.

The festival also illustrates the will and agency of participating countries' nations, territories and cultural groups to mobilise economic and cultural resources to support travel for participation, and the capacity of the host country to successfully mount and manage the dynamic and complex two-week event. Meeting the financial costs is usually challenging on both these fronts, and funds are often raised by participating governments with additional support in the form of international aid. Increasingly, the festival has been examined more closely by the Human Development Programme within the SPC for its economic and development potential, particularly in the context of cultural and creative industries.[2] In the case of the 2012 festival in the Solomon Islands, despite several sceptical news reports that highlighted an alleged lack of preparation, the final organising committee was able to rally resources and inspire the Honiara community to prepare their city for thousands of visitors. This was an impressive achievement that belied the Solomon Islands' regular depiction as a 'failed state', particularly in Australian scholarship and media.[3]

In spite of allegations of corruption and some dissatisfaction from participating provinces and venues, there was a decided air of Solomon Islands independence and pride before, during and after the two-week event in Honiara. In addition to the satellite venues of Doma (Guadalcanal), Auki (Malaita), Tulagi (Central Province) and Gizo (Western Province), two adjacent sites in Honiara, each almost double the size of a rugby field, were transformed to create a 'Pasifika village', stalls for visiting delegations and also a Solomon Islands village with spaces for each province, a fashion runway and a unique stage surrounded by a massive artificial lake.

Within a report conducted by Joycelin Leahy and colleagues, recommendations were made to consider the foreign tourist potential of the festival but as yet this is not the primary focus. Rather, Pacific governments and those in the culture sector prefer to maintain the

---

2   See, for example, David Throsby, 1994, 'The production and consumption of the arts: A view of cultural economics', *Journal of Economic Literature* 32(1) March: 1–29; and Katerina Martina Teaiwa, 2007, 'On sinking, swimming, floating, flying and dancing: The potential for cultural industries in the Pacific Islands', *Pacific Economic Bulletin* 22(2): 140–51.

3   See, for example, 'The Solomon Islands: the Pacific's first failed state?' 2003, *Economist*, 13 February, p. 29; 'Australian government celebrates successes in helping Solomon Islands pull back from failed state', 2013, *Australia Network News*, 21 October. Online: www.abc.net.au/news/2013-10-20/an-sols-failed-state/5034182, (accessed 1 February 2014).

event as an opportunity for intra-regional cultural exchange and expressions of pride.[4] While non–Pacific Islander visitors and tourists were present at the Solomon Islands celebrations in 2012, they were marginal to its production and purpose. Certain venues, however, such as 'VIP stands', became sites of cultural, class and racial distinction that signalled colonial legacies and contemporary geopolitical hierarchies and agendas. While the VIP stands were certainly intended for senior officials representing each of the participating delegations, it was also the case that white tourists and families, and anyone who did not 'look' local, were welcome in these venues, two of which were equipped with refrigerators offering free cold water and other beverages. At the same time, however, the fact that these refreshments were made available to those who presumably represented the most affluent and visibly 'foreign' segment of festival attendees signalled an economic irony that is often apparent throughout the region, especially in tourism industry contexts. Such ironies seemed to contradict the express aims of the event. Free drinks were just one of the many surprising features of this festival in Honiara that many assumed would be challenging for the Solomon Islands government to mount. Even so, as the following student vignettes demonstrate, looking beyond such markers of inequality, the festival's vibrant diversity of expressive arts and performance provided a vital forum for engaging dialogues of culture and identity.

In 2012, Pacific Studies students from The Australian National University, in a course run by Katerina Teaiwa and Nikki Mariner, participated in a project supported by the Secretariat of the Pacific Community and FOPA organising committee. This included interviewing participants for a publication commemorating 40 years of the festival. The students came from diverse disciplines and backgrounds and were excited to attend the festival, and to deepen their knowledge of Oceania by engaging with cultural practitioners from the many islands. For its own part, the SPC viewed this collecting

---

4   See Joycelin Leahy, Joyce Yeap-Holliday and Bill Pennington, 2010, *Evaluation of the Festival of Pacific Arts*, Suva: Secretariat of the Pacific Community; Elise Huffer, 2006, 'Regionalism and cultural identity: Putting the Pacific back into the Plan', in *Globalisation and Governance in the Pacific Islands: State, Society and Governance in Melanesia*, ed. Stewart Firth, pp. 43–55, Canberra: ANU E Press; Teaiwa, 'On sinking, swimming, floating, flying and dancing'; and Katerina M. Teaiwa, 2012, *Implementing, Monitoring and Evaluating Cultural Politics: A Pacific Toolkit*, Suva: Secretariat of the Pacific Community and European Union.

of stories and ideas from participants as key to documenting the festival, especially by highlighting the voices of participants alongside works by academics who regularly write about the iconic event.

The collection of interviews presented here focuses on what scholars might view as minor agents of history or social transformation—everyday peoples who were artists and delegates to the 2012 Festival. The title 'New Pacific Portraits' references two historical projects on 'Pacific Islands Portraits'. *Watriama and Co: Further Pacific Island Portraits* from ANU Press by Hugh Laracy primarily explored the lives and experiences of Europeans in the Pacific, even when focusing on characters such as Kanak William Watriama.[5] *Pacific Islands Portraits* edited by J.W. Davidson and Deryck Scarr[6] included more Pacific Islanders, most of whom were male and leaders in their communities. The framework of 'Pacific portraits', best describes the brief and yet revealing insights into artists' lives and inspirations that are often invisible, or seen as less relevant, in a tourism studies or political studies context.

We have gathered some of the portraits created by students that showcase the experiences of artists and other delegation members on the ground in Honiara. The students' interviews and observations are here presented as written by them with some editing by Teaiwa and Vile. Students' questions focused on participants' thoughts on the festival but also on the importance of culture and arts in their respective local and national contexts. Issues of politics, education and history were regularly raised, reinforcing the fact that the arts in Oceania are mutually entangled with and reflective of many dimensions of Pacific life.

The vignettes demonstrate the festival to be an important site of connection and dialogue, one in which interpretations of personal and collective identity—past, present and future—are communicated and explored. At the same time, each shows how the experience of being a touring representative of a national or cultural collective identity, as expressed through the arts, entails a profound sense of emotionally charged moral reflection and responsibility.

5   Hugh Laracy, 2013, *Watriama and Co: Further Pacific Island Portraits*, Canberra: ANU Press.
6   J.W. Davidson and Deryck Scarr (eds), 1970, *Pacific Islands Portraits*, Canberra: The Australian National University Press.

Portraits of artists and participants by ANU students

Nicholas Neo with Francisco 'Frank' Rabon from Guam

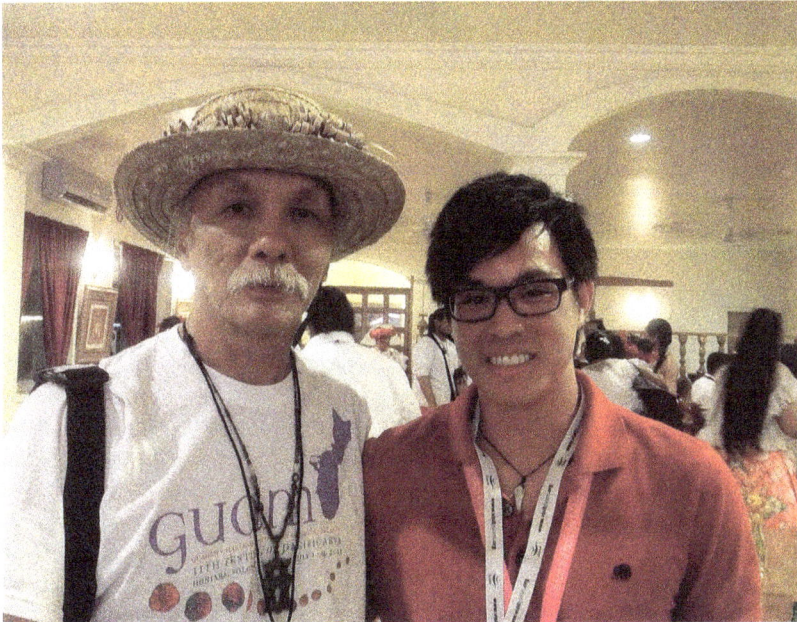

Figure 87. Frank and Nicholas at the Festival of Pacific Arts.
Source. Photograph courtesy of Nicholas Neo, July 2012.

Chamorros are the indigenous people of the Mariana Islands, of which Guam is the largest and southernmost of the island chain. The destructive effects of many waves of colonisation, foreign possession and Guam's current political status has had a huge impact on the loss of cultural practices such as the arts, crafts and those practices originally passed on by men. Through early Spanish colonialism in the sixteenth century, there was also a gradual elimination of Chamorro dances, chants and songs.

> Among the Pacific Islanders, the Chamorro people have the worst struggle in terms of protecting their identity and their indigenous heritage (Francisco Rabon).

Francisco 'Frank' Rabon is the founder and director of the Taotao Tano' Cultural Dancers, which is now synonymous with cultural dance practices in Guam. After founding the dance group in 1983, he continued to advance in the field of cultural dance, most notably to research Chamorro history, origins, migration, connection and the reconstruction of indigenous Chamorro dances, chants and songs. He started his research in 1971 after being exposed to indigenous cultural dancing from other parts of the Pacific in 1970. Frank speaks, writes and reads the Chamorro language fluently and is very familiar with Chamorro customs. It is this upbringing that he credits as the source of his fascination with the history of the islands. He emphasises the importance of his ancestral traditions, knowing just how much has been lost through external influences:

> I'm not an activist; I'm just a person that tries to make changes in a subtle way.

Despite being a United States territory, Guam has closer connections to the Pacific Islands than to America. The Chamorro people are not alone in trying to protect their land, their language and their culture. The Festival of Pacific Arts serves to put out a message of respect to the indigenous people of the Pacific and also the recognition of who they are as people of Oceania. Through FOPA, every individual has a unique experience, a distinctive destiny and different goal. Rabon said:

> It motivates the Pacific Islanders to take hold and cherish and put a value on their indigenous identity and the traditions that makes them unique as Pacific Islanders ... When our world is so hung up on economics, with money being the value of life, then there is no emotion. Arts brings out the emotion, the humanitarian aspect of this world of plenty. Oceania is not a massive land that is glued together, she is a massive land separated by the Pacific Ocean and in many ways the Pacific Islanders are a group of people. The arts in the Pacific is an identity of the people of Oceania. It makes them unique from the other continents.

> Arts is the balance, the humanitarian balance with economics.

Frank's work represents historical, indigenous, colonial and contemporary aspects of the Chamorro people. The performances that he creates are a researched and revitalised product of the 400 years of his people's genocide on culture, songs and music. Over the past 40 years, he has re-established and recreated an identity; what he feels is representative of them in this modern world. For many other countries, their cultures have not been interrupted but the same cannot be said for Guam, or the Marianas.

It is not merely a performance; it is a way of life.

Frank was once a dancer searching and looking for his identity and has since moved on. He is now a leader of his people and feels that he must play his role in what they have entrusted to him. He was bestowed the honour of Master of Chamorro Dance and has received the Lifetime Achievement Award by the Guam Council of the Arts and Humanities in recognition of his accomplishments in cultural dance practices of Guam.

As educators, we have to strive to instill a sense of identity to the people of Guam, and the importance of preserving and perpetuating the traditions of our ancestors. We continue on the path that our ancestors have struggled on before us, knowing that we have only started to rekindle the fire that burns within the hearts of our people.

Kelly Xin Zhang with Sinahemana Hekau from Niue

Coming from a small country, it is actually a big thing to be involved in a big event (Sinahemana Hekau).

Sina came to the 11th Festival of the Pacific Arts with the Niue Dance Group. With a deep understanding of her culture, she is also responsible for the choreography of all Niuean dance performances at this festival. Besides her various roles she also actively participates in different forum discussions on legislation, environment and culture. She was one of the speakers addressing the issue of farmers' rights at the cultural rights symposium organised by the SPC. She felt that this festival offered a great platform for her people to showcase who they are to all other cultures and people.

Figure 88. Sinahemana Hekau.
Source. Photographed by Kelly Xin Zhang, July 2012.

Coming from a small country, Sina appreciated the festival invitation and recognition given to Niue. At the same time, she feels that her participation at the festival was a good development opportunity for her. The need to pay closer attention to her own culture and behaviour in order to positively portray her country and culture acts is a motivation for her to constantly improve the way she does things. Besides the cultural diversity in the Pacific, she also appreciates and enjoys the similarities and connections among different island states and territories.

Sina has a strong passion for dancing and singing, which she learnt at her school and from her family when she was young. At that time, she did not really pay attention to the expression of her performance because she learnt it only for fun. As she grew up, she started to develop her own thinking and integrated it into her performance. Dancing became a way for her to express herself. She has also become more particular about the standard of performance as well as the differences existing among different styles of dance. Dance has also helped her develop self-discipline over the years and she now loves to teach dances to young people. She is happy to see that dance actually helps young people raise their level of confidence in terms of their appearance and self-esteem. She feels that dancing helps her own people to understand their culture and strengthen their identity.

Sina really liked the architecture in the festival village. She was amazed at the traditional styles and concepts of various structures built using natural materials such as bamboo. In particular, the Pasifika Stage, which distinguishes itself from the modern and common architecture of many steel-framed stages, was one of her favourites. She was impressed by the extraordinary amount of effort that the Solomon Islands had dedicated to the construction of the festival sites from scratch. This is her third time participating in the Festival of Pacific Arts and she felt that this has been the best one so far.

> I really appreciate all the learning that I am given. It is so culturally enriched. Each of the countries has their own distinct cultures for different groups of people. To me, it is a bonus coming here to Solomon Islands.

Sina felt that her country's participation in this regional arts festival has helped promote both cultural and national identities among its own people that are crucial to nation-building. She thinks that it will be a slow process for her country to actually realise the benefit of this festival because the development of a creative economy where arts and culture are appreciated requires time. On the other hand, she feels that providing a cultural and authentic experience is very important to the tourism development in her country as its relatively small size offers little room for sightseeing.

Sina believes that this arts festival will contribute to the vitality and continued development of her culture. She feels that participation in festivals like this help people understand their culture better because they are given responsibilities to show and share their cultures with others.

Sina finished her primary and secondary education in Niue and has a diverse and interesting background in many fields of work. With her law background from the University of the South Pacific in Vanuatu, Sina has a keen interest in bringing civil society involvement to the process of law making. Upon her graduation, she returned to her home country to test her knowledge. She has contributed to the legislative development of the Taoga Niue Bill for heritage preservation and use. On the regional level, she represents the interests of small islands and developing states. On the global level, she actively participates in various forums to promote the views of the Pacific region. She has now completed postgraduate study in New Zealand and is looking forward to doing a PhD in the future.

> Art keeps us alive. Arts encourages you to be creative. Science will tell you the rules, the limitations and the boundaries, whereas art has no limitation and boundary.

Anna Pavlakis with Aisea Konrote Faustino from Fiji

Fashion permeates the Festival of Pacific Arts with traditional and contemporary costumes both forming crucial aspects of any cultural performance. However, 2012 was only the second time fashion has been included at the festival.

It is not often that you come across an individual with such enthusiasm and spirit as emerging Fijian fashion designer Aisea Konrote Faustino. His contemporary designs have graced the catwalks of Fiji Fashion Week and now at the Festival of Pacific Arts Fashion Show, and are an outstanding display of the contribution of the vibrant, elegant Fijian culture to the Pacific region. Aisea's passion and zeal for fashion is self-evident in his outfits, but of more significance are the defining aspects of his life that are woven and blended into the patterns and threads of each piece.

Aisea's personal story of identity is inextricably linked with culture and the arts, and he exhibits a profound connection with the Festival of Pacific Arts like few others. He attended the very first festival in Suva, Fiji, as a young boy on his ninth birthday in 1972, and he has fond memories of the colours, talent and arts on display. The 2012 festival in Honiara however, is only the second time he has attended the festival. What happened in the 40 years between was a deeply personal journey of identity construction, such that the festival acts as bookends to perhaps the most important chapter of his life; a period of enlightenment and reclamation of personal heritage.

Figure 89. Aisea with some of his designs at the Fijian delegation hut at the 2012 FOPA.

Source. Photographed by Anna Pavlakis, July 2012.

The son of a seamstress, Aisea's passion for fashion began at a young age and flourished with his experience as a model in his youth. Due to this early exposure to the western world, Aisea was lured by its wealth, prosperity and perceived beauty and sought to explore it more. Trained as a flight attendant, he travelled to some of the most famous cities in the world and considered the life he and others led in Fiji as undeveloped and unsophisticated. Fiji, he believed, paled in comparison to the exquisite cultures and arts he expected to experience through travelling abroad.

Aisea admits that at this time in his life, he willingly shunned his Pacific heritage, however, his quest for wonders did not pan out as planned. The West's splendours, he discovered, were not as rich as expected and his self-entitled 'quest for beauty' had not delivered any significant results. Indeed, he realised that he had found nothing abroad that could not be matched, nor beaten by the simplest of Fiji's natural beauty.

> I searched for beauty in Hollywood, India, Japan but I couldn't find anything beautiful, I shunned Fiji ... but I found that the beauty was right beneath my nose yet I went searching out of my own island (Aisea Konrote Faustino).

Returning to Fiji, Aisea embraced the offerings of his cultural heritage and displayed his first Fijian inspired collection in 2007. With little money for materials and tools, he relied on his mother's old sewing machine to create the initial outfits, entering them in a local competition where he took out first prize. Using his prize money he purchased his very first sewing machine from Australia and created more designs, winning more competitions, and purchasing more materials. Now the proud owner of six sewing machines and countless outfits, Aisea feels that he has reclaimed his Fijian heritage, and that attending 2012's Festival of Pacific Arts sees him come full circle. He perceives the festival as an emotional period of time for him as it represents the culmination of his psychological journey, and an event that secures his position as a Pacific Islander.

> I was lost between the first and current festival ... a lost identity. I was fortunate to have found my identity again and so fortunate to be selected to come over here. I had to go backwards to go forwards.

Fijian fashion has always been a prevalent feature of Fijian livelihoods, with the light and casual clothing designed specifically for the hot, tropical climate. A key traditional item is the sulu, which is considered the trendsetter of Fijian fashion clothing and is worn by both men and women, especially at formal occasions. Only recently, however, has modern Fijian fashion gained respect as a key aspect of Fijian culture. From the late 1990s, interest in contemporary fashion grew until the creation of Fiji's very own Fashion Week in 2008 to the praise of international designers and event chairman Ian Mclean acknowledging that putting fashion into the cultural spotlight has the ability to 'take this country forward'.

Aisea's designs can be described as a fusion of western styles and a Pacific/Fijian style, and he seeks to create contemporary designs that still retain a small aspect of tradition. Nature is his key source of inspiration and whilst it is sometimes not evident in his design's aesthetics, it always plays a large role in the production and thought process of creation as it was this feature of Fiji that drew him back to the islands. Every piece that Aisea creates is a one-of-a-kind as he never duplicates any of his designs because of a desire for uniqueness. In addition, the importance of family is essential in Aisea's designs, and his recent collection at Fiji Fashion Week was dedicated to his late mother and named Hefrani after his grand niece.

Aisea regards Fiji's natural beauty as not only his source of inspiration but as his source of materials, and he accordingly employs natural resources into his designs where possible. He believes that in order to truly appreciate the beauty of the natural environment, one must ensure that it is protected and not misused. Through encouraging the use of natural renewable resources in his designs, Asiea both reduces his individual environmental impact and advocates the utilisation of materials that do not pose a threat to the environment. For this reason he relates wholeheartedly to the 2012 Festival of Pacific Arts' theme 'Culture in Harmony with Nature'.

> The sun, the moon, nature inspires me. All my designs depict the environment from the beginning to the end … I savour the moment when nature's radiance provides inspiration for a new piece … Our natural resources in Fiji are an oyster for fashion design and I intend to use that … My designs are all bold and very provocative … but not too vulgar. I have to respect the culture we are in. I want to learn and absorb as much as I can [at the festival], because I almost lost my identity and I don't want to go through that again. It is not wrong to be in the western world, but do not forget who you are … With the rapid influence of the western world it is our duty to make the youth of today realise that respect is good for culture. If everyone was like me growing up, then culture would be diminished. For this reason I want to teach the children of the Pacific the value of your religion, your skin colour, your looks. You need to be proud to be a Pacific Islander.

Athena Rosabelle Abuan with Stillwest Longden and delegates from the Central Province, Solomon Islands

The Central Province is one of the nine provinces of the Solomon Islands that offers unique and diverse art genres, with its own tales of tribes, chiefs, tradition, culture, and its history of headhunting and tribal wars. A significant traditional dance representing victory during the tribal wars is called the *siokole*.

Figure 90. Central Province dancers gathered for the *siokole*.
Source. Photographed by Athena Abuan, July 2012.

> To our group, the dance really highlights the theme of the festival—
> where land and sea are integrated (Stillwest Longden)

The *siokole* is a traditional dance from Gela in the Central Province—
performed in front of a chief to honour him and the tribe after
a successful battle against tribal enemies. The *siokole* follows a very
meticulous process and dance movements—the vocal tune has to be
regulated in such a way that it is only audible to the Chief, while the
body movements also have to correspond with the song rhythm and
wording to emphasise harmony.

The Central Province is made up of four main tribes: the Gaubata,
Kakau, Hogokiki and Hogokama. In the past, these four tribes fought
against each other for territories and authority over land and ocean.
To complete a chiefly kingdom, victory must be achieved in both land
and sea, and that is why the elements of land and sea are incorporated
into the dance through mimicking the movements of the *sou* (heron),
which dominates the sea with a distinctive movement to hunt for its
prey, and the *puko* (grasshopper), which represents the land.

The movements show how the warriors battled in different environments and in the case of the *sou*, it is how they moved accordingly in sea battles, how warriors incorporate wit in sensing and dealing with enemies and prey, whereas in the case of the land battles, the *puko* represents happiness and celebration as the battle has been conquered. In other words, these movements represent the significant skills and experiences of warriors behind victories.

The order of performance starts with the *totosi*, which gives a picture of the battlefield and how the fights take place. Next are the *sou* and *puko*, as discussed above, and lastly, the *isubela* where the warriors show alertness and caution upon sensing or knowledge that an enemy is close.

Figure 91. The *totosi*—opening sequence of the *siokole* wherein the Chief and warriors make their entrance while a conch shell is blown to signify the beginning of the dance performed at the Pacific Arts Festival.
Source. Photographed by Athena Abuan, July 2012.

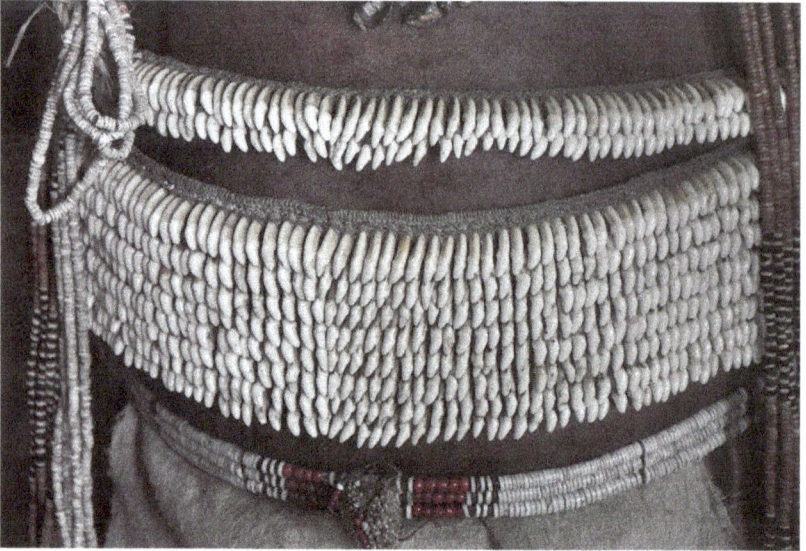

Figure 92. *Na NILAU*—dog's teeth as form of traditional money to signify wealth and power.

Source. Photographed by Athena Abuan, July 2012.

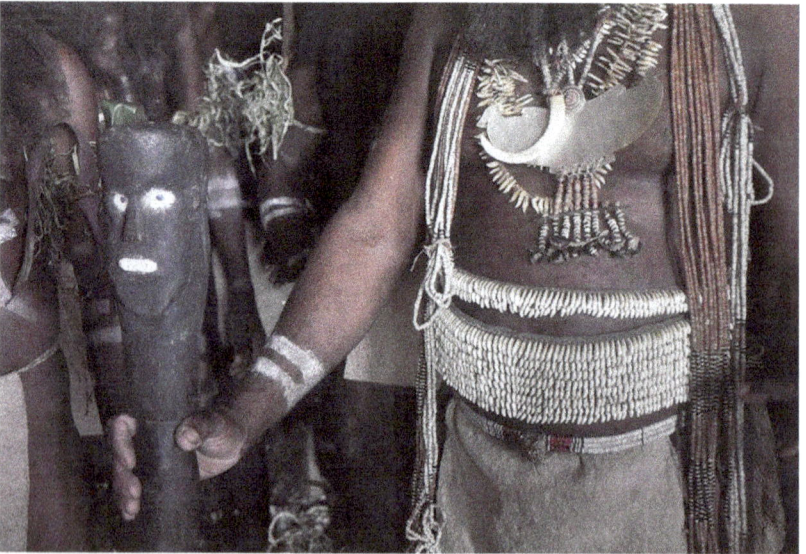

Figure 93. The staff (*totogona*) has faces on both sides to symbolise security and constant vigilance.

Source. Photographed by Athena Abuan, July 2012.

The Chief enters with two warriors on either side of him to offer protection. The front-line warriors enter to symbolise that the fight is over; they serve the Chief during peace and wartime. The Chief's security, chieftaincy and survival depend on their strength, loyalty and skills, as they are bodyguards and act according to his orders, fighters perform leading roles for the *siokole*. The current Chief, Charles Dauasi, hails from the Boli District of Gela in the Central Province. He is the successor of his deceased uncle, the previous Chief, and he will serve his tribe until the day of his death; upon his death, the Chieftainship will be passed to his successor.

The *siokole* highlights and honours the importance and the role of the Chief to a tribe as warriors perform a victory dance upon winning a battle in land and sea to complete the Chief's kingdom. The Chief's clothing and accessories represent his role, power over land and sea, constant vigilance, balance of power, wealth, security, control and status.

> The costumes—it's like their [the dancers'] blessing; whenever the dancers wear these costumes they have this kind of feeling that they have the power.

After a difficult selection process, the FOPA committee announced the need to omit a group from the province and said that their group was not eligible to perform. The group performed in front of the committee member who was from Gela province who was able to understand the concept within the dance; hence they were able to participate.

As explained by Stillwest Longden, one of the organisers and coaches of the group: 'people from other islands cannot be part of a group without understanding what they do'. He added that tribal intermarriages kept the blood ties intact within the province; hence, those from Gela will feel the meaning of the dance.

> We cannot live without being connected to other people and others should respect our identity … To represent the Solomon Islands means so much as it is a means to connect to the world—to display their identity, and to showcase to people around the world that the Solomon Islands is made up of a diverse group of communities. Different groups are showcasing their own cultures, but there should be collaboration and integration as a group. The festival allows them to come together as a group of people of diverse cultures but to boost development, unity is required.

Figure 94. Stillwest Longden, delegation coordinator, Central Province.
Source. Photograph by Athena Abuan, July 2012.

Stillwest reiterated that the festival allowed local people to interact with each other and other ethnic groups, and it changes the perceptions of local people and outside friends of the Solomon Islands after the ethnic tensions and social unrests tarnished their reputation. Stillwest further argued that what they showcase (i.e. dance) is a cultural product and he hopes that this perception is shared by the participants—that they are highlighting what they own, and hopes for a way to market these products to the outside world to boost the economy. But it requires initiatives from the grassroots level— for the government and the region to look at arts as a distinctive product.

> Unity is needed—to be 'one' to compete economically globally; being one economically and culturally. To participate in this sort of event, we are telling the world that we are together; that is when we will be able to compete ... The festival highlights something; that we are here together as Pacific Islanders, not as a different nation; just as one region.

Figure 95. Stillwest Longden and Central Province performers.
Source. Photographed by Athena Abuan, July 2012.

Felicia Lim with Taiwan delegates

Ku Le Le Damuleng belongs to the Taiwan indigenous Paiwan tribe. This is his first time attending the Pacific Arts Festival and he is excited and very much looking forward to visiting the Solomon Islands, and is particularly keen to know more about the culture, tradition and customs of the Solomon Islanders. He had attended the combined worship service at Maranatha Prayer Hall, where he felt honoured to be representing Taiwan indigenous groups at this regional gathering.

He also added that his family and friends were filled with awe and admiration when they learnt about him attending the festival. In addition, he was present for the official opening ceremony held at the stadium and seeing a large sea of people was an eye-opener for him.

Figure 96. Ku Le Le Damuleng.
Source. Photographed by Felicia Lim, July 2012.

Ku Le Le Damuleng has been a trained dancer since the age of 16, and while he had spent most of his time in the city, he was invited by his teacher to join a group, Ping Dong Dance Troupe, consisting of approximately 20 dance members. The best known dance group is Naruwan, which comprises the majority of the Paiwan tribe and the remaining are Rukai tribe. A major difference between dance groups lies in their costume designs. Due to the possible complexities of the 14 tribes, it is often difficult for the Taiwanese government to provide funding to each different tribe to participate. Indigenous Taiwan peoples have both contemporary and traditional dances, embracing diversity but they continue with traditional dance to preserve their roots and unique heritage. Ku Le Le felt that when comparing traditional and contemporary dances, traditional dance would be able to invoke imagination, whereas contemporary dance might not be able to deliver meaning as clearly.

Ku Le Le felt that the arts play a significant role in the Pacific Islands where there is so much sharing and understanding of each other's culture, in order to preserve traditions. His favourite group were the dancers from Tahiti. He hoped that participating countries saw Taiwan as special guests as it is the only country not part of the Pacific Islands. Ku Le Le was also very appreciative of Solomon Islanders' hospitality and kindness.

Figure 97. Amaya Sayfik and an Amis performer at the festival.
Source. Photographed by Felicia Lim, July 2012.

Amaya Sayfik comes from the Amis indigenous tribe and runs a product design company. He designs most of the handicrafts, indigenous costumes and accessories. His pepper and salt containers are inspired by a dance where designs are made to resemble ancestral eyes. Similar to the Rukai, Bunun and Paiwan tribes, a snake is displayed at the front of their houses, which is a symbol of prosperity and security. It is thought that when a snake rises, it protects the tribe. He strongly agrees that both arts and cultures are important and he finds the worthiness in them and preserving one's roots is essential as western influence is becoming rampant. He recommended a mixture of traditional and contemporary aspects of culture so that they can be better integrated into one's daily life. He felt that the indigenous Taiwanese culture has evolved to include the element of innovation. He observed their Solomon Islands counterparts as having a strong foundation in their traditional roots. He added that if Solomon Islands takes up modernisation too quickly, then he fears culture would lose its important links.

Reflections

The late Professor Epeli Hau'ofa, founder of the Oceania Centre for Arts and Culture at the University of the South Pacific, wrote about how what is typically taken for creativity in the Pacific is sometimes viewed as 'the adoption, and occasionally, refinement, of things generated mainly outside Oceania or the unceasing reproduction of the original creations of our forebears in ages past'.[7] However, the creativity to be found in the arts, he argued, actually reflects Pacific principles of reciprocity, cooperation, openness to community, transmission of knowledge and skills through observation, as well as practical experience. If the modern world of art views the field in terms of individualistic expressions of art, the Pacific 'gives priority to the collective'.[8]

The reflections from artists here, as told to ANU students, demonstrate combinations of both individual and collective concerns and hopes that have been there since Europeans first entered the Pacific, and most certainly since Christianity and colonialism resulted in major structural changes to Pacific societies. Many artists spoke of the importance of the preservation of 'tradition', which for many islanders is a combination of both pre- and post-colonial values and practises. Many of the dances, for example, had direct links to ancient social structures and relations.

That binary of tradition and modernity, as critiqued by various scholars in Pacific Studies, anthropology, cultural studies and elsewhere, may not always be useful for thinking about life and art in Oceania today. Past and present surely exist in a fluid continuum inflecting artistic

---

7   Epeli Hau'ofa, 2008, *We are the Ocean: Selected Works*, Honolulu: University of Hawai'i Press, p. 85.
8   Ibid.

choices and presentations. Even so, articulated within a context of creative dialogue, the portraits presented here suggest how dynamic expressions and engagements of and with identity may be effectively and evocatively articulated even while incorporating the much-critiqued and apparently reifying languages of 'tradition'. Indeed, as expressed by these artists and their student biographers, within the context of Pacific arts, diverse traditions may be intimately entwined through understandings of distance and difference as well as identity. As demonstrated across these portraits, the language that artists and delegates use to talk about art forms still reflects epistemological and ontological aspects of Pacific life whereby things are often articulated in terms of perceived differences and perceived anxieties, rather than fluidity. This may demonstrate the actual effectiveness of FOPA over 40 years, to keep strong the initial ideas shaped by the Pacific community, to preserve and safeguard 'traditional' and place-based Pacific cultures in the face of overwhelming changes. This theme continued strongly in the 2016 festival held in Guam in the Northern Pacific along with a political statement from Chamorro activists and artists to 'decolonize Oceania'.

References

Davidson, J.W. and Deryck Scarr (eds). 1970. *Pacific Islands Portraits*. Canberra: Australian National University Press.

Firth, Stewart (ed.). 2006. *Globalisation and Governance in the Pacific Islands: State, Society and Governance in Melanesia*. Canberra: ANU E Press. Online: press.anu.edu.au/publications/series/state-society-and-governance-melanesia/globalisation-and-governance-pacific (accessed 25 February 2016).

Fullagar, Kate (ed.). 2012. *The Atlantic World in the Antipodes*. Newcastle upon Tyne: Cambridge Scholars Press.

Hau'ofa, Epeli. 2008. *We are the Ocean: Selected Works*. Honolulu: University of Hawai'i Press.

Huffer, Elise. 2006. 'Regionalism and cultural identity: Putting the Pacific back into the Plan.' In *Globalisation and Governance in the Pacific Islands: State, Society and Governance in Melanesia*, ed.

Stewart Firth, pp. 43–55. Canberra: ANU E Press. Online: press.anu. edu.au/publications/series/state-society-and-governance-melanesia/ globalisation-and-governance-pacific (accessed 25 February 2016).

Laracy, Hugh. 2013. *Watriama and Co: Further Pacific Island Portraits*. Canberra: ANU Press. Online: press.anu.edu.au?p=260041 (accessed 25 February 2016).

Leahy, Joycelin, Joyce Yeap-Holliday and Bill Pennington. 2010. *Evaluation of the Festival of Pacific Arts*. Suva: Secretariat of the Pacific Community.

Regional Cultural Strategy: Investing in Pacific Cultures. 2010–2020. n.d. Online: www.spc.int/hdp/index2.php?option=com_docman &task=doc_view&gid=382&Itemid=4 (accessed 12 July 2014).

Scarr, Deryck (ed.). 1979. *More Pacific Islands Portraits*. Canberra: Australian National University Press.

Teaiwa, Katerina Martina. 2007. 'On sinking, swimming, floating, flying and dancing: The potential for cultural industries in the Pacific Islands.' *Pacific Economic Bulletin* 22(2): 140–51.

Teaiwa, Katerina M. 2012. *Implementing, Monitoring and Evaluating Cultural Politics: A Pacific Toolkit*. Suva: Secretariat of the Pacific Community and European Union.

Teaiwa Katerina Martina. 2012. 'Cultural development and cultural observatories in the African, Caribbean and Pacific (ACP) group of states.' In *The Atlantic World in the Antipodes*, ed. Kate Fullagar, pp. 256–82. Newcastle upon Tyne: Cambridge Scholars Press.

———. 2014. 'Culture moves? The Festival of Pacific Arts and Dance Remix in Oceania.' *Dance Research Aotearoa* 2: 2–19.

Teaiwa, Katerina and Colin Mercer. 2010. *Pacific Cultural Mapping, Planning and Policy Toolkit*. Noumea: Secretariat of the Pacific Community and European Union.

Throsby, David. 1994. 'The production and consumption of the arts: A view of cultural economics.' *Journal of Economic Literature* 32(1) March: 1–29.

16

Great Works

Courtney Sina Meredith

She has a top knot of black curls, a 105 trench in charcoal, a white linen tunic stopped at her knees revealing black tights running into dark boots with gold points on the heel. Her moleskin is chocolate brown, she takes it from her handbag and continues quietly the conversation with the deity Nafanua, a waterfall of indecipherable pleas running down the page. Inside the Tate Modern, she walks softly and quickly in search of the Henri Matisse exhibition—'The Cut-Outs', a period when Matisse began *cutting* and *carving* into colour.

'Oh there you are … great goddess, I'm here, finally, in front of *L'escargot,* The Snail. Yes, the shapes and the colours are nice but what the fuck, I don't see a snail.' She urges the goddess to help her understand the importance of the collage. From this angle, she shifts her weight to the left hoping for a better view and even slips the handbag over from her right shoulder into her hands, expecting a miracle.

'Nope,' she says under her breath, people close by begin to stare.

'No damn snail anywhere.'

She thinks back to that day in Albert Park with Jan on the lawn, trying to understand criminal law.

'All of the material facts you have to pick out, the precedent or whatever, it's like freaking soup in my head. How am I supposed to remember all of this stuff?

Why are the criminals always brown? And I mean, the whole idea of justice is just a bit cracked. You have these rich lawyers right? They need crime to have a job, and like the police right—if there were no criminals they'd be out of work and hungry! Or maybe they'd be policing real things like oil rigs in the sea and predators of endangered birds and acid rain on heritage buildings.'

'Stop it, surrender, you're just out of your depth Ake.' That was Jan, laughing carelessly, running a hand through her blonde mane.

'When *I* read a case at home, it's with a krispie and a cup of tea. When *you* read a case at your dad's firm, it's with his partners connecting the dots for you.' Jan had glared back at her but eventually they both laughed and headed for the pub.

'Nafanua, are you still there? I think of all the times you must have felt unsure but you stayed fierce and you kept fighting.' By now there was only a rainbow blob and she'd stopping trying to make out any creature, deciding it was a test.

'There was one paper I took in security studies, for politics, I read about the fear underneath most things that shape very simple things, like the direction I'm writing in (left to right). One tutor made us all wear masks down the main road to see how it felt to be different. It didn't feel any different to walking down the street with my own face.'

She surveys the white walls slowly, admires a blue form, considers the snow flower, absorbing the strange looking bodies brought to life at the edge of death. Plinth after plinth a new definition of living unfurls. Nafanua is nowhere to be seen.

'Am I the negress? That idea of exotica, beautiful, two dimensional. This is important, it was important to Matisse. I mean it might be okay to be a monster, an attraction for a while, but the novelty ... it wouldn't take long to wear off, so if I had to be quoted either way, I would have to stay the path of denouncement. They put us up on walls because we *are* works of art, but it's the wrong way round Nafanua, they think they're looking at us.'

She writes with a sleek new pen given to her the day after she arrived in this huge, strange city. He was Polish, the banker, he opened an account for her on Edgeware Road. She didn't feel bad taking it, there were plenty in a glass jar on his desk and she noticed airline tickets.

'Canary Islands,' he said proudly in a thick accent, 'don't worry you'll get used to it here, you miss home at first, then slowly London becomes an even better home.' His teeth were shiny white, like he'd smeared them in vaseline.

Everybody said she had to do the Tate, her boss, her publisher and even her Aunty Sia who jammed her into a booth by the airport departure gate, 'Go to the Tate, especially the show of a master, my mate Emma said it's amazing, the food and the gift shop are really good too, especially the chips and the carrot cake.' Akenese had promised she would go. Everybody looked smaller fanned out in a semicircle waving goodbye, she could see the shared features, how they mirrored each other, wide eyed with excitement. It would've killed her cousin Lisia to know from a distance she looked like she belonged too. A part of her wanted to run back to her grandpa and plead with him not to die while she went off to 'find herself' just like the girls she used to mock at university, especially Jan who had somehow become family. She suddenly wanted to be from that generation before, cheering safely from the sidelines, praying for a future where her daughter or her daughter's daughter would set out into the world all alone. Her uncles didn't cry but her mother was there in the centre shimmering, coming to the fore and disappearing all at once. Akenese remembers the great pang in her chest when she finally walked through to customs, unsure of when she would see them all again.

An intellectual property lawyer enters the Tate Modern to see Kazimir Malevich's first retrospective in 30 years. His thin black glasses give an older appearance but under his arm a lustrous snakeskin folder suggests something else. On the way to contemplate Russian landscapes he takes in the Blue Nude (II) observed by a woman 10 metres long, or so she appears in a crisp linen dress not showing her legs, scribbling into a leather journal. He looks at her in profile, considers the difference between women who witness and women who observe, he takes out his phone and taps on the screen.

Akenese can feel his gaze, she continues in her notebook—*writing is a lot of watching*. Her hands flash across the page, giving truth to the notion she can fit into the scene around her if she just keeps herself busy enough, if she can just capture the moment for Aunty Sia. It will be as the polite Polish banker believed, slowly an even better home. It becomes important to detail the artworks separately for the goddess, she arches her feet inside her boots, takes care to keep them flat, the small hole under the right sole lets in a chill from the marble floors.

She ruminates over her mother's warning, 'You have to notice the subtle changes when you get out there, or else you're going to miss it Ake, you'll go all the way to London for nothing. Just stop and you'll see things aren't the same, they're layered, multi-layered. If you keep looking out you'll miss the journey of stepping inside and while you might feel the temperature change between rooms, how can you question what happens if it appears nothing has changed?'

She sits down on one of those predictable leather seats in the middle of the grand hall, completely dwarfed with ideas of how the world could be. Several German tourists in anoraks nearby move in closer, wetting their lips, approaching with soft greetings 'hello' or 'danke' or 'bitte' as though people from outside Britain are encouraged to band together in the middle of the room for safety. Yellow-haired children drag their feet, tired from all the motionlessness, she senses their urge to break free as one of them blows her a kiss.

'Nafanua, that's another thing. They say children are precious, but the ones here have grown from concrete, out of the shadows, towards a grey sky. I haven't seen the sun in weeks and I'm already starting to feel like an extraterrestrial. It seems unfair watching them miss out on grass and fresh air and sunlight, I don't know, maybe they grow up faster here and it makes them superior adults. I might've stayed in law school and come out the other end an actual lawyer, if I'd grown up somewhere like this.'

She sees him again moving between columns, takes care to watch him without being noticed, she imagines a world of trading markets or perhaps finance. He might be a partner with his own legal firm, who else would have the power to stroll around the gallery so casually, so late in the morning? She sends a text to Lisia—*seeing the Tate in 3D!* When she looks up from her phone he catches her off guard, standing close by gesturing to her notebook, 'Are you in the arts?' This is how you shave a decade off your life, she thinks, or maybe this is how you lose your chances altogether. This must be how easy it is to set out on a new journey that becomes an updated version of the past. Akenese smiles at him, 'The cut-outs were lovely.' She walks out of the Tate with Nafanua assuredly in tow.

Her dark hair catches in the feeble light. Birds overhead are drawn onto the clear sky by hand.

'She's definitely got something, maybe a touch of Arab?' says the older of the men breaking the silence.

'She eats jerk chicken, you can tell by her smile.' Comes the answer. They watch her standing among the flowerbeds, she stares ahead into space. Eating meat pies and drawing on rolled cigarettes, both men slacken their tool belts to relax.

Another cold morning of kerbs and pipes, commuters passing in great hordes. Nobody smiling or saying hello, the usual, the inevitable. Moving each leg slowly as though they have just been discovered, they let out tired sighs, shifting about on the park bench. The younger man opens a can of soda, makes an offering to his workmate who shakes his head with a strong frown. Both pretend to check their phones while keeping watch on the woman across the way, writing beside the sculpture.

More people filter into the square, half expecting rain, desiring sun. At the centre of the garden, the half-timbered hut buzzes with life. A head of golden curls swoops across the lawn, stops in mid-flight, coughs into a sleeve before taking off in a brilliant rush.

'She could be Indian you know?' The younger eager to continue.

'Nice African hips, mind,' he keeps on, 'or she could be some kind of part Chinese, part Japanese, something from that region.'

'I think I might've seen her around here before,' says the older one, his fingers caressing paper around tobacco.

A group of slight women in soft greens sit cross-legged by a great London Plane, under the shadows of leaves they lean into each other with little white notepads. Quarrelling couplings hiss profanities, brilliant shapes of youth, throwing their heads back drinking light, oblivious of their wonder.

'I would introduce her to my mother. I reckon she'd fit right in,' he says watching the plume of smoke rise from his cigarette.

'I would happily take her to my mother's grave.'

'You're sick man.'

'Just the truth.'

Akenese eyes the bronze sculpture, thinks of home and revels in the scene. She takes out her notebook and writes ... 'There is a Plane tree, not an Oak or Kauri or a Pohutakawa but a Plane tree. There are two men mending pipes over by the entrance, the younger of the two talks so loud I can't wait to go home to see if I do look African or like an Indian or even Japanese. You were right Nafanua, there is only me, at the Tate I saw nothing but myself.'

17

Ibu & Tufuga

Courtney Sina Meredith

i

Ibu has made a pork and prawn noodle soup
two loaves of white bread one nutty loaf too
the dough rose with the afternoon sun.

The Tufuga has his sister over from Niu Sila
she wants to see Hogwarts and ghosts
her mokopuna lives in London.

I find a book in the den about thieves
Manu is a good girl she makes a platter
we eat cheese and crackers and read.

ii

The Tufuga apologises to his sister over from Niu Sila
she won't stay any longer she misses her mokopuna
he has to work he has to pack he is sorry.

The local pub is pink with playful bunting
you have to excuse yourself for walking
in the courtyard everybody smokes.

Ibu brings me a cup of chamomile tea
she dyed her hair brown she looks different
we plan to go to the markets.

iii

If a bird flies inside it means someone has died
the garden is in heat all the bees buzz
Ibu loves to plant new trees.

The Tufuga is worried about October
he is teaching an Italian history paper
The Tufuga does not speak Italian.

A new delicatessen has opened on North Parade
it sells boutique meats and hand made cheese
Ibu goes to London for the day.

iv

Manu makes a huge jug of Pimms
the neighbours come over without their kids
we sit outside under the bright blue sky

I show Manu my open wound
seeping every day seeping love
she says my ex was really hot

Ibu watches us from the garden table
she knows exactly who I might become
if only the house could house my spirits.

18

Cross-currents: Teana and Moenau, Tahitian Tourists in Seattle

Miriam Kahn, Teana Gooding and Moenau Holman

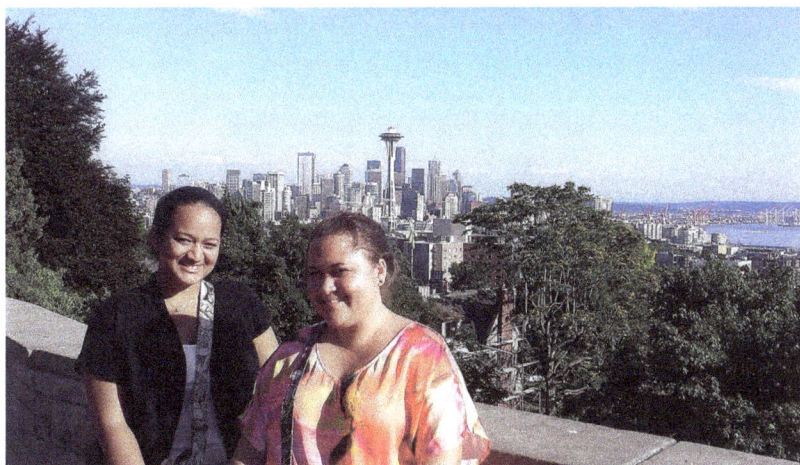

Figure 98. Moenau (left) and Teana (right) at the Kerry Park Lookout, Seattle.

Source. Photographed by Miriam Kahn, 10 August 2013.

Introduction
Miriam Kahn

Moenau Holman and Teana Gooding, from the island of Huahine in French Polynesia, are students at the Université de la Polynésie Française, on the island of Tahiti. Moenau's area of study is social service administration and Teana's is economics.

I've known Teana since she was six years old. Her parents, Hiti and Turia, were our landlords when I began fieldwork on Huahine in 1995. We have continued to enjoy their friendship over the years, visiting with them each time I return to Huahine for my research.

In the summers of 2010 and 2012 I took a group of students from the University of Washington to Huahine for a month-long study abroad trip where students had homestays with Tahitian families. Both Moenau's and Teana's families graciously hosted some of the students (two students each summer). They became very attached to the American students, who established lasting friendships with their Tahitian hosts. Little did I know that a few months after the students left Huahine in 2012, Moenau and Teana would begin planning a big adventure to come to Seattle to visit everyone!

In January 2013, I received the news in an email:

> Nous souhaitons partir sur Seattle pour une durée de trois semaines cet été. Serai ce possible de séjourner chez vous pendant ce temps? Pour la nourriture et le reste on va se débrouiller. Nous attendons votre réponse. (We wish to travel to Seattle for three weeks this summer. Is it possible to stay with you during that time? We can figure out the details about food and other things. We await your response.)

I responded with an enthusiastic *Oui!*

As I later learned, their friends and families on Huahine had been sceptical about their ability to raise the money needed. But they surprised everyone and made a point of being very nonchalant when they told their families that they had purchased their tickets. They arrived in Seattle in July 2013 for their three-week stay. My husband and I, along with several of the University of Washington students who had traveled to Huahine, were overjoyed to welcome them at the airport.

I learned that they had been planning the trip for a year, earning the money by selling plates of home-cooked chicken and rice with vegetables—800 plates in all—which they sold for 500 CFP each (roughly US$6). Because the university is on the island of Tahiti, they could only make and sell the food when they returned home to Huahine during short breaks from school.

Teana and Moenau decided to come to Seattle because they wanted to see new things and have new adventures, and also to see their American friends from the University of Washington. In addition, they wanted to improve their English (what little they knew they had learned from the American students). From the moment they landed in Seattle they insisted that I speak only English with them.

While here, they enjoyed everything immensely. We spent much of the time together, sharing stories and laughter, planning future trips, and fantasising about American ventures that they could institute on Huahine. While driving them around I could see their curiosity and enthusiasm about things that are commonplace for most Americans. As they said, 'Little things make us very happy'. Such things as yellow school buses, police cars and fire engines—all things they knew only from television—caused great excitement. They called the fraternity and sorority houses near the University of Washington campus 'Harry Potter' houses. They made fun of Americans' love of putting peanut butter in everything, but after discovering Cap'n Crunch's Peanut Butter Crunch they insisted on having it every morning for breakfast (along with blueberry pancakes and other American favourites). Their visit to Seattle's Theo Chocolate factory inspired them to think about developing a cacao plantation on Huahine, and they googled information about planting cacao as soon as they got home that day.

Travelling is important to Teana and Moenau (as well as to many Tahitians). As they told me, they can expand their horizons, learn new things, and make things come to life that they had seen only in movies or on television. They can also make new friends. They wanted to try everything, taste everything, and experience everything. As they kept saying, 'We want to benefit from our visit'.

Towards the end of their visit, as we sat together after dinner telling stories and talking about their experiences, I thought about this publication because I had recently been invited to contribute an essay. I explained the idea of the volume to Teana and Moenau, indicating that it might be more interesting if the essay came from them as 'tourists in Seattle', rather than from me. They were delighted at the prospect of collaborating with me on a story for the publication and to 'appear in a book'. We immediately began to sketch out ideas. More focused discussions followed over the next few evenings, as they told me about the things that they enjoyed the most while they were 'tourists in Seattle'. I jotted down their words, translating whenever they switched to French and, eventually (with their approval), I smoothed out the text and provided my own brief commentary (appearing below in italics). Teana and Moenau chose the photos to accompany their stories.

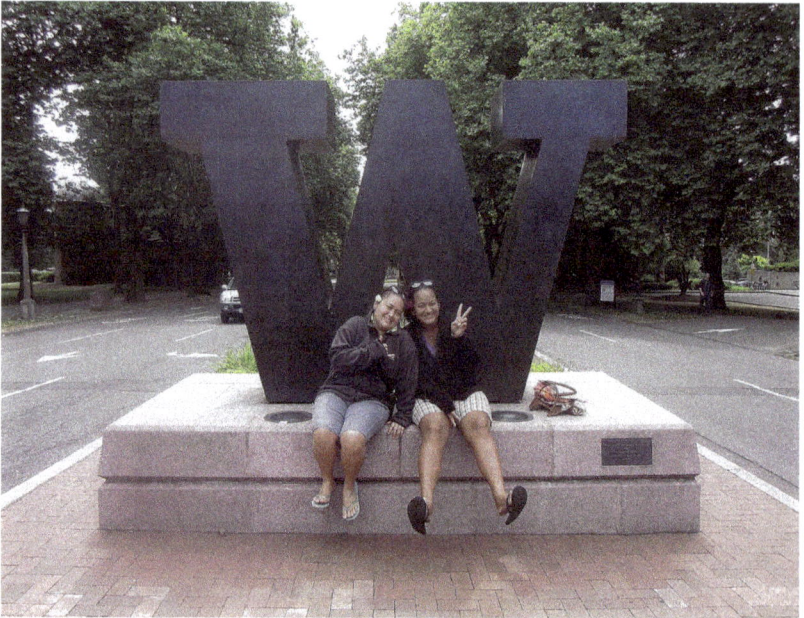

Figure 99. Teana and Moenau at the entrance to the University of Washington.
Source. Photographed by Miriam Khan.

The Pike Place Market

Figure 100. The Pike Place Market.
Source. Photographed by Teana Gooding, 31 July 2013.

'It's very big. There are so many different things at the market. We saw many artists from different countries. We saw people carving in wood and people making jewellery. Here they do a lot of things to attract people to the market. They have people who sing and dance. There are people who toss fish to get your attention. We saw a blind man who played the guitar and a young child who gave him money.'

'Here people are very friendly. When you buy something they ask, "How are you today?" Tahitians are welcoming in some ways, but if they are just doing their job, serving you dinner or selling you something in the market, they don't ask how you are. The vendors in Tahiti just sell you something and tell you the amount you owe them.'

Commentary

Seattle's Pike Place Market, which opened in 1907, is one of the oldest, continuously operated public markets in the United States. It sits on a hill overlooking, and running parallel to, Seattle's waterfront. When it first opened it was used only by farmers selling their produce, but has since grown into one of Seattle's main tourist attractions. Today the market welcomes about 10 million visitors a year.

One of the market's main draws is Pike Place Fish, where an employee stands near the ice-covered fish table and throws large salmon and other fish over the counter to another employee who catches it and prepares it for sale. Although this tradition got started to save employees from having to walk out to the fish table every time someone wanted a fish, it now serves as a major attraction for visitors.

In contrast to the Pike Place Market, the Marché de Pape'ete (Municipal Market), teeming with fresh fish, fruits and vegetables, as well as handicrafts and souvenirs, still serves Pape'ete's urban population, people who may not have access to fishing boats or food gardens. Tourists tend to spend their time on the second storey where the crafts and souvenirs can be found.

Shopping

Figure 101. Teana and Moenau at Costco.
Source. Photographed by Miriam Kahn, 30 July 2013.

'We love to go shopping here! We love the prices. We love the high quality of the clothing. In Tahiti if clothing is cheap it is very poor quality. No regular clothing is produced in Tahiti and everything needs to be imported so it is very, very expensive. Here things are very cheap for us. But then when it comes time to pay they add the tax and it is not as cheap as we had thought. Why don't they just include the tax with the price of the clothing? We like shopping here—the clothing, the styles, the sizes (in Tahiti it is hard to find our sizes), and the many sales!'

Commentary

There are only a few shops that make Tahitian clothing for sale, usually quite expensive. People typically buy imported clothing or have their clothing made by a seamstress (or make it themselves if they know how). Both Teana's and Moenau's mothers are seamstresses and have a steady stream of customers.

Experience Music Project

'For us this museum was very interesting. There were lots of things for people to experience and ways they could express themselves. The visitors could try out different instruments. We think that visitors might develop an interest in music. This way there would be fewer problems with drugs later on because they got interested in music.'

Commentary

Museums in Tahiti, most of which are fairly basic with objects lined up in glass cases, tend to highlight either Tahiti's past or westerners whose fame rests on their adventures and exploits in Tahiti. The main museum is the Musée de Tahiti et ses îles (Museum of Tahiti and its islands), which is a Polynesian ethnographic museum. Other smaller museums include Robert Wan's Black Pearl Museum (attached to a black pearl store), the Paul Gauguin Museum (with relatively poor, small reproductions of some of his paintings), the Seashell Museum (with standard taxonomic exhibits of shells and fish from the lagoon), and the James Norman Hall Home (a replica of the home of the American author of Mutiny on the Bounty *that portrays the writer's life in Tahiti and houses his 3,000-book library).*

Figure 102. Teana and Moenua at the Experience Music Project.
Source. Photographed by Miriam Kahn, 12 August 2013.

The Lighthouse for the Blind, visit with Paula

Figure 103. Teana and Paula Hoffman in a conference room at the Lighthouse.

Source. Photographed by Miriam Kahn, 5 August 2013 and used with Paula Hoffman's permission.

'This was the first time we saw blind people working. They were working at very complicated things, making machines and working with very small objects. In Tahiti blind people don't work. The government just provides some money for them for their bus and things like that. They have to make do with very little. Blind people live with their families but are not very happy because they have to depend on their families for everything. Here we could see that they are happy because they can be independent. We were also impressed that here buses have machines to take a person in a wheelchair. They just lower the machine and pick up the person in the wheelchair. We saw that sidewalks have ramps for wheelchairs. We don't have any of that in Tahiti.'

Commentary

Paula Hoffman, who had been on the study abroad trip in 2010, works at the Lighthouse for the Blind, Inc. Teana and Moenau, both of whom have relatives who are blind, expressed great interest in visiting Paula's place of work.

Since 1918 the Lighthouse has provided employment and support for people who are blind, deaf-blind, and blind with other disabilities. The Lighthouse trains people in precision machining, where they produce an assortment of machined parts and plastic injection molding for aerospace manufacturers, as well as office products and hydration equipment for the US Government and the US Military.

The Woodland Park Zoo

Figure 104. Left to right: Helen Enguerra, Theresa Enguerra, Desiree Bungay, Anaiyah Johnson, Joash Tupufia, Savali Tupufia, Teana and Moenau at the Woodland Park Zoo.

Source. Photographed by Miriam Kahn, 7 August 2013 and used with everybody's permission.

'We were able to see animals that we had only seen in films and in nature programs on TV. It brought us back to our childhood and how when we were little there were many animals we wanted to see but we couldn't. We only saw them in the cartoons. When we were in the zoo we could see the real animals. They were the way we had imagined they would be. We were excited most to see the lions, the penguins and the snakes. We don't have snakes in Tahiti.'

Commentary

The trip to the zoo included two former University of Washington students (Helen and Desiree), who had gone to Huahine in 2010, as well as Helen's sister (Theresa) and cousin (Savali), and their children. There are no zoos in French Polynesia.

Baseball game—Seattle Mariners vs Milwaukee Brewers

Figure 105. Teana and Moenau at the Mariners vs Brewers game at Safeco Field.
Source. Photograhed by Miriam Kahn, 11 August 2013.

'The baseball game was very amazing! The stadium was very big with lots of people! It was just like we had seen in the movies. But now we saw it in real life. And now we can understand the game and how it is played. The big screen was so big. There's a cameraman taking pictures of the spectators and then he puts those pictures on the big screen. But he didn't take pictures of us. When we got out of the train on our way to the baseball game there were so many people all streaming towards the stadium. That was so strange.'

Commentary

In French Polynesia the national sport is va'a (outrigger canoe racing), for which Tahitian teams consistently break world records. Other sports include rugby, basketball, soccer and surfing. Baseball does not exist. Seattle's Safeco Field, with a seating capacity of over 54,000, holds (when full) more than 10 times the number of people who live on the island of Huahine.

Disco dancing at Tia Lou's

Figure 106. Natalie Hart, Moenau, Ashley Bird, Teana at Tia Lou's Lounge.

'At the disco we noticed that all the African-American people were dancing in one area with their own DJ, and everyone else was dancing in a different area. That was strange for us. In Tahiti the Tahitians and the French disagree about political things but there is no segregation. The French people act proud because they feel superior that they are "helping" us Tahitians but we can be together with them. No problem.'

Commentary

Natalie Hart, who had stayed with Teana's family in 2010, and Ashley Bird, who had stayed with them in 2012, were the 'tour guides' for the disco evening. In spite of what many people say about the diversity of Seattle, Teana and Moenau noticed that there is still a lot of economic, social and racial segregation.

Umoja Festival

Figure 107. Teana, Natalie Hart and Moenau at the Umoja Festival.
Source. Photographed by Miriam Kahn, 3 August 2013 and used with their permission.

'We liked the festival where our friend, Natalie, was the queen. We liked that African-American people have a festival just for themselves. It was interesting to learn about Trayvon Martin and how the people brought attention to his case in the festival. We saw that there is still a lot of discrimination here. We could see this in people's eyes.'

'We liked the parade with all the colourful and sparkly costumes and the dancing. We liked the showy way the people walked and danced. We were happy to see Natalie go by in the parade. Natalie later told us that when she heard us call her name as she went by it made her very happy and made her feel important that her two Tahitian friends had come to the festival to see her. One thing was difficult for us—when the African-American people talk it is hard for us to understand their English.'

Commentary

The Umoja Festival is part of Seafair, which is Seattle's annual, month-long summer festival then in its 64th year. Seafair includes community events, parades, drill team marches, a torchlight run, a milk carton derby, pirates and clowns, air shows, and hydroplane and other boat races.

A highlight of the Seafair festival is the Miss Seafair contest, which over the years has come to celebrate the diversity of the greater Seattle area. The Seafair Scholarship Program for Women, for example, has evolved into one that rewards academic ambition, celebrates diversity, and highlights future leaders. The Miss Seafair contestants represent various neighbourhoods and ethnic communities in Seattle. Natalie Hart, who stayed with Teana's family in 2010, was the second runner-up for Miss Seafair 2013, as well as the Queen of the UmojaFest (African-American festival).

The Umoja (a Swahili word meaning 'unity') Festival has been the most unifying celebration in Seattle's African-American community for decades. The parade is just one of many events over a three-day weekend. Numerous religious, educational and civic associations participate in the parade.

19

Carnet de Voyage en Irlande

Flora Aurima-Devatine

Ireland
Homeland
Home
Land
I feel at home
In Ireland

To Elizabeth
My great-grandmother

From my hotel room
By the window to the land

I crossed
Your father's land
Your father's country
Your father's homeland

And I felt at home
In your father's homeland
In your father's homeland

And I thought a lot

I thought strongly
I thought deeply
I thought carefully

I thought of you
I thought landly
Homelandly

I thought a lot
Because I missed you

To Julia
My great-great-grandmother

From my hotel room
By the window to the land

I caught your force
I caught your will
I caught and I understood your nature

I imagined your smile
I imagined your face smiling
I imagined your eyes shining, twinkling

I caught and I imagined a lot
Because I needed you

To Francis
My great-great-grandfather

I saw the descendants of your fellows
I searched your 'dark hair'
I searched your 'blue eyes'

And I found them in our car driver
From Castlewellan to Leitrim
From Leitrim to Legannany
From Leitrim to Castlewellan
From Castlewellan to Newcastle

From a top of the road of Leitrim to Castlewellan
I saw the point of view to the sea of Newcastle
And I thought of you of your dreams
Full of travels by boat by sea full of new countries
Full of a best future full of us your descendants
And I understood you because I felt the same feelings
For all my children and for all of my grandchildren

I tried your Guiness
I drunk in memory of you
Don't be cross with me
I prefer our Hinano beer!

I talked and talked a lot
I thought of you
And I felt happy
Because I admired you

I understood the travels I did
I understood the countries I crossed
I understood the ways I went by
The oceans I passed across
The people I met

It was a never-ending road
An uncompleted way
To you to me to us
It was a boundless, an untiring
A long way to your land
To my ancestor's land

I felt a lot of the past
The travels I had to do
The fields I had to cross
The oceans, to navigate
The roads, to follow
The feelings, to experience

I understood
I believe I understood
I think I believe I understood
I hope I wish to understand

I want to live
I would like to be
I need it
I need so
I need so much.

I needed to see and feel
The Mountains of Mourne
I saw and I felt the land all
The land of my ancestors
I can't say it's enough
Just it's an appreciated part of me
I feel nostalgic about this part of me
But I'm lucky to have had a touch of it
To have had a breeze of it
To have had a sweet smell of it
I feel happy and a little bit on my hunger

To you all
My ancestors

I couldn't express my love
Because I didn't feel it
I didn't know you
But all my thoughts, my spirit,
All my words about you
Only express this tender thing, the feeling
That I love you all.

«- Pourquoi aller voir à quoi ressemble le pays des ancêtres ?
- Quitte à voir, à visiter un pays étranger, autant aller voir aussi celui de ses ancêtres !»

Traduction (2010–2011) de Jean Anderson
Directrice du New Zealand Centre for Literary Translation à
l'Université Victoria de Wellington

20

A Trip from Port Moresby to Suva

Bomai D. Witne

Early in the morning my sister, her husband and Gabriel accompanied me to Jackson's Airport.

'When are you returning?' my sister asked. 'Wednesday, next week,' I replied. 'OK, bring me something from Fiji.'

I smiled and told her I would think about it.

'Do you all have money to pay for your bus home?' I asked them at the airport. They nodded and I asked each of them to reconfirm.

I offered a 10 kina note to my three-year-old nephew and headed for the International Terminal and joined the queue at the check-in counter.

When I fronted the counter, a beautiful woman smiled and asked, 'What's your name?' and put her hands out for my tickets.

'My name is Bomai,' I responded, handing my ticket and passport to her.

'Are you from Simbu?' she asked and I replied, 'How do you know?' 'By looking at your name,' she responded and showed me where to go.

I compared my experience at Goroka Airport's Air Niugini check-in with my first impression of the female staff at Jackson's as I moved on to the money exchange and the immigration counter.

Soon I was in the departure lounge among the other passengers.

I looked around and saw that there were more passengers of Asian origin then all the other races put together. I did not want to think deeper about this observation and took a book from my bag.

As I was reading, the young man I had met in Goroka smiled and walked over to where I was sitting. We shook hands and began a conversation. He spent most of the time on the mobile phone in his hand, so I returned to my book.

Air Niugini flight PX084, scheduled to fly first to Henderson's Airport in Honiara and then on to Nadi Airport in Fiji, was delayed.

I was used to delays and flight cancellations on domestic Air Niugini flights. I saw some passengers becoming impatient and starting little complaining conversations.

A female staff member of Air Niugini walked over to a woman sitting next to me and said, 'The plane is ready to go but we are waiting for one of the pilots to arrive'.

The woman asked, 'Why?' 'Many Air Niugini pilots walked off the job due to some grievances with management and we are low on pilots', the staffer explained.

What I heard was enough to put my mind at rest and I went back into my conversation with the book.

After a while, a young woman dressed in captain's uniform was escorted by a security officer to the waiting plane. I knew she was the co-captain and got ready for departure.

After going through the ticket check, I boarded the plane and sat in seat 19F. After a few minutes, a beautiful woman walked up the aisle and sat next to me. After a moment of silence, she asked, 'Are you Bomai?'

'Yes, I am, and your name, please?' She gave a full smile and said, 'I am Lorna, one of the three writers selected to attend the Pacific Writer's Workshop in Fiji. Nice to meet you.'

'Marlene and I were looking out for you in the departure lounge and mistook someone else for you', Lorna added with a smile.

I laughed and asked for Marlene. Lorna pointed to a seat at the front.

Soon Lorna and I were into a conversation about writing, family, education and many things. The conversation kept us busy over rivers, jungles, mountains, lagoons and atolls through clear blue skies across the Solomon Sea.

I tried listening to Bob Marley and Lucky Dube songs and watching movies on the small screen in front of me but could not find any I liked so decided to listen to songs from Landini Aurelio, who sings and promotes his Garifuna culture.

Midway through the journey, a meal of cold potato was served and I requested coffee. After the meal, I looked around the plane and saw many passengers reading the in-flight magazines or had eyes and ears glued to the mini-screen in front of them.

I smiled to myself at what I saw and went for more music. I switched from Landini to the selection of best local sounds from PNG, seeing someone who looked like my colleague at the University of Goroka, Richard Mogu, among the people in the cover.

I heard a few of his songs among the collection. This gave me a sense of why the University of Goroka was lucky to employ such a talented person to teach music and songs to the students.

My mind tried to describe the varying shapes of the clouds. If the plane was crossing over the Arctic I would have seen one or two Inuit at work.

Other clouds reminded me of the ancient Borobudur temple in Indonesia, some of pictures of Disneyland, flocks of sheep, terraces, kaukau (sweet potato) and mountains in the highlands of Papua New Guinea.

I turned from imagination to songs again. I listened to songs by Eric Clapton and among them was, 'Sky is crying, look at tears down the streets'. I thought the clouds were the way for the sky to form tears and that I was travelling above Clapton's sky.

The music went off as one of the cabin crew announced the plane's preparation for landing at Henderson's at a quarter past two in the afternoon, Solomon Island's time.

Under the clear, blue Solomon sky, I could see a beautiful white coastline below and the roads connecting it to the hinterland. The moving clouds cast shadows on the treetops.

Soon the clouds and forests went out of sight and the plane flew over some human settlements with red soil roads between them, then over several rivers and swamps and then over what appeared to be an extensive oil palm plantation.

It sped over atolls and the bigger islands of the Solomons. An island came into view. It reminded me of Dobu Island in Milne Bay.

A large red ship was floating in the sea with logs on it, which brought to mind the illegal logging in Solomon Islands and other Melanesian countries. The plane descended rapidly and was soon flying over red-roofed buildings and coconut palm–roofed houses. We were soon on the runway, at Henderson International Airport.

The passengers for Solomon Islands were asked to disembark while the Nadi-bound passengers were asked to remain in the plane. From where I was sitting, I could see refuelling trucks settling under the wings of the plane. Another aircraft with 'Virgin Australia' insignia landed and many people disembarked.

Lorna and I walked to Marlene's seat and I introduced myself to her. We were soon getting on as if we had known each other for a long time. We took some photos in the aisle.

We were back on our seats when I noticed a leak in the plane's wing close to me, which I reported to one of the cabin crew. Soon the captain was on the ground. When he returned to his seat he announced it was condensation due to change of temperature. My mind was at case and soon the plane was hitting Henderson's runway.

The plane was soon in the air over the township of Honiara and heading southeast on its way to Nadi. The cabin crew distributed two forms, one on ebola virus and the other labelled 'Fiji arrival card'.

The information revealed that Fiji had strong immigration laws. After filling in the forms, I sat back and listened to more PNG and Celine Dion music. The map on the screen in front of me indicated the plane was flying over Vanuatu.

The sun began to set, painting the clouds with gold and copper. At some points the sun rays described beautiful rainbow-like lines. After a few minutes, the plane was plunging through murky clouds and I could see the lights on the left wing. The crew reminded us that the plane was preparing for landing.

A crew member thoroughly sprayed the interior of the plane from one end to the other for Fiji quarantine. Lorna asked me, 'Why didn't the crew do the same on arrival at Henderson's?' I said, 'Maybe the Solomon Island's government is not serious about quarantine issues'.

It was dark outside and the plane flew over settlements with scattered lights. More lights came into view and we landed at Nadi International airport. Lorna, Marlene and I sorted immigration requirements and raced for the domestic terminal to catch the 8 pm flight to Nausori airport in Suva.

It was raining in Nadi and the airport staff issued us with umbrellas to walk to the plane and the cabin crew greeted us with 'Bula' and gave us a moist towel and water.

I reached out for the *Fiji Sun* and read about Fiji Link's management decision to share its profits with employees. I tried to recall the last time Air Niugini announced it would share its profit with employees. No wonder their airport staff do not care to stand in the rain and distribute umbrellas to passengers.

The flight from Nadi to Nausori was less than 30 minutes and we landed at Nausori around 8.30 pm. The light-skinned young man I'd met in Goroka walked towards his mother who was waiting with a camera. She hugged him.

He introduced me to his mother, who shook hands with me and pointed to a man standing beside us and told us that he was Papua New Guinea's high commissioner to Fiji.

He walked over and shook hands with us.

Lorna, Marlene and I could not find our pick-up car and went to the airport police office to enquire. Two police officers greeted us nicely and asked us to come in and call our contact persons in Fiji.

One police officer offered to call the police boss to assist us. With their help, we were in touch with our contact person in Fiji and the driver arrived in less than 10 minutes to pick us up.

We thanked the police officers and left for the Hotel Peninsula in Suva. The porters at the hotel greeted us with a 'Bula' and carried our luggage to our rooms.

21

Performing Cannibalism in the South Seas

Tracey Banivanua Mar

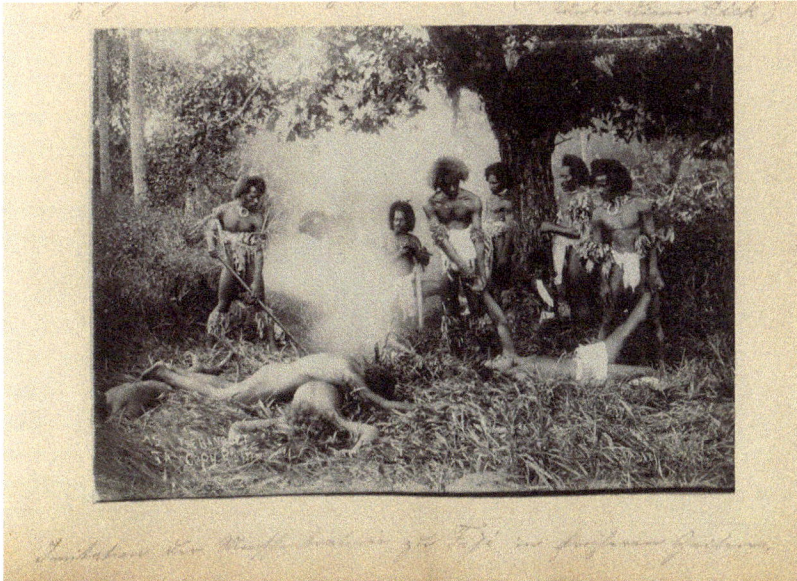

Figure 108. Imitation of roasting humans at Fiji in former times.

Source. Forming part of the library's collection 'Views and portraits of the Pacific Islands' by Paula David; call number PXE 708/item 15b; digital order number a698017, with permission State Library of New South Wales, Mitchell Library, PXE 708.

Climbing the hills out of Sigatoka on Fiji's main island of Viti Levu, the view is stunning. The Sigatoka River snakes its way from the hills to the coast, carving a spectacular valley and sharply steep hills. I was bumping along in a poorly ventilated, muggy as hell minibus with a small group of tourists when I first saw this river. It had been raining for days before. The Sigatoka River was a seething mass of fast-moving water, and the potholed road beneath our bus was only barely attached to the landscape. My fellow travellers were two teenagers, a couple of grey nomads, a sunburnt resort couple and a lady on safari, who was otherwise nondescript except for her archetypal clothing of white linen and a pith-helmet-esque hat, a vision of empire in the tropics. Just out of Sigatoka we had stopped to pick up two more passengers, Fijians Jone and Semi. For some reason they boarded with an inflated tyre tube. They were mates of Sam, our tour guide. Sam had arrived late on this Sunday morning, with bloodshot eyes and a remnant dusting of blue glitter on his face and neck. The camp flourishes with which he waved goodbye to his ride became muted on the bus as he donned his professional tour guide face and welcomed us to a cannibal adventure of a lifetime.

We were going to Fiji's Naihehe Caves, a spectacular and sacred cave system in the hills where, I had read, the Sawaitabu people took refuge against a raging measles epidemic in the 1870s. The measles had arrived from Sydney at the same time as Fiji became a British Crown Colony. It was contracted by chiefs and their entourage at roving ceremonies held to sign the Deed of Cession, the legal instrument ceding Fijian sovereignty to Britain. Infected chiefs unwittingly carried measles back to their villages, devastating their communities. The disease went on to wipe out nearly half the population of Fiji. The Sawaitabu people, viewing the epidemic as a colonial disease, took refuge in the Naihehe Caves, renouncing empire and Christ. In Fiji by the 1870s and 1880s, such resistance was increasingly coupled with the idea of cannibalism and therefore bound for destruction. Protected by the caves with their secret and narrow entrances the Sawaitabu people held out against colonial intrusions until eventually, exhausted by sustained bloody conflict, they surrendered. Today the caves are marketed to tourists as the Cannibal Caves.[1]

---

1   Repeka Nasiko, 2012, 'The caves of Naihehe', *The Fiji Times*, 19 February.

Cannibalism has always been a drawcard for outsiders in the Pacific and for much of the nineteenth century the Fiji islands were nicknamed the 'Cannibal Islands'. A concentration of missionary and planter activity had made them the notorious epicentre of Europe's Pacific craze by mid-century. Travel writers, missionaries, settlers and labour traders published memoirs and travel narratives for ever-attentive audiences. They filled these accounts with titillating tales of cannibal adventures, and illustrated them with pictures of cannibal forks and other paraphernalia.[2] Postcards like 'The Banquet', and travelling human exhibits like the Fiji Cannibal Exhibition of 1873 took the tourist experience to audiences in Europe and America. So, too, accounts of the Pacific's cannibalistic Manners and Customs, as they were nearly always titled, ranged in quality from the formulaic to the absurd, but most simply repeated tales of cannibalism as hearsay of a pagan past. Some writers such as the American William Endicott indulged openly in varying degrees of fantasy many years after their travels, while others, missionaries included, wrote more soberly of practices indicative of a savagery whose days were numbered.

So invested and entwined with colonial projects were the prolific accounts of cannibalism in the Pacific and elsewhere that William Arens was moved in 1979 to controversially—some would say sacrilegiously—claim that cannibalism was a hoax, a projected fantasy.[3] Cannibalism was a meta-myth, he argued, a ritualistic practice specific to colonial encounters. Those whose job it is to document native man-eating practices have been outraged by his suggestion that cannibalism did not and never did exist. But a more subtle point he made endures. Viewing cannibalism says more about the rituals of the viewer than the viewed.

The Naihehe Caves still belong to the people of the Navosa Highlands, and after an hour of travelling we stopped near Natawatawa village to present i-sevusevu, a short ceremony to request and receive permission to visit the caves. We were all asked to wear a sulu for the fairly casual ceremony, receiving at the end a bowl of grog—not the good stuff, the peppery waka, but the touristy muddy yaqona that made Safari Lady wince. After this we crossed the seething Sigatoka

---

2   'Cannibals with Cutlery', 2013, *Daily Mail*, 9 January.
3   William E. Arens, 1979, *The Man-eating Myth: Anthropology and Anthropophagy*, New York: Oxford University Press.

River with our hearts in our throats, and walked the remaining distance along a well-worn and now muddy and slippery path to the opening of the caves. This is a crevice in the hillside and we crouched and shuffled along a stream and through the puckered entry into the long, narrow rock halls beyond. Inside, under torchlight, Sam ramped up the cannibal jokes and stories. As we moved through the halls and taverns of the caves, Sam picked out sparkling formations of limestone and stalagmites, the 'cannibal man' and 'cannibal woman'. Cameras flashed. As we moved through the caves, Sam continually asked us to imagine a whole village living in these spaces, sequestered in the dark, for months on end. Imagine the hunger.

The tour of the cave culminated in a wide and open cavern, the main living space for the village. We were offered more tantalising stories of cannibalism before being shown what had been the kitchen with its natural chimney and oven formation. Here the cannibal stories reached a crescendo. Camera flashes flickered and we were asked to imagine body parts in the oven. Sam acted it out. Safari Lady played along. These cannibals were not evil, she gravely informed us, they just did not know any better. Thank god for the missionaries. Sam pointed at a stalagmite formation with a round flat surface, and suggested maybe it was a cannibal stone, a site of sacrifice, or where bodies were carved and prepared for cooking. He acted it out. He showed us some more chambers, the dining chamber with more references to cannibalism, the sleeping chambers and a secret entrance. The cannibal jokes continued and segued seamlessly into discussion, and more jokes, about lunch. 'Who's for lunch?' Sam said. 'Naah, I meant who wants lunch?' he added, assuring us he had never eaten anyone.

I took this tour nearly 20 years after Dennis O'Rourke's *Cannibal Tours* filmed and framed a group of rich, white travellers 'touring' the Sepik River in Papua New Guinea.[4] Tales of cannibalism had migrated west across the Pacific over time, coming to rest in the late twentieth century on the island that is now split along the 141st Meridian between West Papua and Papua New Guinea. In O'Rourke's film, each tourist has their own agenda, and acts according to latent narratives of savagery and primitiveness. Unsettlingly lingering shots make us observe the tourists observing Papuans. In a pair of loud Americans

---

4   Dennis O'Rourke, 1988, *Cannibal Tours*, directed and produced by Dennis O'Rourke in association with the Institute of Papua New Guinea Studies.

in search of primitive art, and another safari-suited German obsessed with seeking cannibalism and ticking off a checklist of toured, read, conquered regions of the world, we witness an Arens-like ritual being played out. The tourists see what they came to see whether or not Papuans play their part, and Papuans act out their roles knowingly and begrudgingly.

The parallels between cannibal tours up the Sepik River in 1988 and the Cannibal Caves tour 20 years later are all there, even the safari suit. But it was not quite a ritual in which we obediently and religiously replicated a prescribed order. Rather this kind of cultural tourism, which thrives in the Pacific, is more like a performance that has been rehearsed countless times. The script is simple and generic, and is transportable across the islands with empty text-fields that are filled in locally. Cannibalism thrived here among the benighted savages of this place, empire/missionaries arrived in the colonial period, today we are civilised/Christian. Postscript: there may still be some who practice it in the remote hills of the interior.

The present mirrors the past in the Pacific and the promise of encountering cannibals, of the past or in the present, remains alluring. Even as Pacific Islanders have developed sophisticated ways of presenting, celebrating and offering culture to curious tourists, and tourists have developed more nuanced interests, the appeal of discovering, encountering and imagining cannibals endures and has adapted. Tour companies in West Papua sell 'First Contact Tours' as part of a burgeoning adventure tourism trade. They promise to make contact with stone-age primitives and cannibals who have never seen white people before. The tours sell a fantasy of course. And it is lucrative. Since 2000, numerous books, documentaries and Discovery Channel sagas of white men *Going Tribal*[5] amongst cannibals, set in Papua New Guinea or West Papua have fed the market. The UK-based magazine *Zoo Weekly* offered a 'cannibal sex holiday!' in West Papua as a competition prize in 2004.[6] A collection of Fijian cannibal forks sold in the UK for £30,000 in 2013. In the same year international news outlets broadcast under sensational headlines, 'Tourist feared eaten by cannibals' that a German tourist had been killed and eaten

---

5   *Going Tribal* is a popular documentary series, in which the host visits and emulates imagined 'tribal' peoples, that was produced in the early 2000s and aired on the BBC and Discovery Channel.
6   Paul Kingsnorth, 2004, 'Spot the real savages', *New Statesman*, 15 March.

by cannibals in French Polynesia. Social media lit up. On the White Pride website Stormfront, 'Remey74' wondered why white people go to 'these third world countries and not expect' to be eaten.

The reality of cannibal fantasies is stark. Michael Behar, having taken a cannibal contact tour in 2004, wondered in hindsight whether the elaborate feathered headdresses worn by the cannibals he encountered were just a little too ceremonial for a believable casual encounter.[7] In 2004 Benny Wenda, a West Papuan pro-independence leader seeking asylum in the UK, visited the office of *Zoo Weekly*, seeking an apology for the magazine's marketing of West Papua as the titillating home of tribes of cannibals. He did so bearing the torture scars he had received from the Indonesian military, and showing photographs of Papuan torture victims, he reminded the magazine's editor Paul Merrill, that Papuans were actually victims of an unfolding genocide. He received the apology he came for. Finally, the cannibals of the romantic South Seas that ate German tourist Stefan Ramin, was actually the opportunistic and now convicted murderer Henri Haiti.[8] Neither the prosecution nor the defence at his trial took seriously the claims that he was a cannibal. The burnt-out fireplace with charred bones on Nuku Hiva that had prompted sensational claims of cannibalism was merely the site where Haiti had tried to destroy the evidence of his crime.[9]

Pointing out the contextual reality of performances of cannibalism in the Pacific is not about trying to prove that the practice never existed. In a sense that question has become irrelevant. Claims of cannibalism today are a little playful and tongue-in-cheek, and both tourists and the toured play along for mutual gain. At the Naihehe Caves, we all played along, although to varying degrees. Sam played his part as the guide. He helped us as tourists to frame the caves in two dimensions, pointing to the innocuous props to point our cameras at. His jokes about being hungry lightened the mood and invited us to project the simple cannibal narrative on to him. As a guide he was both

---

7   Michael Behar, 2005, 'The selling of the last savage', *Outside Magazine*, 1 February.
8   'Henri Haiti jailed for murder', 2014, *Cook Island News*, 19 May.
9   'Tourist feared eaten by cannibals', 2011, *The Fiji Times Online*, 18 October; 'Tales of cannibalism from the South Pacific', 2011, *Telegraph*, 18 October; 'Hunter suspected of killing and eating mission German Tourist has tattoo of notorious cannibal tribe who ate victims', 2011, *Mail Online*, 21 October; 'Cannibal claims: We'd rather eat hot dogs than humans, say Pacific Islanders', 2011, *Daily Telegraph*, 18 October.

narrator and narrated, embodying the fantasy we had paid for. Safari Lady's accidental or deliberate appearance cast her as Sam's direct counterpart, and she was also narrator and narrated. Such encounters seem both humorous and harmless. They allow tourists who are normally encouraged to stay cloistered in the shelters of sun-drenched resorts to feel they have encountered something of Fijian culture. But as we arrived back at the river and all piled on to a raft for the last part of the tour, the underlying structure of the entire performance became more apparent.

The last part of the Cannibal Caves tour was a short ride on a raft down the Sigatoka River. Normally this would be a leisurely lolling ride propelled by a gentle undertow. But on this day the river was swollen, its water hurtling towards the sea. Our raft looked flimsy, and it strained on its mooring as the water snatched and tugged at it. Jone and Semi had found some more tyre tubes, some of which had been tied to the raft to help it stay afloat. As we all piled on the raft, the two teenagers were invited to hop into the tyres. Jone and Semi swam, pushing the tyres and the teenagers, and Sam towed the rest of us on the raft, holding on to his own tyre. That is how the discomfort I had felt in the caves, and the increasing and unprovoked animosity I was feeling for Safari Lady crystallised. This tour was modern. It respected the customs of landowners, and Sam, Jone and Semi were cosmopolitan urban-dwellers. But there we were dry and high, Safari Lady still pristine and white, and there Sam, Semi and Jone were huffing and puffing in the muddy water to get us across the river. The cannibal tour had cast us all, tourists and toured, outsiders and locals, in a colonial re-enactment.

Touring the Pacific has a history that is tangled up with colonialism. Since at least the nineteenth century, visitors have projected any number of cultural and sexual fantasies onto sites of encounter in the Pacific. Until recently, those visitors arrived on vessels that were threading and weaving the islands of the Pacific evermore tightly into global networks of empire. Escaping the binds of civilisation to the unbound Pacific, whether as a missionary, beachcomber or tortured artist, has been a central trope of travel literature for at least two centuries. Fantasies of, and encounters with, cannibalism belong to the dark heart of these tours. I have written elsewhere about the entanglements of cannibalism and colonialism,[10] as have the authors that contributed to the book *Cannibalism and the Colonial World* in 1998.[11] During the colonial era, touring cannibalism was always about locating virgin sites of conquest, or touring its aftermath. Violence, often extreme, against de-humanised cannibals was eminently just. And encountering ex-cannibals allowed narrators of travel accounts to marvel at the civilisational distance that contact with Europe had afforded. In ex-cannibals they could encounter embodied evolution, living empirical evidence of the benefits of the civilising mission. But this history of cannibalism is elided by fantasy tours of today.

The Cannibal Caves tour ended with the river ride. Miraculously Sam, Semi and Jone got us safely to the other side without being swept away, and afterwards we tourists consumed a prepared lunch together. Our tour guides ate separately. Their performance was over, more or less, and on the bus ride back to the resorts they chatted amongst themselves in Fijian, mostly about their social lives. As the tour receded, our complex subjectivities returned to us all, not least to the caves themselves. In the absence of performances of cannibal tourism, the Naihehe Caves contain the rock art, spirits, stories and legends of their peoples, to whom they provided life-saving refuge from a vicious and uncompromising plague.[12] They are therefore also an important historical site testifying to the ingenuity of the Sawaitabu people who occupied them. They are now a complex site of resistance to and accommodation of colonial rule. But yoked to the enduring narrative of cannibal encounters they lose these layered dimensions.

Cannibal tourism re-stages an uneasy colonial past. The encounters are more than simply a tongue-in-cheek performance in which all actors innocently carry equal agency. Instead, both tourists and the toured engage in a triumphalist animation, a cartoon rehearsal of the colonial encounter, that puts natives back in their place. The jokey humour that almost always accompanies the performance or evocation of cannibal

---

10   Tracey Banivanua Mar, 2008, '"A thousand miles of cannibal lands": Imagining away genocide in the re-colonisation of West Papua', *Journal of Genocide Research* 10(4): 583–602; Tracey Banivanua Mar, 2010, 'Cannibalism and colonialism: Charting colonies and frontiers in Nineteenth-Century Fiji', *Comparative Studies in Society and History* 52(2): 255–81.
11   Francis Barker, Peter Hulme and Margaret Iversen (eds), 1998, *Cannibalism and the Colonial World*, Cambridge: Cambridge University Press.
12   María Cruz Berrocal and Sidsel Millerstrom, 2013, 'The archaeology of rock art in Fiji: Evidence, methods and hypotheses', *Archaeology in Oceania* 48(3): 154–65

tours, moreover, belittles, trivialises and de-humanises complex cultures and histories. Admittedly, the humour is as much directed at the self-conscious tourist as the toured, but they nevertheless call into being the roles of colonised and coloniser, observed and observer, toured and tourist.

References

Arens, William E. 1979. *The Man-eating Myth: Anthropology and Anthropophagy*. New York: Oxford University Press.

Banivanua Mar, Tracey. 2008. '"A thousand miles of cannibal lands": Imagining away genocide in the re-colonisation of West Papua.' *Journal of Genocide Research* 10(4): 583–602.

——. 2010. 'Cannibalism and colonialism: Charting colonies and frontiers in Nineteenth-Century Fiji.' *Comparative Studies in Society and History* 52(2): 255–81.

Barker, Francis, Peter Hulme and Margaret Iversen (eds). 1998. *Cannibalism and the Colonial World*. Cambridge: Cambridge University Press.

Behar, Michael. 2005. 'The selling of the last savage.' *Outside Magazine*. 1 February.

Berrocal, María Cruz and Sidsel Millerstrom. 2013. 'The archaeology of rock art in Fiji: Evidence, methods and hypotheses.' *Archaeology in Oceania* 48(3): 154–65

Cruz Berrocal, María and Sidsel Millerstrom. 2013. 'The archaeology of rock art in Fiji: Evidence, methods and hypotheses.' *Archaeology in Oceania* 48(3): 154–65.

David, Paula. c. 1890–1899. *Views and Portraits of the Pacific Islands*. Mitchell Library, State Library of New South Wales.

O'Rourke, Dennis. 1988. *Cannibal Tours*. Directed and produced by Dennis O'Rourke in association with the Institute of Papua New Guinea Studies.

22

Touring 'Real Life'? Authenticity and Village-based Tourism in the Trobriand Islands of Papua New Guinea

Michelle MacCarthy

Introduction

Tina,[1] a striking young woman of Iranian heritage, travelled on her own from Victoria, Australia, to spend two months in the islands of Milne Bay Province, Papua New Guinea (PNG), with one of those months in the Trobriand Islands. When I spoke with her at length, Tina had been in the Trobriands for about a week and a half. She had stayed in the beachside village of Kaibola for a few days, and then travelled to Tauwema village on Kaileuna Island before returning to the largest island, Kiriwina. Tina organised village stays on the ground by asking around at the guest lodge and in the government station of Losuia. I spoke with Tina outside the small, local bush-materials house she was renting for a few days in Karidakula, the hamlet just

---

1   All participants were given the option, when briefed about my research and offered a Participant Information Sheet (PIS), to indicate their preference for my using their real name or a pseudonym. I have respected their wishes, but do not indicate here in which cases a pseudonym is used.

next to Butia Lodge,[2] where she had just taken a 'bucket shower' in a temporary enclosure built for the purpose. The lodge, a well-established guest house with a generator, beds (as opposed to the mat on the floor on which Tina would have slept), and a kitchen stocked with imported foods, was no more than a few hundred metres away, but staying with a local family in each place was appealing to Tina, who preferred to 'rough it', as she put it, and make her money stretch to allow a longer visit.

Figure 109. Tina, wearing Trobriand dress, enjoying a performance at Karidakula (grounds of Butia Lodge).
Source. Photographed by Michelle MacCarthy, 11 July 2009.

When I asked Tina why she chose to come to the Trobriands, she told me she felt 'an affinity with the culture', which she was familiar with as she had taken some anthropology courses in university and reads 'lots of books on ceremony and ritual in PNG; I'm really interested in myths and legends. It has always fascinated me.' She also has a fascination, she noted, with 'living spaces—how people arrange themselves socially'. Tina told me she has travelled at least once a year since she

---

2   Butia Lodge is one of two established guest houses on Kiriwina, offering basic but comfortable accommodation. Amenities include generators to provide electric fans and even air conditioning, full meal service with a combination of local and imported foods, and a bar. Both, however, are locally owned and operated and in no way reflect a 'resort'-type atmosphere.

was 16, usually on her own for about two months at a time. She had found her experience in PNG thus far safe and easy. She observed that because she stayed in the villages, people were protective, almost treating her like family. 'Here, you'll never feel alone. People worry for you. They're very curious. But I feel so welcome.'[3]

Tina expressed some concern about 'old practises dying out', but says she sees now an interesting melding of Christianity and traditional culture: 'I think it's still a strong culture—you see new influences woven into the old culture.'[4] As her visit coincided with the yam harvest, she was pleased to have seen people carrying yams and stacking them in a heap in the village next to where she stayed in Tauwema, noting the 'visual appeal' of the process. On Kiriwina Island, Tina's experience was also embodied, as she was dressed by her hosts in Trobriand attire to attend the yam harvest festivities carried out during her visit. Tina brought up the issue of authenticity in the course of our discussion, stating that in Thailand, for example, she felt 'sold to'; that everything was about money, and there was little sense that what she was seeing and doing was authentic, which she felt 'devalues the experience—the way you process it, as a traveller'. This word choice, like that of most other tourists I met while in the Trobriands, was deliberate; very few of them would ever refer to themselves as a 'tourist'. While she rinsed out a few pieces of clothing in a basin of water, and wrung them out before hanging them on the line to dry, she continued, 'Things just aren't charged with the same power when they're programmed. You want to feel like you're sharing or witnessing someone's natural practice, not [that it is being done] for your enjoyment. You want them to enjoy it, too.' She told me about having witnessed a School Cultural Day, which was organised 'not for me—for the community. That was nice to see.'[5]

While most visitors to the Trobriand Islands do not stay as long as Tina did, nor do they engage as directly with local hosts, her comments reflect the sentiments of most travellers—whether visiting for a few days or a few weeks, travelling independently or on a group tour. The importance of having an authentic personal experience, in a place with authentic cultural others doing authentically cultural things

---

3   Interview with Tina, Karidakula village, Kiriwina, 4 July 2009.
4   Ibid.
5   Ibid.

(as the visitor perceives it), emerged through my nearly 22 months of fieldwork with residents of and tourists to the Trobriand Islands as of paramount importance to the ways in which visitors assess, understand and narrate their own experiences of intercultural encounters.[6] Visiting a village, whether on a day excursion or for an overnight stay, is seen by most travellers as an opportunity to see and, ideally, take part in 'life as it is really lived'. Such notions are reinforced by tour operators and travel literature, in which the idea of a consumable authentic other is reified. Take, for example, the following excerpt from the brochure of an adventure tourism company based in North America and aimed at 'small group exotic adventures for travellers 50 plus':

> We meet and learn about some of the tribal people of this land including the Asaro Mudmen, the Wahgi, the Simbu, the Kaguel and the fascinating Trobriand Islanders. Our adventure includes many village visits so that we can really meet the people and experience their way of life.[7]

While my fieldwork examined tourism from the perspectives of *both* resident Trobrianders and tourists,[8] I here focus only on the tourists' understanding of, and construction of, an authentic cultural experience in the context of extended village stays. My research indicated that the demographic most likely to engage in village stays of more than a night or two are young (usually, but not exclusively, in their 20s and 30s), independent (that is, not on an organised group tour), and well travelled (often with extensive experience in other less-developed countries). In this chapter, I examine the case of what I refer to as 'unperformance'—village visits in which visitors seek authenticity through experiencing the day-to-day activities of island residents, as against formalised touristic performances or events. I wish to demonstrate how the lack of formal tourist infrastructure,

6   My primary doctoral fieldwork was carried out for 18 months in 2009–2010, facilitated by a Wenner Gren Doctoral Dissertation Fieldwork Grant and the Faculty of Arts at the University of Auckland. A supplemental four months of fieldwork in 2013 was supported by the Gender and Pentecostalism project headed by Annelin Eriksen at the University of Bergen, which was focused on new topics but also permitted follow-up to the initial research.
7   'Papua New Guinea – Adventure Travel For 50 Plus', 2016, *Eldertreks.Com*.
8   Michelle MacCarthy, 2012, '"Before it gets spoiled by tourists": Constructing authenticity in the Trobriand Islands of Papua New Guinea', PhD thesis, Department of Anthropology, University of Auckland; Michelle MacCarthy, 2016, *Making the Modern Primitive: Cultural Tourism in the Trobriand Islands*, Honolulu: University of Hawai'i Press.

the dearth of other tourists, and the opportunities to engage directly with local residents offers an experience interpreted by visitors as more meaningful than those experienced by their peers who travel to more developed touristic destinations. I argue that the grassroots nature of tourism in places lacking 'development' (infrastructure and resources not only for the comfort of tourists, but also reflecting the subsistence-based economy and lack of basic services for the resident population) contributes to a romanticisation of the exotic other and a sense of 'Paradise Lost' in their own societies, and creates an ambiguous distinction between performances orchestrated for the entertainment of visitors, and the quotidian events of daily life in the village. This, I contend, leads to a heightened sense of authenticity, both in terms of their personal experiences in the intercultural interaction, and their objective sense of the authenticity of the people they visit. At the same time, however, the tourist of course knows that he or she is *not* family, and that various comforts and provisions are made, even in the village, on their behalf. There is an inherent tension in the desire to experience 'real life', and the paradox created by the presence of the visitor.

Unperformance

Most existing cultural tourism research has examined places with a fairly formally established tourism infrastructure, focusing on ethnographic theme parks or 'culture villages';[9] dance festivals or floor shows at hotels and resorts featuring 'traditional' dance;[10]

---

9   For example, Edward M. Bruner (ed.), 2005, *Culture on Tour: Ethnographies of Travel*, Chicago: University of Chicago Press; Gerhard Schutte, 2003, 'Tourists and tribes in the "new" South Africa', *Ethnohistory* 50(3): 473–87; Nick Stanley, 1998, *Being Ourselves for You: The Global Display of Cultures*, London: Middlesex University Press.

10   For example, Kalissa Alexeyeff, 2009, *Dancing from the Heart: Movement, Gender, and Cook Islands Globalization*, Honolulu: University of Hawai'i Press; Aurélie Condevaux, 2009, 'Māori culture on stage: Authenticity and identity in tourist interactions', *Anthropological Forum* 19(2): 143–61; Yvonne Payne Daniel, 1996, 'Tourism dance performances: Authenticity and creativity', *Annals of Tourism Research* 23(4): 780–97; Adrienne Kaeppler, 1988, 'Pacific festivals and the promotion of identity, politics, and tourism', in *Come Mek Me Hol'Yu Han': The Impact of Tourism on Traditional Music*, ed. Adrienne Kaeppler and Olive Lewin, pp. 12–38, Kingston, Jamaica: Jamaica Memory Bank.

or the proliferation of 'tourist art'.[11] In these cases, there is a clear separation between performer/producer and audience/consumer, thus reinforcing a sense of the event as 'staged' for both performers and audiences.[12] In the Trobriands, conversely, tourism is highly informal, and such barriers are not clearly established; the fuzziness resulting from this more 'organic' kind of tourism breaks down the separation between performer and audience. This has significant implications for how the experience is conceived, as the following discussion seeks to illustrate.

There are, in fact, few ethnographic examinations of the phenomenon of the village stay. Village stays as an intercultural phenomenon offer an important window into how travellers and the residents of places promoted as exotic and even 'primitive' interact in the sphere of tourism, as they are based on a more intimate interaction than most touristic visits generally provide. Barbara Kirshenblatt-Gimblett, in her examination of museum displays, notes how exhibitions (and, I would argue, experiences in cultural tourism) often 'force us to make comparisons that pierce the membrane of our own quotidian world, allowing us for a brief moment to be spectacles of ourselves, an effect that is also experienced by those on display'.[13] This 'propels the fascination with penetrating the life space of others, getting inside, burrowing deep into the most intimate places, whether the interiors

---

11 For example, Nelson H.H. Graburn (ed.), 1976, *Ethnic and Tourist Arts: Cultural Expressions from the Fourth World*, Berkeley: University of California Press; Nelson H.H. Graburn, 1984, 'The evolution of tourist arts', *Annals of Tourism Research* 11(3): 393–419; Nelson H.H. Graburn, 1999, 'Epilogue: Ethnic and tourist arts revisited', in *Unpacking Culture: Art and Commodity in the Colonial and Postcolonial Worlds*, ed. Ruth B. Phillips and Christopher B. Steiner, pp. 335–54, Berkeley: University of California Press; Eric Kline Silverman, 1999, 'Tourist art as the crafting of identity in the Sepik River (Papua New Guinea)', in *Unpacking Culture: Art and Commodity in Colonial and Postcolonial Worlds*, ed. Ruth B. Phillips and Christopher B. Steiner, pp. 51–66, Berkeley: University of California Press; Eric Kline Silverman, 2004, 'Cannibalizing, commodifying, or creating culture? Power and art in Sepik River tourism', in *Globalization and Culture Change in the Pacific Islands*, ed. Victoria S. Lockwood, pp. 339–57, Upper Saddle River, NJ: Pearson Prentice Hall; Christopher B. Steiner, 1999, 'Authenticity, repetition, and the aesthetics of seriality: The work of tourist art in the age of mechanical reproduction', in *Unpacking Culture: Art and Commodity in Colonial and Postcolonial Worlds*, ed. Ruth B. Phillips and Christopher B. Steiner, pp. 87–103, Berkeley: University of California Press.
12 Erik Cohen, 1988, 'Authenticity and commoditization in tourism', *Annals of Tourism Research* 15(3): 371–86; Dean MacCannell, 1973, 'Staged authenticity: Arrangements of social space in tourist settings', *American Journal of Sociology* 79(3): 589–603.
13 Barbara Kirshenblatt-Gimblett, 1998, *Destination Culture: Tourism, Museums, and Heritage*, Berkeley: University of California Press, p. 48.

of lives or the innermost recesses of bodies'.[14] Examining village stays demonstrates the ways in which such intimacy, whether real or perceived, is both internalised and externalised by visitors.

Figure 110. Trobriand village. Wekuku hamlet, Yalumgwa.
Source. Photographed by Michelle MacCarthy, 21 May 2010.

Authenticity in tourism research

Before I continue with my argument, a few words on definitions and theoretical orientations are necessary regarding the concept of authenticity as both an analytical concept employed by academics and as a trope employed by non-academics. It is important that the reader does not take my approach to be purporting a culturalist agenda, nor validating a reification of authenticity as an essentialist ideal. My interest, rather, is in the way the concept is employed in discourses surrounding tourism, and to what ends.

---

14   Ibid.

Authenticity came to the fore as a key issue in tourism as a result of the publication of Dean MacCannell's groundbreaking work, *The Tourist*.[15] For MacCannell, the quest for authenticity is the primary motivating factor for tourists, who are so alienated by the modern condition that they embark on touristic adventures with a sense of longing for what has been lost in 'simpler' times. MacCannell sees tourism as a ritual that attempts to combat the contradictory, fragmented, and ultimately unsatisfying state of modern society.[16] He argues that the quest for authenticity is doomed to failure, because the search itself compromises the authenticity of the object or experience, assumed to have been previously pristine and untouched.[17] Although MacCannell's thesis has been the subject of much debate, it remains a milestone in the study of tourism as a subject of serious academic inquiry. A problem with MacCannell's approach, however, is that he conflates analytical and lay understandings of the term.

In much of the tourism literature, scholars' use of the concept of authenticity is implicitly objectivist, assuming that there is some essential quality or attribute that makes an entity authentic.[18] This assumption of a true, authentic original presents some methodological and philosophical problems, as many critics have pointed out.[19] For example, how is the pure, unadulterated, authentic original defined when culture, as we know, is dynamic and constantly renegotiated? This idea of a truly authentic object/ritual/culture is inherently flawed, as every anthropologist knows, in that cultures are not, and have never been, static, unchanging entities. Tourists' understanding of the dynamic nature of cultural processes vary, but most cultural tourists, at least as reflected in the dozens of conversations I had with visitors to the Trobriand Islands, implicitly or

---

15 Dean MacCannell, 1976, *The Tourist: A New Theory of the Leisure Class*, New York Schocken Books.

16 MacCannell, *The Tourist*, p. 13.

17 See also, Bruner, 2005, *Culture on Tour*, p. 162; Cohen, 'Authenticity and commoditization in tourism', pp. 272–73; John Taylor, 2001, 'Authenticity and sincerity in tourism', *Annals of Tourism Research* 28(1): 7–26, pp. 11–15.

18 Bruner, 2005, *Culture on Tour*, p. 163; Tazim Jamal and Steve Hill, 2002, 'The home and the world: (Post)touristic spaces of (in)authenticity?' in *The Tourist as a Metaphor of the Social World*, ed. Graham M.S. Dann, pp. 77–108, Wallingford, Oxon: CABI Publishing, p. 79.

19 For example, Edward M. Bruner, 1994, 'Abraham Lincoln as authentic reproduction: A critique of postmodernism', *American Anthropologist* 96(2): 397–415; Bruner, *Culture on Tour*; Cohen, 'Authenticity and commoditization in tourism'; Jamal and Hill, 'The home and the world'; Kjell Olsen, 2002, 'Authenticity as a concept in tourism research', *Tourist Studies* 2(2): 159–82.

explicitly make reference to some tradition-bound, inherent quality of continuity with the past that, to them, signifies an authentic example of 'primitives' in the modern era.

Rather than thinking about authenticity as an analytical concept in objectivist or absolutist terms, I employ a constructivist understanding of the term. Constructivist authenticity takes as its premise the significance of the ways in which people define, recognise and identify a given entity as authentic, even if it is in some way a contrivance, copy, or simulacrum.[20] In this conceptualisation, authenticity is the result of social construction, rather than an objectively measurable quality of an object/event. Thus, things appear authentic not because of some inherent quality of the object, event, or 'culture', but because they are constructed as such in terms of points of view, beliefs, discourses, perspectives, or powers; authenticity is relative, negotiable, contextual, symbolic and ideological.[21] Authenticity is thus a projection of tourists' beliefs, expectations, stereotyped images, and desires. I find the constructivist view useful as it begins to bridge the gap between analytical approaches and lay uses of the term, recognising that people's ideas about authenticity are more important than trying to discern whether a given site, sight, performance, or object is or is not authentic. In my discussion of village-based tourism, my focus is to understand how tourists' conceptualisation of authenticity (and sometimes essentialised ideas of the exotic cultural other) influences their interpretations of their experiences, the cultural other with whom they engage, and ultimately themselves. Both material and semiotic elements are interpreted and reinterpreted in myriad ways to make meaning, and ideas about culture, tradition, and authenticity are points of reference for constructing meaning in the context of cultural tourism.

As an alternative way of conceiving of authenticity, Wang has proposed 'existential authenticity',[22] This is taken to be experience-oriented, and concerns the tourists' personal sense of authenticity

---

20   Bruner, 'Abraham Lincoln as authentic reproduction'; Bruner, *Culture on Tour*; Jamal and Hill, 'The home and the world'; Siân Jones, 2010, 'Negotiating authentic objects and authentic selves', *Journal of Material Culture* 15(2): 181–203; Richard A. Peterson, 2005, 'In search of authenticity', *Journal of Management Studies* 42(5): 1083–98; Ning Wang, 1999, 'Rethinking authenticity in tourism experience', *Annals of Tourism Research* 26(2): 349–70.
21   Edward M. Bruner, 1991, 'Transformation of self in tourism', *Annals of Tourism Research* 18(2): 238–50; Bruner, 'Abraham Lincoln as authentic reproduction'.
22   Wang, 'Rethinking authenticity in tourism experience'.

of the self, achieved through experiencing the liminal process of tourism.[23] As such, like constructivist authenticity, it bears no relation to the (real or perceived) authenticity of objects or events. Wang suggests that constructivist authenticity is object-oriented, rather than experience-oriented, but I interpret constructivist authenticity as more encompassing. I contend that an experiential or even existential understanding of authenticity can easily be incorporated into the constructivist approach, to ensure that the analytical understanding of the authenticity encompasses both an outward-looking and an inward-looking orientation. A constructivist analytical standpoint that allows for the importance of *both* the ways in which tourists perceive cultural difference, *and* the ways in which they perceive their own experience in the village as embodied and sensory (existential authenticity), is a particularly useful conceptual tool for analysing tourist–local interactions in places conceived of in the popular imagination as dramatically and quintessentially other.

'Social distance' in tourism

In most destinations, the infrastructure for visiting 'a culture', as the tour operators and many travellers would have it, is much more formally developed than is the case in PNG. In northern Thailand, for example, hill treks are well established with set routes, trained local guides, and the opportunity to stay with 'real villagers' overnight and offering a series of well-orchestrated examples of Akha, Hmong and/or Karen ways of life. In Lake Titicaca in Peru, groups of foreign tourists visit villages on the reed island of Amantani and, day after day, designated host families welcome tourists, provide the opportunity to wear local dress, and attend a dance in the local community hall, all clearly staged for tourists but designed to provide the visitor not only with a sense of what authentic village life is like, but an embodied experience of dressing up like an Amatani Islander and eating dinner with a local family in their home. Such experiences are clearly a thing apart from floor shows and other formal cultural performances, which are literally presented on a stage with a distinct separation between (local) performer and (foreign) audience. And yet, they are also a performance, and while travellers might willingly suspend disbelief in order to feel that what they are experiencing

---

23   Ibid., p. 352.

is authentic in some way that is meaningful to them, most tourists on some level likely recognise that these exact patterns are repeated daily, that one visits with a large group of other tourists, that the choreography of the interactions is designed to be seamless, and that the actual interactions with individual local hosts are relatively brief. While these experiences can certainly have meaning for tourists, and can offer insight into another way of life and a space for self-reflection, I argue that a place like the Trobriand Islands is conceived, by those relatively few tourists who travel there, as something quite apart from such established tourist experiences. This is especially so for those travellers who stay in a village for part or all of their visits.

A village stay, in practical terms, offers the traveller the opportunity to stay in a local house constructed of bush materials, and to 'rough it' by sleeping on a mat or thin mattress on the floor, using only a lamp for light. They will eat 'local' food (though, in practice, are likely to have more protein and store-bought food than most locals normally eat), and may have the opportunity to engage in activities like visiting the gardens, going fishing, attending a community sporting match or feast, and simply observing the daily rhythm of life for island residents. They can thus feel that they have taken part and seen an aspect of community life that sets them apart from those who visit by cruise ship or group tour.

In the Trobriands, as with many other cultural tourism localities, visiting a village is seen by tourists as a way of interacting with representatives of the cultural other in a more meaningful and 'real' way, though, of course, much of what is exposed to the tourist gaze is orchestrated by tour operators, foreign or local guides, or the village residents themselves.[24] These interactions, too, are a kind of performance. But again, what matters most to tourists is not 'reality', as such, but their own construction of it. Those who, like Tina, organise their own visits—without the intervention or assistance of a tour operator or an accompanying guide, and the hefty payments that are associated with such infrastructure—are most likely to interpret their experiences as truly 'authentic'. I suggest that there is something here akin to Marshall Sahlins' thesis regarding social distance.[25]

24   MacCannell, 'Staged authenticity'; see also Christian S. Hammons, 2015, 'Shamanism, tourism, and secrecy: Revelation and concealment in Siberut, Western Indonesia', *Ethnos: Journal of Anthropology* 80(4): 548–67.
25   Marshall Sahlins, 1972, 'On the sociology of primitive exchange', in *Stone Age Economics*, ed. Marshall Sahlins, pp. 185–276, London: Tavistock.

Sahlins, of course, is addressing general rules governing the kinds of reciprocity between people in very close, kin-based relationships as opposed to those who do not share close social ties. In this case, I suggest that the degree to which tourists conceive of their own experience, and the qualities of the tourism 'products' they consume (including a village stay and the people who provide such services) as authentic is positively correlated with the (perceived, whether or not real in objective terms) 'closeness' of their encounter. This is reflected in terms of both embodied experience (staying in a local house, eating local food, wearing local dress, participating in a local game) and the almost voyeuristic satisfaction of seeing something intended for a local audience rather than a tourist audience, like the school cultural day mentioned by Tina in the opening vignette to this chapter, or attending a village mortuary feast. The absence of other tourists can also lend a sense of closeness not afforded in more established destinations. Let me here provide a few ethnographic examples to demonstrate the ways in which this is conceived by tourists themselves.

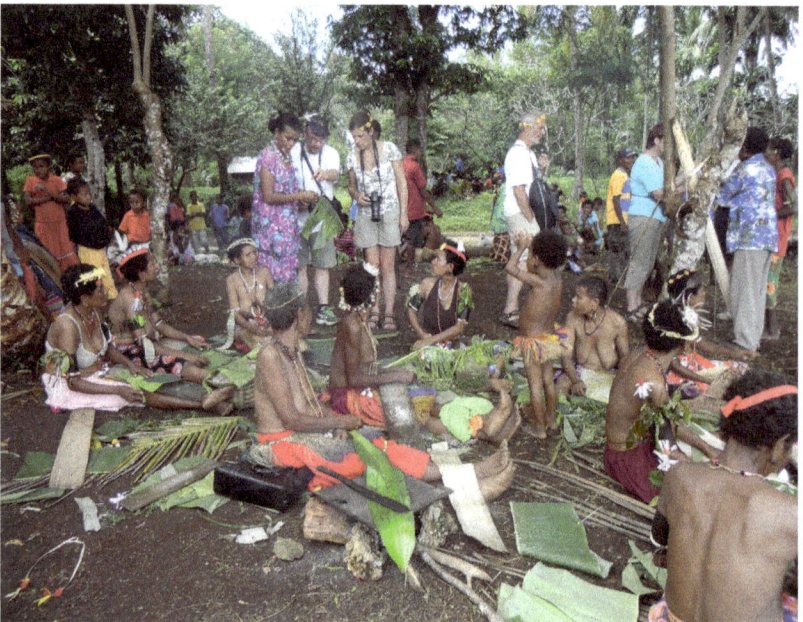

Figure 111. A group tour gets an 'up close' encounter with Trobriand villagers, Yalumgwa Village.

Source. Photographed by Michelle MacCarthy, 23 July 2013.

Figure 112. Visiting tourists participating in a Trobriand cricket match.
Source. Photographed by Michelle MacCarthy, 14 August 2009.

Beyond the stage

In several recent years, a small festival coinciding with the yam harvest period has been organised by Trobriand businesswoman Serah Clark, proprietor of Butia Lodge. The event, called Ugwabwena Festival, generates business for the lodge, often with invited guests representing mid- to high-level public servants and prominent businesspeople from the provincial capital of Alotau, the national capital Port Morseby, and other urban centres. It also attracts a small number of tourists. In 2009, a group of eight expatriate Australians living in Port Morseby and working for AusAID and other development projects came to Kiriwina for the festival. They opted to stay in a village rather than the guest lodge, and this was facilitated by a Trobriand Islander living in Port Moresby, with whom one of the expatriates, Max, had become acquainted. Kebs, their local host, had come back to the village from the city to coordinate and oversee their stay, including organising the construction of bush-materials huts in the local style to house the visitors. I interviewed most of this group, individually or several at a time, and these discussions clearly demonstrated the ways in which this idea of 'social distance' is perceived as significant to tourists' understandings of their experiences. The sentiments expressed by these visitors demonstrate the ways in which their interpretations of their experiences and their assessment of the authenticity of the place and its people were shaped by the 'closeness' they felt they had gained through their village stay.

The festival, of course, is organised in advance, with a number of formal speeches, a schedule of performances from each village and an emcee officiating over the events. A temporary shelter is erected to provide shade to invited guests and tourists, and plastic chairs are available for their comfort. The local audience (Trobrianders from the nearby villages come in droves) squats or sits on the periphery, with only a tree for shade if they are lucky. This demarcation is recognised as signifying a staged event, which made it, to many visitors, inherently inauthentic. For example, Amy said:

> I think, to be honest, in terms of the festival itself, I'd like it to be a more organic experience, I didn't like … the fact that there was a tent [the shaded seating area] … I don't think that used to happen, I just want it to be real. If you [Trobrianders] get out there and you gyrate to the yam, I want to sit in the shade and watch you do that. In the shade of a tree, I don't need a chair. I can sit on the ground in the shade of a tree, just watching, and have it happen the way it would happen, and all these speeches, these long, tedious speeches, from all these random people is unnecessary. I'm sure it didn't happen like that in the old days. Just bring it back to that.[26]

---

26 Interview with Amy, Butia Lodge, Kiriwina Island, 11 July 2009.

The fact that the festival was taking place was identified by this group of Australians as a reason for the timing of the visit, but the interest in the Trobriands as a destination was generated through Max's acquaintance with Kebs, the general reputation of the Trobriand Islands within Papua New Guinea,[27] and the quality of the word carvings that are produced for sale both in Kiriwina and in urban centres like Port Moresby.[28] In addition to taking in some of the events of the organised festival, this group of visitors also undertook excursions from their host village to beaches and other villages, often with their local host as guide. All of these visitors agreed that staying in the village rather than the tourist lodge had given them a greater understanding of 'the culture'; as Max put it:

> It would be so easy to come and stay in one of the lodges, and come and see the staged festival, and have zero interaction with the culture at all. Not saying that we've acculturated or anything, but we've scraped the surface, where it would be quite easy to come here for this weekend and not do that.[29]

The village experience was contrasted starkly with the staged nature of the Ugwabwena Festival, as they saw it. Peta expressed it thus:

> It just sort of opens your eyes to a whole world of complexity, because you don't get answers in five days. [But it] does make you realise some of what's going on. The first day we arrived, too, there was a feast on for some of the aunties who—kind of a funeral feast … So, they took us to see that, and we sat there for about half an hour being completely bamboozled. But that was so much more of the real culture, I guess, than what we've been seeing at the yam festival.[30]

Thus, for tourists, while the *mode* of exchange may not be conditioned by social distance—tourists still pay, in cash, for services rendered—we might paraphrase Sahlins to say that the span of social distance between those who exchange conditions the *meaning* of exchange,

---

27 The 'Islands of Love' trope is well-known throughout the country; see, for example, Katherine Lepani, 2012, *Islands of Love, Islands of Risk: Culture and HIV in the Trobriands*, Nashville, TN: Vanderbilt University Press; Michelle MacCarthy, 2013, '"More than grass skirts and feathers": Negotiating culture in the Trobriand Islands', *International Journal of Heritage Studies* 19(1): 62–77; Michelle MacCarthy, 2016, *Making the Modern Primitive: Cultural Tourism in the Trobriand Islands*, Honolulu: University of Hawai'i Press.
28 Sergio Jarillo de la Torre, 2013, 'Carving the spirits of the wood: An enquiry into Trobriand materialisations', PhD thesis, Department of Anthropology, University of Cambridge.
29 Interview with Max, Butia Lodge, Kiriwina Island, 11 July 2009.
30 Interview with Peta, Butia Lodge, Kiriwina Island, 11 July 2009.

at least from the point of view of the visitor.[31] Further, those experiences that do *not* involve cash payments, such as attending a funeral feast, may also be seen as 'closer' to 'real life' and thus more authentic.[32] We also see here echoes of the frontstage/backstage dichotomy.[33] A further ethnographic example reinforces the commonalities in these discourses, which are particularly uniform amongst the demographic of young, independent travellers I focus on here.

Figure 113. Attending a *sagali* (funeral feast) is a highlight for many cultural tourists to the Trobriands.
Source. Photographed by Michelle MacCarthy, 8 July 2010.

I met Simon, an independent English backpacker in his 30s, when he arrived at the small airstrip in Kiriwina on one of the (then) two weekly commercial flights from Port Moresby, via the provincial capital Alotau. Simon told me he had wanted to come to PNG and the Solomon Islands because he preferred 'off-the-beaten-track' destinations. He considered himself 'intrepid', having climbed PNG's

31   Sahlins, 'On the sociology of primitive exchange', p. 196.
32   For an in-depth discussion of the role of money in tourist transactions, see Michelle MacCarthy, 2015, '"Like playing a game where you don't know the rules": Investing meaning in intercultural cash transactions between tourists and Trobriand Islanders', *Ethnos: Journal of Anthropology* 80(4): 448–71.
33   Erving Goffman, 1971, *The Presentation of Self in Everyday Life*, Harmondsworth: Penguin; MacCannell, 'Staged authenticity'.

highest peak, Mt Wilhelm, without a real guide, just a friend he had made while staying in a settlement in Goroka. He stayed in the settlement rather than in a hotel, because he 'met some nice people' who looked after him. His ability to make 'friends' and fit in was an important part of his narrative, and he felt it set him apart from mere 'tourists' and gave him a greater appreciation of life in the developing world. Like Tina and the group of Australians described above, he feels that staying with local people gives him the opportunity to interact and learn much more about how people live. In his estimation, Europeans have 'less culture' than people in places like the Pacific Islands. 'People in the West have lost sense their sense of community', he reckons;[34] the 'simple life' of people living in the developing world held great romance.

Figure 114. The 'simple life' of the village, as romanticised by visitors.
Source. Photographed by Michelle MacCarthy, 10 December 2009.

These examples, while illuminating and offering a remarkable homogeneity in the ways in which cultural experiences are interpreted and understood by this particular tourist demographic, are not intended to suggest that *all* tourists agree on what is, and what isn't, 'authentic'. Nor do I suggest I have identified some unwavering law

---

34   Interview with Simon, Bweka hamlet, Kiriwina Island, 10 February 2010.

or rule governing tourists' perceptions. Indeed, not all tourists see their experiences in the Trobriands as representing an authentic and unadulterated culture untainted by globalisation; I met several visitors who expressed their dismay at what they interpreted as a *lack* of authenticity. Some are disillusioned with what they see as the corrupting forces of modernity, and especially the scourge (as they see it) of missionisation. Christine, another of the Australian visitors who visited Kiriwina with her friends for Ugwabwena Festival, told me:

> I have found the influence of missionaries disturbing, but that's nothing new. But, the fact that some of the locals were saying the other night when there was a Christian thing in our village that they, that they're taught, that their traditional god is evil and that they need to worship—that there's only one god, and they have to worship that one. Also that there used to be an island that they considered heaven ... But they're not allowed to think that anymore, that they've been told that that's wrong. And, uh, evil.[35]

Christine was not the only visitor who blamed the missionaries for adulterating what would otherwise (they thought) have been a pure and authentic way of life. Two visitors who had come on a small organised tour with a Port Moresby–based tour operator specialising in 'soft adventure experiences'[36] undertook a village stay that they did not see as representing an authentic experience with authentically traditional people, as they had hoped. Olga, a Swiss woman in her 60s, told me that she and her companion had come to the Trobriands with a knowledge of what was in 'the old books' about traditional ways of life, and that she had thus arrived with the hope and expectation of seeing:

> the old traditions. Really the old traditions. And everywhere we were told we don't do this anymore, we cannot talk about it [because of the missionaries]. Even background information, why is this and why is this—to really understand ... nothing could be fulfilled. So my expectations are totally—they hang out in an empty space, in an open empty space—nothing was fulfilled. Sorry to say, but that's the truth.[37]

---

35 Interview with Christine, Butia Lodge, 11 July 2009.
36 'Ecotourism Melanesia – Discover Papua New Guinea and Solomon Islands – Travel and Tourism Arrangements, Escorted Tours, Independent Touring, PNG Tourism Information, Accommodation and Sightseeing', 2016, *Em.Com.Pg*.
37 Interview with Olga, Kiriwina Lodge, 4 August 2009.

Despite Olga's disappointment that she had not found a place frozen in time, where her essentialised ideas of authenticity could be satisfied, it is notable that staying in the village was the one positive thing she had to say in what was otherwise a lengthy tirade about the scourge of modernisation and missionisation. She conceded that amidst all of her failed expectations, staying in a village 'was nice, actually. It was actually a really nice feature, to live with the families … Very warm-hearted, friendly, kind … everything.'[38] Still, for Olga, it was not 'authentic' because it did not meet her preconceived ideas. While their responses to their experiences may have been different from most, visitors like Christine and Olga still demonstrate a concern with authenticity, and their disappointment might be interpreted as a reflection of failing to find the 'closeness' (in this case, to their own idealised expectations of essentialised 'traditional' people) they sought through an encounter with otherness.

'When tourists come here, they don't want Disneyland'

The general *lack* of tourism development and infrastructure in PNG is a feature that sets it apart from many other locations in which ethno-tourism is promoted. The very absence of other tourists increases the sense of authenticity and the self-verification for tourists that one is, indeed, intrepid and has managed to 'get off the beaten track'. Many visitors commented positively on the lack of other tourists in the Trobriands, as tourists are blamed for having 'ruined' so many other destinations by their presence. In a telling comment that demonstrates the other side of the coin, an Australian visitor who arrived by private yacht on the same day that, coincidentally, a group of 16 North American visitors on an ElderTreks tour, an American expatriate working in Port Moresby, and two foreign journalists were also visiting the island, all of whom happened to converge in the northernmost village of Kaibola, observed that the island seemed 'like Disneyland' compared with the other small and relatively untouristed islands they had visited by yacht throughout Milne Bay Province. Too many tourists thus inauthenticate a place, make it a simulacra rather than the 'real thing', and rob the visitor of the experience of

---

38   Ibid.

feeling truly intrepid. Disneyland represents, then, the antithesis of the authentic in which everything is fabrication. Interestingly, the same metaphor was used by Moshe, an elderly Israeli visitor staying at Butia Lodge with his wife, who observed, 'When tourists come here, they want to see that it is authentic. They don't want Disneyland.'[39]

Most people, however, find themselves the only tourists on the island when they visit, and this is itself a great attraction to tourists seeking an unspoiled place, and once again represents a sense of closeness with the place and its people than is available in destinations with heavy tourist traffic. The lack of other tourists and infrastructure validates a sense of difference from home, and a sense of getting a glimpse of 'real life'. Amy, one of the group of Australian expatriates introduced in the previous section, put it like this:

> Here, it's like, they're really interested in you ... there's a curiosity about the tourists, as much as the tourists have a curiosity about the locals. I think there's still that sense of—alright, so there's not the infrastructure that's evident in other tourist locations, but that makes it real, you're still getting a feel for the people. If you're here even for a day, you'll still get a feel for how they live, what they do, their culture, which I think—which is my interest in tourism, and I appreciate [that].[40]

Again, I want to stress that I do not make an argument that one kind of touristic experience is more or less authentic than another, in an empirical sense. That is not my concern. Instead, I seek to demonstrate that the ways in which visitors' *perceptions* of a place, a people, an event, or an object as authentically unique, unusual, or different from the known are directly related, for most cultural tourists, to the value they place on the experience. Like Tina, introduced at the beginning of this chapter, tourists to the Trobriand Islands consistently iterated the importance of feeling that their cultural interactions and touristic experiences were authentic and unusual as markers of their satisfaction with the experience. This 'feeling' is intuitive, and when prompted to explain how they know if a place/experience is authentic, many visitors found it hard to articulate, but yet were confident they knew it when they saw it.

---

39 Interview with Moshe, Butia Lodge, Kiriwina Island, 10 August 2010.
40 Interview with Amy, Butia Lodge, Kiriwina Island, 11 July 2009.

Figure 115. Young girls fetching water, Vakuta Island.
Source. Photographed by Michelle MacCarthy, 10 December 2009.

Herb, an American visitor in his 70s, was more explicit than most visitors about his desire for a singular and authentic cultural experience, and the emotive, intuitive nature of 'feeling' that a cultural experience is 'genuine':

> These dances we see when we travel, sometimes they are authentic, but in some places they're clearly choreographed—here it appears to be genuine ... I don't know how you know, but there is a feeling, it seems natural, but that's just based on my own experience and interpretation. I'm not saying a put-up thing can't be good, it can be entertaining, but if it's not authentic, I won't enjoy it as much. I mean, if a singsing[41] came to New York, it wouldn't really work—there'd be no drama to it.[42]

Regardless of whether visitors interpreted their experiences as authentic, unique, and singular or not, the point is that they are *seeking* such an experience, and *value* the opportunity to engage in a truly singular intercultural interaction.

41 *Singsing* is a PNG pidgin word referring to a cultural show, generally involving traditional dancers in their finery.
42 Interview with Herb, Butia Lodge, Kiriwina Island, 27 August 2010.

Conclusions: Commodifying experience

In cultural tourism, this reified thingness conceived of as culture—sometimes material (i.e. souvenirs, photographs) but more often intangible (performance, interactions with the other) is commodified; tourism is among the world's largest industries. Over a billion people today cross borders for business or leisure travel annually,[43] and if current trends continue, this number could reach 1.8 billion by 2030.[44] Annual expenditures worldwide have since 2012 surpassed US$1 trillion according to the United Nations World Tourism Organization.[45]

The quest for 'close' encounters, meaningful interactions with authentic representatives of otherness, is in many senses an attempt to imagine oneself outside the very infrastructure that makes tourism possible: outside the market, outside modernity, and outside relentless individualism.

Annette Weiner has made a case for some kinds of objects having more 'density' than others, by which she means that objects are cultural constructions that accrue symbolic importance through associations with their owner(s), histories and sacralisation, as well as aesthetic and economic values.[46] I see the experience of a village stay in which the ideal of touring 'real life'—whether merely observed or, more significantly, participated in and experienced as embodied action—as not only 'close', but also symbolically dense for most tourists. For those whose desires are met by these experiences, they encapsulate evidence for the culture-seeking tourist of the existence of the authentic cultural other, and one's own ability to engage in an interaction conceived of as meaningful. Experience, then, may be a special kind of commodity, in which social distance and the expectations for reciprocity are manipulated, in a sense, often through active self-deception. Commodities are treated like gifts, objects and actions are invested with meaning beyond their physical properties,

43   UNWTO, 2014, *UNWTO World Tourism Barometer*, UNWTO.
44   UNWTO, 2014, *UNWTO Tourism Highlights 2013 Edition*, UNWTO.
45   Ibid.; UNWTO, *UNWTO World Tourism Barometer*.
46   Annette B. Weiner, 1994, 'Cultural difference and the density of objects', *American Ethnologist* 21(2): 391–403, p. 394.

and strangers are treated as friends or even family. This inversion provides the perception, if not the reality, of experiencing the life of the cultural other 'as it is really lived'.

References

Alexeyeff, Kalissa. 2009. *Dancing from the Heart: Movement, Gender, and Cook Islands Globalization*. Honolulu: University of Hawai'i Press.

Bruner, Edward M. 1991. 'Transformation of self in tourism.' *Annals of Tourism Research* 18(2): 238–50.

——. 1994. 'Abraham Lincoln as authentic reproduction: A critique of postmodernism.' *American Anthropologist* 96(2): 397–415.

Bruner, Edward M. (ed.). 2005. *Culture on Tour: Ethnographies of Travel*. Chicago: University of Chicago Press.

Cohen, Erik. 1988. 'Authenticity and commoditization in tourism.' *Annals of Tourism Research* 15(3): 371–86.

Condevaux, Aurélie. 2009. 'Māori culture on stage: Authenticity and identity in tourist interactions.' *Anthropological Forum* 19(2): 143–61.

Daniel, Yvonne Payne. 1996. 'Tourism dance performances: Authenticity and creativity.' *Annals of Tourism Research* 23(4): 780–97.

Dann, Graham M.S. (ed.). 2002. *The Tourist as a Metaphor of the Social World*. Wallingford, Oxon: CABI Publishing.

'Ecotourism Melanesia – Discover Papua New Guinea and Solomon Islands – Travel and Tourism Arrangements, Escorted Tours, Independent Touring, PNG Tourism Information, Accommodation and Sightseeing.' 2016. *Em.Com.Pg*. Online: www.em.com.pg/ (accessed 10 March 2016).

Goffman, Erving. 1971. *The Presentation of Self in Everyday Life*. Harmondsworth: Penguin.

Graburn, Nelson H.H. (ed.). 1976. *Ethnic and Tourist Arts: Cultural Expressions from the Fourth World*. Berkeley: University of California Press.

———. 1984. 'The evolution of tourist arts.' *Annals of Tourism Research* 11(3): 393–419.

———. 1999. 'Epilogue: Ethnic and tourist arts revisited.' In *Unpacking Culture: Art and Commodity in the Colonial and Postcolonial Worlds*, ed. Ruth B. Phillips and Christopher B. Steiner, pp. 335–54. Berkeley: University of California Press.

Hammons, Christian S. 2015. 'Shamanism, tourism, and secrecy: Revelation and concealment in Siberut, Western Indonesia.' *Ethnos: Journal of Anthropology* 80(4): 548–67.

Jamal, Tazim and Steve Hill. 2002. 'The home and the world: (Post) touristic spaces of (in)authenticity?' In *The Tourist as a Metaphor of the Social World*, ed. Graham M.S. Dann, pp. 77–108. Wallingford, Oxon: CABI Publishing.

Jarillo de la Torre, Sergio. 2013. 'Carving the spirits of the wood: An enquiry into Trobriand materialisations.' PhD thesis, Department of Anthropology, University of Cambridge.

Jones, Siân. 2010. 'Negotiating authentic objects and authentic selves.' *Journal of Material Culture* 15(2): 181–203.

Kaeppler, Adrienne. 1988. 'Pacific festivals and the promotion of identity, politics, and tourism.' In *Come Mek Me Hol'Yu Han': The Impact of Tourism on Traditional Music*, ed. Adrienne L. Kaeppler and Olive Lewin, pp. 12–38. Kingston, Jamaica: Jamaica Memory Bank.

Kaeppler, Adrienne L. and Olive Lewin (eds). 1988. *Come Mek Me Hol'Yu Han': The Impact of Tourism on Traditional Music*. Kingston, Jamaica: Jamaica Memory Bank.

Kirshenblatt-Gimblett, Barbara. 1998. *Destination Culture: Tourism, Museums, and Heritage*. Berkeley: University of California Press.

Lepani, Katherine. 2012. *Islands of Love, Islands of Risk: Culture and HIV in the Trobriands*. Nashville, TN: Vanderbilt University Press.

Lockwood, Victoria S. (ed.). 2004. *Globalization and Culture Change in the Pacific Islands*. Upper Saddle River, NJ: Pearson Prentice Hall.

MacCannell, Dean. 1973. 'Staged authenticity: Arrangements of social space in tourist settings.' *American Journal of Sociology* 79(3): 589–603.

——. 1976. *The Tourist : A New Theory of the Leisure Class*. New York Schocken Books.

MacCarthy, Michelle. 2012. '"Before it gets spoiled by tourists": Constructing authenticity in the Trobriand Islands of Papua New Guinea.' PhD thesis, Department of Anthropology, University of Auckland.

——. 2013. '"More than grass skirts and feathers": Negotiating culture in the Trobriand Islands.' *International Journal of Heritage Studies* 19(1): 62–77.

——. 2015. '"Like playing a game where you don't know the rules": Investing meaning in intercultural cash transactions between tourists and Trobriand Islanders.' *Ethnos: Journal of Anthropology* 80(4): 448–71.

——. 2016. *Making the Modern Primitive: Cultural Tourism in the Trobriand Islands*. Honolulu: University of Hawai'i Press.

Olsen, Kjell. 2002. 'Authenticity as a concept in tourism research.' *Tourist Studies* 2(2): 159–82.

'Papua New Guinea – Adventure Travel For 50 Plus.' 2016. *Eldertreks. Com*. Online: www.eldertreks.com/tour/ETTD000355 (accessed 9 March 2016).

Peterson, Richard A. 2005. 'In search of authenticity.' *Journal of Management Studies* 42(5): 1083–098.

Phillips Ruth B. and Christopher B. Steiner (eds). 1999. '*Unpacking Culture: Art and Commodity in the Colonial and Postcolonial Worlds*. Berkeley: University of California Press.

Sahlins, Marshal. 1972. 'On the sociology of primitive exchange.' In *Stone Age Economics*, ed. Marshall Sahlins, pp. 185–276. London: Tavistock.

Schutte, Gerhard. 2003. 'Tourists and tribes in the "new" South Africa.' *Ethnohistory* 50(3): 473–87.

Silverman, Eric Kline. 1999. 'Tourist art as the crafting of identity in the Sepik River (Papua New Guinea).' In *Unpacking Culture: Art and Commodity in Colonial and Postcolonial Worlds*, ed. Ruth B. Phillips and Christopher B. Steiner, pp. 51–66. Berkeley: University of California Press.

———. 2004. 'Cannibalizing, commodifying, or creating culture? Power and art in Sepik River tourism.' In *Globalization and Culture Change in the Pacific Islands*, ed. Victoria S. Lockwood, pp. 339–57. Upper Saddle River, NJ: Pearson Prentice Hall.

Stanley, Nick. 1998. *Being Ourselves for You: The Global Display of Cultures*. London: Middlesex University Press.

Steiner, Christopher B. 1999. 'Authenticity, repetition, and the aesthetics of seriality: The work of tourist art in the age of mechanical reproduction.' In *Unpacking Culture: Art and Commodity in Colonial and Postcolonial Worlds*, ed. Ruth B. Phillips and Christopher B. Steiner, pp. 87–103. Berkeley: University of California Press.

Taylor, John. 2001. 'Authenticity and sincerity in tourism.' *Annals of Tourism Research* 28(1): 7–26.

UNWTO. 2014. *UNWTO Tourism Highlights 2013 Edition*. UNWTO. Online: www.e-unwto.org/content/hq4538/fulltext.pdf (accessed 25 February 2015).

———. 2014. *UNWTO World Tourism Barometer*. UNWTO. Online: cf.cdn.unwto.org/sites/all/files/pdf/unwto_barom14_02_apr_excerpt_0.pdf (accessed 25 February 2015).

Wang, Ning. 1999. 'Rethinking authenticity in tourism experience.' *Annals of Tourism Research* 26(2): 349–70.

Weiner, Annette B. 1994. 'Cultural difference and the density of objects.' *American Ethnologist* 21(2): 391–403.

23

Suva, November '97

Anita Jowitt

Nobody smiles for free any more.
The poster says:
'Don't waste your smile on foreigners.'
Empathy as commodity – call it progress.

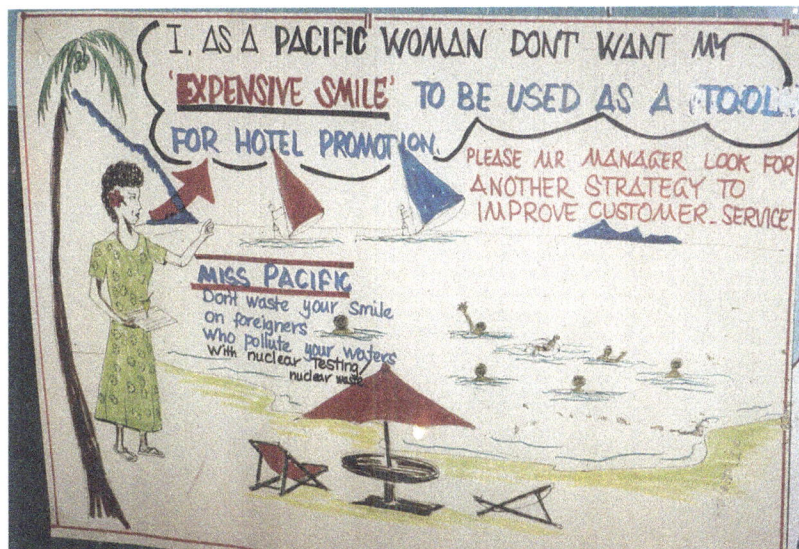

Figure 116. 'Don't waste your smile on foreigners'.
Source. Artist unknown. Produced by a University of the South Pacific, Fiji, student circa 1997 for a geography course (Photograph Anita Jowitt, with permission).

24

Pikinini in Paradise: Photography, Souvenirs and the 'Child Native' in Tourism

John Taylor

Tourism advertising for Vanuatu has in recent years become saturated with images of children. Brochures, in-flight magazines and digital media productions are repeatedly adorned with photographs of ni-Vanuatu 'pikininis' frollicking on the shorelines of sun-drenched beaches or colourfully dressed up in 'native' costumes. In these images, barefoot island fantasies are infused with an alluring innocence and spontaneity, a narrative conjunction that doubly reinscribes the touristic trope of 'escape' from modern adult life. What is more, cruise ship tourists to Vanuatu may purchase souvenir versions of this fantasy 'child native' at the market stalls that greet them, in the form of colourfully adorned plastic baby dolls. They may also consume real life 'pikinini in paradise' in the form of ni-Vanuatu children who are exhorted by their parents to play dress-up, strike smiling poses, and trade photographic opportunities for 'donations'.

As this chapter explores, far from representing a simple replication or circulation of imagery, such performances reflect the ambiguities and ambivalences that may occur when touristic images of ethnicity become miniaturised in the production of souvenirs and enacted by locals for photographic consumption by visiting tourists. By obscuring rather than making visible the radically unequal political-economic relations that define many tourism settings, especially in developing countries, as well as the means of production that bring those settings into being, the majority of such advertising and souvenirs constitute classic commodity fetishes. Indeed, in Vanuatu, obscuring massive economic inequalities behind welcoming smiles, resort opulence and sandy beaches, tourism and tourism advertising is currently encouraging and facilitating the alienation of indigenous-owned land to expatriate 'investors',[1] thus furthering the large divide between expatriate haves and ni-Vanuatu have nots in that country. However, increasingly disinherited locals are also taking up such imagery in the pursuit of capital. As argued here, indigenous appropriations of the neo-colonial imagery of tourism may sometimes threaten to break open the efficacy of the fantasy image of a Pacific paradise. In the case examined, by presenting an ambiguous and for some confrontational blend of touristic fantasy and 'photogenic poverty',[2] real-life performances of the 'pikinini in paradise' are seen to provoke a cognitive dissonance that may disrupt the carefree pleasure of the tourist gaze. In doing so, they invite tourists to consider the inequalities that lie behind the tourism fetish.

Performances such as these may be seen to epitomise the negative effects of what has been dubbed a 'hermeneutic circle of tourism photography': a feedback loop that circulates between; the tourism industry, which produces saleable images of places and people for tourists to consume through travel; tourists, who desire to consume those images through the 'I was there' evidence production of photography; and locals, who likewise aim to reproduce a credible version of such images, and thus satisfy those tourist desires in order to get their hands on a slice of the tourist dollar.[3] But as I argue further below, the dissonance produced in this instance also continually

---

1   Claire Slatter, 2006, *The Con/Dominium of Vanuatu?: Paying the Price of Investment and Land Liberalisation—A Case Study of Vanuatu's Tourism Industry*, New Zealand: Oxfam.

2   John Hutnyk, 2004, 'Photogenic poverty: Souvenirs and infantilism', *Journal of Visual Research* 3(1): 77–94.

3   For recent usages, see Kellee Caton and Carla Almeida Santos, 2007, 'Closing the hermeneutic circle: Photographic encounters with the other', *Annals of Tourism Research* 35(1): 7–26; Olivia Jenkins, 2003, 'Photography and travel brochures: The circle of representation', *Tourism Geographies* 5(3): 305–28; and for a critical discussion with regards to Vanuatu, John Taylor, 2011, 'Photogenic authenticity and the spectacular in tourism', in *Indigenous Tourism and the Intricacies of Cross-cultural Understanding*, special issue of *La Ricerca Folkorica* 61: 32–40.

threatens to fracture the idealised image, break or at least unsettle the circle of reproduction, and allow tourists a perhaps unsettling opportunity to glance beyond the tourist bubble.

Children and photography in Vanuatu tourism advertising

Images of children have a long history in tourism-related publications for Vanuatu, and have featured, for example, on postcards from the early twentieth century onward. Over the course of the last two decades, however, they have come to assume a central role across all major forms of advertising. Photographs of ni-Vanuatu children sitting with tourists in outrigger canoes are especially prevalent, as are those of children colourfully adorned in 'native' dress. Most popular, however, are images of children engaged in joyous play in the shallows of a white sand beach. Such images communicate the generic Pacific Island frame of fun, sun and sand, as well as a sense of playful, carefree and spontaneous happiness that is evidently of great value to selling Vanuatu as a tourism product. Along with the images themselves, children often feature prominently in the psuedo-journalistic stories that also sometimes feature in tourism publications. In doing so, albeit sometimes unwittingly, they also encourage tourists to take souvenir snapshots of children while on their travels.

So apparently popular have images of ni-Vanuatu children become in such contexts that they form the basis of entire publications, such as the 2008 wall calendar that provides the title for this chapter, *Vanuatu: Pikinini in Paradise*.[4] As stated on the back cover, interaction with smiling children appears as an intrinsic aspect of holidays to Vanuatu:

> In Vanuatu—where the name for children is pikinini—it's hard not to be captivated by the smiles and laughter that surrounds you. Says international photographer, David Kirkland, wherever you go in this tiny island nation, you're likely to find a welcoming smile or an entourage of excited kids keen to engage you. This 2008 Wall Calendar is the celebration of the genuine warmth and friendliness of the

---

4   David Kirkland, 2008, *Vanuatu: Pikinini in Paradise*, Brisbane: Hema Maps.

Ni-Vanuatu children—a souvenir to hang in your home and remind you of the special holiday you are likely to have had in these so-called timeless islands of the South Pacific.[5]

While instances such as these are in many ways reflective of the casual gaze of tourism and tourism-related image production everywhere, the emphasis on children brings the often radically unequal power relations that underpin such acts of voyeurism into sharp relief. Others run the risk of slipping into more explicitly exploitative territory. The feature article of one issue of Air Vanuatu's in-flight publication, *Island Spirit*, presents a case in point. Here images of children playing in the shallows of a sandy beach and a portrait of a wide-eyed 'pot-bellied pikinini' gazing innocently and inquisitively up at the viewer—presumably the child described in the passage below—were accompanied by the following opening passage:

A small hand awoke me from my heat-induced slumber. Two large brown eyes peeked over the edge of the fabric and I saw a one-eyed teddy next to me in the hammock.

'Swing-swing?' the request came with a smile. This pot-bellied pikinini was clearly skilled at the art of wrapping visitors around her chubby little finger.

I dragged her in beside me and she propped two bare, sandy feet on my belly, as if they'd been there a million times before. We top-and-tailed in the shade of an old cyclon tree, silently looking out across a languid sea. I sighed deeply, letting go of my old fabricated world and drinking in this newfound reality.[6]

Such romantic imagery plainly reflects the patronising and exoticising voice of colonialism. However vague and unwitting, there is also the suggestion of a potentially sexualised encounter between tourist and child that is deeply problematic. The passage also strongly articulates a further key theme that repeatedly attaches itself to such imagery. This is the idea that meeting and interacting with indigenous children in tropical island settings may help tourists to unlock and set free their own 'inner child', and in doing so magically liberate them from the 'fabricated world' of modernity.

5   Kirkland, *Vanuatu: Pikinini in Paradise.*
6   Chantal Dunbar, 2015, 'Secluded Santo', *Island Spirit*, Air Vanuatu's in-flight publication, pp. 20–23.

'Tabu blong pass'

Let us turn to a specific ethnographic example, that of 'cruise ship day' in Luganville. Cruise ships with carrying capacities of up to 2,000 passengers or more, including P&O's *Pacific Jewel*, *Pacific Pearl* and *Pacific Sun*, stop at the northern Vanuatu town of Luganville around 10 times a year, swelling its local population of some 15,000 by more than 10 per cent. While the nation's capital Port Vila is the primary and more frequent port of call,[7] Luganville is one of several secondary stopping points in cruises that typically last for one to two weeks. Here, at the threshold between cruise ship and shore, disembarking passengers are met by a male string band who strum out familiarly clichéd picture postcard songs that celebrate 'my beautiful island home' and 'smiling friendly people' (Figure 117). Such lyrics echo tourism imagery for Vanuatu and the Pacific region, as do the hibiscus print Hawiian shirts, lava-lavas and the plastic flower leis that are worn by the performers and are on sale in the marketplace beyond. The string band faces a small sign in bold letters stating the legal injunction, 'TABU BLONG PASS' (ILLEGAL TO ENTER).

Another sign, handwritten on cardboard, is placed in front of the performers. Diverting from the stock signifiers of a tropical island paradise, for observant travellers these signs foreground the key elements of ambivalence and even contradiction that follow. The sign reads:

> Tourism development became priority in Vanuatu & policies and also in provinces. Therefor tourism has a wide rangs of capacity buildings in order to provide better service and effective services in tourism industry. Therefore as a part of this services we want to make it more easy and enjoyable by providing you some C.D. cleaps is our dreams. So we really need your help. Thank you for your coberation. God Bless [original spelling retained].

---

7   For an in-depth study of cruise ship tourism to Port Vila, see Anne Lucy Naitu, 2007, 'Dosalsal, the floating ones: Exploring the socio-cultural impacts of cruise ship tourism on Port Vila, Vanuatu residents, and their coping strategies', Masters of Tourism Management thesis, Lincoln University, Christchurch.

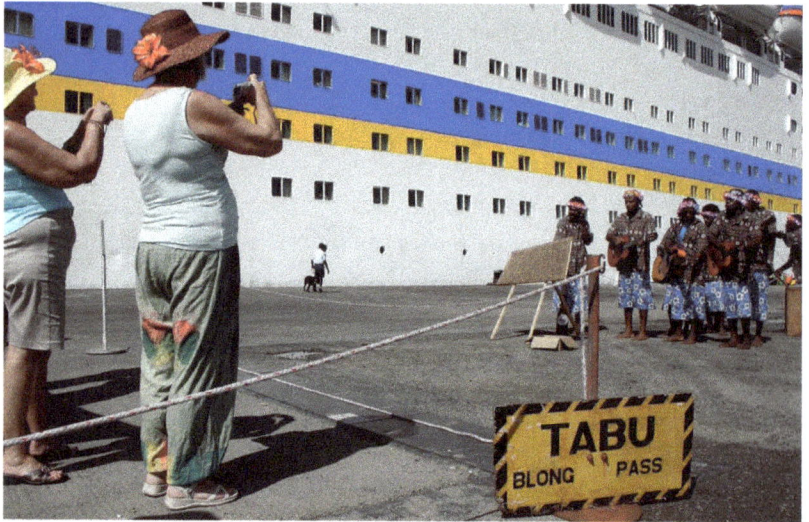

Figure 117. String band greeting *Pacific Sun* to Luganville.
Source. Photographed by John Taylor, May 2007.

Apparently, for some, the incorrect English displayed on the sign seems to prompt responses that call to mind the legacy of the same western evolutionary trope that posited Melanesians as a 'child race'. As I overheard one woman remarking to her friend, 'My kids can write better than that!' Rather than a simple avowal of the image of happy and childlike 'natives', however, such statements might equally be taken as an acknowledgement by such tourists of the imbalance of economic, educational and aspirational opportunity that is one key feature of contemporary difference that separates them from vast majority of ni-Vanuatu locals. Indeed, such imbalances are amply present in the content of the statement. They are also highlighted by the presence of a donations collection box that sits on the ground in front of the performers.

Appropriating a mixture of tourism and development industry jargon in describing their own island 'dreams' for increased economic growth, such that would contribute to the provision of 'better services', the string band comes to embody the potentiality of 'capacity building'. In this way, looking temporally beyond a promise of 'native servitude', a more distant future of enlightened equality is suggested, such that tourism industry development would bring. Indeed, temporally defined difference and distance is a key feature here, and one that by way of parallel tends to naturalise the abundantly apparent economic differences.

In Luganville, mainly expatriate business owners coordinate pre-booked mini-tours ashore, ensuring that the movement of tourists is closely regulated, as is the flow of their dollars. For tourists who opt to take one of these tours—the vast majority—there leaves just enough time to take a leisurely walk along a stall-lined avenue of some 100 metres that leads from the dock to the town's main street. Beyond the welcoming string band, several similar performances are encountered that also seek to prompt acts of charity; a cardboard collection box in front of one group of children, flowers in their hair and singing 'Jesus is the Living God', asks for 'Sunday School donations', while another solicits donations for 'School Fees'. Facilitating as they do the opportunity for tourists to 'donate' a few coins, and thus contribute to the project of development already suggested in the string band sign, such performances offer the 'added value' of providing what John Hutnyk describes as a 'cheap entrée to virtue'.[8] It also offers a context in which the tourists may legitimately take their own photographs of ni-Vanuatu children. Overall, given the sense that such photographic opportunities are paid for with 'donations', especially, an ambiguously fraught conjunction of references is generated, one that comprises the imaginary island escapism on one hand and 'photogenic poverty' on the other.[9]

Souveniring children in the cruise ship marketplace

Markets are central to most short-term destination travel experiences. Indeed, it is in marketplaces that tourists are often most easily able to experience a sense of sincere interaction with the everyday life of locals. For this reason, souvenirs purchased in market contexts may not necessarily represent a real 'piece of the wall' or product of local 'traditions' to be effective, but rather act as a memento and proof of face-to-face encounter. Eschewing one of the master analytic tropes

---

8   Hutnyk, 'Photogenic poverty', p. 81.
9   Hutnyk, 'Photogenic poverty'.

of both tourism and tourism studies,[10] any need to evaluate the relative 'authenticity' of the items on sale appears to be largely irrelevant in this market context. To be effective as souvenirs, however, they do need to signify a generalised sense of place, and/or recall some aspect of the relationship between their new possessors and the perceived sense of otherness from which they are extracted.[11] On these terms, the souvenirs on sale do not only encapsulate and communicate the idea of tourist site and market as 'meeting ground',[12] they also signify and enhance the sense of leisure and play that is present in the market as a whole, and of course encompass a key aspect of cruise ship tourism as a whole. Thus, finely woven pandanus baskets and exquisitely carved miniatures based on local artistic traditions are on sale. Yet the primary stock-in-trade of the market stalls is rack upon rack of brightly coloured 'calico' or lava-lavas, cloth bags, plastic flower leis and beaded necklaces, items that vendors produce from materials purchased from the multitude of 'Chinese' trade stores that comprise the town's primary retail industry. As their brochure advertising indicates, large-scale and short-term cruise ship journeys such as those offered by P&O do not offer touristic searches for 'tradition' or pilgrimages into the 'real'. These are, after all, island escapes where the 'customs and cannibals' do not frighten,[13] but are all part of the front-page theme of 'No hassles and no worries. Fun for the whole family.'[14] Collectively, the colourful stock items on sale in Luganville appeal to this overarching sense of childish fantasy play that permeates the cruise ship tourism experience more generally. This is seen most explicitly in the humorously titillating coconut bras and colourful plastic dolls that are also on sale. On these terms, rather than encouraging serious cultural, historical or political-economic reflection, the market as a whole appears as a kind of fun fair.

---

10   Carol Steiner and Yvette Reisinger, 2006, 'Understanding existential authenticity', *Annals of Tourism Research* 33(2): 299–318; John Taylor, 2001, 'Authenticity and sincerity in tourism', *Annals of Tourism Research* 28(1): 7–26; Ning Wang, 1999, 'Rethinking authenticity in tourism experience', *Annals of Tourism Research* 26(2): 349–70.
11   John Taylor, 1998, *Consuming Identity: Modernity and Tourism in New Zealand*, Auckland: Department of Anthropology, University of Auckland, p. 44.
12   Graeme Evans, 2000, 'Contemporary crafts as souvenirs, artifacts and functional goods and the role in local economic diversification and cultural development', in *Souvenirs: The Material Culture of Tourism*, ed. Michael Hitchcock and Ken Teague, pp. 127–45. Aldershot: Ashgate, p. 129.
13   P&O Cruises, 2011, *2011–2013 Pacific – Australia – Asia* [Cruises Departures Brochure], Sydney: Carnival, trading as P&O Cruises, p. 16.
14   Ibid., p. 1.

Figure 118. Dolls and handicrafts for sale at a roadside 'cruise ship day' market, Luganville.

Source. Photographed by John Taylor, May 2007.

Also working to obscure the means of production, the (mainly) women who run the stalls appear as the primary artisan producers of the items on sale.[15] Occasionally seen working at manual sewing machines, and typically dressed in brightly coloured 'island dresses'[16] comprising the same colourful fabric of the lava-lavas and bags they stitch and sell, these women blend seamlessly into the market world and indeed appear as an intimate source of the products on sale. Their presence is also reflected in another miniaturised form, for nestled amongst the strings of beads, the coconut bras, and rack upon rack of colourful lava-lavas, sit miniaturised plastic versions of 'market mamas', and more predominantly, the 'pikinini in paradise' as South Seas golliwog/hula doll.

---

15   For a discussion of the Port Vila handicrafts industry, see Haidy Geismar, 2003, 'Museums, markets and material culture: Prestations and presentations in rural and urban Vanuatu', PhD thesis, University College London.

16   See Lissant Bolton, 2003, 'Gender, status and introduced clothing in Vanuatu', in *Clothing in the Pacific*, ed. Chloë Colchester, pp. 119–40, Oxford: Berg.

The sense of childlike play referred to above is reinforced in these souvenirs. However, given the evocation of dual 'semiotics of nostalgia'[17] involving ideas of human evolution and the life-course of individuals—a narrative through which such images or objects come to represent a simplicity that the tourists are themselves supposed to have lost, yet that may be regained through childlike play—rather than the native/savage other it is the lost child of the tourist that these souvenirs more properly represent.

The fantasy 'child native' as photographic fetish

In tourism, photography is intimately connected to the processes and products of souveniring practice. Since the advent of digital photography, selfie sticks and social media, especially, taking photographs has also become an important focus for play. It is therefore not surprising to find that photography plays a key role in the context discussed here.

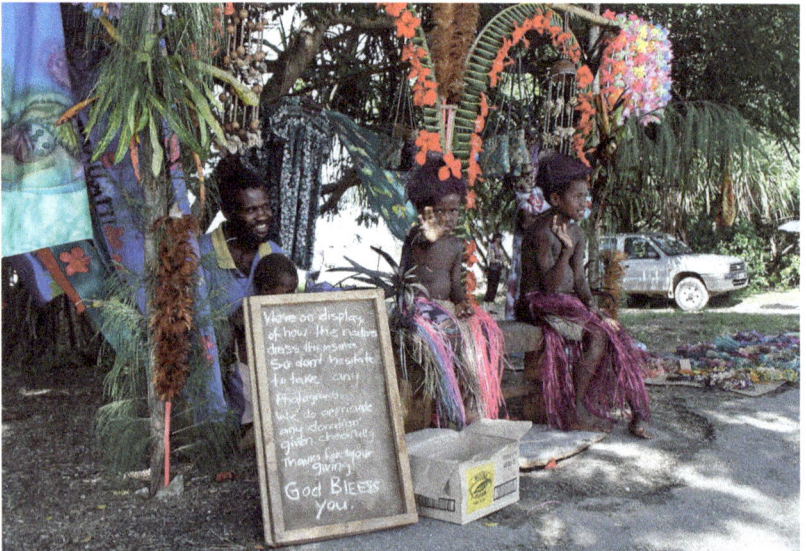

Figure 119. Children posing for photographs, Luganville.
Source. Photographed by John Taylor, May 2007.

---

17   John Frow, 1991, 'Tourism and the semiotics of nostalgia', *October* 57: 123–51.

In general, photographic practise in this street market context assumes the familiar touristic form famously described by Susan Sontag: the photographer, an 'armed version' of Walter Benjamin's 'voyeuristic stroller', discovers around them a picturesque 'landscape of voluptuous extremes'.[18] As has already been suggested, however, the tourists in this market do not only stroll, watch and take photographs, they also encounter, interact, and in doing so consume aspects of their own imagined identity.

Rather than paying the short-term business licence of 1,000vt that is required for those operating 'legitimate' market stalls, and as already seen in the string band and other performances, here some locals offer photographic opportunities in return for 'donations'. Alongside opportunities to pose with examples of local wildlife, such as birds, snakes, lizards and turtles, tourists may take photographs of and pose with brightly costumed children who are exhorted by their parents to smile for 'donations'. One mother, for example, dresses up her daughter in bright tinsel to pose with a clipped-wing bird behind the following words:

> My name is Mweikensery. I am female and wants to say Hellow and wants to welcome you all. And here with me to my thatched house of my fascinating and attractive birds. So anyone is welcome and feeling free to take films about it. Any way your help will be much appreciated to me in advance. Thank you very much. God Bless.

Further down the market street, two children sit on a bench beneath an archway that is brightly decorated with hibiscus flowers, their parents inviting tourists to pose with them:

> We're on display of how the natives dress themselves. So don't hesitate to take any photographs. We do appriciate any donation given cheerfully. Thanks for your giving. God Bleess you [original spelling retained].

Here, like the dolls, the tourist brochure image of the fantasy 'child native' is again replicated. However, in this instance, profound dissonances emerge. The primary basis for these are signalled in the slippage from first to third person in the sign quoted above—'We're

---

18   Susan Sontag, 1979, *On Photography*, London: Penguin Books, p. 55.

on display of how the natives dress themselves'—such that signals the ambiguous position between indigenous subject and tourist role that the children are exhorted to assume.

Like the souvenirs that surround the children, these performances do not seek to reproduce the 'stret *kastom*' found in longer-term 'eco-tourism' excursions to the Ambrym *'rom* ceremony', the *toka* of Tanna, or at the famous Pentecost island *gol* (land dive).[19] Rather, in keeping with the values of the cruise ship market more generally, the native body is instead presented as a prettily decorated trinket— the souvenir fetish is brought to life.

Once again, the narrative that connects the child performer and souvenir fetish to the tourist self—the key structural component of souvenir 'use value'—are the entwined meanings of childhood and primitive 'nativeness'. This suggestion of a primordial connection linking western tourist and native child operates through the equation of ideas of the life-course to the myth of evolutionary progress. This is the same aetiological framework by which indigenous people under colonialism everywhere were confined to 'the past of which the white man is the future'.[20] As one tourist told me as she sat with 'Mweikensery', handing her camera to me so I could take her picture and mimicking with amazing clarity the clichéd jargon of tourism advertising, 'They're just like little children of paradise. So happy! They seem to have something we've lost.' A few minutes later, I encountered a more blatantly racist statement that also echoed this sense of temporal disjuncture as an expatriate tourism operator described to me how a tourist had questioned him for reprimanding a member of his adult staff. His justification, he told me, 'They have to realise, it's like talking to 12 year olds!'[21]

Of course not all tourists believe the industry-produced catalogue images are in any way 'real'. Nor do they necessarily wish to consume them as a part of their own tourism experiences. Just as many tourists are drawn towards the brightly costumed and painted children,

---

19   Margaret Jolly, 1994, *'Kastom* as commodity: The land dive as indigenous rite and tourist spectacle in Vanuatu', in *Culture – Kastom – Tradition: Developing Cultural Policy in Melanesia*, ed. Lamont Lindstrom and Geoffrey M. White, pp. 131–44, Suva, Fiji: Institute of Pacific Studies, University of the South Pacific; Taylor, 'Photogenic authenticity and the spectacular in tourism'.
20   Homi K. Bhabha, 1994, *The Location of Culture*, London: Routledge, p. 238.
21   Author's fieldnotes, May 2007.

others find the displays 'weird', even distasteful. Yet the dissonance of these performances not only has to do with any resonances of a 'human zoo'. Given the immediate economic context in which photographic opportunities are offered in exchange for 'donations', they may also disconcertingly evoke what Hutnyk has described as 'photogenic poverty'.[22] Ubiquitously found in UNICEF and other aid or charity brochures, images of a poor indigenous or ethnic children provide, as he puts it, 'the necessary motivator for even just a gesture (send just a few coins) of care or concern for dispossessed human beings'.[23] But in this particular context of producing touristic 'added-value' there is an additional double bind. That as a demonstration of 'victimology', such performances may expose to tourists the very inequality between touring tourist and toured indigenous subject that the souvenir fetish would otherwise ideally seek to hide. No wonder many local people I spoke to about the practice were so quick to denigrate it as a form of begging. No wonder, too, that many tourists give the children a wide berth, skirting or quickly distancing themselves from the disconcerting scene.

As numerous commentators have argued, toured places the world over are continually reproduced according to tense processes of negotiation.[24] Local people must wrestle with the desire of the tourism industry that their pre-existing habitats and practices be 'dressed up' according to its own specific aesthetic requirements. As articulated in the case presented here, however, and extending beyond Hutnyk's text-based examples, performances reflecting processes such as these often come to inhabit an uncomfortable and uncanny non-space, hovering uncomfortably between touristic visual 'fantasy' and socio-economic 'reality'. Such displays of ethnicity or culture are not only at odds with everyday realities, past and present, but often conflict with the moral judgement or aesthetic tastes of tourists on the ground.

Whether they are viewed as ironic, humorous, or tragic, such blended instances of photogenic poverty and touristic fantasy also demonstrate how cultural stereotypes may be hijacked, reiterated and transformed

---

22   Hutnyk, 'Photogenic poverty'.
23   Ibid., p. 79.
24   For example, Dean MacCannell, 1976, *The Tourist: A New Theory of the Leisure Class*, New York: Schocken Books; John Urry, 1990, *The Tourist Gaze: Leisure and Travel in Contemporary Societies*, London: Sage Publications; Chris Rojek and John Urry, 1997, *Touring Cultures: Transformations of Travel and Theory*, London: Routledge.

by local people. If the images produced are sometimes discomforting, then perhaps this is as it should be. Indeed, we might consider that the often forced photographic smiles that are produced in so much tourism advertising get to very heart of the problematic relationship between 'object authenticity' and 'existential authenticity' discussed by Ning Wang on the one hand,[25] and of the relationship of these to the rather distinct notion of sincerity,[26] or a congruence between avowal and actual feeling on the other. Far from representing objects of authenticity, they bring into question the sincerity of the intersubjective encounter that defines such photographic exchanges. Further, they may expose their basis in economic and political inequality. Yet, in the costumed children prodded by their parents to smile in exchange for 'donations' there is in equal measure a sense of the agency of a real life photographic subject who likewise seeks to capture the gaze of the tourist in the interest of profit.

Paradise lost and found: Lands behind the tourist fetish

This chapter has explored the workings of the souvenir fetish within the context of cruise ship tourism to Vanuatu, focusing especially on the ubiquitous image of the smiling fantasy 'child native'. I have argued that at its most effective the souvenir fetish seeks to magically obscure the unequal relations of power that underpin the mode of production by which it is produced. As Claire Slatter has so forcefully revealed, perhaps the most pressing concern relating to tourism in Vanuatu is the indelible linkage of that industry to the rampant and ongoing alienation of indigenous-owned land.[27] As she suggests, the current tourist boom, triggered by a mixture of international development industry-led investment liberalisation policies, may be seen to have spurred positive economic growth in Vanuatu. And yet ni-Vanuatu are being increasingly marginalised economically and dispossessed of their land in the process.[28]

25   Wang, 'Rethinking authenticity in tourism experience'.
26   Taylor, *Consuming Identity*.
27   Slatter, *The Con/Dominium of Vanuatu?*
28   Ibid., p. 3.

On this key point I note that in the Americas where the term is ultimately derived, the image of the smiling 'pikinini' appears to have been crucially linked to such processes of dispossession and denial of sovereignty historically. Likewise in Australia, as argued by Liz Connor, black child beauty has acted since the eighteenth century as a 'commodity form for white consumption', providing 'a fetish which disavowed the injury of these children's disinheritance and delimited their cultural presence to cute domestic and tourist bric-a-brac'.[29] As the beachfront properties around Vanuatu's main towns of Port Vila and Luganville are bought up by expatriate 'sea changers', it becomes apparent that Vanuatu is not an idyllic playground for ni-Vanuatu, but rather, as one young ni-Vanuatu man suggested to me with more than a hint of irony, a *'paradaes blong waetman'* (a 'whiteman's paradise'). At its most effective, the souvenir fetish would erase from view the unequal relations that constitute tourism production as a whole. However, as this chapter has also shown, where the souveniring of destinations involves the visual consumption of photogenic fantasy alongside 'photogenic poverty',[30] an unsettling and uncanny tension between the 'really real' and 'really imagined' may occur, and with it a cognitive dissonance that disrupts both the pleasure of the tourist gaze and the efficacy of the fetish. In these fractured and unsettling performances resides the potential to unravel those hermeneutic circles of tourism image production, and in doing so render visible the very inequalities that the tourism industry produces yet also seeks to hide.

Acknowledgements

Versions of this paper have been presented at the Association for Social Anthropology in Oceania (ASAO) session at the La Trobe University School of Social Sciences Seminar Series, the Monash University Anthropology Seminar Series, and at The Australian National University Anthropology Seminar Series. I am appreciative of and sensitive to concerns raised in those sessions, especially regarding 'proper fieldwork' and the perils of reifying images and image-making processes of inequality such as those explored here. I especially thank

29   Elizabeth Connor, 2012, 'The "Piccaninny": Racialised childhood, disinheritance, acquisition and child beauty', *Postcolonial Studies* 15(1): 45–68.
30   Hutnyk, 'Photogenic poverty'.

Kalissa Alexeyeff, Stewart Muir, Lucy Pickering, Margaret Jolly, Katerina Teaiwa, Bob Foster, Matt Tomlinson, Matthew Spriggs and Nicolas Peterson for providing insightful comments, criticisms and suggestions.

References

Bhabha, Homi K. 1994. *The Location of Culture*. London: Routledge.

Bolton, Lissant. 2003. 'Gender, status and introduced clothing in Vanuatu.' In *Clothing in the Pacific*, ed. Chloë Colchester, pp. 119–40. Oxford: Berg.

British Broadcasting Corporation News. 1996. 'Happiness doesn't cost the earth.' Online: news.bbc.co.uk/2/hi/5169448.stm (accessed 6 May 2011).

Caton, Kellee and Carla Almeida Santos. 2007. 'Closing the hermeneutic circle: Photographic encounters with the other.' *Annals of Tourism Research* 35(1): 7–26.

Connor, Elizabeth. 2012. 'The "Piccaninny": Racialised childhood, disinheritance, acquisition and child beauty.' *Postcolonial Studies* 15(1): 45–68.

Evans, Graeme. 2000. 'Contemporary crafts as souvenirs, artifacts and functional goods and the role in local economic diversification and cultural development.' In *Souvenirs: The Material Culture of Tourism*, ed. Michael Hitchcock and Ken Teague, pp. 127–45. Aldershot: Ashgate.

Frow, John. 1991. 'Tourism and the semiotics of nostalgia.' *October* 57: 123–51.

Geismar, Haidy. 2003. 'Museums, markets and material culture: Prestations and presentations in rural and urban Vanuatu.' PhD thesis, University College London.

Hutnyk, John. 2004. 'Photogenic poverty: Souvenirs and infantilism.' *Journal of Visual Research* 3(1): 77–94.

Island Spirit. Air Vanuatu's in-flight publication. Online: issuu.com/ pacific-island-living/docs/island-spirit (accessed 29 April 2016).

Jenkins, Olivia. 2003. 'Photography and travel brochures: The circle of representation.' *Tourism Geographies* 5(3): 305–28.

Jolly, Margaret. 1994. '*Kastom* as commodity: The land dive as indigenous rite and tourist spectacle in Vanuatu.' In *Culture – Kastom – Tradition: Developing Cultural Policy in Melanesia*, ed. Lamont Lindstrom and Geoffrey M. White, pp. 131–44. Suva, Fiji: Institute of Pacific Studies, University of the South Pacific.

Kirkland, David. 2008. *Vanuatu: Pikinini in Paradise*. Brisbane: Hema Maps.

Lindstrom, Lamont and Geoffrey M. White (eds). 1994. *Culture – Kastom – Tradition: Developing Cultural Policy in Melanesia*. Suva, Fiji: Institute of Pacific Studies, University of the South Pacific.

MacCannell, Dean. 1976. *The Tourist: A New Theory of the Leisure Class*. New York: Schocken Books.

Naitu, Anne Lucy. 2007. 'Dosalsal, the floating ones: Exploring the socio-cultural impacts of cruise ship tourism on Port Vila, Vanuatu residents, and their coping strategies.' Masters of Tourism Management thesis, Lincoln University, Christchurch.

P&O Cruises. 2011. *2011–2013 Pacific – Australia – Asia* [Cruises Departures Brochure]. Sydney: Carnival, trading as P&O Cruises.

Rojek, Chris and John Urry. 1997. *Touring Cultures: Transformations of Travel and Theory*. London: Routledge.

Slatter, Claire. 2006. *The Con/Dominium of Vanuatu?: Paying the Price of Investment and Land Liberalisation—A Case Study of Vanuatu's Tourism Industry*. Oxfam New Zealand.

Sontag, Susan. 1979. *On Photography*. London: Penguin Books.

Steiner, Carol and Yvette Reisinger. 2006. 'Understanding existential authenticity.' *Annals of Tourism Research* 33(2): 299–318.

Tabani, Marc. 2010. 'The carnival of custom: Land dives, millenarian parades and other spectacular ritualizations in Vanuatu.' *Oceania* 80(3): 309–28.

Taylor, John. 1998. *Consuming Identity: Modernity and Tourism in New Zealand*. Auckland: Department of Anthropology, The University of Auckland.

———. 2001. 'Authenticity and sincerity in tourism.' *Annals of Tourism Research* 28(1): 7–26.

———. 2010. 'The troubled histories of a stranger god: Religious crossing, sacred power and Anglican colonialism in Vanuatu.' *Comparative Studies in Society and History* 5(2): 418–46.

———. 2011. 'Photogenic authenticity and the spectacular in tourism.' *Indigenous Tourism and the Intricacies of Cross-cultural Understanding*. Special issue of *La Ricerca Folkorica* 61: 32–40.

Urry, John. 1990. *The Tourist Gaze: Leisure and Travel in Contemporary Societies*. London: Sage Publications.

Wang, Ning. 1999. 'Rethinking authenticity in tourism experience.' *Annals of Tourism Research* 26(2): 349–70.

25

Bandit *Singsing*: The Tourism Unexperience

John Cox

We left on Friday morning but this short weekend trip now seems much longer. Our neighbours, Nick and Irina, who live across from us on campus at Divine Word University, had told us that there was a *singsing* (dance festival) being held at a Rai Coast village. They have been exploring every suggestion of the Tourism Bureau with some energy, so their invitation to join them at the *singsing* was most welcome.

Through the week, we visited the Tourism Bureau and found the staff very friendly and helpful, although one of them looked like she was about to burst into tears and run away if anyone asked her anything! A few repeat visits and phone calls confirmed arrangements for the trip and in the end we added Monica, another neighbour with several years experience of living in Papua New Guinea (PNG), to the list of guests.

We were told to get ourselves to the Tourism Bureau by 'eight o'clock, maybe seven-thirty' so that they could take us down to the wharf for a two- or three-hour boat trip to Saidor on the Rai Coast. We would need to leave early in the morning because the sea would be too rough later on. So, at quarter to eight, we met in the space between our three houses and Nick dropped us off. The security guards there gave us a blank look as no one had arrived to open the place but then we saw Joanne, one of the more outgoing tourism people, across the road, waiting to hail our transport. She came over and began ringing around to try and contact the driver with apparently little success.

I amused myself by watching Madang's peak hour traffic. It is by no means insubstantial. Every minute or so at least 10 vehicles carrying 10 people passed by, so I think that between 7:30 and 9 am, perhaps some 10,000 people come into Madang town. Hard to imagine that there could be so much work or activity here.

By 8:30 Joanne had given up on the driver and so decided that we should get a PMV (bus) down to the wharf. This was the cue for rain to start falling and, by the time we got to the wharf, the rain was heavy and prolonged. Some friendly betel nut sellers offered us shelter under their umbrella but we still got wet because of the angle and strength of the rain.

The rain cleared and, after an hour or so, the boat arrived, having come all the way from Saidor. We went off and got some provisions (bread, roast chicken and banana) before setting out just after 10:30. Not quite the early morning start envisaged (I could have slept another two hours and avoided getting rained on) but a reliable guide to the progress of the weekend.

We were farewelled by some tourism bigwig and joined by Melchior, a local councillor wearing shoes and socks and long pants, who was 'escorting' us to the *singsing*—and with some pride. The boat trip was unremarkable and a little uncomfortable. Many things were familiar from other banana boat trips around the Pacific: the steely eyed driver, smoking during the fuel tank refills; leaving the palms and looking back to the pastel greys and purples of the coast; flying fish zipping past; and of course the choppy crash of the boat against the waves and the discipline of not checking the time.

At Saidor, we beached the boat, interrupting a village full of playing children. Oniel, our hostess from the Tourism Bureau, had come down from the *singsing* to meet us. We sat in the shade, to the great fascination of 20 or 30 children and adults, before walking through the village towards the cocoa and coconut plantations that surround it. I got talking to a man about cocoa and the economic struggle of daily life. He cut a cocoa pod to show us the sweet pulp inside that bears no discernable relationship to chocolate.

On the boat, we had been told we'd have to walk two (or three) hours up a mountain to the village. News to us, as we'd thought the *singsing* was being held in Saidor itself. None of us had suitable footwear. One might think that a two- to three-hour walk was a fairly important detail that might have been passed on to us in advance. Monica almost certainly would not have come had she known of such a walk. Irina only had strappy sandals.

To our relief, a decrepit Land Rover turned up and drove us up steep and heavily rutted roads to our destination. Every 20 minutes or so, we had to stop to refill the radiator to stop it from overheating. In steep stops, a rock was placed under the wheels to stop it from sliding backwards down the hill. At the first of these stops, by a river and just past a former soccer field, now covered in metre-high rushes, we took photos of the entourage on the back of the truck, including the delightful Rudolph, a teacher from Bandit village. His contribution to the discussion of what the Tok Pisin word for 'smile' was, 'smael long mi!', accompanied by a great and winning betel nut smile.

The road became steeper and steeper and eventually we arrived in Bandit village. We looked up at a delightful freshly thatched house with arabesque weaving for windows and, before we knew it, had decamped. Our luggage was taken from us and we were rushed up the hill to catch the remainder of the day's program.

We passed through a few family compounds and soon could hear singing and drums. As we came closer, groups of people in dancing costumes and smeared with a copper-red body paint stopped to wave at us. Here was a field full of dozens of people and surrounded by stalls. We were taken to a makeshift pavilion which the Governor had recently delivered an address, before quickly heading back down to Saidor and boarding a chartered flight back to Madang. We were welcomed as VIPs and a man in a large suit jacket (several times larger than his proper size) stopped the dancing to introduce us as 'tourists from Australia and Divine Word University' through a megaphone. The dancing resumed but we hadn't eaten and so opened up our chicken and bread and filled our faces while trying to be inconspicuous. Soon the handful of other tourists came in and without hesitation made us welcome: Elsa and Julian from France, Kathleen and Tom and their teenage children Jenna, Kali and Ben—American yachties who have been sailing the Pacific for the last seven years. All were smeared with the copper-red paint. Descending to the field, we took some photos of one of the dance groups who recommenced their dances for us but only after daubing our faces with the now ubiquitous red paint.

Figure 120. The beautiful guest house at Bandit village.
Source. Photo courtesy of Dr Georgina Phillips, 30 May 2009.

Walking back down the hill, we returned to the guest house, found our rooms, showered and made ready for the evening program. Our hosts served up a large meal of taro, cooked bananas, greens, rice and *tinpis* (canned fish). At 8:30 or so, several of us headed up to the *singsing* ground. Tom stayed behind to help his two girls dress for dancing. Already they were being absorbed into the village, not least due to Jenna's complete lack of social skills beyond an innocent and enthusiastic affection for everyone she meets. Monica and Irina decided to miss the all night festivities in favour of sleep and the prospect of a full day and night of dancing ahead.

Soon after nine, the first group entered the field. We could hear their drumming and *singsing* from afar but this did not prepare us for the amazing sight of their headdresses shimmering in the darkness. The *singsing* is a *kangal* festival, *kangal* being Tok Pisin for 'feather' and the distinctive headdress of the Rai Coast peoples. These are bamboo frames dressed with cockatoo and other feathers. They are mostly crescent-shaped and designed to sway from side to side as the dancers circle around, skipping to the beat of *kundu* (handheld stretched hide) drums. Others are very long, almost like flagpoles, and certainly up to five metres high. It is quite extraordinary to see how the dancers balance these great works on their heads. One group had headdresses boasting images of fish and other sea creatures, including a stylised canoe prow. Another had a stylised horse but the meaning of these symbols was lost to us beyond the most obvious. They were most eerie emerging from the drumming and the darkness with their white feathers luminescent. We were quite awestruck.

Figure 121. Dancers emerging from the darkness.
Source. Photo courtesy of Dr Georgina Phillips, 30 May 2009.

Dancers wore mostly red paint, often with black facepaint and tapa loincloths, beads and pig tusk decorations. To our surprise, Jenna and Kali danced bare breasted in their group and Tom emerged drenched in red paint, wearing only a loincloth, pig tusk necklace, sandals and a bird of paradise on his head to complement his own blonde mane.

Figure 122. Kangal headdresses.
Source. Photo courtesy of Dr Georgina Phillips, 30 May 2009.

The dancing was cumulative, not sequential. Each new group of 20 or 30 dancers would arrive out of the night, dance a few turns under the pavilion and the only spotlight and then head off to the corners of the field to continue dancing and singing. New groups would come in with new and amazing *kangals* and simply add a new hypnotic drum beat to the several already beating through the darkness. Watching on the field, the audience would swarm around each new group and then be swept out of the way by the next one arriving. Hundreds of people were there crowding together in the dark.

Somehow amidst this foment of people, I struck up a long and serious conversation with Timothy, a pastor in the Evangelical Church from a nearby village. He sidled up to me and we got talking about dancing and church cultures and this led on to many other things. He told me about U-Vistract, the pyramid scheme I had come to study.[1] Years earlier, the promoter of the U-Vistract scam on Manus Island had had to flee to Bougainville for fear of reprisals. We talked at some length about the Bible and his suspicion of Pentecostals and their prosperity

---

1   John Cox, 2011, 'Prosperity, nation and consumption. Fast money schemes in Papua New Guinea', in *Managing Modernity in the Western Pacific*, ed. Mary Patterson and Martha Macintyre, pp. 172–200, St Lucia: University of Queensland Press.

theology. This led on to questions of reconciling culture and Christianity, divisions and tolerance of diversity within the church. I showed a bit of knowledge and he must have thought me a Christian, even though I explained that I was studying anthropology. We also ventured into politics and the lack of services in PNG. He wanted the Australian Government to come back and take over, so they would get good services. I thought he was up for it, so tried my hand at explaining how the free market ideology was responsible for governments globally relinquishing their responsibility for services.

Knowing that the dancing would go on all night, we rested in the pavilion from time to time. Early on we decided to get some coffee from one of the stalls. This provoked a megaphone announcement and a police escort across to the coffee shop. I guess if you have a megaphone, you may as well use it! It was used again at the end of our night to summon our police escort again to walk us down the hill. The place seemed entirely safe to us. We left at about 1 am, after all the dance groups had arrived and been performing for a while. The dancing continued for several hours longer, our American friends retiring at 4 am.

The next day we slept in a little, knowing that the dancing would not start until the afternoon and would go all night. But as we woke, we became aware of a committee meeting under the house in which we were sleeping. We could only catch the gist of the discussion but the tone was of disappointment. Money was clearly involved. We thought of the other tourists telling us how uncomfortable they felt as the megaphone introduced them and told all present that the tourists would bring money. By the time we rose, they'd forgotten we were staying there and were quite were surprised to see us, as we in turn were surprised to see some 30 men sitting underneath the house, the leaders talking in hushed tones.

Things were clearly not going according to plans. For some reason, we were discouraged from going up to the field. A much smaller dance group from the village began performing next to the guest house. Before long the hidden tensions became apparent. An angry man entered the crowd and denounced the dancing, saying that the field above was the proper place for the *singsing*. Nobody replied to him and security guards tried to shepherd him away from the group. The dancers and drummers looked on waiting to resume without inflaming the man's anger. Eventually he stormed off. I was surprised, because it seemed that he had made such a fool of himself for so little return.

No one was volunteering explanations and our curiosity was not rewarded in further inquiries. The big, bald-headed man who seemed to chair the organising committee and who had a prominent stall on the dancing ground with a generator and a fridge was dismissive of any concerns. Our Tourism Bureau escorts did not know how to begin explaining what was becoming a debacle. Nevertheless, it became clear that the other villages were expecting a share of the K2,000 donated by the Governor the previous day. Given as a cheque, this money could not possibly be cashed and was therefore not suitable for redistribution. Perhaps there was also a longer history behind these resentments.

As the day went on, another angry man came down from the top and demanded to speak with the leaders. Another pointed performance of anger: no one responded as he berated the villagers and he eventually tired of his tirade and left. Clearly there was going to be no dance program for the rest of the weekend and it was now unwise to venture up the hill.

So, we lazed about, opened some tins of sardines and had them with stale bread from the previous day. Opening the first tin was OK but the point of the knife bent, making it impossible to open any other tins. Or so I thought: I took the knife and sardines out of the guest house compound across to the group of villagers hanging out across the way. Rudolph took the knife and slid it into the tin as if the steel were soft as a pawpaw. His wife Ruth explained to me that white people didn't know the 'way of the knife'. Fair call, although I've never thought of Papua New Guineans as Melanesian Samurai.

Soon after we'd finished the sardines, a cooked lunch was served up to us and the Americans returned from their walk. Another example of the poor sense of timing and mixed up expectations that characterised the weekend.

It was very disappointing to realise that there really would be no more dancing. There was little else to do in this small mountain village but walk up and down the road. Rudolph and his wife Rose took us up past the dancing field and up to their hilltop school. We rested at the summit and looked out at the sea and the approaching mist. Rose is from Bandit village and Rudolph from the coast north of Madang. They wish to stay here but have no security of tenure. As teachers, they can be moved to other schools each year—a huge disruption, expense and waste of bureaucratic resources almost deliberately designed to ensure low morale.

As we came back through the dance field, it was obvious that the pavilion and some of the stalls had been burnt down, indicating the strength of the feud. Rudolph explained that many of the villagers had spent up to K10,000 in their preparations and had been led to believe that there would be government funding to reward their contributions. At the previous year's festival, a representative from the National Museum had made a promise he had no chance of keeping and, in his absence, the *singsing* groups from other villages blamed the organising committee.

The tourists' perceptions of the weekend's events chopped and changed. On Friday night, Elsa and Julian, who work in humanitarian emergencies in Africa and who had just come from trekking through remote West Papuan villages, were amazed at the *singsing* being organised without the input of foreigners behind the scenes: no UNICEF funding! For the backpackers, they had met some interesting and welcoming Papua New Guineans and felt that the K600 or so that our accommodation amounted to would have been fair compensation to the guest house owners.

For Tom and Kathleen, this was an experience of an untouched culture that they admire and were privileged to participate in before it was thoroughly spoiled by the approach of the capitalist system. They said the dancing was a highlight of their seven years of travel, just as they turn their thoughts homewards, returning to a society whose materialistic values they reject. Their daughters were drawn into participation before it even became an option, particularly the gregarious Jenna, who was commandeered by Rita, a local teenager who hardly left her side.

Monica's resignation and ennui was salted with genuine affection and good humour. She had quickly decided she didn't want to be there and shouldn't have come but one never had the sense that she didn't want to be living in PNG. Irina only became more disoriented as she attempted to make sense of what was going on. Nowhere was this clearer than in her sense of time, where her requests assumed an association between events and specific time commitments. Seven o'clock meant seven o'clock for her, not an approximation meaning 'sometime in the morning'. Neither of them saw the dancing that night, so enjoyed all the petty discomforts without the compensation of such a magnificent spectacle.

For us, the expectations of the villagers and our ill-preparedness to meet any of these or even to adequately provision our own expectations (tea and coffee for instance but at least we had a torch and toilet paper!) were a failing of the Tourism Bureau, whom we'd allowed to give us an inadequately interrogated impression of what to expect. But, of course, I must also blame myself for ignoring what I know about travelling to a village.

Had we just been going on our own, we would have been much better prepared but we consented to the very silly idea that we didn't need to bring anything and stupidly accepted answers from the wrong people without question. We had specifically asked about footwear and were told there was no need to bring walking shoes (no mention of the 2–3-hour walk). I asked about mosquito nets and was told the guesthouse would have them (they didn't but thankfully there weren't any mosquitoes to speak of). Really we should—and do—know much better.

We allowed ourselves to believe that all food would be provided, not thinking that that might be fried bananas for breakfast and lunch. What on Earth were we thinking? We also submitted to an idea of preposterously low costs—K70 per person each way for the canoe, K20 per night for accommodation and food and K5 per person for the village museum. We were already in the habit of carrying minimal cash so, while there wasn't much to buy, we shouldn't have let ourselves swallow the idea that 'they don't need money in the village', as Oniel and Joanne told us. Fortunately we did have enough for a nice Madang style *bilum* (woven bag) but we fell far short of the promise of tourists bringing the kind of money that would support a cottage industry.

I feel particular regret at not having brought anything with us that could have represented a show of practical appreciation of the efforts the village had gone to for our entertainment and comfort. Just weeks ago we visited a north coast village and took a hand of betel nut in appreciation of their hospitality but somehow that kind of intuition left us for this journey.

For all the hospitality we received, we gave little in return, beyond the prestige of having white people come to the village. We were celebrated as the first tourists there, heralding many more to come. People were shy to approach us so milled about whispering to each other and occasionally coming over to make conversation. It would have been so easy for us to bring some bags of rice and tinpis to show our gratitude but this did not occur to us (or the tourism people) until it was far too late. Instead, the Americans received dancing skirts, bilums, tapa cloth and necklaces, leaving with a sense of 'how generous these people are', seemingly blind to the possibility that the gifts were intended to provoke something in the way of reciprocity. In fairness to some very decent and adventurous people, the yachties had been generous in other ways; not least in the spirit in which they immersed themselves in the dancing.

With a colder economic eye, it was hard to see much potential for tourism in Bandit. While the *singsing* was magnificent and a true privilege to watch, the remoteness of the village and the small-scale facilities there make it unlikely that more people will come. This presumes that village resentments can be resolved amicably enough to organise another festival. Many Madang expatriates will be turned off by the long canoe journey alone, not to mention the walk. Only so many tourists have the adventurous spirit shown by our French and American friends. That aside, the lowly charges for accommodation, the modest standard of the food, and the lack of an admission charge make commensurate tourism revenue for this particular activity impossible. If six dance groups want K10,000 each—not such an unreasonable claim for weeks of preparation, travel, food and accommodation for the dozens of people in each group—then that makes for a hefty charge for the few visitors intrepid enough to make the trip. It seems grossly irresponsible for local and national authorities to encourage dreams of tourism as a money-making venture. For the tourist, such expectations make the stay rather discomforting, particularly when local disputes become visible.

By the end, the transparency of this conflict shamed the village. They clearly felt that they had failed the tourists and were ashamed. As we left, we were lined up to be presented with bilums and to shake hands with everyone from Bandit. I detected an apologetic tone in our hosts and a wish to ensure that we would not leave angry with them.

We piled onto the back of the decrepit Land Rover, knowing this was unsafe; but none of us wanted to walk down the mountain in the wrong shoes! The truck set off and immediately lost control of the brakes. We careened around the first corner, in front of our guest house, where one of the locals leapt off with a frightened look on his face. The truck was clearly out of control and I was worried it would tip over. I saw Julian leaping off the side before we crashed through a low rock wall and into the bush that stopped us.

It was a relief to stop uninjured. As we came back to the road, the mamas of the village began wailing and ran towards us crying hysterically and hugging each of us who emerged alive. Julian had landed badly and dislocated his knee, which fortunately had snapped back into position. People swarmed around him as he sat there in shock. Eventually we bandaged him up and treated his abrasions. He and Elsa waited for a stretcher to carry him down the mountain and the rest of us set off on foot with women carrying our backpacks on their heads.

Actually the walk down was very pleasant, not the ordeal we had dreaded. Having the women to carry our luggage certainly made it an easy trip, even in the wrong footwear. We were foolish to insist on a vehicle. A steep and sometimes slippery road and the odd blister were more than compensated for by beautiful trees and a river stop where we cooled our feet and drank coconut juice.

The river was also where the stretcher caught up with us. Julian would need some recuperation and would not be able to continue his tour of PNG as planned but was otherwise in good spirits. Rudolph and Oniel both attributed his injury to him jumping too soon—he should have held on or leapt into the bush as Oniel did! In this version, the driver did a good job (yes …) to steer away from the slope into bush that stopped us and didn't damage the vehicle.

Figure 123. The author at the end of the 'unexperience'.
Source. Photo courtesy of Dr Georgina Phillips, 30 May 2009.

But that's not how the white people saw the risks: the more we think about it, the more incredible it seems that this was the only injury. Someone could have so easily been killed or seriously hurt with just a slightly different turn of the wheel or slip of the road. We imagine the horror of bodies (ours and our companions) thrown into trees, crushed under the truck, or of trying to stabilise someone's neck, instead of knee.

The village will not remember the accident in terms of risks and possible disasters that didn't happen. I asked Rudolph about sorcery (in fact we had joked about it the previous day) and it was clear that others would believe that the accident was sorcery and therefore connected to the conflict of the weekend. Indeed, Rudolph himself believed that sorcery was involved ('There are many strange powers operating in this area'). He says they had tested the Land Rover's brakes the previous night, so the malfunction was not the result of the condition of the vehicle or its overloading. That leaves malicious sorcery as the only remaining explanation. No doubt this event will fuel the animosities of the *singsing* with sorcery accusations and make future Kangal festivals impossible.

The son of one of PNG's most famous artists sells his works outside the Madang Resort. Several have the caption, 'Papua New Guinea, Land of the Unexpected: Experience the Unexperience [*sic*]'. The Bandit *singsing* was certainly a tourism unexperience.

References

Cox, John. 2011. 'Prosperity, nation and consumption. Fast money schemes in Papua New Guinea.' In *Managing Modernity in the Western Pacific*, ed. Mary Patterson and Martha Macintyre, pp. 172–200. St Lucia: University of Queensland Press.

Patterson, Mary and Martha Macintyre (eds). 2011. *Managing Modernity in the Western Pacific*. St Lucia: University of Queensland Press.

26

The Friendly Islands? Tonga's Ambivalent Relationship with Tourism

Helen Lee

The Tongan woman sitting behind the counter in the Tongan Visitors Bureau didn't look up as I entered the dimly lit building and perused the display of tattered brochures and fading maps pinned to noticeboards on rickety stands. I was the only visitor but she continued to focus on her mobile phone as I wandered around then headed back along the path to Vuna Road, one of the main streets of Tonga's capital, Nuku'alofa. Her lack of interest didn't surprise me; I already knew tourists in Tonga are often regarded as vaguely annoying intrusions rather than enthusiastically welcomed visitors. For many years there have been attempts by the Tongan Government and budding entrepreneurs to boost tourism, supported by sporadic injections of large amounts of foreign aid for tourism projects. Despite these efforts, most Tongans have never really embraced tourism as a source of revenue and have long viewed tourists with ambivalence.

In 1980, when I was living in Tonga and teaching at Queen Sālote College, a girls' high school, I would occasionally wander down to the waterfront when a cruise ship was docked and watch as it disgorged its passengers onto the dusty streets of Nuku'alofa. Where the Visitors Bureau now stands was a park in which Tongans would set up stalls to sell handicrafts to tourists and I would sit with women I knew and observe their encounters with foreigners. Ignoring the cultural briefings provided on board ship before disembarking, these *pālangi* (the common term for white foreigners) offended Tongans' cultural sensibilities in many ways. They often wore skimpy, immodest clothing and couples were openly affectionate, which clashed with Tongan morality. For Tongans these behaviours were even harder to bear than relatively wealthy tourists haggling for ridiculously low prices. The Tongan women did a great job of meeting the tourists' expectations of Friendly Islanders; little did the foreigners know the comments the Tongan women made to each other with shrieks of laughter were always at their expense. In town, some of the shopkeepers were not as willing to encounter these offensive tourists and simply shut up shop when the cruise ships came to town.

By 2013, when I wandered into the Visitors Bureau, there had been a steady increase in foreign visitors to Tonga but only a fraction of the number heading to Pacific nations like Fiji and the Cook Islands, for which tourism is a significant source of revenue. For a long time cruise ships stopped visiting Tonga, but the recent construction of Vuna Wharf aimed to attract the international cruise liners, whose passengers will disembark 'to stroll through the new city and its modern and traditional delights in sidewalk stalls selling handicrafts and local produce, retail shopping, cafes, restaurants and eateries offering island-style cuisine'.[1] Instead, I was told by frustrated cafe owners, the few cruise ships that now dock in Nuku'alofa are met at the wharf by buses that take the passengers on a quick tour of the island then return them to the ship; they often don't have time to go into town or even stop to look at any stalls set up on the wharf.

The handicraft market moved years ago to a small section of the Talamahu market in the centre of town, which sells mainly produce to locals. Other markets are full of second-hand clothes and household goods sent by the container-load by Tongans living overseas and are by no means intended to be tourist attractions. The majority of visitors to the country are now diasporic Tongans who are 'VFR tourists'

---

1   Teen Brown Pulu, 2011, *Shoot the Messenger: The Report on the Nuku'alofa Reconstruction Project and why the Government of Tonga Dumped it*, Nuku'alofa: Taimi Publishers, p. 136.

(visiting friends and relatives).[2] In 2011, for example, 43 per cent of arrivals by air were VFR tourists, compared to 39 per cent arriving for a vacation, and by November 2012 these figures were 56.3 per cent compared to 30.8 per cent.[3] Tongan visitors make up much of the clientele of the cafes and restaurants of the main towns and are the main buyers of Tongan handicrafts, particularly the decorated tapa cloth (*ngatu*) and finely woven pandanus mats (*kie*) that are still gifted in Tonga and throughout the diaspora at important events. Many of the visiting Tongans stay in hotels and guest houses to avoid the constant demands of relatives and to have some of the comforts to which they've become accustomed.

As for foreign tourists, the Tongans remaining in Tonga have grown used to them ignoring their preference for modest clothing and behaviour and, besides, some younger Tongans now dress and behave much like *pālangi* youth, especially those visiting from the diaspora. Yet the ambivalence remains and a Lonely Planet guide observes: 'You may get the impression that most Tongans would prefer visitors to donate their dollars and not leave the airport; expats seem determined to build a tourist industry, but most of the locals just don't seem to care.'[4]

Tongatapu, where about 80 per cent of Tongans remaining in the Kingdom now live, is littered with the remnants of attempts to cater for tourists by both locals and foreign investors. The Tongan Cultural Centre on the outskirts of Nuku'alofa had a brief existence as a tourist attraction with a museum display and Tongans demonstrating various crafts and activities like coconut-husking and mat-weaving but it quickly fell into disrepair. The once popular beachside hotel and restaurant, The Good Samaritan, lies derelict and abandoned and even Nuku'alofa's International Dateline Hotel, once a hub of

---

2   On VFR tourism in the Caribbean, see David Timothy Duval Duval, 2003, 'When hosts become guests: Return visits and diasporic identities in a Commonwealth Eastern Caribbean community', *Current Issues in Tourism* 6(4): 267–307; David Timothy Duval, 2004, 'Linking return visits and return migration among Commonwealth Eastern Caribbean migrants in Toronto', *Global Networks* 4(1): 51–67.

3   Government of Tonga, 2012, *International Arrivals, Departures and Migration*, Statistical Bulletin Series No: SDT:38.13, Statistics Department, Nuku'alofa; Government of Tonga, 2013, *Migration Monthly Bulletin November 2012*, Series No: SDT: 38–M06, Statistics Department, Nuku'alofa.

4   Craig McLachlan, Brett Atkinson and Celeste Brash, 2012, *Lonely Planet: Rarotonga, Samoa and Tonga*, Melbourne: Lonely Planet Publications, p. 53.

activity for tourists, expats and Tongans alike, had trouble filling its rooms for many years. In 2012, I walked through its empty foyer, past a termite-eaten column, unusable pool and dark, empty restaurant and was shown into a poorly constructed new wing with water damaged ceilings and no guests. Having changed ownership several times, it was taken over in early 2015 by the Tanoa Hotel Group from Fiji and won't reopen until mid-2017. One of the newest hotels in Tonga, the Scenic Hotel, was originally planned as a casino by Sam Wong, a shady Hong Kong Chinese businessman who at one time also had plans to build a shopping plaza complete with extravagant fountain in Nuku'alofa. After sitting half-built for many years the hotel has been completed, but with its 76 rooms and pristine swimming pool it sits alone in the fields opposite the entrance to the airport, far from town and largely deserted apart from its bored staff.

Any foreign visitor to Tonga could not help but notice that very little has been done to accommodate them beyond the few hotels and guest houses. Sites that might attract tourists, like the viewing area for the dramatic blowholes in the rocks along part of the southwest coast, are badly neglected. Many of the roads are similarly neglected, including the road along that coast, which is the route to the best beaches. Apart from the beaches in front of the few 'resorts' sprinkled along that coast, most are near impossible for tourists to find as they are hidden down unmarked, narrow tracks that run through plantations. Those tracks are even more potholed than the 'main' road and at intervals along them people have dumped piles of rubbish on either side. Public events like the Heilala Festival that runs for a week in July every year are very much for Tongans, not tourists; information about upcoming events is difficult to find and usually gives scant details of locations and schedules. Those events run on 'Tongan time' anyway, leaving the few tourists who find out about them waiting hours for them to begin. After all, under the heading 'True Culture' the Kingdom of Tonga's tourism website has the opening line: 'Welcome to life in the slow lane.'[5]

Having observed tourism in Tonga struggling along for so many years, I can't help but wonder if many Tongans would really prefer not to have tourists at all, at least not in their towns and villages where

---

5   Tonga Tourism Authority, 2014, 'Kingdom of Tonga: True culture'.

Tongans are getting on with their daily lives. Tongans are intensely proud that their islands were never formally colonised, that they have a Constitution that prevents Tonga's land from being purchased and that until a recent influx of Chinese immigrants the country has remained largely monocultural. This history may hold the key to Tonga's very different engagements with tourism than those of its close neighbour, Fiji, or other popular Pacific tourist destinations such as the Cook Islands, Tahiti and Hawai'i. Fiji, for example, had a difficult colonial history that profoundly reshaped its society, but it has chosen to embrace tourism. The constant enthusiastic cries of 'Bula!' you encounter as a visitor in tourist areas mask any traces of post-colonial resentment and in the towns you simply blend into the multicultural population. Even in New Zealand, many Maori help support the thriving tourism industry, pragmatically accepting the presence of foreign visitors in order to reap the financial rewards of tourism. Yet Tonga has remained aloof, struggling along on the verge of economic collapse but refusing to pander to foreign tourists in order to survive.

A comparison between Fiji and Tonga was made by Iliesa Tora, the Fijian editor of *Koe Ita*, a Tongan newspaper published in 2012 by the Ita Media Network in Nuku'alofa. In his editorial 'Marketing Tonga to the World', he blames the lack of tourism in Tonga on the 'lazy population' who rely on their relatives for money.[6] He compares Tonga to Fiji where 'there are happy faces greeting you almost everywhere'. In the same issue of *Koe Ita*, Cook Islander Hakaoro Hakaoro, married to a Tongan woman and living in New Zealand, complains that visitors are not made welcome in Tonga, in contrast to the Cook Islands.[7] Many Tongans do rely on the remittances their relatives send from overseas— due to lack of employment opportunities rather than laziness—and it's certainly true that some visitors may feel they are not welcome. However, it is simplistic to argue that if Tongans just put in the hard work, and put on the friendly faces, tourism will flourish and save the economy. A complete overhaul of Tonga's infrastructure would be required to support more tourism than already exists and the ecological implications are frightening for a country already struggling with

---

6   Iliesa Tora, 2012, 'Marketing Tonga to the world', *Koe Ita*, 28 November, p. 6.
7   See Hakaoro Hakaoro, 2012, 'A challenge for church leaders in Tonga', *Koe Ita*, 28 November p. 6; cf. Kalissa Alexeyeff, 2008, 'Are you being served? Sex, humour and globalisation in the Cook Islands', *Anthropological Forum* 18(3): 287–93.

multiple environmental problems. Even if these practical problems somehow could be overcome, Tongans are understandably wary about the social and cultural impact of large numbers of foreign visitors.

Speaking out against large-scale tourism more than 20 years ago, Tongan academic Konai Helu-Thaman warned that tourism is 'a major contributor to, as well as manifestation of, a process of cultural invasion' from colonisation and the impact of missionaries to 'the universalization of Western ... culture'.[8] Like the articles in *Koe Ita*, she also compared Tonga and Fiji, but points out that since tourism began in Fiji in the colonial era it has been dominated by foreign business. In comparison, tourism only began in Tonga with the opening of the International Dateline Hotel in 1966. At that time the Dateline was government-owned and was built to provide accommodation for visitors to the coronation of King Taufa'ahou Tupou V. The 'gradual but cautious growth of tourism over the years',[9] Helu-Thaman describes for Tonga, has continued but with many setbacks including destructive hurricanes and the riots of 2006, during which more than half of central Nuku'alofa burnt to the ground. Unless they have yachts, many tourists don't make it beyond Tongatapu and a few small islands nearby with accommodation. There have been many attempts to run domestic airlines, usually with problems of erratic flight times and cancellations that leave tourists stranded. In 2013, New Zealand had suspended NZ$10.5 million in tourism development aid to Tonga because of its concerns about the safety of the Chinese-made MA60 plane donated by China for the newly established Real Tonga domestic airline.[10] Tonga has played the trump card of sovereignty, refusing to comply with New Zealand's demand that the aircraft meet international safety standards and certifying the aircraft under Tongan laws. It has remained grounded ever since, although in August 2015 a tender process for operating the aircraft commenced.

This issue of sovereignty and Tongans' pride in their independence may make it impossible for Tonga ever to build the kind of tourist industry seen in Pacific countries like Fiji. Most Tongans simply don't want to be subservient to tourists; in fact, they often seem

---

8   See Konai Helu-Thaman, 1993, 'Beyond hula, hotels, and handicrafts: A Pacific Islander's perspective on tourism development', *The Contemporary Pacific* 5(1): 104–11, p. 104.

9   Ibid., p. 108.

10   Pesi Fonua, 2013, 'Sovereignty not a bargaining chip', *Matangi Tonga Online*, 15 July. Online matangitonga.to/2013/07/15/sovereignty-not-bargaining-chip (accessed 3 March 2016).

uncomfortable working for *pālangi* bosses in any context. When I've discussed tourism with Tongans they also frequently mention the risk of 'losing our culture'. Since the rule of the revered Queen Sālote, Tongans have paid heed to her constant encouragement to maintain their traditions and their 'authenticity' is another source of pride. Of course Tongan culture has changed in many ways already; the country is firmly embedded in the world economy and Tongans are exposed to global popular culture. Yet driving from the airport into town in mid-2015, Tonga looked much the same as when I first travelled that road in 1979. The same sleepy villages dotted with churches, with skinny dogs and huge black pigs wandering across the road, bored young men hanging around and school children in their variously coloured uniforms trudging home. The little village shops (*fale koloa*) may be painted bright red now with advertising for the Digicel mobile phone company, but behind their counters are still stacks of tinned fish, two-minute noodles, bags of sugar and assorted other basic goods. On Sundays the country still slows down even further, with laws preventing commercial trade and families spending the day going to church, feasting and resting. Of course, for tourists, it comes as a shock to find central Nuku'alofa completely deserted on Sundays and I've often observed backpackers and family groups hovering uncertainly outside closed cafes and staring in bewilderment at the empty streets.

Tonga's first TV tourism campaign was held in 2013, developed by an advertising agency in New Zealand and using the slogan the 'True South Pacific'. The Prime Minister in 2013, Lord Tu'ivakano, said of the campaign: 'Tonga is less developed when compared to some other South Pacific countries and offers visitors a truly authentic South Pacific experience.'[11] Whether this brings a flood of tourists seeking authenticity rather than luxury remains to be seen, but I know many Tongans who remain unconvinced this is the way to solve their economic woes. In any case, the YouTube channel set up for the campaign has not been updated since 2013 and generated no public comments at all on the site. As long as Tongans overseas continue to support the economy with remittances and their visits home, the stranded MA60 aircraft will symbolise Tongans' approach to tourism. It has to happen on their own terms, or not at all.

---

11   Steven Raeburn, 2013, 'New Zealand agency designs Tonga's first TV campaign', *The Drum*, 15 May; Travel Monitor, 2013, 'New Tonga tourism campaign – 'True South Pacific', 16 May.

References

Alexeyeff, Kalissa. 2008. 'Are you being served? Sex, humour and globalisation in the Cook Islands.' *Anthropological Forum* 18(3): 287–93.

Brown Pulu, Teen. 2011. *Shoot the Messenger: The Report on the Nuku'alofa Reconstruction Project and why the Government of Tonga Dumped it*. Nuku'alofa: Taimi Publishers.

Duval, David Timothy. 2003. 'When hosts become guests: Return visits and diasporic identities in a Commonwealth Eastern Caribbean community.' *Current Issues in Tourism* 6(4): 267–307.

Duval, David Timothy. 2004. 'Linking return visits and return migration among Commonwealth Eastern Caribbean migrants in Toronto.' *Global Networks* 4(1): 51–67.

Government of Tonga. 2012. *International Arrivals, Departures and Migration*. Statistical Bulletin Series No: SDT:38.13. Statistics Department, Nuku'alofa.

Government of Tonga. 2013. *Migration Monthly Bulletin November 2012*. Series No: SDT: 38–M06. Statistics Department, Nuku'alofa.

Hakaoro Hakaoro. 2012. 'A challenge for church leaders in Tonga.' *Koe Ita*, 28 November.

Helu-Thaman, Konai. 1993. 'Beyond hula, hotels, and handicrafts: A Pacific Islander's perspective on tourism development.' *The Contemporary Pacific* 5(1): 104–111.

McLachlan, Craig, Brett Atkinson and Celeste Brash. 2012. *Lonely Planet: Rarotonga, Samoa and Tonga*. Melbourne: Lonely Planet Publications.

Raeburn, Steven. 2013. 'New Zealand agency designs Tonga's first TV campaign.' *The Drum*, 15 May.

Tonga Tourism Authority. 2014. 'Kingdom of Tonga: True culture.' Online: www.thekingdomoftonga.com/index.php/discover/true-culture/ (accessed 3 March 2016).

Tora, Iliesa. 2012. 'Marketing Tonga to the world.' *Koe Ita*, 28 November.

Travel Monitor. 2013. 'New Tonga tourism campaign – 'True South Pacific.' 16 May. Online: www.travelmonitor.com.au/tonga-tourism-campaign-targets-aussies-and-kiwis/ (accessed 3 March 2016).

27

Re-purposing Paradise: Tourism, Image and Affect

Kalissa Alexeyeff

The words 'Pacific', 'island', and 'paradise' are synonymous with each other in the western imaginary. It is an association that has a long trajectory originating in sixteenth-century Spanish expeditions and culminating in the travels of eighteenth- and nineteenth-century explorers, evangelists, traders and settlers. Collectively, these European 'tours' generated—through their images, texts, and collections—what might be termed the first 'paradise tourism' in the region. Occurring relatively late on the colonial stage, these incursions reinforced the 'utopian significance of the Pacific islands as the last "unspoiled" locations on the earth'.[1] It is a significance that has been retraced and retracked in the (post)colonial period through literature, popular film and music, media and particularly, through the material culture of mass-tourism.

As a persistent and ubiquitous trope 'Pacific paradise' fuels fantasies of abundance and bounty. Images of crystal clear lagoons, iridescent sand and gently swaying palm trees that shade beckoning young women have been critiqued by academics for their racist and sexist

---

1   Sharae Decard, 2010, *Paradise Discourse, Imperialism and Globalization: Exploiting Eden*, New York and London: Routledge, p. 12.

underpinnings.[2] Artists have thoroughly deconstructed stereotypical images of paradise for example, through reimagining the 'dusky maiden' in the works of Rosanna Raymond, Yuki Kihara and Sue Pearson.[3] Here I build on the insights developed in this body of work as well as exploring another highly potent, and somewhat curious, aspect of the 'Pacific paradise' trope. In this paper, I explore how images and imaginaries of 'Pacific paradise', especially via the material culture of tourism, are adopted by locals across a transnational Pacific community, to articulate heartfelt emotions about their homeland, their families and personal aspirations. In doing so, they bundle together political, economic and affective economies and make 'paradise' a key register of what has usefully been called 'felt modernity'.[4]

What emerges is a wide and often ambivalent range of local engagement with 'Pacific paradise' that amounts to more than outright rejection of this trope (although there are certainly contexts in which this refusal occurs). Some of the examples I present both deconstruct and adopt 'paradise' ironically, as many scholars and artists have done previously. But they engage less in a process of escaping or subverting than speaking through this trope. In these instances, generic images of paradise are re-purposed to express personal and community attachments and desires. I choose the word 're-purpose' carefully in order to emphasise the ambivalence attached to this trope.[5] In the examples below, 'Pacific paradise' is not simply taken up and given new meaning as terms such as 'appropriation' and 're-appropriation'

2   Patty O'Brien, 2006, *The Pacific Muse: Exotic Femininity and the Colonial Pacific*, Seattle: University of Washington Press; Jane C. Desmond, 1999, *Staging Tourism: Bodies on Display from Waikiki to Sea World*, Chicago: University of Chicago Press; Margaret Jolly, 1997, 'From Point Venus to Bali Ha'i: Eroticism and exoticism in representations of the Pacific', in *Sites of Desire, Economies of Pleasure: Sexualities in Asia and the Pacific*, ed.Lorraine Manderson and Margaret Jolly, pp. 99–122, Chicago: University of Chicago Press; Teresia Teaiwa, 1994, 'Bikinis and other S/pacific N/oceans', *The Contemporary Pacific* 6(1): 87–109; Haunani-Kay Trask, 1993, '"Lovely hula hands": Corporate tourism and the prostitution of Hawaiian culture', in *From a Native Daughter: Colonialism and Sovereignty in Hawai'i*, pp. 179–97, Maine: Common Courage Press.
3   See Marata A. Tamaira, 2010, 'From full dusk to full tusk: Reimagining the "dusky maiden" through the visual arts', *The Contemporary Pacific* 22(1): 1–35; and also Yuki Kihara, 2013, *Undressing the Pacific*, Dunedin: Hocken Collection, University of Otago; Selina Tusitala Marsh, 'Hawai'i: Prelude to a Journey', this volume; Courtney Sina Meredith, 'Ibu & Tufuga' and 'Great Works', this volume.
4   Koichi Iwabuchi (ed.), 2004, *Feeling Asian Modernities: Transnational Consumption of Japanese TV Drama*, Hong Kong: University of Hong Kong Press.
5   I have John Taylor to thank for suggesting the term after reading an early version of this paper.

tend to suggest, but rather 'paradise' retains the traces of gendered and raced (post)colonial histories as well as marks of the political economy in the global present.

Paradise as commodity fetishism

'As a destination for the tourist, the Pacific is a creation of capitalism', Michael Hall incisively remarks in an early discussion of myths of the Pacific as untouched paradise.[6] Tropes of virginal yet bountiful landscapes create an 'imperial politics of place'[7] that are intertwined with the global political economy and, most significantly, serve to mask histories of exploitation of land and people.[8] Teresia Teaiwa's work on Bikini Atoll is still the most striking example of this masking process. In this piece, she outlines how the 'bikini' bathing suit named after the atoll was created from myths of the island paradise as a pacific and feminised space.[9] Crucially, this 'bikini' served to strategically conceal the nuclear testing that occurred on Bikini Atoll, rendering the history of colonialism and ecological racism invisible to a western audience.

Beyond the Pacific, the paradise trope has similarly functioned to both mark and mask colonial and capitalist enterprise. The original theological meaning of 'paradise' underwent both religious and secular transformations and gained increased traction in response to fifteenth-century European colonial expansion, serving to both produce and veil the material exploitation of newly acquired colonies in the Americas.[10] Paradise, Sharae Decard's argues in *Paradise Discourse, Imperialism and Globalization: Exploiting Eden*:

6   C. Michael Hall, 1998, 'Making the Pacific: Globalisation, modernity and myth', in *Destinations: Cultural Landscapes of Tourism*, ed. Greg Ringer, pp. 140–53, London and New York: Routledge, p. 141.
7   John Connell, 2003, 'Island dreaming: The contemplation of Polynesian paradise', *Journal of Historical Geography* 29(4): 554–81, p. 555.
8   Miriam Kahn, 2011, *Tahiti Beyond the Postcard: Power, Place, and Everyday Life*, Seattle: University of Washington Press.
9   Teaiwa, 'Bikinis and other S/pacific N/oceans'.
10   See Decard, *Paradise Discourse, Imperialism and Globalization*.

is a value-laden discourse related to profit, labour, and exploitation of resources both human and environmental whose very appearance or irrelevance or 'death by ubiquity' shields the process it perniciously conceals. Paradise is inextricably linked to the long modernity of the capitalist world-system.[11]

Here the trope of paradise operates as a form of commodity fetishism that both emerges from, and mystifies, the material conditions to which it is attached. As the early colonial fantasy of paradise as labour-free profit and accumulation of wealth was enabled by forced labour and land alienation, so too in the twenty-first century we witness the economic transition from slavery and indenture to tourism and a refiguration of tropes of paradise. Paradise as bounty and abundance works to obscure exploitative relations of the present day as tourism resorts displace local homes, and fresh towels, flowers and fruit appear in hotel rooms as if by magic.[12] Contemporary images of paradise are no longer sites ripe for extraction of material goods (gold, sugar, cotton) but are now 'sights'. That is, commodified spectacles of luxury and leisure.[13]

The ways in which paradise discourse enables, legitimises and obscures relations of global capitalism informs the following analysis of Cook Islands tourism imagery. I extend this analysis to explore the role of 'paradise' in local rather than western imaginaries. While much has been said about the instrumental potency of 'paradise' for 'the West', it is often implicitly assumed that local engagement amounts to simple rejection or dismissal of the notion of 'paradise'. Especially in tourism scholarship, 'Pacific paradise' is portrayed principally as myth drummed up by the tourist industry. This assumption is implicit in analyses that aim to look 'beyond the postcard' or 'behind the smile', and is also more broadly evident in ideas of 'staged authenticity' and the commodification of experience that continue to dominate tourism

---

11 Ibid., p. 2.
12 'Paradise discourse' operates through oppositional imagery of Eden and apocalypse (ibid., p. 3). This is a point clearly demonstrated in Teaiwa's work and it is a distinction that is potentially useful for thinking through the classificatory divides between Melanesia and Polynesia, as well as ideas about 'failed states' and environmental disasters such as hurricanes and global warming as they are inflected in the Pacific. See Teaiwa, 'Bikinis and other S/pacific N/oceans'.
13 Decard, *Paradise Discourse, Imperialism and Globalization*, p. 16.

studies.[14] In contrast to this line of argument, the examples below demonstrate that 'paradise' operates as an affective geography for local expression of what is valued, including ideas of personal success and failure and, significantly, ways of imagining and managing the contradictions of modern life. These contradictions coalesce on the experiences of the global tourist industry as well as those of migration and transnationalism produced by global capital.

Touring paradise

In the Cook Islands, as throughout much of the Pacific, tourism is the primary industry accounting for at least 70 per cent of the nations' Gross Domestic Product (GDP). The Cook Islands is a group of 15 islands in central Polynesia with a resident population of approximately 18,000.[15] Rarotonga, the main island of the group and destination of most tourists, has dramatic volcanic peaks, a large lagoon and lush tropical vegetation (as well as large-scale hotels and requisite services). Approximately 90,000 tourists visit every year and, on Rarotonga, they make up one fifth of the population at any given time.[16] Tourism and tourists are thus highly visible all over the island, and the industry plays a major role in employment. At least one person from every family works in the tourism industry in some capacity or another. Tourism also plays a major role in the presentation of self on a daily basis. Tourists outnumber locals on the bus, at retail outlets and especially on the beach. The tourist gaze is also to be negotiated. Cook Islanders complain about how tourists stare at locals whilst engaging in mundane activities such as shopping at the supermarket. It is as if 'they expect us to live in grass huts', one Cook Islander friend explained with exasperation, 'they think we should be living in the Stone Age'.[17]

---

14   Dean MacCannell, 1976, *The Tourist: A New Theory of the Leisure Class*, New York: Schocken Books; see also Erik Cohen's critique, 1998, 'Authenticity and commoditization in tourism', *Annals of Tourism Research* 15: 371–86; and Edward M. Bruner, 2005, *Culture on Tour: Ethnographies of Travel*, Chicago: University of Chicago Press.
15   Cook Islands Statistics Office, Ministry of Finance and Economic Management, 2010, *Rarotonga: Cook Islands*.
16   Ibid.
17   Conversation with 'Odile', 8 May 2011. Pseudonyms are adopted throughout this chapter and all potentially identifying material (images, locations and people) have been de-identified.

Tourism is the main destination for development aid and assistance to the Cook Islands and it provides jobs in service, agriculture, construction and further, informal sectors such as craft and cultural production including dance and music. As well as these direct material impacts and conditions, tourism ensures regular international air-flights and somewhat less regular national transport between the smaller islands of the group. 'Island life' continues in a large part because of the income tourism generates and the infrastructure it provides. For example, it is not uncommon to see tourist buses, boats and venues being utilised for local events and activities such as weddings, school excursions, or even a trip to the taro plantation. Furthermore, cultural performances are said to take place far more often than they used to in pre-tourism days, and thus the industry is both seen as an opportunity to maintain cultural traditions, providing money and a reason to dance, sing, drum and carve. But tourism is also considered to represent the vanguard of western influences that are viewed as eroding traditional local forms. These contradictory and concurrently held views about the positive and negative dimensions of tourism reflect deep ambivalence about the tourism industry evidenced in debates about 'culture for sale', land alienation and, increasingly, environmental pollution. The often employed phrases 'prostitution' and 'bastardisation' point to the ambivalence felt towards tourism and tourists, and to the global processes of commodification and perceived loss of cultural ownership.[18]

As in many tropical islands, the 'paradise' trope is a central signifier of the Cook Islands tourist industry; 'Welcome to Paradise' or 'Kia Orana from Paradise' are stock phrases repeated at tourist shows, lagoon cruises, on postcards and on t-shirts. In this scenario, where tourism is ubiquitous and saturates everyday life on the Cook Islands, the trope functions intertextually as it is adopted by many Cook Islanders to summarise their world view and perception of their geographical surrounds. Cook Islanders often wax lyrical about their home as 'paradise'. A woman I lived with on Rarotonga in the late 1990s would often greet her neighbour: 'Ah, another beautiful day in paradise!' The phrase expressed both a genuine utterance that spoke

---

18   Kalissa Alexeyeff, 2008, 'Are you being served? Sex, humour and globalisation in the Cook Islands', *Anthropological Forum* 18(3): 287–93.

to the warmth, light and smell of the day at hand as well as a partly ironic sentiment in its self-conscious mimicry of tourism advertising campaigns.

'Paradise' now also features prominently in status updates on Facebook as the medium that is hugely popular with transnational communities in the Cook Islands as elsewhere. The following post tellingly includes the phrase in English preceded by an update in Cook Islands Māori, reassuring friends that they have not been forgotten and that everything is well on the island. Indeed, the island is so abundant that the person has been too busy picking up all the rubbish (a phrase used to refer to overgrown grass and fallen leaves, palm fronds and nuts) to find time to go online:

> Tangi Ke e te au taeake ... Kare kotou i ngaropoina iaku ... Kua tae meitaki ua mai ki te enua nei. E ngao angaanga, kua roa rava te aere anga kua roaroa te tita. Ka pukapuka akaou tatou a teia nga ra. Beautiful Day here in Paradise!

This lush 'paradise' references both the natural environment and, in other contexts, the people who live there, especially local women. Islanders are proud of their beautiful young women; national and regional beauty pageants are hugely popular amongst locals and winners retain their fame and celebrity throughout their lives. While these beautiful young women featured in tourism advertising during the 1990s, advertising campaigns during the 2000s attempted a shift from these stock images of feminised paradise filled with 'dusky maidens' towards more 'realistic' experiential images based around the slogan 'Cook Islands, Live Differently'. In an interview I conducted with the Tourism Cook Islands' marketing director who oversaw the new campaign, she described how this proved disconcerting for local audiences. Locals, she said, were 'appalled' by the campaign featuring exuberant larger women. They asked her, 'Why are you putting fat mamas in the picture? We have such beautiful girls. What [a] shame!'[19]

---

19 Interview with Glenda Tuaine, 4 July 2008. Colleen Ballerino Cohen has dubbed sentiments such as these as 'marketing paradise, making nation' a process by which 'island nations market feminised paradise landscapes to western tourists while encouraging their own citizens to identify with these as patriotic expressions'. Cohen, 'Marketing paradise, making nation', *Annals of Tourism Research* 22 (2): 404–21, cited in Decard, *Paradise Discourse, Imperialism and Globalization*, p. 21.

Figure 124. Tourism Cook Islands image of laughing mamas, 2015.
Source. Photo courtesy of Cook Islands Tourism Corporation.

The 'paradise' trope assumes a particular poignancy for Cook Islanders who have moved abroad. As a former New Zealand colony, the Cook Islands has an 'associated state' relationship, which means among other things that Cook Islanders travel on New Zealand passports and have automatic citizenship rights. Opportunity, in the form of higher wages, education and social welfare 'pull' Cook Islanders abroad, and now the vast majority of Cook Islanders live abroad, an estimated 60,000 in New Zealand and 15,000 in Australia (compared to 18,000 in the nation-state). Tourism and migration are intertwined in the Cook Islands' postcolonial history. Since the international airport opened on Rarotonga in 1974, tourism was earmarked as a key national growth area and concurrently locals began to migrate in unprecedented numbers to New Zealand. The majority of migrants settle permanently abroad but participate in transnational networks that encompass family who reside at home and those living in other countries. The images associated with Cook Islands tourism advertising provide a backdrop for those who have migrated to imagine their return home and to narrativise their experience of migration.

Picturing paradise

As I visited various Cook Islanders in New Zealand one winter, I was struck that the images used to decorate the walls were the tourist posters and postcards of the Cook Islands as well as more generic prints depicting palms leaning into the lagoon at sunset. By contrast, these interiors were inhabited by people dressed in layers of warm clothing to combat the cold weather. This cold was exacerbated by the lack of insulation and limited heating. These images of paradise where not ironic appropriations of tourism advertising it seemed, but rather they appeared to starkly represent how the migrant dream of self-advancement and wealth was as illusory as the goal of returning to make paradise home.

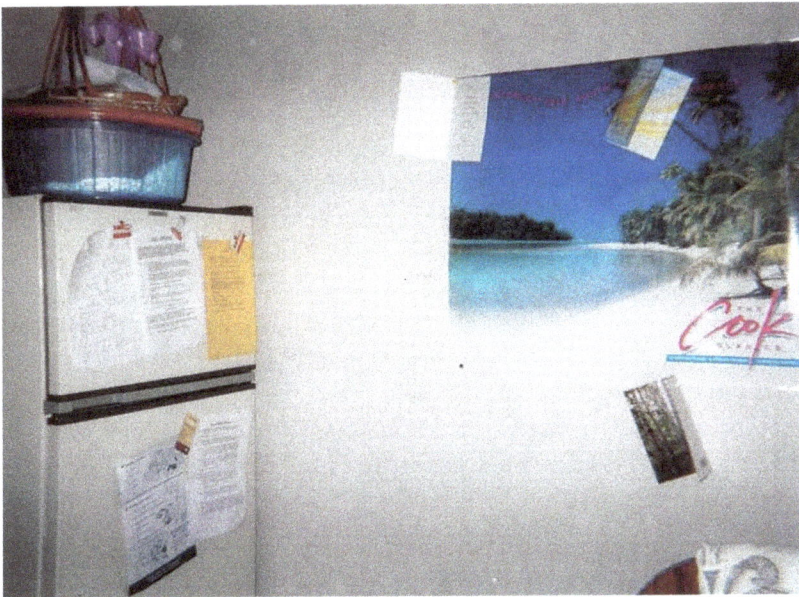

Figure 125. A kitchen with paradise poster.
Source. Photographed by Kalissa Alexeyeff, Otara, Auckland, 12 August 2000.

One house in which I frequently stayed in South Auckland was a particularly arresting example of this decorative style of re-purposing 'Pacific paradise'. The small house was rented by a woman, who lived there with her 80-year-old father who was visiting from the islands for medical treatment, and two of her teenage children. The elderly father first migrated to New Zealand to work in the timber industry. He came along with many Pacific Islander men, to fill labour shortages during the post–World War II period. He had returned to his home island after five years work and had only recently arrived back in New Zealand because of his ailing health and access to free and comprehensive health care. This move was to become permanent despite his wish to eventually die at home. Like all of his eight children, the woman who rented the house had grown up in the Cook Islands but she had moved to New Zealand in her early 20s (and now, all but one sibling lives abroad). She married, had children and worked on an assembly line at an electronics factory. After this industry suffered a decline in the late 1990s, she found work as a car park attendant. Although she returned annually to her home island for Christmas festivities and family reunions and expressed a deep sadness on these occasions that she didn't reside there, she felt she was 'too used to New Zealand' and besides, her three teenage children had been born and raised in Auckland had no desire to return 'home'. These children accompanied family members on trips to the Cook Islands sitting in rapt attention listening to their parents reminiscing together about 'the olden days'. These children also maintained transnational relationships with cousins through Facebook, phone texts and travel. While their ancestral home featured significantly in their self-identifications, they also felt they would be incredibly bored if they had to live there. Alongside boredom they expressed a certain awkwardness in their habitus at 'home'. One professed to me that they felt like a 'tourist' when they went on these trips home, 'because I take photos and have more money and better clothes than my cousins. But also because I want to go to the beach and I can't husk a coconut properly. My aunty called me a tourist once, she was laughing at me, and I felt pretty shamed.'[20]

These conflicting attitudes to 'home' should not suggest that New Zealand, and Auckland in particular, is divorced from 'Island life'. Two-thirds of all Pacific people residing in New Zealand (7.4 per cent of the population, 295,941 people identified with one or more Pacific ethnic group),[21] live in South and West Auckland. Retail outlets and markets in these areas provide local produce, garments,

---

20   Personal communication, 'Tangi', 30 March 2012.
21   Statistics New Zealand, 2014, *2013 Census Quick Stats about Culture and Identity*.

music and wealth such as fine mats in abundance. Samoan, Tongan and Cook Islander churches and community halls figure prominently on the main roads, and performing arts, sports competitions and other community festivals are dotted throughout the year. These activities and objects attest to the 'super-vibrancy' of Pacific Islander cultural production and consumption abroad.[22] Back home and outside of tourism contexts, these practices continue in largely attenuated forms or for 'export' to family who lived abroad.

A proliferation of local cultural forms does little however to ameliorate longing for homeland at the level of lived experience and in familial narratives across generations. One might suggest that this cultural production, consumption and the sentiments they engender feeds this yearning. For example, the large taro industry that operates from the Pacific Islands to New Zealand supplies nostalgic demands, but also people invariably comment that taro doesn't 'taste the same as it does at home'. Songs written by string band groups that proliferate in the diaspora (and are hugely popular with 'home' audiences as well), similarly voice sentiments of loss and yearning for a home often signified as a paradisial landscape.

Island paradise as trope of home as well as that which is displaced was evident in my friend's house in South Auckland. Shell 'ei (necklaces) hung in long curtains from each doorway, softly chinking as one passed through them. In the main rooms of the house, woven hats and fans and plastic flowers adorned the architraves, and posters of the 'paradise' produced by Tourism Cook Islands decorated the walls. These touristic images were framed with shell necklaces, invitations to Cook Islander events such as weddings and community fundraisers, and photographs of family members at these events.

---

22   Cathy A. Small, 2011 [1997], *Voyages: From Tongan Villages to American Suburbs*, Ithaca and London: Cornell University Press, p. 151.

Figure 126. Living room wall, South Auckland.
Source. Photographed by Kalissa Alexeyeff, Otara, Auckland, 12 August 2000.

Embedding global mass-produced and generic images in local histories via personal photographs, significant objects and text is a phenomenon observed by Christopher Pinney and others,[23] who view these practices as acts that link material objects to practices of memorialisation and projection.[24] As a visual tableau, these images and objets d'art act as repositories of both memory and aspiration; visually communicating collective and personal history and future identifications and trajectories.

Similarly at the South Auckland house, the images and artefacts display collective and personal histories by channelling the affective force of the 'paradise' trope. 'Paradise' in this tableau represents natural beauty and the smiling warmth of its people. It communicates genuine love for homeland and pride in cultural heritage. Framing and layering images of 'paradise' with photographs of people and gifted objects also visually gestures to a form of sociality in which family, community, and culturally styled generosity are central values.

23   Christopher Pinney, 1997, *Camera Indica: The Social Life of Indian Photographs*, London: Reaktion Books.
24   Daniel Miller, 2008, 'Migration, material culture and tragedy: Four moments in Caribbean migration', *Mobilities* 3(3): 397–413.

Figure 127. 'Endless summer': A Cook Islands Tourism poster on a kichen wall.

Source. Photographed by Kalissa Alexeyeff, Otara, Auckland, 12 August 2000.

Paradise is, however, an elusive destination. Paradise is always elsewhere; registering nostalgia for a place that has once been, as well as, and crucially, encapsulating future anticipatory longing.[25] For many Cook Islanders, including the inhabitants of this particular South Auckland house, the dream of the future is narrated through the paradise trope as a yearning to earn enough money to return and build a home on their family land. For many this land, especially beachfront sections, is leased on 99-year contracts to local elites and to foreign interests to develop tourism enterprises. Back in New Zealand, individuals who migrated to 'better themselves' through education and higher paying jobs may find the high cost of living and debt often trap them at the lower end of New Zealand's socio-economic scale. 'Paradise' home is a place of both projected love and longing and a location that is always deferred, a site to which one returns only briefly for events such as Christmas celebrations and in one's dreams.

Figure 128. 'Autumnal crying woman' poster and family photos.
Source. Photographed by Kalissa Alexeyeff, Otara, Auckland, 12 August 2000.

In the South Auckland house, longing and nostalgia for a paradise deferred were visually represented through the placement of tourist images, souvenirs and family photographs alongside poster art of

---

25   Decard, *Paradise Discourse, Imperialism and Globalization*, p. 4.

(white) women and young girls crying, the latter often embracing soft toys for comfort. These crying images made for an unusual juxtaposition with the far more upbeat images of 'paradise' expressed through tourist posters. It was a juxtaposition that visiting family would comment upon and tease the woman with comments such as, 'Are you trying to make us all sad?' The owner in turn, could not, or would not, fully articulate her interest in these pictures beyond saying she liked them, and that she liked that they were crying. She acknowledged they were a bit unusual compared to other Cook Islands interiors, although she stated that she did not find them sad but rather found these images aesthetically pleasing and somehow comforting.[26]

The woman's frequent reminiscing and also singing about her homeland, further articulated this juxtaposition. Her small backyard in the Auckland suburb was often cold and wet but nevertheless she coaxed cuttings of gardenia and *rauti* (Cordyline Terminalis) and even taro to grow. It is an image I cannot resist comparing to the expansive view of the sun-drenched lagoon that one could watch from her family house back home—a view that is in some ways a reflection of 'paradise' visual imagery, and one that is made more poignant by the fact that the 100-year-old family home from which I took the photo was destroyed by a cyclone in the mid-2000s.

---

26 'Crying art' is a popular genre of painting and mass-produced posters and prints. They most famous is *The Crying Boy* painting by Italian painter Bruno Amadio, also known as Bragolin, in the 1950s. In urban legend the image is thought to be cursed, bringing bad luck and fire to owners' homes. The Hollywood movie *Big Eyes*, directed by Tom Burton (2014), recounts another notorious story of artist Margaret Keane, who painted often teary-eyed girls, and whose work was passed off by her husband, Walter, as his own.

Figure 129. South Auckland backyard.
Source. Photographed by Kalissa Alexeyeff, Otara, Auckland, 12 August 2000.

Figure 130. View from the family land looking out across the lagoon, Rarotonga.
Source. Photographed by Kalissa Alexeyeff, Rarotonga, Cook Islands, 2 January 1997.

Re-purposing paradise

Both the exterior and interior of the South Auckland house presented a vivid contrast between the 'endless summer' of 'paradise' and the cold, outer-suburban reality of many Cook Islands migrants in New Zealand. Daniel Miller similarly details 'the tragedy of migration' and the role of material cultural in evoking and enabling related sentiments.[27] Particular houses of Caribbean migrants in London with whom he worked indexed key contradictions in migrant trajectories, including aspirations to improve one's lot in life, the 'myth of return home', success and failure, as well as broader historical and economic stratification that mark these personal narratives. Like some of Miller's more 'quirky' individuals and their interior decoration styles, the woman living in the South Auckland house was unusual in the care she took to decorate her interiors. While many Cook Islands migrants will casually stick family photos and memorabilia to walls of their rental house, more permanent ornamentation is usually minimal. Nevertheless, I feel confident suggesting (on the back of Miller's work) that the 'Pacific paradise' represented in tourist imagery of smiling, bikini-clad *brown* girls interspersed with pictures of crying *white* girls was not a haphazard arrangement nor simply an idiosyncratic decorative style. This arrangement drew upon the racialised and gendered dimensions of the paradise trope, re-purposing it to inflect her experience of migration, but nevertheless revealing and masking the contradictions in her life-history—her sense of self and place. For this woman, her house expressed her deeply held familial and cultural bonds, as well enacting a longing for that which was beyond her reach. Taking on board the idea that 'paradise discourse' has been repeatedly mobilised in the service of capitalist modes of production, exploitation of labour and capital accumulation,[28] it is not an especially large leap to argue that the South Auckland house serves both to reveal, as well as revel in, the contradictions of a racialised capitalist modernity— the promises of great economic mobility, expanded horizons and freedom in contrast to the more truncated reality of structural poverty embedded in formations of racism that characterises settler colonial societies globally.

'Paradise' has a long historical trajectory in the Pacific as the emblem of Pacific tourism. It is a trope that is embedded in local everyday social life and lived experience. As such, tourism—and its material culture—is entwined with local economics, politics and sensibilities as much as it is a vehicle of global capitalism and other macro trends such as emigration and patterns of labour mobility and national economic development. In the little South Auckland house, as well as in the practices of Cook Islanders at home, 'paradise' serves as

---

27   Miller, 'Migration, material culture and tragedy'.
28   Decard, *Paradise Discourse, Imperialism and Globalization*, p. 21.

a backdrop to register the contradictions of economic, social and affective modernities poignantly illustrating how 'paradise' is not simply an image for outsiders but also a story upon which locals may map a geography of longing concerning here and there, now and then, and into spaces of the future.

References

Alexeyeff, Kalissa. 2008. 'Are you being served? Sex, humour and globalisation in the Cook Islands.' *Anthropological Forum* 18(3): 287–93.

Big Eyes. 2014. Directed by Tom Burton.

Bruner, Edward M. 2005. *Culture on Tour: Ethnographies of Travel*. Chicago: University of Chicago Press.

Cohen, Erik. 1998. 'Authenticity and commoditization in tourism.' *Annals of Tourism Research* 15: 371-86.

Connell, John. 2003. 'Island dreaming: The contemplation of Polynesian paradise.' *Journal of Historical Geography* 29(4): 554–81.

Cook Islands Statistics Office, Ministry of Finance and Economic Management. 2010. *Rarotonga: Cook Islands*. Online: www.mfem. gov.ck/statistics (accessed 3 March 2016).

Decard, Sharae. 2010. *Paradise Discourse, Imperialism and Globalization: Exploiting Eden*. New York and London: Routledge.

Desmond, Jane C. 1999. *Staging Tourism: Bodies on Display from Waikiki to Sea World*. Chicago: University of Chicago Press.

Hall, C. Michael. 1998. 'Making the Pacific: Globalisation, modernity and myth.' In *Destinations: Cultural Landscapes of Tourism*, ed. Greg Ringer, pp. 140–53. London and New York: Routledge.

Iwabuchi, Koichi (ed.). 2004. *Feeling Asian Modernities: Transnational Consumption of Japanese TV Drama*. Hong Kong: University of Hong Kong Press.

Jolly, Margaret. 1997. 'From Point Venus to Bali Ha'i: Eroticism and exoticism in representations of the Pacific.' In *Sites of Desire, Economies of Pleasure: Sexualities in Asia and the Pacific*, ed. Lorraine Manderson and Margaret Jolly, pp. 99–122. Chicago: University of Chicago Press.

Kahn, Miriam. 2011. *Tahiti Beyond the Postcard: Power, Place, and Everyday Life*. Seattle: University of Washington Press.

Kihara, Yuki. 2013. *Undressing the Pacific*. Dunedin: Hocken Collection, University of Otago. Online: shigeyukikihara.files.wordpress.com/2013/04/kihara-ecatalogue.pdf (accessed 3 March 2016).

MacCannell, Dean. 1976. *The Tourist: A New Theory of the Leisure Class*. New York: Schocken Books.

Miller, Daniel. 2008. 'Migration, material culture and tragedy: Four moments in Caribbean migration.' *Mobilities* 3(3): 397–413.

O'Brien, Patty. 2006. *The Pacific Muse: Exotic Femininity and the Colonial Pacific*. Seattle: University of Washington Press.

Pinney, Christopher. 1997. *Camera Indica: The Social Life of Indian Photographs*. London: Reaktion Books.

Small, Cathy A. 2011 [1997]. *Voyages: From Tongan Villages to American Suburbs*. Ithaca and London: Cornell University Press.

Statistics New Zealand, 2014. *2013 Census Quick Stats about Culture and Identity*. Online: www.stats.govt.nz/Census/2013-census/profile-and-summary-reports/quickstats-culture-identity/pacific-peoples.aspx (accessed 3 March 2016).

Tamaira, Marata A. 2010. 'From full dusk to full tusk: Reimagining the "dusky maiden" through the visual arts.' *The Contemporary Pacific* 22(1): 1–35.

Teaiwa, Teresia. 1994. 'Bikinis and other S/pacific N/oceans.' *The Contemporary Pacific* 6(1): 87–109.

Trask, Haunani-Kay. 1993. '"Lovely hula hands": Corporate tourism and the prostitution of Hawaiian culture.' In *From a Native Daughter: Colonialism and Sovereignty in Hawai'i*, pp. 179–97. Maine: Common Courage Press.

28

Local Tourist on a Bus Ride Home

Audrey Brown-Pereira

cool breeze sweeping sweet sweat of sadness
(through the cold hot air of the open closed window)

look   'sweet-e'
                not with your i i dar-ling

?   (anonymous object sits silently inside palm of her head)

the mist kisses the mountains
the mountains kiss the sky
                coloured pockets of green & gold & blue
                sing her a familiar song she thought she could
                never understand

(fault?)   *tuatua maori*   *no*
                church   *no*
                ura   *kare?*

echoed an even more familiar voice inside her head 2 herself
                        the bird flies over the sun
                        the sun flies in2 the sea

thoughts (r) / evolve as the km (s) clock from papa joe's watch & the
o-do-me-ter
of the yellow – yellow/jam packed/yellow/jam packed bus

(on the $\frac{1}{2}$ hr anti-clock-wise of course)

10 9 8 7 6 5 4

watch the c   through the trees
                                   through the houses

through the stones that paint each stop with a story of a somebody
a n d   a   s o m e w h e r e   t h a t   a   s o m e o n e (s)   s t i l l
l o v e s

can u c?

as they pass herstory in arorangi & tupapa

teuki ©

29

Mixed Bag of Tropical Sweets Sitting Outside the Hotel R & R

Audrey Brown-Pereira

n is a g of the c
walking peeping like his prother kaukan
whose lost in islands of imagined para-dices
panting, pounding, desperately waiting
hiding in the nut-less tree

e is still in the never never y
waiting 4 decisions on the unknown x

>
> denial
> bereavement
> the sensitive issue
> yes?

hmmm still-awaiting the pigs 2 fly & grow wings

o is an aa with gold chains and a moo-stache

>
> (ie donkey beyond the limit+)

drinking & driving & driving & drinking with balls and balls and no
balls – to say stop!

keys will fall upon graves soon
just as blood, just as time, just as day

m is queen b (jnr)
flying upon aotearoa's wings
breathless she trips upon her uncustomary arrival
squashing the yellow tipani & pink tipani & white tipani in2 pools
of oil spoiled plue
mummy queen B (snr) coronates daughter queen b (jnr) with
a specially prepared & recycled
paper cut crown

ceremonially wearing her golden lathen kikau plastic t-shirt
magnificently star studded in plack pearls & plue pearls & preen pearls
forming the ohh so humble words 'she came from me!'

bc brigade
march barefoot in trench coats
with their writing pads & their writing pens & their writing hands
that do not write
accompanied by their lists of 4gotten witnesses
with their no names & their non accounts of incidences non-4seen

inside the mixed bag of tropical sweets
sitting outside the hotel r & r
white cockroaches walk & fly & play
as the chaos of bottomless chastity sings his vowels of virtue to the
airport with no wings

kia orana!

30

Fiji: Reflections in the Infinity Pool

John Connell

Figure 131. An infinity pool.

Source. Photo by Pacific Resort Hotel Group, Pacific Resort Aitutaki, Cook Islands and used with permission.

The infinity pool extends into the distance beyond blue seas and under blue skies—the rest of the world and its indignities are banished beyond the horizon and space is seemingly endless—until only another distant island intrudes. Purpose-built pools in small islands, naturally surrounded by water, constitute the ultimate architecture of pleasure. The sea is domesticated—harmful creatures are gone, abrasive corals are absent, waves and currents are without threat. Tourism is a sentient, stress-free, mildly emotional experience.

The lure of water is everywhere: water is therapy, it anchors resort existence—warm, clean, soothing, languorous, soporific even. In the midst of a sea of islands—resort and landscape blend together, into the increasingly bland face of island tourism, where any sense of place has gone.

The tourist Pacific has come to exemplify placelessness—ironic and even paradoxical here, when smiling Fijians grace every brochure—yet resorts isolate visitors and tourists in ever strengthening cocoons and bubbles, a small 'p' pacific rather than a distinctive and differentiated Pacific.

Reflections on space and place are drawn from five years of Australian newspaper articles on Fiji (2009–13), a suite of contemporary (mid-2014) websites and multiple current travel brochures, simply differentiated as newspaper (N), website (W) and brochure (B) since all conspire and combine to create a distinctive, introspective world of infinite pleasure and uninhibited delight. They are repetitious in an uncritical journalistic and PR oeuvre that knows only positives and superlatives, and that rarely offers alternative or critical discourses. Specific sites and stories have largely been rendered anonymous, to protect the guilty.

Advertising islands

Promoting Fiji as a tourist destination has always involved three themes: tropical island South Seas imagery, cultural and scenic attractions unique to Fiji, and experiences quite distinct from urbanised metropolitan lifestyles.[1] These have scarcely changed in half a century, but have intensified, gone upmarket, displaced culture and rebalanced Fiji from the mainland to small outlying islands and

---

1   Stephen G. Britton, 1983, *Tourism and Underdevelopment in Fiji*, Monograph No. 31, Canberra: Development Studies Centre, The Australian National University, p. 36.

resorts.[2] Through that process place has faded away. While resorts are certainly in Fiji, they are not necessarily of it. Brochures and websites rarely offer even the most diagrammatic of maps. Only fine print (or 'an easy helicopter trip from Nadi') suggest an actual location.

'Fiji: the way the world should be' (taken up directly by more than one resort) has been the longest standing national marketing slogan. Though ironic in a nation that has been dealt recurrent coups and economic crises, it has served the country well. And silenced and excluded the daily world. Coups and crises are another world: all the more reason to be apart from that. So utopian adjectives are overworked, clichés pile up and hyperbole abounds—pristine, blissful, unique, exclusive, peaceful—'Palm trees with the obligatory hammock hanging from them' (N)—as Fiji gently disappears.

In the midst of generic attributes there are only rare mentions of Fiji: 'a true island oasis, Fiji is an intoxicating land' (B). Elsewhere destinations are 'in the heart of the Pacific' (W), 'the ultimate island paradise' (B), 'impenetrable jungle, coconut plantations and amazing coral reefs' (B), 'if the untouched South Pacific is what you seek then you'll find it' (B), and 'our own little piece of paradise' (W).

Tourism is shaped by the picturesque. Resorts are only exceptionally located in place—'a small market town is nearby' (W)—but more frequently 'nestled amongst tropical gardens' (W) or 'set on a coral and sand-fringed atoll within a vibrant marine sanctuary' (W). Natural landscapes abound, typically remote from markets and towns. Coconut palms sway, crabs scuttle and fish glide through variously azure, turquoise, ultramarine and (albeit on one occasion) Listerine blue waters. 'This Eden like isle is ringed by tropical waters' (W) or perhaps by 'our trademark aqua waters' (W). This combines into 'an idyllic location for discerning travellers seeking an exotic beachside getaway' (W). So much is tropical-universal that Fiji gradually recedes into infinity.

Banal and mundane 'destination branding' ensures similarity rather than marking any distinctive island experience; 'mainlands' are small enough to become islands, and resorts are increasingly all-embracing.

---

2   John Connell, 2015, 'Competing islands? The Mamanuca and Yasawa Islands, Fiji', in *Archipelago Tourism. Policies and Practices*, ed. Godfrey Baldacchino, pp. 183–97, Farnham: Ashgate.

> Treasure Island is one of Fiji's most iconic resorts, with extensive experience in providing hospitality and friendship to travellers from across the globe. This resort is specially designed for honeymooners, couples and families seeking a unique and unforgettable island holiday experience (B),

which covers most possibilities. On the next page of the brochure, Castaway Island is described as

> an iconic private island and one of the most popular resorts in the Mamanucas. Surrounded by white sandy beaches with a pristine natural environment, vibrant coral reefs and a great resort atmosphere … the perfect escape for families and couples alike (B).

The extent of differentiation between such resorts is trivial. Repetitive descriptions and positive attitudes proliferate and degenerate into an amorphous mass where the attributes of particular islands are minimised with reference to descriptions of the resort itself. Water soothes and surrounds. Words wash by like waves. The island world is awash with images that conform with, confirm and reinforce tourist expectations. Islands and resorts are different yet familiar, everywhere but nowhere.

Islands apart

Despite the need for ease of accessibility, separation is necessary to invoke difference and even exclusiveness, hence repeated invocations to 'charming and remote' (B), 'blissful isolation' (B) and 'A sense of privilege and exclusion, of blissful isolation from the rest of the world' (N). Creative destination branding becomes introspective and rather less than innovative.

Solitude and separation engender peace: 'Sail to uninhabited tropical islands, anchor in private lagoons' (B) where the resort 'epitomises the seclusion and graceful hospitality for which the Fijian archipelago is famed' (W). The Pacific polis is now without danger, terrestrial or marine. It has become 'A place with no crowds, commitments or deadlines. A place where you can be yourself and re-connect with the natural way of life while being wrapped in luxury and romance. Wake up to the sound of whistling birds and magical rain forests. Unwind, relax and submerge yourself in the simplicity of pristine tropical paradise sanctuary' (W).

To meet 'your desire for seclusion, for splendour, for authenticity' (W) several resorts have simply banished others, or imposed numerical constraints. Resorts may cater to couples only, hopefully 'romantic couples' (if not—'rekindle the romance' (W)), while others exclude children under 16, or are off-limits to non-guests. 'Tokoriki prides itself on being an idyllic adults-only retreat for those who want to escape the stresses of everyday life, swapping offices and commuting for a week or two of non-stop luxury' (W). Luxury may even be defined as the absence of others. 'Whatever you choose to do at Yasawa, you'll do it in complete seclusion' (W). Better still 'why book a hotel room when you can have an entire island?' (W). And even better again: on Turtle Island, 'this entirely all-inclusive, exotic tropical paradise can be rented for a week at a time' (W). Pleasure derives from the absence and exclusion of others.

Air-conditioning and surround sound exclude the world. Seclusion and isolation offer social stability, safety and sameness—a fleeting release from the seething, congested capitalist maelstrom into a demographically diminished world.

Pristine

Tourism takes place in an environment that naturally is neither tarnished nor trashed by capitalism. Pollution is far beyond such an innocent, unchanging landscape. Indeed 'it appears as if the garden of Eden does exist after all' (W). All that is predictable: 'spend a single moment here ... and you will be convinced that the words "paradise found" were first spoken with our secluded beaches and authentic luxury in mind' (W), 'a pristine aqua lagoon and dazzling white sand beach' (W), 'lush tropical vegetation surrounded by white sandy beaches' (N). 'Once upon a time across the bluest of oceans, an island was born of lava and sand—an untouched paradise whose heart was a turquoise lagoon of unimaginable beauty and tranquility. The first visitors came and explored' (W) yet must have left no imprint.

Of course, once again, it is advisable to escape other tourists, their tawdry resorts and their worlds. 'Away from over-populated tourist destinations and the frantic pace of preoccupied modern living ... another world. This is not just escapism, more a return to nature' (W) but a once-wild nature, tamed, subdued and rendered sublime.

One resort is 'the last pristine place on earth' (W) and 'paradise perfected' (W); since nightly rates start at US$2,280 it may be that 'fantasy becomes reality' (W).

Resorts are created and designed to 'blur the boundary between architecture, interiors and landscape' (N), as interior and exterior are fused, to evoke an ethos of simplicity that might capture a supposedly idyllic past time. 'It is a unique and special place designed with integrity to Fijian cultural values, traditional designs and architecture, and is embraced by the renowned warmth of the Fijian people' (W). The core of resorts is the mock *bure* (traditional thatched Fijian house) in a sanitised paradise with invisible modernity. 'Likuliku embodies the richness of an ancient culture with vibrant present-day lifestyle touches. Welcome to Fiji's most unique luxury escape for couples. Welcome to your magical sanctuary' (W). *Bures* evoke 'nostalgia, fantasy and the exotic'.[3] Likuliku is 'built and decorated in the traditional island style, located directly on stilts in the water, on the beachfront' (W), although 'traditional' islanders were far too wary of the vagaries of oceans and cyclones to build anything close to the coast.

Architecturally choreographed views across pools and oceans extend to the 'horizon aflame with the kind of sunset you might see in a brochure' (N). And is seen in brochures. Mimicry is multiplied. 'I watch the sun slowly set from my plunge pool' (N) and 'I'm in love with the salt infinity pool that has all the dreaminess of a larger resort pool while being small enough to feel like your own back yard in paradise' (W). 'There are no clouds, the sky is crystal clear and there's nothing between me and the big blue sea' (N). 'The dream of an unworked natural landscape is very much the fantasy of people who have never themselves had to work the land to make a living.'[4] Such is readily evident and actively constructed.

---

3   Brian King and Peter Spearritt, 2001, 'Resort curtilages: The creation of physical and psychological tourism spaces', in *Virtual Globalization. Virtual Space/Tourist Space*, ed. David Holmes, pp. 245–61, London: Routledge, p. 252.
4   William Cronon, 1995, 'The trouble with wilderness: Or, getting back to the wrong nature', in *Uncommon Ground: Rethinking the Human Place in Nature*, ed. William Cronon, pp. 69–90, New York: Norton, p. 80.

Timeless

Locked into a natural pristine environment, tourism is quite timeless: 'Where would you go if you just wanted to turn the world off? This is it' (W) and so experience 'no idea what day or time it is' (W). History is banished into infinity where nothing changes or is likely to change: 'just as the mainland of Viti Levu was like 50 years ago' (W) is as close as it gets.

Tourists are constantly enjoined to embrace 'Fiji time', abandon watches and the internet, since 'everything here happens in Fiji time' (N) or simply 'island time'. That then means that 'Time seems to slow down as I adjust to the easy-going rhythm' (N). With luck the present becomes timeless. 'Time has a way of dissolving on a tropical island' (N). Even in the timeless tropics going back in time is invaluable.

'Being out in nature brings a chance to realign yourself with some of the deepest roots of being. Build your day around the rhythms of the day. Forget clock-time, and make time to respond to what the day presents you. The greatest symphony in the world happens as the pre-dawn light rises into day and the sun come up to the song of birds' (W). 'Stop, take a deep breath and let life pass by' (N). Technology is unstated but subtly presumed. Money itself is unnecessary at the most upmarket resorts: a modern subsistence world. The landscape has been tamed, appropriated and rendered authentic.

Languid

Without time urgency disappears. 'Calm warm turquoise water is as close to the perfect tropical moment I've experienced' (N). Water is the real and metaphorical key: 'immerse yourself in a realm of relaxation' and 'retreat to the serenity' (W), or more generally 'immerse yourself in award-winning luxury' (W). For this provides opportunities, while 'surrounded by serenity' (W) to 'wash the soul' (W), 'awaken the senses' (W) and 'rejuvenate the mind body and spirit' (W) or merely relax and indulge.

Activity is condoned but scarcely encouraged. 'Do as much or as little as you like. We'll help you slot in to your zone of yearning' (W). Quite so. 'If you are seeking to do more than just relax and soak up the sun [we] offer numerous activities to give you a memorable touch of adventure in paradise' (W). These are islands of consumption not production, other than of handicrafts, where resorts stage 'performances' of handicraft manufacture, and 'local people will bring their fascinating handicrafts to you' (W) just frequently enough to provide a measure of cultural capital and a few photographs. Organised excursions and beach activities exist but, as so much is built in (three meals a day, golf courses, kava ceremonies and more), that endeavour and leaving the resort are slightly improbable.

Trivial connections, whether of environment, society or economy, embrace the local. Only occasionally does 'culture' intrude. 'Immerse yourself in a Pacific cultural experience at the Marau Village. Enjoy a lavish lovo feast of Fijian specialties cooked in earth ovens (lovo). The evening opens with our exotic Polynesian dance performances and knife and fire dancing show by the Shangri-La Fijian Firedancers and culminates with the Fijian Beqa firewalkers showcasing the mystical art of firewalking' (W). Water reconstitutes jaded bodies, where spas might draw on suggestions of tradition and timelessness: 'indulgent treatments inspired by ancient wisdoms and healing traditions' (W). 'Its modern and traditional treatments draw on indigenous plants and herbs that have been used to heal for generations' (W) with 'warm seashell massage, banana leaf wraps, locally produced virgin coconut oil' (W). But, failing that, 'a total spa escape and ritual to allow your mind and body to be rejuvenated, replenished and nourished' (W). 'The day spa is incredible, to be pampered by skilled spa therapists whilst listening to the sounds of a waterfall' (W). Waterfalls and shops are drawn indoors, precluding any need to venture beyond. Spectacle, performance and purchases are internalised as the resort gradually evolves into theme park.

A glorified global may intrude selectively. 'Incorporating traditional Fijian bure architecture with Balinese pavilion architecture [to] feature open plan layout, taking advantage of the spectacular views creating fluid indoor/outdoor ambience while ensuring complete privacy' (W). One resort is named as 'a Tibetan exclamation of wonder' (W). Globalism is inevitable where the Pacific scales few cuisine peaks, 'island nights' of local specialties can disappoint (though 'Native foods are worth a taste' (B)) yet good food and wine are integral components of good tourism. Menus do find Pacific adjectives and 'the recipes are inspired by a distinctive culinary style blending international gourmet cuisine with traditional Fijian flavours. The meals are a true reflection of the colourful tropical setting [and] the retreat's own organic garden' (W). More probably 'Dishes are infused with Polynesian, European, Chinese and Indian flavours, often with a tropical twist for authentic Fijian flair' (B) or 'The menu does a carousel from Japan to Vietnam to Italy and France' (N). International chefs can produce a 'signature crabmeat omelet' matched by a 'fine wine list' balanced by a lagoon-facing spa (N): 'island warmth mixed with western savoir-faire' (N). Introspection and infinity collude.

Displaced islanders

It is a cliché that islanders and culture are a backdrop—though Indo-Fijians are neither to be seen nor referred to—but are necessarily and helpfully there: 'a unique nation of colourful religious festivals, ritualistic tribal ceremonies and fascinating archaeological finds' (B) with 'sacred space, ancient wisdom' (W). Kava ceremonies and *meke* dances are inescapable. No resort is without a cultural performance of impressive and noisy staged inauthenticity, contemporary examples of Boorstin's (1964) 'pseudo-event'.[5] 'Watch the children dance their traditional spear-waving war dance with gentle movements' (W); an implausible tradition is constantly reinvented as the soft primitivism of good savages.[6] The exotic is tamed, lingering only as painted performance faces and hibiscuses behind the ear. Smiles and 'bula' are minimalist place markers of tourism: the 'commodification of the smile'.[7]

Islanders serve and smile, yelling *bula* (hello), paddling canoes and child-minding, having made the painless transition from ancient warriors and cannibals (whose sanitised knives and forks make kitsch souvenirs) to the way the world should be. 'Come and be pampered, our caring Fijian staff are here to make your stay unforgettable' (W)

5   Daniel J. Boorstin, 1964, *The Image. A Guide to Pseudo-Events in America*, New York: Harper.
6   Yoko Kanemasu, 2008, 'Weapons of the workers. Employees in the Fiji hotel scene', in *Tourism at the Grassroots: Villagers and Visitors in the Asia-Pacific*, ed. John Connell and Barbara Rugendyke, pp. 114–30, London: Routledge, p. 114.
7   Miriam Kahn, 2011, *Tahiti. Beyond the Postcard: Power, Place and Everyday Life*, Seattle: University of Washington Press, p. 146; Kanemasu, 'Weapons of the workers'.

while 'Our friendly and discreet butler is everywhere' (W) all part of 'a revolving cast of smiling wait staff, a seamless parade of polite Fijians' (N). Infinity acquires human dimensions.

The revolving cast, and unobtrusive locals who know their place, ensure there is no sense of real participation, perception, understanding and belonging. Perhaps there is scope to tangle with an idealised environment: on Taveuni 'I've discovered the real Fiji, where villagers still feel at home, fishing, planting their gardens, thatching bures and hunting wild boar' (N). But adult social interaction is missing and tourism is isolated from any real Fiji. Fortuitously, while tourism rarely intrudes into that world, it makes some beneficial financial contribution to it, even stimulating environmental management, especially in smaller, more remote islands.[8] But it is a suppliant, menial and uneven form of development that has provoked a quiet and subtle Fijian resentment towards servicing the leisure aristocracy.[9]

Tourism in infinity

As imagery and practice move upmarket, an infinity begins to separate tourists from Fiji, which lies further beyond a physical and psychological horizon. Tourist gazes are directed into space and ignore the local place. Fiji has become a generic Pacific—as place is gradually abolished—crushed under the weight of multimedia imagery. Resorts represent narratives of loss—and the simultaneous disappearance of culture, history and geography—and of authenticity—tradition has been reinvented over and over again, until nothing is left. Only pseudo-events in non-places remain.[10]

In a global age we withdraw and are encouraged to withdraw into ourselves and into sybaritic luxury. This is no place of distinctive culture—nothing more than a familiar, generic destination—static, immobile, sheltered even from the Pacific. The expense of isolation and exclusivity has permitted luxuriant anonymity. Dream, imagine and relax. Participate energetically and beyond only if you must.

---

8   Connell, 'Competing islands?'
9   Kanemasu, 'Weapons of the workers'.
10   Marc Augé, 1995, *Non-Places. Introduction to an Anthropology of SuperModernity*, London: Verso.

Islanders and children are absent, unless servants or photogenic objects, for these are places of middle-class, middle-aged solace and morality—and of indolence, isolation and privacy. Enclosed resorts are introspective pseudo-places—preferable to 'real' places and real experiences—a determined and organised retreat from everyday life, replicating familiar pleasures through an ensemble of standardised and barely differentiated components. Image subsumes and overwhelms novelty and difference.

Resorts are designed and described to satisfy anticipated gazes with just enough that is exotic to hint at difference. Yet innocent plagiarism and infinite clichés, and the uniformity of advertisements, of language and of smiles, are underpinned by repetition and familiarity, creating one more category of non-places, gradually devoid of local specificity within the super-modern leisure world. Island resorts are the spaces typically encountered when travelling, to be marketed, portrayed, experienced and remembered in generic terms. Unique no longer. Connection with place is fading fast. Culture cannot linger in non-places. Islands and resorts vary and though each has particular attributes, all are subsumed into a pleasure periphery. Difference is demarcated by the materiality of commerce—and price—rather than by physical and social landscapes. Space, time and Fiji are eroded, empty of meaning, vanquished and vanished into infinity.

References

Augé, Marc. 1995. *Non-Places. Introduction to an Anthropology of SuperModernity*. London: Verso.

Baldacchino, Godfrey (ed.). 2015. *Tourist Archipelagoes: Policies and Practices*. Farnham: Ashgate.

Boorstin, Daniel J. 1964. *The Image. A Guide to Pseudo-Events in America*. New York: Harper.

Britton, Stephen G. 1983. *Tourism and Underdevelopment in Fiji*. Monograph No. 31. Canberra: Development Studies Centre, The Australian National University.

Connell, John and Barbara Rugendyke (eds). 2008. *Tourism at the Grassroots: Villagers and Visitors in the Asia-Pacific*. London: Routledge.

Connell, John. 2015. 'Competing islands? The Mamanuca and Yasawa Islands, Fiji.' In *Archipelago Tourism. Policies and Practices*, ed. Godfrey Baldacchino, pp. 183–97. Farnham: Ashgate.

Cronon, William. 1995. 'The trouble with wilderness: Or, getting back to the wrong nature.' In *Uncommon Ground: Rethinking the Human Place in Nature*, ed. William Cronon, pp. 69–90. New York: Norton.

Cronon, William (ed.). 1995. *Uncommon Ground: Rethinking the Human Place in Nature*. New York: Norton.

Holmes, David (ed.). 2001. *Virtual Globalization. Virtual Space/Tourist Space*. London: Routledge.

Kahn, Mirian. 2011. *Tahiti. Beyond the Postcard: Power, Place and Everyday Life*. Seattle: University of Washington Press.

Kanemasu, Yoko. 2008. 'Weapons of the workers. Employees in the Fiji hotel scene.' In *Tourism at the Grassroots: Villagers and Visitors in the Asia-Pacific*, ed. John Connell and Barbara Rugendyke, pp. 114–30. London: Routledge.

King, Brian and Peter Spearritt. 2001. 'Resort curtilages: The creation of physical and psychological tourism spaces.' In *Virtual Globalization. Virtual Space/Tourist Space,* ed. David Holmes, pp. 245–61. London: Routledge.

31

Afterword: Ambivalence, Ambiguity and the 'Wicked Problem' of Pacific Tourist Studies

Jane C. Desmond

'The Pacific …'—it is a sweeping term that pulls up a host of images reiterated over and over on tourist brochures: limitless blue sea, swaying palm trees, pristine beaches, warm breezes and warmly welcoming, happy inhabitants. 'Paradise found!'

The reality is quite different and much more complex—co-existing with all of those elements are many languages and many communities, sovereignty movements, under-employment and poverty, and, for some, a dependence on remittances sent home from family members working far away and, for others, elaborate homes of local elites. There are also universities, artists, writers, scholars, sustainable fishing initiatives, factories, labourers, business owners, a continuing US military presence, and rusting planes, Japanese or American, from World War II. There is, in short, a complex history of mobile indigenous peoples, colonial crossings and imperial relations, intensive labour immigration and ex-migration, and post- and neo-colonial realities. Tourism, not simply as a global industry but *as an embodied social practice*, usually writes out this complexity to tell simplified narratives anchored in a physical place. And, in the Pacific at least, these tourist narratives rarely embrace the complexity and mobilities of the present.

The European cultural imaginaries that form much of the framework for tourism in the Pacific draw on images, ideas, fantasies, and political presumptions that have been circulating widely since the eighteenth century. Lamont Lindstrom's chapter in this book, on early photography in the mid-nineteenth century in what was then known as the New Hebrides (now, Vanuatu), demonstrates the long reach of these ideologies of primitivism (whether celebrated as paradise lost, or condemned as 'heathen' in need of salvation) and their visualisation by Europeans for other Europeans. The islands of the Pacific are still framed to non-residents, to potential tourists, as an 'escape' from modernity for weary moderns.

Unlike the touristic allure of hyper-modernity associated with Abu Dhabi, or Tokyo, or New York, centres of global commerce, home to skyscrapers and financial hubs, Honiara, Rarotonga, and even the large city of Honolulu are painted as 'laid back', a place to get away from it all. That the local inhabitants may also be weary moderns, and wanting to get away from the 'it all' of tourists, and often doing so through their own travel (detailed, for example, in Miriam Kahn, Teana Gooding, and Moenau Holman's chapter on the experiences of two contemporary Tahitian women—Gooding and Holman—touring the city of Seattle in the United States), is a flip of the ideological coin that rarely surfaces, indeed must not, in economically successful touristic frames of encounter.

In this unique book, *Touring Pacific Cultures*, editors Kalissa Alexeyeff and John Taylor foreground these multiple mobilities, and ask us to take a *regional* approach to tourism in the Pacific. The implicit question the book raises is this: What do we gain, as scholars of tourism, as artists responding to tourism, and as residents of Pacific nations engaged with tourism, by taking a regional approach? Why not just study tourism at the community or national level, as is so often the case?

The editors construct their experiment in regionalism by anchoring that breadth in the specificity of case studies from many sites and many nations across the region. This is essential. As these many on-the-ground studies show, their blend of overarching regional similarities is countered by the historical, geographical and cultural specificity that necessarily marks each of the locations and communities the authors engage with—from Tahiti to Papua New Guinea, from Hawai'i to the Marshall Islands. A regional approach makes explicit the necessity of understanding how historical differences and similarities are played out on the ground. It reminds us that sweeping generalisations are often wrong even when they appear on the surface to be right. Only through engagement with residents, with how they craft meaning and lives in places strikingly marked by tourism, can we begin to grasp the larger contours of this shared phenomenon and its complementary distinctive specificity of lived experience.

For example, in the discussion by Helen Lee of what some might call Tonga's 'failed' tourism industry, we find that some Tongans explicitly reject the service worker role of tending to tourists' needs, or the foreign investments in infrastructure that could lure sightseers, despite the money it could bring to a faltering economy. Such arrangements they say, would be neo-colonial, and they are proud of not having ever been formally colonised. As Tongan scholar Konai Helu-Thaman warned in 1993, tourism can be seen as a form of cultural invasion,[1] as a threat to Tongan ways of life. Hotels sit half empty, and the majority of visitors who do use them are of Tongan descent, visiting family from abroad or tending to business. Taking this instance to heart, should it prod us, as scholars of tourism, to redefine our categories?

Perhaps we should define tourism not by the 'who' but by the 'what'. Many of the hotel-staying Tongan returnees, or their children born off-island, may spend some of their time doing the same things that 'tourists' do—visiting special sites, eating at restaurants to enjoy Tongan specialties they can't get at 'home', and purchasing market handicrafts like woven pandanus mats (kie) that are difficult to find abroad but still used for important gifting occasions. Their frame of reference and interpretation, and indeed their motivation, is different from those without Tongan ties, including a sense of (perhaps) both ownership and estrangement—but some of the actions at least may outwardly be the same.

---

1   Konai Helu-Thaman, 1993, 'Beyond hula, hotels, and handicrafts: A Pacific Islander's perspective on tourism development', *The Contemporary Pacific* 5(1): 104–111, cited in Helen Lee, 'The Friendly Islands?', this volume.

Is tourism then not a set of actions but of attitudes towards those actions? Of claims to belonging or not? Can people be both tourists and non-tourists at the same time and in the same places? If so, then we need to consider tourism as a complex matrix of people, place and practices, temporally charged but not spatially determined. As an attitude, a touristic stance elicits attention to and calibrations of (and valuations of) perceived similarities and difference—of landscape, of histories, of beliefs and practices, and of embodied presences in specific time and place.

Frances Steel's intriguing chapter on early cruise ship tourism out of Australia to ports in Samoa and Fiji and Tonga in the 1880s reconstructs accounts of local and visitor encounters on shipboard, revealing the touristic attitude going both ways. Reconstructing these encounters from historical documents, Steel notes how some local residents board the ship from canoes, and physically engage with the new Euro-Australian arrivals—touching their hair, pronouncing them 'good', and expressing an appetite for difference as strong as those of the Europeans who came to see them. This is not to imply that such encounters, then or now, take place on some ahistorical utopian ground of equal political power. It would be foolish to deny that vast differences of wealth and global power underpin such pleasure travel. But it would be equally foolish to deny the agential roles inhabited by all parties to such an encounter. As Steel puts it, early colonial touring was 'an inherently open, negotiated and unstable practice, one of cross-cutting mobilities, improvisations, and multi-sensorial encounters'.

Although heightened through touristic infrastructure and ideologies of difference, such open, unstable, and improvisatory attitudes, or modes of attending to the world around us and calibrating our place in it, can surface, theoretically at least, anywhere and anytime. For instance, this attentiveness might surface when as individuals we cross our home cities to another neighbourhood, just as when we cross thousands of miles to visit another nation. Expanding on Jonathan Urry's foundational notion of the 'tourist gaze',[2] we can think instead of the 'tourist attitude'. This reformulation works against the more static, reified categories of 'host/visitor' or 'exploited/exploitee' that

---

2   Jonathan Urry, 1990, *The Tourist Gaze*, New York: Sage Publishers.

earlier formulations imply. It takes up the editors' challenge to put the notion of mobilities—of ideas, of objects and images, of people, and of practices—at the forefront of our analyses.

Yet physical co-presence remains an essential component even within this widened formulation of touristic modes of encountering each other. For all of their geographic and temporal variety of foci, none of the articles in this book imply that tourism as physical displacement through space is dead. Rather, a long but changing history of visual images (from lantern slides by missionaries to photographic 'selfies' by today's teens) creates a visual virtual landscape that engages with, counters and articulates or at least suggests ideological networks of interpretation. Yet the actual bodily act of touring—that is, of moving physically from one place to another with the purpose of encountering the new place for pleasure as opposed to seeking political refuge or labour opportunities, remains a defining criterion for tourism and our study of it.

Therefore, while keeping in mind the editors' call to theorise mobilities more generally, we must hone our abilities to theorise and understand more deeply the defining nature of physical proximity. Documentary films, live streaming 'cams' and skyping have not replaced 'tourism' in the classical sense. Why? What is at stake, what is gained, by whom, and under what conditions, in this consummated urge to *move the physical self* and not just our vision or auditory capacity, to another site? Given all the other modes of vision and connection available now across the world, why do people still engage in tourism—in mobility for pleasure? This is a crucial question for tourism studies now.

Newer takes on tourism have urged us to uncover the affective and sensorial aspects of touring, and this is surely an important part of it. But even so, we need to press more strongly on this aspect of tourism: the 'you are here' component that is the ground not only of sensorial experience (trade winds, gustatory delights, sonic melodies, the grit of sand, the smell of detritus) but also of encounters (speech, hearing, vision, touch, conversation, arguments) with other people in other places. There is no need to adopt the 'reality TV' fiction of unbiased reporting, hoping that the body will somehow be a pre-discursive site of 'authenticity'. Rather we should embrace the ways that these physical and interactive experiences are narrativised and given meaning both by tourists and those who encounter them, as well as by the infrastructures and businesses that service their needs. The result is often a mix of 'ambivalence and ambiguity' as long-standing ideological frames meet contemporary co-presence. John Taylor deploys this generative phrase in his study of photography and local children in cruise tourism in Vanuatu in the Solomon Islands for this volume. I want to mobilise it more broadly here in the context of ethics, leisure, and the possibilities for social change through tourism.

A 'wicked problems' approach

If ambivalence and ambiguity are at the heart of touristic practices, as so many of the articles in this book reveal, how do we frame them as an object of study? Artists may be somewhat more attuned to this, and better equipped to respond, because aesthetic practices embrace the polysemic elements of sound, image and object. Scholarly work too is just as resonant, but we often try to work against the activation of multiple registers of meaning, honing down to a carefully sharpened point, rather than opening out to those multiple registers of evocation like a poet or a painter. Recognising this, this book brings together a range of responses to tourism in the Pacific, including not only poetry by Audrey Brown-Pereira, but a very good discussion of the complex politics and specific image-based negotiations in the use of and commissioning of Native Hawaiian artists' works as part of the design of Disney's Aulani Resort & Spa on the island of Oahu in Hawai'i. The resort, opened in 2011 with great fanfare, is now the site of the largest collection of visual art by Native Hawaiian artists in the world. Necessarily entailing complex engagements between artist, object and viewer as co-constituents of meaning production, artistic work is not neatly contained in simplistic narratives. There is always an 'excess', and in this excess lies both complexity and the potential for engagement.

For non-artists, for scholars, activists, even policymakers, taking a 'wicked problems' approach can be a productive way to approach the ambivalence and ambiguity of tourism. A concept often used in engineering, or urban planning, a wicked problem approach starts from the assumption that important social issues are necessarily complex and contradictory, with various, often competing stakeholders. Deborah Curran notes that 'wicked' problems, or social challenges, are different from other types of more easily identifiable problems, 'tame' ones with clear, if difficult to attain, solutions.[3] 'Wicked' challenges, on the other hand, have no one single definition, the definition of the problem often depends on the viewpoint of the definer. Their solutions are not true or false, right or wrong, but better or worse. Solutions may bring about their own unanticipated problems that then need to be addressed in turn. And there is no ending point: 'Wicked' problems evolve and change over long periods of time, demanding new solutions, new interventions as relations among people, resources, ideas and political power change.

The social relations of tourism in the Pacific pose a classic 'wicked problem'. Evolving over long periods of time from complex and multiple histories of interactions, tourism is seen as positive or negative depending on various points of view. Does tourism promise a better life for island populations in the Pacific, as some proponents of 'development' through the growth of tourism imply? Or, as critics suggest, is it merely a neo-liberal form of neo-colonialism that continues the exploitation of local residents while retreading long-enduring tropes of primitivism and paradise as a source of pleasure for residents of former colonial powers? If we take a wicked problem approach, we would acknowledge that rather than an 'either/or' equation we must accept, conceptually, that it is quite possibly a 'both/and'. In this volume, the discussion by Marata Tamaira about the display of artworks by Native Hawaiian artists in the Disney Aulani resort is a perfect example. Some artists embraced the opportunity to reach wide audiences, and others criticised them for 'selling out'. We won't grasp the effects of these artworks in this particular corporate setting for those particular guests without further fieldwork. How does the Disney narrative of 'culture' shape or limit the potential power of the works? What counter-discourses might prevail?

One motivation for research on tourism by scholars, or interventions in a touristic landscape by artists, is to look to a future of less social and economic inequality in the world. If so, how does that shape our future investigations?

---

3   Deborah Curran, 2009, 'Wicked', *Alternatives Journal* 35(5): 8–11.

At the very bottom of tourism as a social practice is a physical leaving 'home', wherever home may be, for an experience that (the tourist assumes) cannot be found at home. It comprises an experience of geography, of cultural expression, of urban architecture and rural landscapes, of foods, and of populations, all of which can be experienced as 'different'. This attention to and construction of difference, for pleasure, can take innumerable forms depending on whom the addressee is. My mundane is, perhaps, your exotic, your intriguing.

Are there ways to make this appetite for difference not simply reinscriptions of old inequities—in the case of the Pacific, retreadings of colonial ideologies dressed up in twenty-first-century prose? Is it possible that the juggernaut of tourism as a global social practice, infrastructure, and industry could potentially provide progressive pathways to new more equitable relations?

Is it possible, for example, to conceive of a touristic parallel to the notion of 'fair trade' in commodities like coffee, but here extended to intangible realms of experience?

Given stark and enduring inequalities in the distribution of material resources and political power, such a format may be easily abjured as naïve. Yet, tourists spend billions of dollars each year and invest enormous amounts of intellectual, physical and (as Kalissa Alexeyeff tells us in her chapter) affective work, on tourism. In what ways might it be possible to recapture some of those resources, to make tourism more sustainable in the broadest sense of that term—not just in terms of renewable environmental resources, but in terms of ethically acceptable practices, sustaining health and welfare of the humans and landscapes and animals involved?

We see this in 'alternative tourism' sites, small enterprises, often spearheaded by creative indigenous leaders, that seek to connect progressive visitors with progressive local residents. But, by definition, these remain a marginal part of the larger industry. They depend on building intimate, small-scale opportunities for connection and thus for experiencing and articulating the complexities of ambivalent relations and difficult histories. Small-scale tourism usually attracts elites with high cultural capital and significant expendable income to customise their experiences. Can this apply to mass tourism with its vertically integrated infrastructures of hotels, airplanes, and tour agencies, owed by foreign corporations? Is this a scalable model?

To start to think about this question, I turn away from tourism to other global infrastructures that commodify not only experience but material goods: behemouths like McDonald's fast food restaurants and Walmart, the largest retailer on the planet. Before turning away in dismay, stay with me for a moment here, for new thinking often requires thinking with and not simply against the previously unthinkable.

A wicked problems approach to tourism assumes several things. First, tourism industries are not going to just go away; capitalism will not just wither on the vine; and social inequality will not disappear just because it is immoral. Second, tourism is comprised of actions by many groups of stakeholders, often with deeply conflicting beliefs and desires; therefore change is possible but may yield unexpected, even negative outcomes, which themselves then need to be addressed. Change is always a process never a completed event. Today, dramatic overhauls in short terms are unlikely, given the enormous numbers of moving parts in complex global social, geographical and financial imbrications. However, the very complexity of these systems means they are always in flux and thus always available for change.

One of the available tools for both tourists and touring infrastructures and populations is the ability to shift interpretive frames. Several years ago, researching Hawaiian hula performances in the tourist context, I was struck by the bold vision of highly respected Native Hawaiian hula master, or 'kumu hula', Frank Kawaikapuokalani Hewitt in designing his troupe's tourist performances at an important hotel complex on the island of Kaua'i. Drawing on the sonic histories of the 1950s US *Hawai'i Calls* radio show, Hewitt staged a spectacle of continental US images of the islands, drawing on historical depictions from stage and screen. Then, in an astute 'bait and switch' move, just when the largely Euro-American audience was swooning into the 1950s memories of 'paradise', he juxtaposed those to the practice of hula in the islands today. Still working within the framework of tourist 'pleasure' and 'cultural shows', he managed to instigate self-reflexivity in his audience and to draw them into the present of Hawaiian politics. He did so by reproducing and revealing the ideological history of island imaginaries, then pointing out how they came to be. This is just one example, and a small one. Hewitt's troupe was in residence at the time in an upscale hotel, so this did not reach the masses that seaside lu'aus would do, where bus loads of US tourists were driven out from Waikiki to local beaches for doses of 'culture' in large-scale feasts.

When and to what transformative degree might such imputations of self-reflexivity become possible?

Ultimately, ownership of the means of production may give the greatest ideological control. As long as tourism in the Pacific is largely framed by external forces, the power of local residents to determine the terms of interaction and interpretation will be attenuated. But, from a 'wicked problems' point of view, that does not mean that no change is possible. Rather it demands the opposite. Indeed, change is always present, it is a constituent component of living systems of social formations. To the extent that Pacific tourism sells 'the cultures of the Pacific' as part of its distinctive allure, differentiating it from other sun and sand destinations, then the bargaining power for self-representation is at least there in theory. A 'wicked problems' approach calls on participants to make change even when it cannot result in a complete, dramatic political overhaul.

Facilitating the conscious recalibration of power over time in the Pacific tourist industry is one of the goals of progressive scholarship. First, we must endeavour to understand ever more deeply what is going on—a complex wicked problems approach combined with the editors' insistence on the flux of mobilities, and anchored in the physical reality of embodied presence, provide us a map from which to move forward. Then, it is up to the actors to imagine differently, to rearticulate the frames of interpretation.

Taking our cue from large-scale international business in other realms, we might imagine, for example, deploying a notion of 'fair trade tourism'. Bringing morality explicitly into coffee drinking, the notion of 'fair trade' recognises the colonial legacies of extractive agriculture that built the coffee-drinking habit in the richest parts of the world. It keeps that history present for today's consumers, asking (offering?) them to work against a colonial legacy to build a new future. 'Fair trade' coffee, which guarantees a modest yet liveable wage to the suppliers, connects specific coffee drinkers in New York or Sydney, for example, willing to pay a premium, with specific producers in Colombia or Brazil through a matrix of shared desire for a more equitable world. Is it conceivable that something like 'fair trade' mass tourism could catch hold?

We have seen other massive shifts due to retail giants' change of policy when we consider, for example, the surprising leading role that global McDonald's Restaurant Corporation now plays in requiring increasing vigilance in animal welfare from its producers. Driven by consumers' demands and resulting legislation, such a move nonetheless has positive material effects on the lives of animals and of workers in animal agriculture. When a global giant like McDonald's moves, it shifts the landscape of the possible. Analysing such massive global retail changes may provide one instructive avenue for modelling change in a contemporary global business-scape, and ultimately even suggest modes of rearticulation in a tourism sphere.

In the realms of Pacific tourism, a 'wicked problems' approach suggests that we could investigate the potential for progressive outcomes based on carefully crafted alliances with capitalist enterprises, enterprises, like large multinational hotel chains, that are unlikely to go away in the next decade. The power of moral and ethical claims, when backed by consumer support, could, *could*, be an arena of potential change. This is especially true because the wider political landscape is also always in motion, with ongoing legal battles for land restitution and renegotiations of long-term military treaties just two areas of change. Available discourses of rights, restitution and respect grow stronger, invariably edging into the framing of tourism. A number of years ago in Honolulu I was stunned to watch a poolside hula show at a major multinational hotel chain as part of my fieldwork when an entire section of the show became devoted to issues of Native Hawaiian sovereignty and land claims, and contemporary hulas that harked back to the time of colonial usurpation. A highly regarded kumu hula had been hired by the Sheraton Hotel chain, and (a key point) had negotiated to retain control over the script for her performance. Lulled by the welcoming patter and the sweet strains of ukulele music, suddenly the tenor shifted and tourists lounging by a pool were blindsided by songs about sovereignty politics, stunned into an awareness of co-temporary with the performers, and forced into an ambivalent state of comfort and discomfort. We might call this a sort of 'stealth politics' of tourism encounters, and it was very effective.

It may be that today's infrastructure and the lingering historical legacies of tourism in the Pacific region call for just this sort of stealth politics, a way to intervene in the 'wicked problem' of the tourist industry which is fundamentally built on ambivalence and ambiguity. Embracing that ambivalence, and seizing that ambiguity, can be a key to progressive change through a continual rethinking and re-doing of tourism in the Pacific.

References

Curran, Deborah. 2009. 'Wicked.' *Alternatives Journal* 35(5): 8–11.

Konai Helu-Thaman. 1993. 'Beyond hula, hotels, and handicrafts: a Pacific Islander's perspective on tourism development.' *The Contemporary Pacific* 5(1): 104–111.

Urry, Jonathan. 1990. *The Tourist Gaze*. New York: Sage Publishers.

Contributors

Kalissa Alexeyeff is an Australian Research Council (ARC) Future Fellow at the University of Melbourne. Her present project examines globalisation, migration and gendered affect in the Pacific. She is the author of *Dancing from the Heart: Gender, Movement and Cook Islands Globalization* (2009) and with Niko Besnier, *Gender on the Edge: Transgender, Gay, and Other Pacific Islanders* (2014).

Maria Amoamo is a Research Fellow in the Department of Management, Otago University. Her current research draws on social anthropology to examine aspects of cultural change, resilience and sustainable development in small island states. Her longitudinal ethnographic fieldwork focuses on issues affecting Pitcairn as a Subnational Island Jurisdiction, Britain's only Pacific Overseas Territory. Maria has also published works on Māori and Indigenous tourism with particular interest in exploring the interface of post-colonialism and hybridity theory in relation to the transformation, production and mobility of cultures.

Flora Aurima-Devatine has been a member of the Tahitian Academy since 1972. She is an Indigenous Tahitian writer, poet, orator and researcher, and the author of traditional poems in Tahitian, which are published on her own website *Flora Aurima-Devatine* (www.lehman. cuny.edu/ile.en.ile/media/5questions_aurima-devatine.html) and of *Tergiversations et Rêveries de l'Ecriture Orale. Te Pahu a Hono'ura* (Au Vent des îles, 1998). Her free-verse poems in French and essays on Tahitian culture have been published in journals and anthologies in Canada, France, and Hawai'i.

Tracey Banivanua Mar is an Australian Research Council Future Fellow at La Trobe University. She has written about and researches on transnational indigenous histories in the Pacific and Pacific basin. Her publications include *Violence and Colonial Dialogue: the Australia-Pacific Labor Trade* (2007) and *Decolonisation and the Pacific: Indigenous globalisation and the Ends of Empire* (2016).

Audrey Brown-Pereira is an innovative poet, who is of Cook Island Māori and Samoan descent. Her poetry collections include 'Threads of Tivaevae: Kaleidoskope of Kolours' with new media artist Veronica Vaevae; and 'Passages in Between I(s)lands', recently published by Ala Press in 2014. Her work appears in anthologies *Whetu Moana: Contemporary Polynesian Poems in English* and *Mauri Ola: Contemporary Polynesian Poems in English*, and she has performed at the New Zealand Fringe Festival and Poetry Parnassus in London. Audrey is a graduate of Auckland University and is a postgraduate student in the Development Studies Programme at the National University of Samoa.

William C. Clarke's academic career in geography and anthropology led him from Berkeley to Papua New Guinea, Australia and Fiji. Throughout his life (1929–2013) he read, wrote and published poetry. He encouraged a generation of Pacific Islanders to do the same, by his interest in their writing and facilitation of its publication.

John Connell is Professor of Human Geography in the School of Geosciences, University of Sydney. Prior to the University of Sydney he was at the Institute of Development Studies, University of Sussex, and the Department of Economics, Research School of Pacific Studies, The Australian National University. He has been a consultant to the International Labor Organization, the World Health Organization, the South Pacific Commission, the Secretariat of the Pacific Regional Environment Programme, the World Bank and the Asian Development Bank. He has written various books including *Papua New Guinea. The Struggle for Development*; *The Last Colonies* (1997, with R. Aldrich); *Urbanisation in the Island Pacific. Towards Sustainable Development* (2002, with J. Lea); *Music and Tourism. On the Road Again* (2005, with C. Gibson); *The Global Health Care Chain. From the Pacific to the World*; *Tourism at the Grassroots. Villagers and Visitors in the Asia-Pacific* (2009, with B. Rugendyke) and *Islands at Risk? Environment, Economies and Contemporary Change* (2013). When he is not engaged in these loosely academic activities he plays football in the Eastern Suburbs (Sydney) Over 45s League—without great success.

John Cox has worked in the Pacific region for the last 20 years, as a volunteer, NGO program manager, consultant and anthropologist. His PhD research on fast money schemes in Papua New Guinea was awarded the Australian Anthropological Society's Prize for Best PhD thesis in 2012. He is currently finalising a monograph on this topic with Indiana University Press. John is a Research Fellow at the Institute for Human Security and Social Change at La Trobe University.

Jane C. Desmond is currently Professor of Anthropology and Gender/Women's Studies at the University of Illinois at Urbana-Champaign, where she also directs the International Forum for US Studies: a Center for Transnational Study of the United States, which she co-founded with Virginia Dominguez. Formerly a professional modern dancer and choreographer, her scholarly work focuses broadly on issues of embodiment and social identity, which grounds her work in social history, cultural studies, animal studies, performance studies and the arenas of visual culture and tourism. Her books include *Staging Tourism: Bodies on Display from Waikiki to Sea World* (1999), and the influential edited collections *Meaning in Motion: New Cultural Studies of Dance* (1997) and *Dancing Desires: Choreographing Sexuality On and Off the Stage* (2002), as well as several edited special issues for journals. Her latest book *Displaying Death and Animating Life* (2016) is published with the University of Chicago Press.

Jo Diamond is a Māori woman of Ngapuhi descent. She has a PhD from The Australian National University and is currently a Senior Lecturer at the University of Canterbury, New Zealand. She is also a New Zealand Fulbright Lecturer Alumnus, having taught sophomore students Indigenous art at Georgetown University, Washington DC, in 2008. Her teaching and publication record is extensive and diverse, covering numerous aspects of Maori and other Indigenous art and culture. Her latest book on the *pari* is expected to be published in 2016.

Greg Dvorak received his masters degree from the University of Hawai'i at Mānoa and his PhD from The Australian National University. He is an Associate Professor of Pacific/Asian cultural studies and history at Hitotsubashi University in Tokyo. He is also an adjunct lecturer in Pacific Islands Studies at Waseda University. His book, *Coral and Concrete*, forthcoming from the University of Hawai'i Press, deals with themes of memory and resistance between Japanese and American imperialism in the Marshall Islands.

Margaret Jolly (FASSA) is an Australian Research Council Laureate Fellow and Professor in the School of Culture, History and Language in the College of Asia and the Pacific at The Australian National University. She has taught at Macquarie University in Sydney, the University of Hawai'i and the University of California, Santa Cruz, and has been a visiting scholar in Anthropology in Cambridge University and at Centre de recherche et documentation sur l'Océanie (CREDO) in Marseille. In 2009 she held a Poste Rouge with the Centre national de la recherche scientifique (CNRS) in France. She is an historical anthropologist who has written extensively on gender in the Pacific, on exploratory voyages and travel writing, missions and contemporary Christianity, maternity and sexuality, cinema and art. Her most recent book is *Divine Domesticities: Christian Paradoxes in Asia and the Pacific* (ed. with Hyaeweol Choi, 2014).

Anita Jowitt joined the University of the South Pacific as a lecturer in law in 1997, and is based in Vanuatu. She is of mixed New Zealand and Indo-Fijian heritage.

Miriam Kahn is Professor of Anthropology at the University of Washington, Seattle. Her research interests include the anthropology of place, colonial and post-colonial politics, nuclear testing, tourism and cultural representations in the Pacific. She has done fieldwork in both Papua New Guinea (1976–95) and French Polynesia (1993–present). She is the author of three books: *Always Hungry, Never Greedy: Food and the Expression of Gender in a Melanesian Society* (1986), *Pacific Voices: Keeping Our Cultures Alive* (2005) and *Tahiti Beyond the Postcard: Power, Place and Everyday Life* (2011).

Helen Lee is Professor of Anthropology at La Trobe University in Melbourne. Since the 1980s her research has focused on the people of Tonga. Helen's doctoral research was published as *Becoming Tongan: An Ethnography of Childhood* (1996). She has published widely on migration and transnationalism, with a particular focus on the children of migrants, including *Tongans Overseas: Between Two Shores* (2003); *Ties the Homeland: Second Generation Transnationalism* (2008); and *Migration and Transnationalism: Pacific Perspectives* (ed. with Steve Francis 2009). Her current research focuses on overseas-born Tongan youth attending high schools in Tonga.

Lamont Lindstrom, Kendall Professor of Anthropology at the University of Tulsa, has long-term research interests in Vanuatu and other Melanesian countries focused on local knowledge systems and social movements, kava, World War II ethnohistory, contemporary chiefs and the politics of tradition, cultural policy development, sociolinguistics, urban migration and personhood, and early Pacific photography.

Michelle MacCarthy is a postdoctoral fellow at the University of Bergen, Norway. Her fieldwork in the Trobriand Islands of Papua New Guinea since 2009 began with a focus on the dynamics of cultural or 'primitivist' tourism in a place sacralised in anthropology and branded as 'culturally unique' for visitors. This research has been published in *Ethnos, The International Journal of Heritage Studies,* and the book *Art/Artifact/Commodity: Perspectives on the P.G.T. Black Collection* (in press), edited by Robert J. Foster and Kathryn H. Leacock. Her first monograph, available in June 2016 from the University of Hawai'i Press, is entitled *Making the Modern Primitive: Cultural Tourism in the Trobriand Islands.* Currently, she is taking up new research on gender and Pentecostal Christianity in a comparative perspective, collaborating with colleagues working elsewhere in Melanesia and in Africa.

Selina Tusitala Marsh is a poet and Senior Lecturer in the English Department at the University of Auckland, where she teaches New Zealand and Pacific Literature and Creative Writing. Of Samoan, Tuvaluan, English and French descent, her critical and creative work focuses on giving voice to Pacific communities. She is author of the award-winning poetry collection *Fast Talking PI* (2009) and *Dark Sparring* (2013).

Courtney Sina Meredith is a poet, playwright, fiction writer and musician of Samoan, Mangaian and Irish descent. Meredith describes her writing as an 'ongoing discussion of contemporary urban life with an underlying Pacific politique.' She was the first New Zealander and first writer of Pacific descent to hold the LiteraturRaum Blebitreu Berlin residency in 2011. In 2016 Meredith was New Zealand's representative for the University of Iowa's International Writing Program Fall Residency, after which she was the Writer in Residence for the Island Institute in Sitka, Alaska. Meredith launched her first book of short stories *Tail of the Taniwha* (Beatnik Publishing) in 2016, following her award-winning play *Rushing Dolls* (Playmarket, 2012) and her much lauded collection of poems *Brown Girls in Bright Red Lipstick* (Beatnik, 2012).

Peter Phipps is a senior lecturer in Global Studies at RMIT University, Director of the Honours Program and a founding member and on the executive committee of the Globalism Research Centre. He undertook post-graduate training in cultural anthropology at the University of California Berkeley, and completed a PhD on the cultural politics of post-colonial theory in the School of Anthropology, Philosophy and Social Enquiry at the University of Melbourne. He has published a number of book chapters, industry reports, policy recommendations and articles on Indigenous festivals, tourism and the politics of cultural globalisation. He has consulted to a number of organisations and government bodies, including the Papua New Guinea Department for Community Development, Aboriginal and Torres Strait Islander Commission, Aboriginal and Torres Strait Islanders Arts Board (Australia Council), United Nations Development Program (Sarajevo) and the Yothu Yindi Foundation. Most recently he wrote on ethnic cultural precincts for the City of Melbourne and Victorian Multicultural Commission, and a project at Warlayirti Art Centre in the West Australian desert.

Frances Steel teaches Pacific History at the University of Wollongong. Her research connects cultures of empire, shipping and mobility in the Pacific world. She is currently writing a trans-Pacific history of British and American imperialisms using the passenger liner trades between Australasia and North America as a framework (c.1870s – 1950s). She is the author of *Oceania under Steam: Sea Transport and the Cultures of Colonialism, c.1870–1914* (2011).

A. Marata Tamaira hails from Aotearoa New Zealand and has genealogical ties with the central North Island tribe of Ngāti Tūwharetoa. She recently completed a PhD in Gender, Media and Cultural Studies at The Australian National University in which she examined how contemporary Kānaka Maoli (Native Hawaiians) use the visual arts as a tool to assert their socio-political aspirations and affirm their sovereign identity in the context of ongoing US colonialism in Hawai'i. Her research interests include settler colonial visual representations in the Pacific, the politics and aesthetics of contemporary Hawaiian art, and articulations of visual sovereignty in contemporary indigenous art. She edited the University of Hawai'i at Mānoa Center for Pacific Islands Studies publication *The Space Between: Negotiating Culture, Place, and Identity in the Pacific*.

John Taylor is Senior Lecturer and Anthropology Program Convener in the Department of Social Inquiry, La Trobe University, Melbourne. He is the author of two books, *Consuming Identity: Modernity and Tourism in New Zealand*, and *The Other Side: Ways of Being and Place in Vanuatu*, and co-editor of *Working Together in Vanuatu: Research Histories, Collaborations, Projects and Reflections*. He is currently undertaking an Australian Research Council Discovery Project on the relationship between spirituality and healthcare in the western Pacific.

Katerina Teaiwa is Associate Professor in the School of Culture, History and Language, in the College of Asia and the Pacific at The Australian National University. She is author of *Consuming Ocean Island: Stories of People and Phosphate from Banaba* (Indiana University Press, 2015).

Mandy Treagus is Associate Professor in English and Creative Writing at the University of Adelaide, where she teaches nineteenth- and twentieth-century literature, culture and visual studies. Her recent book, *Empire Girls: The Colonial Heroine Comes of Age*, examines narratives of development in colonial settings. She has also recently co-edited *Changing the Victorian Subject*, a collection re-examining Victorian studies in both metropolis and empire. She has also published widely in Pacific literary, historical and visual studies.

Joseph Vile took part in the Pacific Islands Field School course taught by Katerina Teaiwa and Nicola Mariner at the Festival of Pacific Arts in Honiara, and is now an ANU graduate on an Australian Volunteers for International Development assignment in Vietnam.

Bomai D. Witne is a lecturer in Political Science at the University of Goroka, Papua New Guinea. He likes freelance writing during his free time.

www.ingramcontent.com/pod-product-compliance
Lightning Source LLC
Chambersburg PA
CBHW040151270326
41926CB00079B/4560